T0144307

Hawaiian
Antiquities

Hawaiian Antiquities

(Moolelo Hawaii)

David Malo

MINT EDITIONS

Hawaiian Antiquities was first published in 1898.

This edition published by Mint Editions 2021.

ISBN 9781513299532 | E-ISBN 9781513223872

Published by Mint Editions®

 MINT EDITIONS

MintEditionBooks.com

Publishing Director: Jennifer Newens
Design & Production: Rachel Lopez Metzger
Project Manager: Micaela Clark
Translated By: Dr. N.B. Emerson
Typesetting: Westchester Publishing Services

To

Bernice Pauabi Bishop

The Mother of Hawaiian Industrial Education

I Dedicate this Volume in appreciation of her efforts to keep alive a knowledge of the Antiquities and Mysteries of Hawaiian History

Contents

List of Illustrations

BIOGRAPHICAL SKETCH OF DAVID MALO

It is a commentary on the fleeting character of fame and human distinction that, even at this short remove from the life of one of Hawaii's most distinguished sons, it is with no little difficulty that one can obtain correct data as to the details of his career; it is also an index of the rapidity with which the plough-share of evolution has obliterated old landmarks.

The materials from which this sketch of David Malo's life is pieced together have been derived from many sources, both oral and written, as will be indicated in the course of the narrative.

Malo was the son of Aoao and his wife Heone, and was born at the seaside town of Keauhou, North Kona, Hawaii, not many miles distant from the historic bay of Kealakeakua, where Captain Cook, only a few years before, had come to his death. The exact year of his birth cannot be fixed, but it was about 1793, the period of Vancouver's second visit to the islands. It was the time of a breathing spell in the struggle for military and political supremacy over the entire group in which the chief actors were Kahekili, the old war-horse and veteran of Maui, Kalanikupule, his son, the weak and ill-fated king of Oahu, and Kamehameha, the oncoming conqueror of the group.

Aoao, the father, was attached as a follower in some capacity to the court and army of Kamehameha and moved west with the tide of invasion; but I have found no evidence that his travels took him so far as Oahu, which was the western limit of his master's operations.

During his early life Malo was connected with the high chief Kuakini (Governor Adams), who was a brother of Queen Kaahu-manu, and it was during this period specially that he was placed in an environment the most favorable to forming an intimate acquaintance with the history, traditions, legends and myths of old Hawaii, as well as with the *meles, pules* and *oils* that belong to the hula and that form so important and prominent a feature in the poesy and unwritten literature of Hawaii. But his attainments in these directions are even more to be ascribed to his happy endowment with a shrewd and inquiring mind as well as a tenacious memory, which had to serve in the place of writing and of all mnemonic tablets. If we may trust the authority of the writer of a brief sketch of Malo (See *The Polynesian* of Nov. 5, 1853), it was largely from association with one Auwai, a favorite chief of Kamehameha I, who excelled in knowledge of Hawaiian lore, including an acquaintance with the genealogies (kuauhau) of the chiefs, the religious ceremonials under the tabu system, and the old myths and traditions, that Malo was enabled to acquire his knowledge of these matters. In ancient Hawaii it was at the king's court that were gathered the notable bards, poets, and those in whose minds were stored the traditional lore of the nation.

Brought up under circumstances well fitted to saturate his mind with the old forms of thought and feeling, it would be surprising if he had not at some time given evidence of ability in that form of composition, the *mele*, which represents the highest literary attainment of the old regime. Such a production by him we have,—a threnody celebrating the death of the beloved regent, Queen Kaahumanu, who died June 5, 1832. It is entitled, *He Kanikau no Kaahumanu*, a poem of real merit that combines in itself a large measure of the mystery of ancient pagan allusions with a tincture of such feelings as belong to one newly introduced to the stand-point of a Christian civilization. (A copy of this poem will be found in *The Friend* of Aug., 1859, together with a translation by C. J. Lyons.)

Such good use did Malo make of his opportunities that he came to be universally regarded as the great authority and repository of Hawaiian lore.

As a natural result of his proficiency in these matters, Malo came to be in great demand as a raconteur of the old-time traditions, *meles*, and genealogies, as a master in the arrangement of the hula, as well as of the nobler sports of the Hawaiian arena, a person of no little importance about court. In after years, when his mind had been impregnated with the vivifying influence of the new faith from across the ocean, his affections were so entirely turned against the whole system, not only of idol-worship, but all the entertainments of song, dance and sport as well, that his judgment seems often to be warped, causing him to confound together the evil and the good, the innocent and the guilty, the harmless and the depraved in one sweeping condemnation, thus constraining him to put under the ban of his reprobation things which a more enlightened judgment would have tolerated or even taken innocent pleasure in, or to cover with the veil of contemptuous silence matters, which, if preserved, would now be of inestimable value and interest to the ethnologist, the historian and the scholar.

It is a matter of vain regret from the stand-point of the student that this should have been the case, and that there should not have survived in him a greater toleration for the beauties and sublimities, as well as the darker mysteries, of that unwritten literature, which the student of today finds dimly shadowed in the cast-off systems of heathendom. But it is not to be wondered at that David Malo should have been unable to appreciate at its true value the lore of which he was one of the few repositories. It could be expected only of a foreign and broadly cultivated mind to occupy the stand-point necessary to such an appraisal. The basis of this criticism will be evident to every attentive reader of this book.

The attitude of David Malo's mind toward the system of thought - from which he was delivered, "the pit from which he was digged," as some would put it, was, from the circumstances of the case, one of complete alienation not to say intolerance, and gives ground for the generalization that it is hopleless to expect a recent convert to occupy a positon of judicial fairness to the system of religion and thought from which he has been rescued. While this may be reckoned as a tribute to the depth and sincerity of his nature, it cannot but be deemed an index of the necessarily somewhat narrow view of the mystic and the convert. The application of Malo's energies to the task of setting forth in an orderly manner his knowledge of the history and antiquities of his people was due to the urgent persuasions of his teachers, and shows their broad-minded appreciation of the value of such information.

While still a young man and before leaving Hawaii, Malo was married to a widow-woman of alii blood, by the name of A'a-lai-oa, who was much older than himself and said to have been a daughter of Kahekili, the great king of Maui; but it seems hardly probable that she was so closely related to that distinguished monarch. The marriage with this woman was in the language of the time called a *ho-ao*. This, though not according to Christian rites and forms, was none the less a regular, honorable and legitimate form of marriage, according to the ideas and customs of the time. One may conjecture, however, that in this case the union was one in which the husband was the chosen rather than the chooser. Such marriages were not at all uncommon in ancient Hawaii, it being considered that the woman made up by her wealth and position what she lacked in physical attractiveness. There was no issue, and the woman died while Malo was still at Keauhou, on Hawaii.

The date of Malo's removal to Lahaina, Maui, marks an important epoch in his life; for it was there he came under the inspiring influence and instruction of the Rev. William Richards, who had settled as a missionary in that place in the year 1823, at the invitation of the queen-mother, Keopuolani. Under the teachings of this warm-hearted leader of men, to whom he formed an attachment that lasted through life, he was converted to Christianity, and on his reception into the church was given the baptismal name of David. There seems to have been in Mr. Richards' strong and attractive personality just that mental and moral stimulus which Malo needed in order to bring out his own strength and develop the best elements of his nature. In the case of one of such decided strength of character and purpose there could be no half-way work; in whatever direction the current of will turned, it flowed as one full and undivided stream.

From his first contact with the new light and knowledge of Christian civilization, David Malo was fired with an enthusiasm for the acquisition of all the benefits it had to confer. He made efforts to acquire the English language, but met with no great success: his talents did not lie in that direction; one writer ascribes his failure to the rigidity of his vocal organs. His mental activity, which was naturally of the strenuous sort, under the influence of his new environment seemed now to be brought to a white heat.

In his search for information he became an eager reader of books; every printed thing that was struck off at the newly established mission press at Honolulu, or afterwards at Lahaina-luna, was eagerly sought after and devoured by his hungry and thirsty soul. He accumulated a library which is said to have included all the books published in his own language. In taking account of David Malo's acquirements as well as his mental range and activity of thought, it is necessary to remember that the output of the Hawaiian press in those days, though not productive of the newspaper, was far richer in works of thought and those of an educational and informational value than at the present time. It was pre-eminently the time in the history of the American Protestant Mission to Hawaii when its intellectual force was being directed to the production of a body of literature that should include not only the textbooks of primary and general education, but should also give access to a portion of the field of general information. It was also the time when the scholars of the Mission, aided by visiting friends from the South, were diligently engaged in the heavy task of translating the Bible into the Hawaiian vernacular, the completed result of which by itself formed a body of literature, which for elevation and excellence of style formed a standard and model of written language worthy to rank with the best.

On the establishment of the high school at Lahaina-luna in 1831, Malo entered as one of the first pupils, being at the time about thirty-eight years of age, and there he remained for several years, pursuing the various branches of study with great assiduity.

It was while at Lahaina, before entering the school at Lahainaluna, that he for the second time entered into marriage; and as before so on this occasion, it was with a woman of chiefish blood and older than himself that he formed an alliance; she was named Pahia. The marriage ceremony was conducted in accordance with the Christian forms by his friend and spiritual father, Mr. Richards. Like his former union, this was non-fruitful; and after the death of Pahia, Malo married a young woman of Lahaina named Lepeka (Rebecca) by whom he became the father of a daughter, whom he named A'a-laioa, in memory of his first wife. To anticipate and bring to a close this part of the narrative, his union with this young woman proved most disastrous; her dissilute ways were a constant thorn in the side of her husband, driving him well nigh to distraction, and ultimately proved the cause of his death.

Having been ordained to the Christian ministry and settled over a church in the district of Kula, Maui, David Malo made his home at the forlorn seaside village of Kalepolepo, on the lee of East Maui, where he continued in the duties of the Christian ministry and in the pastorate of the little church there located during the remaining few years of his life. The shame and disgrace of his wife's conduct told upon him, and at length came to weigh so heavily on his mind that he could not throw it off. He refused all food and became reduced to such a state of weakness that his life was despaired of. The members of his church gathered about his bedside, and with prayer and entreaties sought to turn him from his purpose, but without avail. His last request was to be taken in a canoe to Lahaina, that thus he might be near the site which he had selected as the resting place of his body, which he had indicated to be Pa'u-pa'u, on the hill called Mount Ball that stands back of Lahaina-luna. It would, he had hoped, be above and secure from the rising tide of foreign invasion, which his imagination had pictured as destined to overwhelm the whole land.

His request was fulfilled, and after his death, which took place October 21, 1853, his body was deposited in a tomb on the summit of Mt. Ball, where for nearly half a century it has remained as a beacon to his people.

Lahaina appears to have been the continued place of residence of David Malo from the time of his first coming thither—on leaving

Keauhou—probably some time in the twenties—till he went to the final scene of his labors at Kalepolepo, a period that must have extended over about twenty-five years and included the most useful activities of his life.

*It was during the period of Malo's stay at Lahaina that certain lawless spirits among the sea-rovers collected in that port instituted attacks on the new order of civilization that was winning its way, which were directed—most naturally—against its foremost representative, Mr. Richards. The result was an investigation, a trial, it might be termed in which the issue practically resolved itself into the question whether Mr. Richards was in the right and to be defended or in the wrong and to be punished. Malo was present at the conference and it was no doubt largely due to his native wit and the incisive common sense displayed in his putting of the question that justice speedily prevailed and the cause of law and order triumphed.

While at Lahaina David Malo also occupied for a time the position of school-agent, a post of some responsibility and in which one could usefully exercise an unlimited amount of common sense and business tact; there also was the chief scene of his labors for the preservation in literary form of the history and antiquities of his people.

To confine one's self to that division of David Malo's life-work which is to be classed as literary and historical, the contributions made by him to our knowledge of the ancient history and antiquities of the Hawaiian Islands may be embraced under three heads: First, a small book entitled "Moolelo Hawaii," compiled by Rev. Mr. Pogue from materials largely furnished by the scholars of the Lahaina-luna Seminary. (The reasons for crediting Malo with having lent his hand in this work are to be found in the general similiarity of style and manner of treatment of the historical part of this book with the one next to be mentioned; and still more conclusive evidence is to be seen in the absolute identity of the language in many passages of the two books.) Second, the work, a translation of which is here presented, which is also entitled Moolelo

---

* Here Dr. Emerson refers to the outrages perpetrated by lawless sailors from the whaleships at Lahaina during the years 1825, 1826 and 1827, and to the trial of Mr. Richards held at Honolulu in November, 1827, for the crime of having reported the facts in the United States.

During this trial, David Malo on being consulted by the Queen-Regent, Kaahumanu, said "In what country is it the practice to condemn the man who gives true information of crimes committed, and to let the criminal go uncensured and unpunished?"

See Dibble's History p. 225.

W.D.A.

Hawaii, though it contains many things which do not properly belong to history. The historical part brings us down only to the times of Umi, the son of Liloa. There was also a third, a History of Kamehameha, a work specially undertaken at the request of the learned historian and lexicographer, Rev. Lorrin Andrews, and completed by David Malo after a year's application, during which he made an extended visit to the island of Hawaii for the purpose of consulting the living authorities who were the repositories of the facts or eye-witnesses of the events to be recorded. This book was side-tracked very soon after its completion— even before reaching the hands of Mr. Andrews—and spirited away, since which time it has been hidden from the public eye.

David Malo was a man of strong character, deep and earnest in his convictions, capable of precipitate and violent prejudices, inclining to be austere and at times passionate in temper, yet kind and loving withal, with a gift of pleasantry and having at bottom a warmth of heart which not only made friends but held him fast to friendships once formed. Though nurtured in the superstitious faith and cult of old Hawaii, and though a man of tenacious opinions, when the light reached him, the old errors were dissipated with the darkness, as clouds are dissolved by the rising sun, and his whole intellectual and moral nature felt the stimulus and burst forth with a new growth. Judging from frequent references to such matters in his writings, there must have existed to a more than usual degree in Malo's nature and spiritual makeup that special hunger and thirst which was to be met and more or less assuaged by what was contained in the message of Christian civilization from across the water. So great was the ardor of his quest after knowledge that it is said to have been his custom to catechize the members of his family not only on points of doctrine and belief, but along the lines of general information, on such points as were of interest to himself: the whale, the lion, the zebra, the elephant, the first man, the wind, the weather, the geography of the world—these were some of the topics on which he quizzed the young men and women, as well as the older ones, who gathered in his family. There was room for no educational laggards under his roof.

Malo was one of that class to whom the prophetic vision of the oncoming tide of invasion—peaceful thought it was to be—that was destined to overflow his native land and supplant in a measure its indigenous population, was acutely painful and not to be contemplated with any degree of philosophic calm; and this in spite of the fact that he fully recognized the immense physical, moral and intellectual benefits that had accrued and were still further to accrue to him and his people from the coming of the white man to his shores. And this sentiment, which was like a division of councils in his nature, controlled many of his actions during his life, and decided the place of his burial after death.

David Malo was not only a man of industry, but was able so to shape his enterprises as to make them serve as guides and incentives to a people who stood greatly in need of such leading. At a time when a movement was on foot looking to the industrial development of the resources of the islands, he entered heartily into the notion—it could not be called a scheme—and endeavored to illustrate it by his own efforts, to such an extent that he went into the planting of cotton—on a small scale, of course—purchased a loom and had the fibre spun and woven by the members of his own family under the direction of Mrs. Richards and Miss Ogden. Afterwards, when walking about arrayed in a suit of his own homespun, on being asked where he had obtained the fabric—it was not of the finest—with beaming satisfaction he pointed to the earth as the source of its origin. At the time also when the sugar industry was yet in its earliest infancy in this country, he turned his hand in that direction also, and so far succeeded as to produce an excellent syrup from sugar cane of his own raising.

In the "Narrative of the United States Exploring Expedition," by Charles Wilkes, U. S. N., while commenting upon observations made during the year 1840, Admiral Wilkes, *apropos* of the book-making work under the care of the American missionaries and the writers of the various publications, says, "Some of them are by native authors. Of these I cannot pass at least one without naming him. This is David Malo, who is highly esteemed by all who know him, and who lends the missionaries his aid, in mind as well as example, in ameliorating the condition of his people and checking licentiousness. At the same time he sets an example of industry, by farming with his own hands, and manufactures from his own sugar cane an excellent molasses."

In physique Malo was tall and of spare frame, active, energetic, a good man of business, eloquent of speech, independent in his utterances. He was of a type of mind inclined to be jealous and quick to resent any seeming slight in the way of disparagement or injustice that might be shown to his people or nation, and was one who held tenaciously to the doctrine of national integrity and independence.

The real value of David Malo's contributions to the written history and antiquities of ancient Hawaii is something that must be left for appraisal to the historian, the critic and student of Hawaiian affairs. The lapse of years will no doubt sensibly appreciate this valuation, as well as the regret, which many even at the present time feel most keenly, that more was not saved from the foundering bark of ancient Hawaii. If the student has to mourn the loss of bag and baggage, he may at least congratulate himself on the saving of a portion of the scrip and scrippage—half a loaf is better than no bread.

The result of Malo's labors would no doubt have been much more satisfactory if they had been performed under the immediate supervision and guidance of some mentor capable of looking at the subject from a broad standpoint, ready with wise suggestion; inviting the extension of his labors to greater length and specificness, with greater abundance of detail along certain lines, perhaps calling for the answer to certain questions that now remain unanswered.

As a writer David Malo was handicapped not only by the character and limitations of the language which was his organ of literary expression, but also by the rawness of his experience in the use of the pen. It was only about half a score of years before he broke ground as a literary man that scholars, with serious intent, had taken in hand his mother tongue and, after giving it such symbols of written expression as were deemed suitable to its needs, clothing its literary nakedness with a garb, which in homely simplicity and utility might be compared to the national holoku—the gift of the white woman to her Polynesian sister—and then, having sought out and culled from many sources the idioms and expressions that were pertinent and harmonious to the purpose, had grappled the difficult undertaking of translating the Christian Bible into the Hawaiian language. The result of these scholarly labors was indeed a book, which in fitness, dignity and sublimity of expression might ofttimes be an inspiration to one whose mother tongue is none other than the Anglo-Saxon speech. But this work was not fully completed until 1839, at which time Malo must have been several years at his labors; and though its effect is clearly discernible in the form in which he has cast his thought, yet it would be too much to expect that its influence should have availed to form in him a style representing the best power and range of the language; certainly not to heal the infirmities and make amends for the evolutionary weaknesses of the Hawaiian speech.

N.B. Emerson

I do not suppose the following history to be free from mistakes, in that the material for it has come from oral traditions; consequently it is marred by errors of human judgment and does not approach the accuracy of the word of God.

Davida Malo

Introduction

The trustees of the Bernice Pauahi Museum, by publishing Dr. N.B. Emerson's translation of David Malo's Hawaiian Antiquities, are rendering an important service to all Polynesian scholars.

It will form a valuable contribution not only to Hawaiian archaeology, but also to Polynesian ethnology in general.

It is extremely difficult at this late day to obtain any reliable information in regard to the primitive condition of any branch of the Polynesian race. It rarely happens in any part of the world that an alien can succeed in winning the confidence and gaining an insight into the actual thoughts and feelings of a people separated from himself by profound differences of race, environment and education. But here another difficulty arises from the rapidity of the changes which are taking place throughout the Pacific Ocean, and from the inevitable mingling of old and new, which discredits much of the testimony of natives born and educated under the new regime.

In the following work, however, we have the testimony of one who was born and grew up to manhood under the tabu system, who had himself been a devout worshipper of the old gods, who had been brought up at the royal court, and who was considered by his countrymen as an authority on the subjects on which he afterwards wrote.

His statements are confirmed in many particulars by those of John Ii of Kekuanaoa, of the elder Kamakau of Kaawaloa, and of the historian, S. M. Kamakau, the latter of whom, however, did not always keep his versions of the ancient traditions free from foreign admixture.

Although David Malo evidently needed judicious advice as to his choice and treatment of subjects, some important topics having been omitted, and although his work is unfinished, yet it contains materials of great value for the "noblest study of mankind." Its value is very much enhanced by the learned notes and appendices with which Dr. Emerson has enriched it.

The following statement may serve to clear away some misapprehensions. The first "Moolelo Hawaii" (*i.e.,* Hawaiian History), was written at Lahainaluna about 1835–36 by some of the older students, among whom was David Malo, then 42 years of age. They formed what may be called the first Hawaiian Historical Society. The work was revised by Rev. Sheldon Dibble, and was published at Lahainaluna in

1838. A translation of it into English by Rev. R. Tinker was published in the *Hawaiian Spectator* in 1839. It has also been translated into French by M. Jules Remy, and was published in Paris in 1862.

The second edition of the Moolelo Hawaii, which appeared in 1858, was compiled by Rev. J. F. Pogue, who added to the first edition extensive extracts from the manuscript of the present work, which was then the property of Rev. Lorrin Andrews, for whom it had been written, probably about 1840.

David Malo's Life of Kamehameha I, which is mentioned by Dr. Emerson in his life of Malo, must have been written before that time, as it passed through the hands of Rev. W. Richards and of Nahienaena, who died December 30, 1836. Its disappearance is much to be deplored.

W.D. ALEXANDER

I

General Remarks on Hawaiian History

1. The traditions about the Hawaiian Islands handed down from remote antiquity are not entirely definite; there is much obscurity as to the facts, and the traditions themselves are not clear. Some of the matters reported are clear and intelligible, but the larger part are vague.

2. The reason for this obscurity and vagueness is that the ancients were not possessed of the art of letters, and thus were unable to record the events they witnessed, the traditions handed down to them from their forefathers and the names of the lands in which their ancestors were born. They do, however, mention by name the lands in which they sojourned, but not the towns and the rivers. Because of the lack of a record of these matters it is impossible at the present time to make them out clearly.

3. The ancients left no records of the lands of their birth, of what people drove them out, who were their guides and leaders, of the canoes that transported them, what lands they visited in their wanderings, and what gods they worshipped. Certain oral traditions do, however, give us the names of the idols of our ancestors.

4. Memory was the only means possessed by our ancestors of preserving historical knowledge; it served them in place of books and chronicles.

5. No doubt this fact explains the vagueness and uncertainty of the more ancient traditions, of which some are handed down correctly, but the great mass incorrectly. It is likely there is greater accuracy and less error in the traditions of a later date.

6. Faults of memory in part explain the contradictions that appear in the ancient traditions, for we know by experience that "the heart* is the most deceitful of all things."

7. When traditions are carried in the memory it leads to contradictory versions. One set think the way they heard the story is the true version; another set think theirs is the truth; a third set very likely purposely falsify. Thus it comes to pass that the traditions are split up and made worthless.

8. The same cause no doubt produced contradictions in the genealogies (*moo-kuanhau*). The initial ancestor in one genealogy differed from that in

another, the advocate of each genealogy claiming his own version to be the correct one. This cause also operated in the same way in producing contradictions in the historical traditions; one party received the tradition in one way, another party received it in another way.

9. In regard to the worship of the gods, different people had different gods, and both the worship and the articles tabued differed the one from the other. Each man did what seemed to him right, thus causing disagreement and confusion.

10. The genealogies have many separate lines, each one different from the other, but running into each other. Some of the genealogies begin with *Kumu-lipo*[1] as the initial point; others with *Pali-ku*[2]; others with *Lolo*[3]; still others with *Pu-anue*[4]; and others with *Ka-po-hihi*.[5] This is not like the genealogy from Adam, which is one unbroken line without any stems.

11. There are, however, three genealogies that are greatly thought of as indicating the Hawaiian people as well as their kings, These are *Kumu-lipo, Pali-ku,* and *Lolo*. And it would seem as if the Tahitians and Nuuhivans had perhaps the same origin, for their genealogies agree with these.

Notes to Chapter I

(* *Naau,* literally bowels, is the word used for heart or moral nature. To commit to memory was *hoopaa naau*).

1. Sect. 10. *Kumu-lipo,* origin in darkness, chaos. *Ripo-ripo* is a Polynesian word meaning vortex, abyss. In Hawaiian, with a change of the Maori and Tahitian *r* to *l*, it was applied to the blackness of the deep sea. Origin by *Kumu-lipo* may by a little stretch of imagination be regarded as implying the nebular hypothesis.

2. Sect. 10. *Pali-ku* meant literally vertical precipice. There is in the phrase a tacit allusion to a riving of the mountains by earthquake—cataclysmal theory of cosmogony. "*Pali-ku na mauna*" is an expression used in a *pule*.

3. Sect. 10. *Lolo,* brains in modern Hawaiian parlance; more anciently perhaps it meant the oily meat of the cocoanut prepared for making scented oil. (See Maori Comp. Dict., Tregear).

I have taken the liberty to omit the article *o*, which Mr. Malo had mistakenly incorporated with the word, thus leaving only the bare substantive.

4. Sect. 10. *Pu-anue;* Mr. S. Percy Smith kindly suggests, *Pu*, stem, root, origin. *Anue,* the rainbow. Cf. Samoan account of the origin of mankind from the *Fue-sa,* or sacred vine, which developed worms (iloilo), from which came mankind.

5. Sect. 10. *Ka-po-hihi*: The branching out or darting forth of *po*, *i.e.*, night or chaos. *Po* was one of the cosmic formative forces of Polynesia. *Hihi*: to branch forth or spread out, as a growing vine. *Po-hi-hi-hi* means obscure, puzzling, mysterious. In Maori, Tahitian and Marquesan *hihi* means a sunbeam, a ray of the sun. N. B. The cosmogony of Southern Polynesia also included *Kore*, void or nothingness, as one of the primal cosmic forces. (See *Kore*, Maori Comp. Dict., Tregear).

II

Formation of the Land

(*Cosmogony*)

1. It is very surprising to hear how contradictory are the accounts given by the ancients of the origin of the land here in Hawaii.

2. It is in their genealogies (*moo-ku-auhau*) that we shall see the disagreement of their ideas in this regard.

3. In the *moo-kuauhan*, or genealogy named *Pu-anue*, it is said that the earth and the heavens were begotten (*hanau maoli mai*).

4. It was *Kumukumu-ke-kaa* who gave birth to them, her husband being *Paia-a-ka-lani*. Another genealogy declares that *Ka-mai-eli* gave birth to the foundations of the earth (*mole o ka honua*), the father being *Kumu-honua*.

5. In the genealogy of *Wakea* it is said that *Papa* gave birth to these Islands. Another account has it that this group of islands were not begotten, but really made by the hands of *Wakea* himself.

6. We now perceive their error. If the women in that ancient time gave birth to countries then indeed would they do so in these days; and if at that time they were made by the hands of *Wakea*, doubtless the same thing would be done now.

7. In the genealogy called *Kumu-lipo* it is said that the land grew up of itself, not that it was begotten, nor that it was made by hand.

8. Perhaps this is the true account and these Hawaiian islands did grow up of themselves, and after that human beings appeared on them. Perhaps this is the best solution of the mistaken views held by the ancients; who knows?

9. In these days certain learned men have searched into and studied up the origin of the Hawaiian Islands, but whether their views are correct no one can say, because they are but speculations.

10. These scientists from other lands have advanced a theory and expressed the opinion that there was probably no land here in ancient times, only ocean; and they think that the Islands rose up out of the ocean as a result of volcanic action.

11. Their reasons for this opinion are that certain islands are known which have risen up out of the ocean and which present features similar

to Hawaii nei. Again a sure indication is that the soil of these Islands is wholly volcanic. All the islands of this ocean are volcanic, and the rocks, unlike those of the continents, have been melted in fire. Such are their speculations and their reasoning.

12. The rocks of this country are entirely of volcanic origin. Most of the volcanoes are now extinct, but in past ages there were volcanoes on Maui and on all the Islands. For this reason it is believed that these Islands were thrown up from beneath the ocean. This view may not be entirely correct; it is only a speculation.

13. It is possible, however, that there has always been land here from the beginning, but we cannot be sure because the traditions of the ancients are utterly unreliable and astray in their vagaries.

Note to Chapter II

1. Sect. 4. *Paia-a-ka-lani*: *Paia* was a Maori goddess, daughter of *Rangi* and *Papa*, sister of *Tane, Tu, Tanga-loa* and *Rongo*.

III

The Origin of the Primitive Inhabitants of Hawaii nei

1. In Hawaiian ancestral genealogies it is said that the earliest inhabitants of these Islands were the progenitors of all the Hawaiian people.

2. In the genealogy called *Kumu-lipo* it is said that the first human being was a woman named *La'ila'i* and that her ancestors and parents were of the night (*he po wale no*), that she was the progenitor of the (Hawaiian) race.

3. The husband of this *La'ila'i* was named *Ke-alii-wahi-lani* (the king who opens heaven); but it is not stated who were the parents of *Ke-alii-wahi-lani*, only that he was from the heavens; that he looked down and beheld a beautiful woman, *La'ila'i*, dwelling in *Lalawaia;* that he came down and took her to wife, and from the union of these two was begotten one of the ancestors of this race.

4. And after *La'ila'i* and her company it is again stated in the genealogy called *Lolo* that the first native Hawaiian (*kanaka*) was a man named *Kahiko*. His ancestry and parentage are given, but without defining their character; it is only said he was a human being (*kanaka*).

5. *Kupulanakehau* was the name of Kahiko's wife; they begot *Lihauula and Wakea.* Wakea had a wife named *Haumea*, who was the same as *Papa*. In the genealogy called *Pali-ku* it is said that the parents and ancestors of Haumea the wife of Wakea were *pali, i.e.,* precipices. With her the race of men was definitely established.

6. These are the only people spoken of in the Hawaiian genealogies; they are therefore presumably the earliest progenitors of the Hawaiian race. It is not stated that they were born here in Hawaii. Probably all of these persons named were born in foreign lands, while their genealogies were preserved here in Hawaii.

7. One reason for thinking so is that the countries where these people lived are given by name and no places in Hawaii are called by the same names. La'ila'i and Ke-alii-wahi-lani lived in Lalowaia; Kahiko and Kupu-lana-ke-hau lived in Kamawae-lua-lani: Wakea and Papa lived in *Lolo-i-mehani.*[1]

8. There is another fact mentioned in the genealogies, to-wit: that when Wakea and Papa were divorced from each other, Papa went away and dwelt in *Nuu-meha-lani.*[2] There is no place here in Hawaii called Nuu-meha-lani. The probability is that these names belong to some foreign country.

Notes to Chapter III

1. Sect. 7. *Lolo–i–mehani*: *Te Mehani* in Raiatea was the Tahitian Hades.
2. Sect. 8. *Nuu–meha–lani*: undoubtedly the same as Nuu-mea-lani.

IV

OF THE GENERATIONS DESCENDED FROM WAKEA

1. It is said that from Wakea down to the death of *Haumea* there were six generations, and that these generations all lived in Lolo-i-mehani; but it is not stated that they lived in any other place; nor is it stated that they came here to Hawaii to live.

2. Following these six generations of men came nineteen generations, one of which, it is supposed, migrated hither and lived here in Hawaii, because it is stated that a man named Kapawa, of the twentieth generation, was born in Kukaniloko, in Waialua, on Oahu.

3. It is clearly established that from Kapawa down to the present time generations of men continued to be born here in Hawaii; but it is not stated that people came to this country from Lolo-i-mehani; nor is it stated who they were that first came and settled here in Hawaii; nor that they came in canoes, *waa;* nor at what time they arrived here in Hawaii.

4. It is thought that this people came from lands near Tahiti and from Tahiti itself, because the ancient Hawaiians at an early date mentioned the name of Tahiti in their *meles,* prayers, and legends.

5. I will mention some of the geographical names given in meles: *Kahiki-honua-kele,*[1] *Anana-i-malu,*[2] *Holani,*[3] *Hawa-ii, Nuu-hiwa;* in legends or *kaaos, Upolu, Wawau, Kukapuaiku, Kuaihelani;* in prayers, *Uliuli, Melemele, Polapola, Haehac, Maokuululu, Hanakalauai.*

6. Perhaps these names belong to lands in Tahiti. Where, indeed, are they? Very likely our ancestors sojourned in these lands before they came hither to Hawaii.

7. Perhaps because of their affection for Tahiti and Hawaii they applied the name Kahiki—nui to a district of Maui, and named this group (*pae-aina*) Hawaii. If not that, possibly the names of the first men to settle on these shores were Hawaii, Maui, Oahu, Kauai, and at their death the islands were called by their names.

8. The following is one way by which knowledge regarding Tahiti actually did reach these shores: We are informed (by historical tradition) that two men named Paao and Makuakaumana, with a company of

others, voyaged hither, observing the stars as a compass; and that Paao remained in Kohala, while Makua-kaumana returned to Tahiti.

9. Paao arrived at Hawaii during the reign of *Lono-ka-wai*,[4] the king of Hawaii. He (Lono-ka-wai) was the sixteenth in that line of kings, succeeding Kapawa.

10. Paao continued to live in Kohala until the kings of Hawaii became degraded and corrupted (*hewa*); then he sailed away to Tahiti to fetch a king from thence. *Pili*[5] (Kaaiea) was that king and he became one in Hawaii's line of kings (*papa alii*).

11. It is thought that Kapua in Kona was the point of Paao's departure, whence he sailed away in his canoe; but it is not stated what kind of a canoe it was. In his voyage to Hawaii, Pili was accompanied by Paao and Makua-kaumana and others. The canoes (probably two coupled together as a double canoe—Translator) were named *Ka-nalo-a-mu-ia*. We have no information as to whether these canoes were of the kind called *Pahi*.

12. Tradition has it that on his voyage to this country Pili was accompanied by two schools of fish, one of *opelu* and another of *aku*, and when the wind kicked up a sea, the *aku* would frisk and the *opelu* would assemble together, as a result of which the ocean would entirely calm down. In this way Pili and his company were enabled to voyage till they reached Hawaii. On this account the *opelu* and the *aku* were subject to a tabu in ancient times. After his arrival at Hawaii, Pili was established as king over the land, and his name was one of the ancestors in Hawaii's line of kings.

13. There is also a tradition of a man named Moikeha, who came to this country from Tahiti in the reign of Kalapana, king of Hawaii.

14. After his arrival Moikeha went to Kauai to live and took to wife a woman of that island named Hinauulua, by whom he had a son, to whom he gave the name Kila.

15. When Kila was grown up he in turn sailed on an expedition to Tahiti, taking his departure, it is said, from the western point of Kahoolawe, for which reason that cape is to this day called *Ke-ala-i-kahiki* (the route to Tahiti).

16. Kila arrived in safety at Tahiti and on his return to these shores brought back with him *Laa-mai-kahiki*.[7] On the arrival of Laa was introduced the use of the *kaekeeke*[8] drum. An impetus was given at the same time to the use of sinnet in canoe lashing (*aha hoa waa*), together with improvements in the plaited ornamental knots or lashings, called

lanalana.[9] The names I have mentioned are to be numbered among the ancestors of Hawaiian kings and people, and such was the knowledge and information obtained from Tahiti in ancient times, and by such means as I have described was it received.

17. The Hawaiians are thought to be of one race with the people of Tahiti and the Islands adjacent to it. The reason for this belief is that the people closely resemble each other in their physical features, language, genealogies, traditions (and legends), as well as in (the names of) their deities. It is thought that very likely they came to Hawaii in small detachments.

19. It seems probable that this was the case from the fact that in Tahiti they have large canoes called *pahi;* and it seems likely that its possession enabled them to make their long voyages to Hawaii. The ancients are said to have been skilled also in observing the stars, which served them as a mariner's compass in directing their course.

20. The very earliest and most primitive canoes of the Hawaiians were not termed *pahi,* nor yet were they called *moku* (ships); the ancients called them *waa.*

21. It has been said, however, that this race of people came from the *lewa,*[10] the firmament, the atmosphere; from the windward or back of the island (*kua o ka moku*).

22. The meaning of these expressions is that they came from a foreign land, that is the region of air, and the front of that land is at the back of these islands.

23. Perhaps this was a people forced to flee hither by war, or driven in this direction by bad winds and storms. Perhaps by the expression *lewa,* or regions of air, Asia is referred to; perhaps this expression refers to islands they visited on their way hither; so that on their arrival they declared they came from the back (the windward) of these islands.

24. Perhaps this race of people was derived from the Israelites, because we know that certain customs of the Israelites were practiced here in Hawaii.

25. Circumcision, places of refuge, tabus (and ceremonies of purification) relating to dead bodies and their burial, tabus and restrictions pertaining to a flowing woman, and the tabu that secluded a woman as defiled during the seven days after childbirth—all these customs were formerly practiced by the people of Hawaii.

26. Perhaps these people are those spoken of in the Word of God as "the lost sheep of the House of Israel," because on inspection we clearly

see that the people of Asia are just like the inhabitants of these islands, of Tahiti and the lands adjacent.

Notes to Chapter IV

1. Sect. 5. *Kahiki-honua-kele:* In Hawaiian the root *kele* is part of the word *kele-kele* meaning muddy, miry, or fat, greasy. In Tonga the meaning also is muddy. It is a word applied to the soil.

2. Sect. 5. *Anana-i-malu:* Mr. S. P. Smith suggests that *Anana* is the same as ngangana, an ancient name for some part of *Hawa-iki raro,* or the Fiji and Samoan groups.

3. Sect. 5. *Holani:* It is suggested that this is the same as *Herangi,* the Maori name for a place believed to be in Malaysia.

4. According to the ULU GENEALOGY, given by Fornander, "The Polynesian Race," Vol. I, p. 191, *Lana-ka-wai* is the seventeenth name after *Hele-i-pawa.* It seems probable, as implied by Fornander, loc. cit. Vol. II, p. 21, that *Hele-i-pawa* and *Ka-pawa* were the same person; also that *Lana-ka-wai* is an erroneous orthography for *Lono-ka-wai.* (Granting these emendations, the problem of reconciling the tangled skein of Hawaiian genealogies is made a little easier.)

5. Sect. 10. *Pili (Kaaiea):* Pili is an ancient Samoan name.

6. *Pahi* is the Tahitian or Paumotuan for boat, ship, or canoe. (In Mangarevan *pahi* means ship.)

7. Laa was a son of Moikeha who had remained in Tahiti.

8. The *haekeeke* was a carved, hollow log, covered with sharkskin at one end and used as a drum to accompany the hula.

9. *Lanalana* is the name applied to the lashing that bound the *amo* or float to the curved cross-pieces of the canoe's outrigger. These lashings were often highly ornamental. One of them was called *pa'u-o-luukia,* a very decorative affair, said to have been so styled from the corset, or woven contrivance, by which Moikeha's paramour, the beautiful Luukia, defended herself against the assaults of her lover, when she had become alienated from him. *Aha* is used substantively to mean sinnet, or the lashing of a canoe made from sinnet, *Lanalana* is not used substantively to mean sinnet.

10. According to Wm. Wyatt Gill the Mangaians represent all ships as breaking through from the sky. This expression is in strict accordance with the cosmogony of the time, that the earth was a plain, the sky a dome, and the horizon a solid wall—*kukulu*—on which the heavens rested.

V

Names Given to Directions or the Points of the Compass

1. The ancients named directions or the points of the compass from the course of the sun. The point where the sun rose was called *kukulu*[1] *hikina*, and where the sun set was called *kukulu komohana*.

2. If a man faces towards the sunset his left hand will point to the south, *kukulu hema*, his right to the north *kukulu akau*. These names apply only to the heavens (*lani*), not[2] to the land or island (*mokupuni*).

3. These points were named differently when regard was had to the borders or coasts (*aoao*) of an island. If a man lived on the western side of an island the direction of sun-rising was termed *uka*, and the direction of sun-setting *kai*, so termed because he had to ascend a height in going inland, uka, and descend to a lower level in going to the sea, kai.[3]

4. Again, north, *kukulu akau*, is also spoken of as *luna*, or *i-luna*, up and south is spoken of as *lalo* down, the reason being that that quarter of the heavens, north, when the (prevailing) wind blows is spoken of as up, and the southern quarter, towards which it blows, is spoken of as down.

5. As to the heavens, they are called the solid above, *ka paa iluna*,[4] the parts attached to the earth are termed *ka paa ilalo*, the solid below; the space between the heavens and the earth is sometimes termd *ka lewa*, the space in which things hang or swing. Another name is *ka hookui*,[5] the point of juncture, and another still is *ka halawai*,[5] *i.e.*, the meeting.

6. To a man living on the coast of an island the names applied to the points of compass, or direction, varied according to the side of the island on which he lived.

7. If he lived on the eastern side of the island he spoke of the west as *uka*, the east as *kai*. This was when he lived on the side looking east. For the same reason he would term South *akau*, because his right hand pointed in that direction, and north he would term *hema*,[8] *i.e.*, left, because his left hand pointed that way.

9. In the same way by one living on the southern exposure of an island, facing squarely to the south, the east would be called *hema*, left, *akau*, the west.

10. So also to one living on the northern face of an island the names applied to the points of compass are correspondingly all changed about.

11. Here is another style of naming the east: from the coming of the sun it is called the sun arrived, *ka-la-hiki*, and the place of the sun's setting is called *ka-la-kau*, the sun lodged. Accordingly they had the expression *mai ka la hiki a ka la kau* from the sun arrived to the sun lodged; or they said *mai kela paa a keia paa*,[7] from that solid to this solid.

12. These terms applied only to the borders, or coasts, of an island, not to the points of the heavens, for it was a saying "O Hawaii ka la hiki, o Kauai ka la kau," Hawaii is the sun arrived, Kauai is the sun lodged. The north of the islands was spoken of as "that solid," *kela paa*, and the south of the group as "this solid," *keia paa*. It was in this sense they used the expression "from that firmament—or solid—to this firmament."

13. According to another way of speaking of directions (*kukulu*), the circle of the horizon encompassing the earth at the borders of the ocean, where the sea meets the base of the heavens, *kumu lani*, this circle was termed *kukulu o ka honua*, the compass of the earth.

14. The border of the sky where it meets the ocean-horizon is termed the *kukulu-o-ka-lani*, the walls of heaven.

15. The circle or zone of the earth's surface, whether sea or land, which the eye traverses in looking to the horizon is called *Kahikimoe*.

16. The circle of the sky which bends upwards from the horizon is *Kahiki-ku*; above Kahiki-ku is a zone called *Kahiki-ke-papa-nuu;* and above that is *Kahiki-ke-papa-lani;* and directly over head is *Kahiki-kapui-holani-ke-kuina.*

17. The space directly beneath the heavens is called *lewa-lani;* beneath that, where the birds fly, is called *lewa-nuu;* beneath that is *lewa-lani-lewa;* and beneath that, the space in which a man's body would swing were he suspended from a tree, with his feet clear of the earth, was termed *lewa-hoomakua.* By such a terminology as this did the ancients designate direction.

Notes to Chapter V

1. Sect. 1. *Kukulu* was a wall or vertical erection, such as was supposed to stand at the limits of the horizon and support the dome of heaven. *Hikina* is the contracted form of *hiki ana* coming, appearing. *Komohana* is the contracted form of *komo* and *hana*, which latter is represented in modern Hawaiian by *ana*, the present participial ending.

3. Sect. 3. The explanation given of this terminology is a complete begging of the question, and is no explanation at all.

4. Sect. 5. *Ka paa iluna* is literally the upper *firmament,* taking this word in its original and proper meaning.

6. Sect. 5. *Ka halawai.* This last expression is probably applied to the horizon, the line where the walls of heaven join the plain of the earth.

2. Sect. 2. I think Malo is mistaken in this statement. The terms *hikina*, or *kukulu-hikina, komohana,* etc., as designating East, West, North, South, were of general application, on sea and on land; whereas, the expressions *uka* and *kai,* with their prefixes *ma* and *i,* making *makai* and *ikai, mauka* and *iuka,* etc., had sole reference to position on or tendency towards land or sea, towards or away from the centre of the island. The primitive and generic meaning of the word *uka,* judging from its uses in the Southern languages, was that of stickiness, solidity, standing ground. Where a man's feet stood on solid ground was *uka.* Nowhere in the world more than in the Pacific could the distinction between *terra firma* and the continent of waters that surrounded it be of greater importance, and the necessity for nicely and definitely distinguishing it in language be more urgent. The makers of the Hawaiian tongue and speech well understood their own needs.

5. Sect. 5. *Hookui* is undoubtedly that part of the vault of heaven, the zenith, where the sweeping curves of heaven's arches meet; the *halawai* was probably the line of junction between the *kukulu,* walls or pillars on which rested the celestial dome, and the plane of the earth. The use of these two terms is illustrated in the following:

Pule Hoola

> *Na Au-makua mai ka la hiki a ka la kau,*
> *Mai ka hoo-kui a ka halawai!*
> *Na Au-makua ia ka-hina-kua, ia ka-hina-alo,*
> *la kaa-akau i ka lani,*
> *O kiha i ka lani,*
> *Owe i ka lani,*
> *Nunulu i ka lani,*
> *Kaholo i ka lani,*
> *Eia ka pulapula a oukou, o Mahoe.*
> *E malama oukou iaia.,* etc., etc.

Ye ancestral deities from the rising to the setting of the sun!
From the zenith to the horizon!
Ye ancestral deities who stand at our back and at our front!
Ye gods who stand at our right hand!
A breathing in the heavens,
An utterance in the heavens,

A clear, ringing voice in the heavens,
A voice reverberating in the heavens!
Here comes your child, Mahoe.
Safeguard him! etc., etc.

7. Sect. 11. *Mai kela paa a keia paa,* literally from one firmament to another firmament, direction in a vertical line.

I should be remarked that the Hawaiian of today is utterly and entirely unacquainted with these terms. He may have heard them used by his grandmother, or some wise person, but not one in a thousand can explain their use or meaning.

8. Sect. 8. There certainly has been no such confusion in the use of these terms among the Hawaiians of the present generation as to lead one to think that David Malo's statements are not mistaken. The Hawaiians, as a race of navigators from their earliest traditional recollection, are now and must have been eminently clear-headed in all that concerned matters of direction. I do not believe their terminology of direction was quite so confused as would appear from Malo's statements. The Hawaiian, in common with other Polynesians, was alive to the importance of marking the right-handed and left-handed direction of things relative to himself, and it is easy to believe that for temporary and supplemental purposes he might for the moment indicate a northerly direction by reference to his left side, but that it was more than a temporary, or incidental use I do not credit. It is true that his term for North was *Akau,* the same as was used to express the right; but it must be observed that in designating the points of the compass they coupled with the *Hema,* or *Akau,* the word *kukulu.*

VI

Terms Used to Designate Space Above and Below

1. The ancients applied the following names to the divisions of space above us. The space immediately above one's head when standing erect is spoken of as *luna-ae;* above that *luna-aku;* above that *luna-loa-aku;* above that *luna-lilo-aku;* above that *luna-lilo-loa;* and above that, in the firmament where the clouds float, is *luna-o-ke-ao;* and above that were three divisions called respectively *ke-ao-ulu, ka-lani-uli* and *ka-lani-paa,* the solid heavens.

2. *Ka-lani-paa* is that region in the heavens which seems so remote when one looks up into the sky. The ancients imagined that in it was situated the track along which the sun travelled until it set beneath the ocean, then turning back in its course below till it climbed up again at the east. The orbits of the moon and the stars also were thought to be in the same region with that of the sun, but the earth was supposed to be solid and motionless.

3. The clouds, which are objects of importance in the sky, were named from their color or appearance. A black cloud was termed *eleele,* if blue-black it was called *uliuli,* if glossy black *hiwahiwa,* or *polo-hiwa.* Another name for such a cloud was *panopano.*

4. A white cloud was called *keokeo,* or *kea.* If a cloud had a greenish tinge it was termed *maomao,* if a yellowish tinge *lena.* A red cloud was termed *ao ula,* or *kiawe-ula* or *onohi-ula,* red eye-ball. If a cloud hung low in the sky it was termed *hoo-lewa-lewa,* or the term *hoo-pehu-pehu,* swollen, was applied to it. A sheltering cloud was called *hoo-malu-malu,* a thick black cloud *hoo-koko-lii,* a threatening cloud *hoo-weli-weli.* Clouds were named according to their character.

5. If a cloud was narrow and long, hanging low in the horizon, it was termed *opua,* a bunch or cluster. There were many kinds of *opua* each being named according to its appearance. If the leaves of the *opua* pointed downwards it might indicate wind or storm, but if the leaves pointed upwards, calm weather. If the cloud was yellowish and hung low in the horizon it was called *newe-newe,* plump, and was a sign of very calm weather.

6. If the sky in the western horizon was blue-black, *uli-uli,* at sunset it was said to be *pa-uli* and was regarded as prognosticating a high surf, *kai-koo.* If there was an opening in the cloud, like the jaw of the *a'u,* (sword fish), it was called *ena* and was considered a sign of rain.

7. When the clouds in the eastern heavens were red in patches before sunrise it was called *kahea* (a call) and was a sign of rain. If the cloud lay smooth over the mountains in the morning it was termed *papala* and foretokened rain. It was also a sign of rain when the mountains were shut in with blue-black clouds, and this appearance was termed *pala-moa.* There were many other signs that betokened rain.

8. If the sky was entirely overcast, with almost no wind, it was said to be *poi-pu* (shut up), or *hoo-ha-ha,* or *hoo-lu-luhi;* and if the wind started up the expression *hoo-ka-kaa,* a rolling together, was used. If the sky was shut in with thick, heavy clouds it was termed *hakuma,* and if the clouds that covered the sky were exceedingly black it was thought that *Ku-lani-ha-koi* was in them, the place whence came thunder, lightning, wind, rain, violent storms.

9. When it rained, if it was with wind, thunder, lightning and perhaps a rainbow, the rain-storm would probably not continue long. But if the rain was unaccompanied by wind it would probably be a prolonged storm. When the western heavens are red at sunset the appearance is termed *aka-ula* (red shadow or glow) and is loooked upon as a sign that the rain will clear up.

10. When the stars fade away and disappear it is *ao,* daylight, and when the sun rises day has come, we call it *la;* and when the sun becomes warm, morning is past. When the sun is directly overhead it is *awakea,* noon; and when the sun inclines to the west in the afternoon the expression is *ua aui ka la.* After that comes evening, called *ahi-ahi* (*ahi* is fire) and then sunset, *napoo ka la,* and then comes *po,* the night, and the stars shine out.

11. Midnight, the period when men are wrapped in sleep, is called *au-moe,* (the tide of sleep). When the milky way passes the meridian and inclines to the west, people say *ua huli ka i'a,* the fish has turned. *Ua ala-ula mai o kua, ua moku ka pawa o ke ao; a kcokeo mauka, a wehe ke ala-ula, a pua-lena, a ao loa, i.e.,* there comes a glimmer of color in the mountains, the curtains of night are parted; the mountains light up; day breaks; the east blooms with yellow; it is broad daylight.

12. Rain is an important phenomenon from above; it lowers the temperature. The ancients thought that smoke from below turned into

clouds and produced rain. Some rain-storms have their origin at a distance. The *kona* was a storm of rain with wind from the south, a heavy rain. The *hoolua*-storm was likewise attended with heavy rain, but with wind from the north. The *naulu*, accompanied with rain, is violent but of short duration.

13. The rain called *awa* is confined to the mountains, while that called *kualau* occurs at sea. There is also a variety of rain termed *a-oku*. A water-spout was termed *wai-pui-lani*. There were many names used by the ancients to designate appropriately the varieties of rain peculiar to each part of the island coast; the people of each region naming the varieties of rain as they deemed fitting. A protracted rain-storm was termed *ua-loa*, one of short duration *ua poko*, a cold rain *ua hea*.

14. The ancients also had names for the different winds.[1]

15. Wind always produced a coolness in the air. There was the *kona*, a wind from the south, of great violence and of wide extent. It affected all sides of an island, east, west, north and south, and continued for many days. It was felt as a gentle wind on the *Koolau*—the north-eastern or trade-wind—side of an island, but violent and tempestuous on the southern coast, or the front of the islands, (*ke alo o na mokupuni*).

16. The kona wind often brings rain, though sometimes it is rainless. There are many different names applied to this wind. The *kona-ku* is accompanied with an abundance of rain; but the *kona-mae,* the withering kona, is a cold wind. The *kona-lani* brings slight showers; the *kona-hea* is a cold storm; and the *kona hili-maia*—the banana-thrashing kona—blows directly from the mountains.

17. The *hoolua*, a wind that blows from the north, sometimes brings rain and sometimes is rainless.

18. The *hau* is a wind from the mountains, and they are thought to be the cause of it, because this wind invariably blows from the mountains outwards towards the circumference of the island.[2]

19. There is a wind which blows from the sea, and is thought to be the current of the land-breeze returning again to the mountains. This wind blows only on the leeward exposure or front (*alo*) of an island. In some parts this wind is named *eka* (a name used in Kona, Hawaii), in others *aa,* (a name used at Lahaina and elsewhere,), in others *kai-a-ulu,* and in others still *inu-wai.*[3] There was a great variety of names applied to the winds by the ancients as the people saw fit to name them in different places.

20. The place beneath where we stand is called *lalo;* below that is *lalo-o-ka-lcpo* (under ground); still below that is *lalo-liloa* (the full form

of the expression would be *lalo-lilo-loa); the region still further below the one last mentioned was called *lalo-ka-papa-ku.*[4]

21. A place in the ocean was said to be *maloko o ke kai,* that is where fish always live. Where the ocean looks black it is very deep and there live the great fish. The birds make their home in the air; some birds live in the mountains.

Notes to Chapter VI

1. Sect. 14. It would be a hopeless task to enumerate all the names use din designating the winds on the different islands. The same wind was often called by as many names on the same island as there were capes and headlands along the coast of that island. See the legend of *Kamapuaa* for a list of names of winds about Oahu, also the story of Paka'a.

2. Sect. 18. *Hau.* Evidently the land-breeze.

3. Sect. 19. *Inu-wai,* water-drinking, is a name not frequently applied to a rainless wind that wilts and dries up the herbage.

4. Sect. 20. "The general support of tradition is given to the idea that *Papa* is the same person as *Papa-tu-a-nuku* (earth standing in space); but White gives legends affirming that *Papa-tu a-nuku* was really the wife of Tangaroa, and that Rangi and Tangaroa fought for her possession (mythically ocean and sky claiming and warring for earth). Tangaroa was the victor," etc. Maori Comp. Dict., Edward Tregear. Article on *Papa, Papa-tu-a-nuku* (mythological).

5. Sect. 20. In a song of rejoicing by Kukaloloa, celebrating the escape of Keoua-kuhauula and Keawe-mauhili, after the battle of Mokuohai, in which Kamehameha I was victorious, I find the following:

> *Moku ka ia i ka papa-ku o Wakea,*
> *O Wakea hauli i ka lani,*
> *Hauli i ka papa-ku o Lono.*

MSS. Notes on the Waa p. 14.

This ancient mele has two meanings, like very many Hawaiian meles. The archaic meaning I cannot yet make out. Polikapa gives me the following, which seems to me ingenious, but modern.

> Torn is the fish from the embrace of Wakea,
> Wakea who has fallen from heaven,
> Fallen to the level of the hard world.

The phrase *moku ia* is generally used to mean the turning of the milky way towards the west at midnight, and *papa-ku* the underground stratum that would have to be passed before one reached Milu or Hades, if any one can tell which that is. In the modern meaning, which is the one I have given, *ia* (literally a fish) means a woman, while *papa-ku o Wakea* means the breast, *i.e.,* the embrace of Wakea.

Hauli i ka lani, literally has fallen from heaven, may mean has been robbed of his paradise, that is, his companion. *Papa-ku o Lono,* I am told, means the back of a man, a slang phrase, archaic slang, *i.e.,* a figurative form of expression, such as abound in the wilderness of Hawaiian poetic phraseology. But into plain speech, the meaning of this poetical fragment is, the woman has been torn from the embrace of Wakea; Wakea has lost his paradise; his consort has been carried away on the back of another.

The interpretation of the passage has apparently led me far afield and landed me in unknown territory. I can see in it a possible allusion to the separation of Wakea from his wife Papa, which according to Southern Polynesian myth was the lifting up of the vault of heaven from the plain of the Earth, Papa; but in Hawaiian tradition was often spoken of as the divorce of the woman Papa by the man, her husband, Wakea.

VII

NATURAL AND ARTIFICIAL DIVISIONS OF THE LAND

1. The ancients gave names to the natural features of the land according to their ideas of fitness. Two names were used to indicate an island; one was *moku*, another was *aina*. As separated from other islands by the sea, the term *moku* (cut off) was applied to it; as the stable dwelling place of men, it was called *aina*, land, (place of food).

2. When many islands were grouped together, as in Hawaii nei, they were called *pae-moku* or *pae-aina;* if but one *moku* or *aina*.

3. If one (easily) voyaged in a canoe from one island to another, the island from which he went and that from which he sailed were termed *moku kele i ka waa*, an island to be reached by a canoe, because they were both to be reached by voyaging in a canoe.

4. Each of the larger divisions of this group, like Hawaii, Maui and the others, is called a *moku-puni* (*moku*, cut off, and *puni*, surrounded).

5. An island is divided up into districts called *apana*, pieces, or *moku-o-loko*, interior divisions, for instance Kona on Hawaii, or Hana on Maui, and so with the other islands.

6. These districts are subdivided into other sections which are termed sometimes *okana* and sometimes *kalana*. A further subdivision within the *okana* is the *poko*.

7. By still further subdivision of these sections was obtained a tract of land called the *ahu-puaa*, and the *ahu-puaa* was in turn divided up into pieces called *ili-aina*.

8. The *ili-aina* were subdivided into pieces called *moo-aina*, and these into smaller pieces called *puuku-aina* (joints of land), and the *pauku-aina* into patches or farms called *kihapai*. Below these subdivisions came the *koele*,[1] the *hake-one*[2] and the *kuakua*.[3]

9. According to another classification of the features of an island the mountains in its centre are called *kua-hiwi*, back-bone, and the name *kua-lono*[4] is applied to the peaks or ridges which form their summits. The rounded abysses beneath are (extinct) craters, *lua pele*.

10. Below the *kua-hiwi* comes a belt adjoining the rounded swell of the mountain called *kua-mauna* or *mauna*, the mountainside.

11. The belt below the *kua-mauna,* in which small trees grow, is called *kua-hea,* and the belt below the *kua-hea,* where the larger sized forest-trees grow is called *wao,*[5] or *wao-nahele,* or *wao-eiwa.*

12. The belt below the *wao-eiwa* was the one in which the monarchs of the forest grew, and was called *wao-maukele,* and the belt below that, in which again trees of smaller size grew was called *wao-akua,*[6] and below the *wao-akua* comes the belt called *wao-kanaka* or *ma'u.* Here grows the *am'au*-fern and here men cultivate the land.

13. Below the *ma'u* comes the belt called *apaa* (probably because the region is likely to be hard, baked, sterile), and below this comes a belt called *ilima*[7] and below the *ilima* comes a belt called *pahee,* slippery,[8] and below that comes a belt called *kula* (plain, open country) near to the habitations of men, and still below this comes the belt bordering the ocean called *kahakai,* the mark of the ocean (*kaha,* mark, and *kai,* sea).

14. There are also other names to designate the features of the land: The hills that stand here and there on the island are called *puu,* a lump or protuberance; if the hills stand in line they are designated as a *lalani puu* or *pae puu;* if they form a cluster of hills they are designated *kini-kini puu* or *olowalu puu.*

15. A place of less eminence was called an *ahua;* or if it was lower still an *ohu,* or if of still less eminence (a plateau) it was termed kahua.[9]

16. A narrow strip of high land, that is a ridge, was called a *lapa* or a *kua-lapa,* and a region abounding in ridges was called *olapa-lapa.*

17. A long depression in the land, a valley, was called a *kahawai;* it was also called *awawa* or *owawa.*

18. Those places where the land rises up abrupt and steep like the side of a house are named *pali;*[10] if less decided precipitous they are spoken of as *opalipali.*

19. A place where runs a long and narorw stretch of beaten earth, a road namely, is turmed *ala-nui;* another name is *kua-moo* (lizard-back). When a road passed around the circumference of the island it was called the *ala-loa.* A place where the road climbed an ascent was termed *pii'na;* another name was *hoopii'na;* another name still was *koo-ku,* and still another name was *auku.*

20. Where a road passed down a descent it was termed *iho'na,* or *alu,* or *ka-olo* (*olo-kaa,* to roll down hill), or *ka-lua* or *hooi-ho'na.* The terraces or stopping places on a (steep) road where people are wont to halt and rest are called *oi-o-ina.*

21. A (natural) water-course or a stream of water was called a *kahawai* (scratch of water); its source or head was called *kumuwai;* its outlet or mouth was called *nuku-wai.* An (artificial) ditch or stream of water for irrigating land is called *au wai.* When a stream mingles with sea water (as in the slack water of a creek) it is termed a *muli-wai.* A body of water enclosed by land, *i.e.,* a lake or pond, is called a *loko.*

Notes to Chapter VII

1. Sect. 8. A *koele* was a piece of land seized by an *alii* while under cultivation by serf or peasant. The peasant was required to keep it still under cultivation, but the land and the crops went to the *alii.* The work devoted to its cultivation was called *hana po-alima,* because Friday was the day generally given up to work for the *alii.*

2. Sect. 8. *Haku-one* was the small piece of land under cultivation by the peasant which the *konohiki* seized for his own use, though the peasant had to continue its cultivation. A peasant, for instance, had six taro-patches; the *alii* appropriated the best one for himself, and that was called *koele.* The *konohiki,* or *haku-aina,* took another for himself and that was called *haku-one.*

3. Sect. 8. The *kua-kua* was a broad *kuauna* or embankment between two wet patches which was kept under cultivation.

4. Sect. 9. I am informed on good authority that a *kua-lono* was a *broad* plateau between two vallies, while a *kua-lapa* was a narrow ridge.

5. Sect. 11. *Wao* is the name of any kind of a wilderness or uninhabited region, the abode of gods, spirits and ghosts.

6. Sect. 12. *Wao-akua.* In this phrase, which means wilderness of gods, we have embodied the popular idea that gods and ghosts chiefly inhabit the waste places of the earth.

7. Sect. 13. The *leis* or garlands of beautiful chrome-yellow flowers which the flower girl of Honolulu on "steamer day" offers to you for a price, are from the *ilima* or Sida fallax.

8. Sect. 13. *Pahee,* slippery. Probably because of a peculiar species of grass that grows in such places.

9. Sect. 15. *Kahua* is also the term used to denote a foundation.

10. Sect. 18. According to Lieutenant Younghusband, author of an interesting book of travel, entitled "Through the Heart of a Continent," the word *pali* is used in North India as in the Hawaiian Islands, to designate a mountain wall or precipice.

11. Sect. 21. *Muli* means remainder, and *muliwai* therefore means remainder of the water. The explanation is that at the mouth of many Hawaiian streams is a bar of sand or mud. At low tide water still remains standing within this retaining bar, and this water caused the whole stream to be called *muliwai.*

VIII

Concerning the Rocks

1. The ancients applied to various hard, or mineral, substances the term *pohaku*, rocks or stones. A rocky cliff was called a *pali-pohaku:* a smaller boulder or mass of rock would be termed *pohaku uuku iho.* The term *a-a* was applied to stones of a somewhat smaller size. Below them came *iliili* or pebbles. When of still smaller size, such as gravel or sand, the name *one* was applied, and if still more finely comminuted it was called *lepo*, dirt.

2. A great many names were used to distinguish the different kinds of rocks. In the mountains were found some very hard rocks which probably had never been melted by the volcanic fires of *Pele.* Axes were fashioned from some of these rocks, of which one kind was named *uli-uli*, another *ehu-ehu.* There were many varieties.

3. The stones used for axes were of the following varieties: *ke-i, ke-pue, ala-mca, kai-alii, humu-ula, pi-wai, awa-lii, lau-kea, mauna.* All of these are very hard, superior to other stones in this respect, and not vesiculated like the stone called *ala.*

4. The stones used in making *lu-hee* for squid-fishing are peculiar and were of many distinct vareties. Their names are *hiena, ma-heu, hau, pa-pa, lae-koloa, lei-ole, ha-pou, kawau-puu, ma-ili, au, nani-nui, ma-ki-ki, pa-pohaku, kaua-ula, wai-anuu-kole, hono-ke-a-a, kupa-oa, poli-poli, ho-one, no-hu, lu-au, wai-mano, hule-ia, maka-wela.*

5. The stones used for *maikas* were the *ma-ka (maka-a?), hiu-pa iki-makua, kumu-one,*[1] *ma-ki-ki, kumu-mao-mao, ka-lama-ula,* and *paa-kea.*[2]

6. Volcanic *pa-hoe-hoe* is a class of rocks that have been melted by the fires of Pele. *Elc-ku* and *a-na*, pumice, are very light and porous rocks. Another kind of stone is the *a-la*[3] and the *pa-ea.*

7. The following kinds of stone were used in smoothing and polishing canoes and wooden dishes, coral stones (*puna*), a vesiculated stone called *o-ahi, o-la-i* or pumice, *po-huehue, ka-wae-wae, o-i-o,* and *a-na.*

8. The kinds of stone used in making poi-pounders were *a-la, lua-u, kohe-nalo*, the white sand-stone called *kumu-one,* and the coral-stone called *koa.* There is also a stone that is cast down from heaven by lightning. No doubt there are many other stones that have failed of mention.

Notes to Chapter VIII

1. Sect. 5. *Kamu-one:* A white sand-stone composed of sea-sand. It cuts and works up well.

2. Sect. 5. *Paa-kea* is volcanic sinter A *maika* of this species of stone which is in the writer's collection had been used as a fetish or medicine-charm.

3. Sect. 6. *A-la* is the hardest and densest kind of basalt to be found on the islands. It is the stone from which the best axes are made. It seems unaccountable that Mr. Malo should omit this most important of all the stones from his rambling and very unsatisfactory list. If any stone might be considered to have escaped the melting action of Pele's fires by reason of its hardness it would certainly be this one.

In the Maori language the same dark, close-grained basalt is named *ka-ra* and is used in making the finest axes.

IX

Plants and Trees

1. The ancients gave the name *laau* to every plant that grows in the earth of which there are a great many kinds (*ano*). The name *laau* was, however, applied *par eminence* to large trees; plants of a smaller growth were termed *laa-lau;* the term *nahele* (or *nahele-hele*) was used to indicate such small growths as brush, shrubs, and chapparal. Plants of a still smaller growth were termed *weu-weu;* grasses were termed *mauu.*

2. The *pupu-keawe*[1] (same as *pu-keawe*), another name for which is *mai-eli,* is a sort of brush, *nahele,* that grows on the mountain sides. It was used in incremating the body of any one who had made himself an outlaw beyond the protection of the tabu.

9. Further down the mountain grows the *ohia* (same as the *lehua*), a large tree. In it the bird-catchers practiced their art of bird-snaring. It was much used for making idols, also hewn into posts and rafters for houses, used in making the enclosures about temples, and for fuel, also from it were made the sticks to couple together the double canoes, besides which it had many other uses.

4. The *koa*[2] was the tree that grew to be of the largest size in all the islands. It was made into canoes, surf-boards, paddles, spears, and (in modern times) into boards and shingles for houses. The koa is a tree of many uses. It has a seed and its leaf is crescent-shaped.

5. The *ahakca*[3] is a tree of smaller size than the *koa.* It is valued in canoe-making, the fabrication of poi-boards, paddles, and for many other uses.

6. The *kawau* was a tree useful for canoe-timber and for tapa-logs. The *manono* and *aica* were trees that also furnished canoe-timber.

7. The *kopiko* was a tree that furnished wood that was useful for making tapa-logs (*kua kuku kapa*) and that also furnished good fuel. The *kolea* was a tree the wood of which was used in making tapa-logs and as timber for houses. Its charcoal was used in making black dye for tapa. The *naia* was a tree the wood of which was used in canoe-making.[4] The sandal-wood, *ili-ahi,* has a fragrant wood which is of great commercial value at the present time. The *naio* also is a sweet-scented wood and

of great hardness. The *pua* is a hard wood. The *kauila* is a hard wood, excellent for spears, tapa-beaters and a variety of other similar purposes.[5]

8. The *mamane* and *uhi-uhi* were firm woods used in making the runners for *holua*-sleds and spades, *o-o*, used by the farmers. The *alani* was one of the woods used for poles employed in rigging canoes.

9. The *olomea* was a wood much used in rubbing for fire; the *ku-kui* a wood sometimes used in making the dug-out or canoe; the bark of its roots, mixed with several other things, was used in making the black paint for canoes, and its nuts are strung into torches called *ku-kui*.[6]

10. The *paihi* is a wood useful as fuel and in house-making. It has a flower similar to that of the *lehua* and its bark is used in staining tapa of a black color. The *alii* is a solid wood used for house posts. The *koaie* is a strong wood useful as house-timber and in old times used in making shark hooks.

11. The *ohe*, or bamboo, which has a jointed stem (*pona-pona*), was used as fishing poles to take the aku—or any other fish—and formerly its splinters served instead of knives.

12. The *wili-wili* is a very buoyant wood, for which reason it is largely used in making surf boards (*papa-hee-nalu*), and outrigger floats (*ama*) for canoes. The *olapa* was a tree from which spears such as were used in bird-liming or bird-snaring were obtained. The *lama* is a tree whose wood is used in the construction of houses and enclosures for (certain) idols. The *awa* is the plant whose root supplies the intoxicating drink (so extensively used by the Polynesians).

13. The *ulu* or bread-fruit is a tree whose wood is much used in the construction of the doors of houses and the bodies of canoes. Its fruit is made into a delicious *poi*.[7] The *ohia*—so-called mountain apple—is a tree with scarlet flowers and a fruit agreeable to the taste. The *hawane*, or loulu-palm, is a tree the wood of which was used for battle spears; its nuts were eaten and its leaves are now used in making hats.

14. The *kou* is a tree of considerable size, the wood of which is specially used in making all sorts of platters, bowls and dishes, and a variety of other utensils. The *milo*[8] and the *pua* were (useful) trees. The *niu*—coco-palm—is a tree that bears a delicious nut, besides serving many other useful purposes. The (fleshy) stems of the *hapuu* fern, and the tender shoots of the *a-ma-u* fern and the *i-i-i* fern afforded a food that served in time of famine.

15. The *wauke* is one of the plants the bark of which is beaten into *tapa*.[9] The *wauke* had many other uses. The hibiscus, called *hau*,[10]

furnished a (light) wood that was put to many uses. Of its bark was made rope or cordage. The *ohe*-tree produced a soft wood, similar to the kukui (or American bass—Translator), and was sometimes used in making stilts, or *kukuluaeo*.

16. The *olona* and the *hopue* were plants from whose bark were made lines and fishing nets and a great many other things. The *mamaki* and the *maa-loa* were plants that supplied a bark that was made into tapa. The *keki* and the *pala* fern were used as food in times of famine. The (hard leaf stalks) of the *ama'u-ma'u* fern were used as a stylus for marking tapa (*mea palu hole kapa*).

17. The *ma'o* was a plant whose flower was used as a dye to colored tapa and the loin cloths of the women, etc. The *noni* was a tree (the bark and roots of) which furnished a yellowish-brown dye (resembling madder) much used in staining the tapa caleld *kua-uia*. Its fruit (a drupe) was eaten in time of famine. The (yellow) flowers of the *ilima*[11] were much desired by the women to be strung into *leis* or garlands.

18. The *hala*—pandanus or screw pine—was a tree the drupe of which was extremely fragrant and was strung into wreaths. Its leaves were braided into mats and sails. The *ulei* was a tree whose wood was highly valued for its toughness, and of it were made thick, heavy darts—*ihe-pahee*—for skating over the ground in a game of that name. It also furnished the small poles with which the mouth of the bag-net, *upena-aei*, was kept open. The *a-e* and the *po-ola* were trees the wood of which was used in spear-making. The wood of the *wala-hee* was formerly much used in making a sort of adze (to cut the soft *wili-wili* wood); it also furnished sticks used in keeping open the mouth of the *paki-kii* net.

19. The banana, *maia*, was a plant that bore a delicious fruit. There were many species of the banana and it had a great variety of uses. The *maua* was a tree suitable for timber (literally boards or planks *papa*). The *haa, ho-awa, hao,* and many other trees I have not mentioned in this account were no doubt good for fuel. Besides there were many more trees that I have not mentioned.

20. The *pili*—a grass much used for thatching houses—the *koo-koo-lau*—an herb used in modern times as a tea—these and various other plants in the wilderness, such as the *i.e.,* the *pala* fern, the *kupn-kupu*, mana, akolea, ama-u-ma'u-fern, etc., etc., were termed *nahele-hele*,[12] *i.e.,* weeds or things that spread.

21. The *hono-hono*, wandering Jew, the *kukae-puaa*,[13] the *kakona-kona*, the *pili, manicnie*,[14] the *kulohia, puu-koa, pili-pili-ula, kaluha,* the

moko-loa, the *ahu-awa*, the *mahiki-hiki*, and the *kohe-kohe* were grasses, *mauu*.

22. The *popolo*, the *pakai*, the *aweo-weo, nau-nau, haio, nena* and the *palula* were cooked and eaten as greens (*luau*). The gourd was a vine highly prized for the calabashes it produced.

Notes of Chapter IX

2. Sect. 4. *Koa.* In ancient times the *koa* found its ch chief use in making the canoe. In these days its greatest usefulness is found as a cabinet wood. It is capable of a very high polish.

3. Sect. 5. *Ahakea.* It furnished the material chiefly used in making the carved pieces that adorned the bow and stern of every old-time Hawaiian canoe, also the top rail on the gunwale of the canoe.

4. Sect. 7. *Naia* Not for the body of the craft, but in trimming it.

5. Sect. 7. *Kauila.* Kamehameha I armed his legions with spears of *kauila* wood.

6. Sect. 9. *Kukui.* The Samoan name for this tree is *tui-tui*, to sew or to thread or to string, as to string beads or flowers. *Tui* is needle and *tui-tui* is to sew or to string. The name of the tree and of the torches or candles produced from its nuts, as indicated in both the Hawaiian and Samoan word-forms, was undoubtedly derived from *ini*, a needle or thorn.

7. Sect. 13. *Poi* in the great majority of cases means the article of food made from taro: but the Hawaiians also applied that name to the product of the breadfruit and of the potato as well, when cooked, pounded, and mixed with water.

8. Sect. 14. The *milo* like the *kou*, made excellent dishes. The wood of the *pua*, which was very hard, burned with a hot flame, like hickory, even when green. Every woodman or mountaineer will know what that means.

9. Sect. 15. *Kapa* or *tapa.* In the form of sheets used as a blanket to cover one at night, or as a toga for dignity and comfort by day, or made into the *malo*, the garment of modesty of the men, or the *pa-u*, which was the garment of modesty of the women.

10. Sect. 15. *Hau.* It was the favorite wood for making firesticks, and was much used at handles for axes.

11. Sect. 17. *Ilima.* At the present day it is cultivated by the Hawaiians.

12. Sect. 20. *Nahclehele.* From *hele*, to go? As to the derivation of this word, in Maori *nga-here-here* means the forest, not the creeping plants in it. This is certainly not the case in the Hawaiian language. In Hawaiian the word is applied to weeds, brush, under-growth, chapparal, whether that is found in the woods, beneath the forest trees, in the open, standing alone, or in cultivated fields.

13. Sect. 21. *Kukac-puaa.* A rich and delicate grass, said to have sprung up wherever the great pig-god, Kama-puaa, left his mark.

14. Sect. 21. *Manieme.* A modern grass, probably introduced by Vancouver from Mexico or South America. It makes a fine lawn grass.

15. Sect. 21. *Mokoloa.* Also known as Makaloa, a small rush used in making the famous Niihau *pawche* mats.

1. Sect. 2. *Pu-keawe.* When a kapu-chief found it convenient to lay aside his dread exclusiveness for a time, that he might perhaps mingle with people on equal terms without injury to them or to himself, it was the custom for him—and according to one authority those with whom he intended to mingle joined with him in the ceremony—to shut himself into a little house and smudge himself with the smoke from a fire of this same *pu-keawe.* At the conclusion of this fumigation a priest recited the following:

Pule Huikala

> *I Kane ma, laua o Kanaloa,*
> *O kahi ka po,*
> *O lua ka po,*
> *O kolu ka po,*
> *O ha ka po,*
> *O lima ka po,*
> *O ono ka po,*
> *O hiku ka po,*
> *O walu ka po,*
> *O iwa ka po,*
> *A umi ka po,*
> *Holo aku oe i kai,*
> *Noa aku oe i kai,*
> *Pau ko'u kapu ia oe, Lono.*
> *Amama. Ua noa ia Umi.*

Prayer for a Dispensation

To Kane and his fellow Kanaloa,
For one night,
For two nights,
For three nights,
For four nights,
For five nights,
For six nights,
For seven nights,
For eight nights,
For nine nights,
For ten nights,
You shall sail out to sea,

And the tabu shall not rest upon you at sea.
My tabu shall be done away with by you, o Lono!
It is lifted! There is freedom to Umi!

(Informant Waialeale of Waimanalo, O.)

Apropos of this same shrub, or small tree rather, the following story has been communicated to me (by J. K. K.).

In the time of *Ulu-lani,* who was then the king in that part of Hilo—the northern part—which was called *Hilo pali-ku,* a certain woman caused him to be very angry, so that he threatened to put her to death, for the simple reason that she had stepped on his bathing stone. He was restrained from this purpose, however, by his *kahuna,* who had spiritual insight, as a *makaula,* and recognized the woman to be of royal lineage. This woman had come down from the interior and, reaching the ocean, went in to bathe. Having finished her salt water bath, she entered the river for the purpose of cleansing her body of the salt, and wishing to assert her royal blood, on coming out of the water she deliberately occupied the flat stone on which the king was accustomed to stand after bathing in the same stream. When the king learned of this insult he felt greatly enraged and determined to put the woman to death. His priest, however, said to him, "You can't kill her for this." "Why not?" asked he. "Because she had an *alii* on her back." "Who was that *alii?*" asked the king. "It was *Mai-eli-lani,* king of *pupu keawe* (*ka lani o pupu keawe*). When a man dies what wood do you use to make the fire to consume his body with?"

"No, you'd better not kill that woman," said the priest.

"Why?" persisted the king. "As you know, I am the king of *Hilo pali-ku,* a native of the land, a descendant from the very earliest line of kings (*he kupa au a he apaakuma*)."

"Yes, and for that very reason, because you are an *apaakuma,* an autochthon, you will be put to death." The king was silenced and could make no further answer, because he knew that only with this sort of wood was a human body reduced to ashes. The *kahuna* then repeated the following ancient *mele*:

> *O Mai-eli, lani o Uli,*
> *O Uli ku huihui lau, lau o Ikuo,*
> *O Iku-lani** *naha;*
> *Naha ke poo o Pupu-keawe,*
> *O Keawe ia a Ka-lani-Hilo, hilo e make.*
> *A make! a make i ka Hilo pali-ku.*
> *Eia la o Mai-eli! he alii no A,*
> *A Uli! a make!*
> *A make o ia Pupu-Keawe!*

> *Mai-eli,* king of *Uli,*
> *Uli,* the active, the multiform, offshoot of *Iku,*

> *Iku*, king of kings in heaven, broken for others;
> Broken was the body of *Pupu-keawe;*
> It is *Keawe*, king of *Hilo* who must die.
> He dies! Lo he dies in *Hilo-pali-ku!*
> Here too is *Mai-eli*, king of fuel.
> Burn *Uli!* Burn to death!
> You are consumed by *Pupu-keawe.*

* The term *Iku* is used by the *Nauwa* Society in the modern word *Iku-hai.*
Iku-lani, the ancient word, means the highest, head of all.

'So it is by the *Mai-eli* that 1 am to die and the *Mai-eli* is a king. I command that henceforth no man, woman or child gather this shrub on my land or use it to make a fire for common purposes."

Then the king ordered all the men in seven ahupuaas to go up into the mountains and bring a quantity of this brush to make a fence of. The fence when first made was called *ka pa o na Hiku*. But they had great difficulty in finding any of the brush long enough to be used in making a fence, and they had to go repeatedly; consequently they changed the name to *ka pa o na hiku ai-kukae, i.e.,* the fence of the seven who eat dirt.

N. B.—It is not an uncommon thing for Polynesian yarns to wallow like a hog in the mire at the end of their journey.

X

Divisions of the Ocean

1. The ancients applied the name *kai* to the ocean and all its parts. That strip of the beach over which the waves ran after they had broken was called *a'e-kai*.[1]

2. A little further out where the waves break was called *poii'na-kui*.[2] The name *pue-one* was likewise applied to this place.[3] But the same expressions were not used of places where shoal water extended to a great distance, and which were called *kaikohala* (such as largely prevail for instance at Waikiki).

3. Outside of the *poi-na-kai* lay a belt called the *kai-hele-ku*, or *kai-papau*, that is, water in which one could stand, shoal water; another name given it was *kai-ohua*.[4]

4. Beyond this lies a belt called *kua-au* where the shoal water ended; and outside of the *kua-au* was a belt called *kai-au, ho-au, kai-o-kilo-hee*, that is, swimming deep or sea for spearing squid, or *kai-hee-nalu*,[5] that is, a surf-swimming region. Another name still for this belt was *kai kohala*.[6]

5. Outside of this was a belt called *kai-uli*, blue sea, squid-fishing sea *kai-lu-hee*, or sea-of-the flying-fish, *kai-malolo*, or sea-of-the opelu, *kai-opelu*.

6. Beyond this lies a belt called *kai-hi-aku*, sea for trolling the *aku*, and outside of this lay a belt called *kai-kohola*, where swim the whales, monsters of the sea; beyond this lay the deep ocean, *moana*, which was variously termed *waho-lilo*, far out to sea, or *lepo*, under ground, or *lewa*, floating, or *lipo*, blue-black, which reach *Kahiki-moe*, the utmost bounds of the ocean.

7. When the sea is tossed into billows they are termed *ale*. The breakers which roll in are termed *nalu*. The currents that move through the ocean are called *au* or *wili-au*.

8. Portions of the sea that enter into recesses of the land are *kai-hee-naiu*,[6] that is a surf-swimming region. Another name still *kai-o-kilo-hee*, that is swimming deep, or sea for spearing squid, or called *kai-kuono*; that belt of shoal where the breakers curl is called *pu-ao;* another name for it is *ko-aka*.

9. A blow-hole where the ocean spouts up through a hole in the rocks is called a *puhi* (to blow). A place where the ocean is sucked with force down through a cavity in the rocks is called a *mimili*, whirlpool; it is also called a *mimiki* or an *aaka*.

10. The rising of the ocean-tide is called by such names as *ka-pii*, rising sea, *kai-nui*, big sea, *kai-piha*, full sea, and *kai-apo*, surrounding sea.

11. When the tide remains stationary, neither rising nor falling, it is called *kai-ku*, standing sea; when it ebbs it is called *kai-moku*, the parted sea, or *kai-emi*, ebbing sea, or *kai-hoi*, retiring sea, or *kai-make*, defeated sea.

12. A violent, raging surf is called *kai-koo*. When the surf beats violently against a sharp point of land, that is a cape, *lae*, it is termed *kai-ma-ka-ka-lae*.

13. A calm in the ocean is termed a *lai* or a *malino* or a *pa-e-a-e-a* or a *point*.

Notes on Chapter X

1. Sect. 1. *A'e-kai*. In the N. Z. *aki-tai* means the dash of the waves. A well known tribe, now extinct, was named *Aki-tai*, because their ancestor was dashed to pieces on the rocks of the sea-shore. Mr. S. Percy Smith of New Zealand, remarks that if this word is actually *a'e* in the Hawaiian, it forms an exception to the rule of vowel-changes. As stated by Mr. Smith, this rule is as follows, "vowels change in the Polynesian language according to the following law, *a, e, o* form one series which may interchange without altering the meaning of the word. *I* and *u* form another series. Very rarely do the two series change with each other." The phrase *a'e-one* was also used when it concerned a sand-beach.

2. Sect. 2. *Poana-kai* is the expression in the text. But I am informed from many sources that *poi'na-kai* is the correct expression, that *poana-kai* is applied to the place where the breakers scoop out the sand near the shore.

3. Sect. 2. *Pue-one*, sand-heap, from the heaping up of the sand by the action of the waves.

4. Sect. 3. *Kai-ohua*. Because there was found a small fish called *ohua*. I am informed it was also termed *kai-o hee*, because the squid is there speared.

5. Sect. 4. *Kai-hee-nalu*. Because there the rollers from the ocean look head and it was there that the surf-rider lay in wait for a big wave to carry him in on its back.

6. Sect. 4. *Kai-kohola*. This is clearly a mistake. *Kohola* is applied only to the shoal water inside the surf where it reaches out in a long stretch as at Waikiki. (See Sect. 2.)

XI

Eating Under the Kapu System

1. The task of food-providing and eating under the kapu-system in Hawaii nei was very burdensome, a grievous tax on husband and wife, an iniquitous imposition, at war with domestic peace. The husband was burdened and wearied with the preparation of two ovens of food, one for himself and a separate one for his wife.

2. The man first started an oven of food for his wife, and, when that was done, he went to the house *mua* and started an oven of food for himself.

3. Then he would return to the house and open his wife's oven, peel the taro, pound it into poi, knead it and put it into the calabash. This ended the food-cooking for his wife.

4. Then he must return to *mua*, open his own oven, peel the taro, pound and knead it into poi, put the mass into a (separate) calabash for himself and remove the lumps. Thus did he prepare his food (*ai*, vegetable food); and thus was he ever compelled to do so long as he and his wife lived.

5. Another burden that fell to the lot of the man was thatching the houses for himself and his wife; because the houses for the man must be other than those for the woman. The man had first to thatch a house for himself to eat in and another house as a sanctuary (*heiau*) in which to worship his idols.

6. And, that accomplished, he had to prepare a third house for himself and his wife to sleep in. After that he must build and thatch an eating house for his wife, and lastly he had to prepare a *hale kua*, a place for his wife to beat tapa in (as well as to engage in other domestic occupations.—Translator). While the husband was busy and exhausted with all these labors, the wife had to cook and serve the food for her husband, and thus it fell that the burdens that lay upon the woman were even heavier than those allotted to the man.

7. During the days of religious tabu, when the gods were specially worshipped, many women were put to death by reason of infraction of some tabu. According to the tabu a woman must live entirely apart from her husband, during the period of her infirmity: she always ate in her

own house, and the man ate in the house called *mua*. As a result of this custom, the mutual love of the man and his wife was not kept warm; the man might use the opportunity to associate with another woman, likewise the woman with another man. It has not been stated who was the author of this tabu that prohibited the mingling of the sexes while partaking of food. It was no doubt a very ancient practice; possibly it dates from the time of Wakea; but it may be subsequent to that.

8. There is, however, a tradition accepted by some that Wakea himself was the originator of this tabu that restricts eating; others have it that it was initiated by *Luhau-kapawa*. It is not certain where the truth lies between these two statements. No information on this point is given by the genealogies of these two characters, and every one seems to be ignorant in the matter. Perhaps, however, there are persons now living who know the truth about this matter; if so they should speak out.

9. It is stated in one of the traditions relating to the gods that the motive of the tabu restricting eating was the desire on the part of Wakea to keep secret his incestuous intercourse with *Hoo-hoku-ka-lani*. For this reason he devised a plan by which he might escape the observation of Papa; and he accordingly appointed certain nights for prayer and religious observance, and at the same time tabued certain articles of food to women. The reason for this arrangement was not communicated to Papa, and she incautiously consented to it, and thus the tabu was established. The truth of the story I cannot vouch for.

10. If it was indeed Wakea who instituted this tabu then it was a very ancient one. It was abolished by *Kamchameha II,* known as *Liholiho,* at Kailua, Hawaii, on the third or fourth day of October, 1819. On that day the tabu putting restrictions on eating in common ceased to be regarded here in Hawaii. The effect of this tabu, which bore equally on men and women, was to separate men and women, husbands and wives from each other when partaking of food.

11. Certain places were see apart for the husband's sole and exclusive use; such were the sanctuary in which he worshipped and the eating-house in which he took his food. The wife might not enter these places while her husband was worshipping or while he was eating; nor might she enter the sanctuary or eating-house of another man; and if she did so she must suffer the penalty of death, if her action was discovered.

12. Certain places also were set apart for the woman alone. These were the *hale pea,* where she stayed during her period of monthly infirmity—at which time it was tabu for a man to associate with his

own wife, or with any other woman. The penalty was death if he were discovered in the act of approaching any woman during such a period. A flowing woman was looked upon as both unclean and unlucky (*haumia, poino*).

13. Among the articles of food that were set apart for the exclusive use of man, of which it was forbidden the woman to eat, were pork, bananas, cocoanuts, also certain fishes, the *ulua, kumu* (a red fish used in sacrifice), the *niuhi*-shark, the sea turtle, the *e-a*, (the sea-turtle that furnished the tortoise-shell), the *pahu*, the *naia*, (porpoise), the whale, the *nuao, hahalua hihimanu*, (the ray) and the *hailepo*. If a woman was clearly detected in the act of eating any of these things, as well as a number of other articles that were tabu, which I have not enumerated, she was put to death.

14. The house in which the men ate was called the *mua;* the sanctuary where they worshipped was called *heiau*, and it was a very tabu place. The house in which the women ate was called the *hale ai'na.* These houses were the ones to which the restrictions and tabu applied, but in the common dwelling house, *hale noa*, the man and his wife met freely together.

15. The house in which the wife and husband slept together was also called *hale-moe.* It was there they met and lived and worked together and associated with their children. The man, however, was permitted to enter his wife's eating house, but the woman was forbidden to enter her husband's *mua.*

16. Another house also was put up for the woman called *hale kuku*, the place where she beat out tapa-cloth into blankets, into *paus* for herself, *malos* for her husband, in fact, the clothing for the whole family as well as for her friends, not forgetting the landlord and chiefs (to whom no doubt these things went in lieu of rent, or as presents.— Translator).

17. The out-of-door work fell mostly upon the man, while the in-door work was done by the woman—that is provided she was not a worthless and profligate woman.

18. I must mention that certain men were appointed to an office in the service of the female chiefs and women of high station which was termed *ai-noa*. It was their duty to prepare the food of these chiefish women and it was permitted them at all times to eat in their presence, for which reason they were termed *ai-noa*—to eat in common—or *ai-puhiu.*

XII

The Divisions of the Year

1. The seasons and months of the year were appropriately divided and designated by the ancients.

2. The year was divided into two seasons *Kau* and *Hoo-ilo*. *Kau* was the season when the sun was directly overhead, when daylight was prolonged, when the trade-wind, *makani noa'e*, prevailed, when days and nights alike were warm and the vegetation put forth fresh leaves.

3. *Hoo-ilo* was the season when the sun declined towards the south, when the nights lengthened, when days and nights were cool, when herbage (literally, vines) died away.

4. There were six months in Kau and six in Hoo-ilo.

5. The months in Kau were *Iki-iki*, answering to May, at which time the constellation of the Pleiades—*huhui hoku* set at sunrise. *Kaa-ona*, answering to June,—in ancient times this was the month in which fishermen got their *a-ei* nets in readiness for catching the opelu, procuring in advance the sticks to use in keeping its mouth open; *Hina-ia-eleele*, answering to July, the month in which the *ohia* fruit began to ripen; *Mahoe-mua*, answering to August,—this was the season when the ohia fruit ripened abundantly; *Mahoe-hope*, answering to September, the time when the plume of the sugar-cane began to unsheath itself; *Ikuwa*, corresponding to October, which was the sixth and last month of the season of *Kau*.

6. The months in *Hoo-ilo* were *Weleehu*, answering to November, which was the season when people, for sport, darted arrows made of the flower-stalk of the sugar-cane; *Makalii*, corresponding to December, at which time trailing plants died down and the south-wind, the Kona, prevailed; *Kaelo*, corresponding to Januuary, the time when appeared the *enuhe*,[1] when also the vines began to put forth fresh leaves; *Kaulua*, answering to February, the time when the mullet, *anae*, spawned; *Nana*, corresponding to March, the season when the flying-fish, the *malolo*, swarmed in the ocean; *Welo*, answering to April, which was the last of the six months belonging to *Hooilo*.

7. These two seasons of six months each made up a year of twelve months,[2] equal to nine times forty days and nights—but the ancients reckoned by nights instead of days.

8. There were thirty nights and days in each month; seventeen of these days had compound names (*inoa huhui*) and thirteen had simple names (*inoa pakahi*) given to them.

9. These names were given to the different nights to correspond to the phases of the moon. There were three phases—*ano*—marking the moon's increase and decrease of size, namely, (1) the first appearance of the new moon in the west at evening:

10. (2) The time of full-moon when it stood directly overhead (literally, over the island) at midnight.

11. (3) The period when the moon was waning, when it showed itself in the east late at night. It was with reference to these three phases of the moon that names were given to the nights that made up the month.

12. The first appearance of the moon at evening in the west marked the first day of the month. It was called *Hilo* on account of the moon's slender, twisted form.

13. The second night when the moon had become more distinct in outline was called *Hoaka;* and the third when its form had grown still thicker, was called *Ku-kahi;* so also the foutrh was called *Ku-lua.* Then came *Ku-kolu,* followed by *Ku-pau* which was the last of the four nights named *Ku.*

14. The 7th, when the moon had grown still larger, was called *Ole-ku-kahi;* the 8th, *Ole-ku-lua;* the 9th, *Ole-ku-kolu;* the 10th, *Olepau,*[3] making four in all of these nights, which, added to the previous four, brings the number of nights with compound names up to eight.

15. As soon as the sharp points of the moon's horns were hidden the name *Huna* (hidden) was given to that night—the 11th. The 12th night, by which time the moon had grown still more full, was called *Mohalu,* The 13th night was called *Hua,* because its form had then become quite egg-shaped (*hua* an egg); and the 14th night, by which time the shape of the moon had become distinctly round, was called *Akua* (God), this being the second night in which the circular form of the moon was evident.

16. The next night, the 15th, had two names applied to it. If the moon set before daylight *ke ao ana*—it was called *hoku palemo,* sinking star, but if when daylight came it was still above the horizon it was called *hoku ili,* stranded star.

17. The second of the nights in which the moon did not set until after sunrise—16th—was called *Mahea-lani.* When the moon's rising was

delayed until after the darkness of night had set in, it was called *Kulua*, and the second of the nights in which the moon made its appearance after dark was called *Laau-ku-kahi* (18th); this was the night when the moon had so much waned in size as to again show sharp horns.

18. The 19th showed still further waning and was called *Laau-ku-lua;* then came *Laau-pau* (20th), which ended this group of compound names, three in number. The name given to the next night of the still waning moon was *Ole-ku-kahi*, Then in order came *Ole-ku-lua* and *Ole-pau*, making three of this set of compound names (21st, 22nd and 23rd).

19. Still further waning, the moon was called *Kaloa-ku-kahi;* then *Kaloa-ku-lua;* and lastly, completing this set of compound names, three in number, *Kaloa-pau* (24th, 25th and 26th).

20. The night when the moon rose at dawn of day (27th) was called *Kane*, and the following night, in which the moon rose only as the day was breaking (28th), was called *Lono*. When the moon delayed its rising until daylight had come it was called *Mauli*—fainting;[4] and when its rising was so late that it could no longer be seen for the light of the sun, it was called *Muku*—cut off. Thus was accomplished the thirty[5] nights and days of the month.

21. Of these thirty days some were set apart as tabu, to be devoted to religious ceremonies and the worship of the gods. There were four tabu-periods in each moon.

22. The first of these tabu-periods was called that of *Ku*, the second that of *Hua*, the third that of *Kaloa* (abbreviated from *Kana-loa*), the fourth that of *Kane*.

23. The tabu of *Ku* included three nights; it was imposed on the night of Hilo and lifted on the morning of *Kulua*. The tabu of *Hua* included two nights; it was imposed on the night of *Mohalu* and lifted on the morning of *Akua*. The tabu of *Kaloa* included two nights; it was imposed on the night of *Ole-pau* and raised on the morning of *Kaloa-ku-lua*. The tabu of *Kane* included two nights; being imposed on the night of *Kane* and lifted on the morning of *Mauli*.

24. These tabu-seasons were observed during eight months of the year, and in each year thirty-two[6] days were devoted to the idolatrous worship of the gods.

25. There were now four months devoted to the observances of the Makahiki, during which time the ordinary religious ceremonies were omitted, the only ones that were observed being those connected

with the Makahiki festival. The prescribed rites and ceremonies of the people at large were concluded in the month of *Mahoe-hope*. The keepers of the idols, however, kept up their prayers and ceremonies throughout the year.

26. In the month of *Ikuwa* the signal was given for the observance of Makahiki, at which time the people rested from their prescribed prayers and ceremonies to resume them in the month of Kau-lua. Then the chiefs and some of the people took up again their prayers and incantations, and so it was during every period in the year.

Notes on Chapter XII

1. Sect. 6. *Enuhc,* a worm very destructive to vegetation.

3. Sect. 14. *Ole-ku-pau* is the full and correct orthography, the one also given by W. D. Alexander in his History, p. 315.

4. Sect. 20. *Mauli.* "To faint in the light of the sun."—Tennyson.

Divisions of the Makahiki

2. Sect. 7. There were considerable differences in the nomenclature of the months and divisions of the year of the Hawaiian people. The differences attached to the different islands, as will be seen by reference to the following table:

MONTHS AND OTHER DIVISIONS OF THE HAWAIIAN YEAR

	HAWAII.	MOLOKAI.	OAHU.
HOOILO	1. Welehu . . . . Nov	1. Ikuwa. . . . . . .Jan	1 Nana. . . . . . . .Jan
	2. Makalii . . . . Dec	2. Hina-ia eleele	2. Welo . . . . . . Feb
	3. Kaelo . . . . . . .Jan	. . . . Feb	3. Ikiiki . . . . . .Mar
	4. Ka'u-lua . . . . Feb	3. Welo . . . . . .Mar	4. Kaaona. . . . . Apr
	5. Nana . . . . . .Mar	4. Makalii . . . . Apr	5. Hina-ia-eleele
	6. Welo . . . . . . Apr	5. Kaelo . . . . . .May	. . . . .May
KAU	7. Ikiiki . . . . . .May	6. Ka'u-lua . . . .June	6. Mahoe-mua
	8. Kaaona. . . . .June	7. Nana . . . . . . July	. . . . .June
	9. Hina-ia-eleele	8. Ikiiki . . . . . .Aug	7. Mahoe-hope July
	. . . . July	9. Kaaona. . . . .Sept	8. Ikuwa. . . . . .Aug
	10. Mahoe mua . Aug	10. Hili-na-ehu	9. Welehu . . . . Sep
	11. Mahoe-hope	. . . . Oct	10. Makalii . . . . Oct
	. . . . .Sept	11. Hili-na-ma . Nov	11. Kaelo . . . . . .Nov
	12. Ikuwa. . . . . . Oct	12. Welehu . . . . Dec	12. Ka'u lua . . . . Dec

Kauai.	
1. Ikuwa . . . . Apr	The year was divided into two seasons, Mahoemua
2. Welehu . . . . May	and Mahoe hope. The former included the
3. Kaelo . . . . June	six months from the beginning of Ikuwa,
4. Ikiiki . . . . July	corresponding to April, to the end of Mahoe-
5. Hina-ia-eleele . . . . Aug	mua, corresponding to September. Mahoe-hope
6. Mahoe-mua . . . . . Sept	included the other six months of the year. My
7. Mahoe-hope . . . . . Oct	informant obtained this statement from an old
8. Hili-na-ma . . . . . . Nov	man of Waimea, Kauai, who was a famous
9. Hili-nehu . . . . Dec	*Kaka-olelo*.
10. Hili-o-holo . . . . . . Jan	
11. Hili o-nalu . . . . Feb	
12. Huki-pau . . . . .Mar	

HAWAIIAN NAMES OF MONTHS
FROM W. D. ALEXANDER'S HISTORY

1. Makalii . . . . . Nov . . . . Dec	After considering this radical diversity that
2. Kaelo . . . . .Dec . . . . .Jan	obtained among the peoples of the different
3. Kaulua . . . . Jan . . . . Feb	islands that made up the Hawaiian group
4. Nana . . . . Feb . . . .Mar	as to the nomenclature of the divisions,
5. Welo . . . . Mar . . . . Apr	and the initial point, of the year, it would
6. Ikiiki . . . . .Apr . . . .May	seem as if the only generalized statement
7. Kaaona . . . . . May . . . .June	that could be made in regard to it was that
8. Hinaieleele . . June . . . . July	it was divided into twelve months.
9. Hilinaehu . . . .July . . . .Aug	
10. Hilinama . . . . Aug . . . .Sept	
11. Ikuwa . . . . . . Sept . . . . Oct	
12. Welehu . . . . . .Oct . . . . Nov	

5. Sect. 20. The Hawaiians evidently hit upon the synodic month and made it their standard. Their close approximation to it can not fail to inspire respect for the powers of observation and the scientific faculty of the ancient Hawaiians. It was an easy matter to eke out the reckoning by omitting the last day in every other month, the synodic lunar month being 29½ days.

NAMES OF THE DAYS IN THE MONTH

The *Ku* tabu. {	1. Hilo.	6. Ku-pau.
	2. Hoaka.	7. Ole ku-kahi.
	3. Kukahi.	8. Ole-ku-lua.
	4. Ku-lua.	9. Ole-ku-kolu.
	5. Ku-kolu.	10. Ole-pau.

	11. Huna.		21. Ole-ku-kahi.
	12. Mohalu.		22. Ule-ku-lua.
The *Hua* tabu. {	13. Hua.	The *KANALOA* or {	23. Ole-pau.
	14. Akua.	*KALOA* tabu, {	24. Kaloa-ku-kahi.
	15. Hoku.		25. Kalo-ku-lua,
	16. Mahea-laui.		26 Kaloa-pau.
	17. Ku-lua.	The *KANE* tabu. {	27. Kane
	18 Laau-ku-kahi.		28 Lono.
	19. Laau-ku-lua		29. Mauli.
	20. Laau pau		30. Muku.

As if to prove that even on *the same island* there might be more than one nomenclature, a Hawaiian well skilled in the ancient lore of his country (Kaunamano) gives me the following list of months in the Hawaiian year:

	1. Iku wa . . . . Oct-Nov	*Ikuwa*—The noisy month, clamor of ocean, thunder, storm.
	2. Ka ulua . . . . . . Nov-Dec	*Ka-ubia*—The two stars called *Ka-ulua* then rose in the East.
	3. Nana . . . . .Dec-Jan	
HOOILO.	4. Welo . . . . Jan-Feb	*Nana*—The young birds then stir and rustled about (*uanana*) in their nests and coverts.
	5. Ikiiki . . . . Feb-Mar	
	6. Kaaona. . . . . . . Mar-Apr	*Welo*—The leaves are torn to shreds by the *enuhe*.
	7. Mahee-mua . . . Apr-May	
	8. Mahoe-hope . May-June	*Ikiiki*—Warm and sticky from being shut up in doors, by weather.
MAKALII.	9. Hina-ia-eleele . June-July	
	10. Welehu . . . . . . July-Aug	*Kaaona*— (Dry) sugar-cane flower-stalks, etc., put away in the top of the house have now become very dry.
	11. Makalii . . . . . .Aug-Sept	
	12. Kaelo . . . . Sept-Oct	

An old woman of Kipahulu, Maui, gives me the following as the names of the months of the Hawaiian year according to Maui-nomenclature:

1. Ikuwa	She volunteered the information that each month had
2 Welehu	thirty days, save that four months, two in Hooilo aud
3. Makalii	two in Kau, had thirty-one days apiece, thus giving three-
4. Kaelo	hundred and sixty four days in each year. This is the first
5. Ka-ulua	time I have heard this important statement made by a
6. Nana	Hawaiian. The name of this intelligent old lady, whose
7. Welo	neck and head, when I called upon her, were encircled with
8. Ikiiki	fillets of *ti* leaf, deserves to be recorded—Nawahineelua,

9. Kaaona	of Kipahulu, Maui, the place where the hero Laka made
10 Hina-ia-eleele	the canoe in which to sail in search of his father's bones.
11. Hili-nehu	I omitted to state that the four supplementary days were
12. Hili-na-ma	called *na Mahoe*, the twins. Ikuwa was the same as January.

Whether by this she meant merely that it was the first month in the year, or that its place in the seasons was the same as that of January I could not make out.

The above statement cannot be correct, for such months would not be lunar months, and the days would not correspond to the phases of the moon.

6. Sect. 24. The arithmetic of this calculation is all out. By referring to the table showing the days of the month and the tabu periods it will be seen that there were nine tabu days in each month. There must have been therefore seventy-two regular or canonical fast-days in each year, not to mention the days appointed from time to time by the king or priests.

7. Sect. 20. In considering the ancient Hawaiian calendar, it must be remembered that the synodical lunar month equals 29.53 days. Hence it is necessary in any calendar based upon the moon's phases to reckon alternately 29 and 30 days to a month, which was done by the Hawaiians, as is correctly stated in Dibble's history, p. 108. For the night of Hilo always had to coincide with the first appearance of the new moon in the west, and that of Akua or Hoku with the full moon.

Again, as twelve lunar months fall about eleven days, (more exactly 10.875 days), short of the solar year, it was necessary to intercalate three lunar months in the course of eight years, in order to combine the two reckonings, as was done by the ancient Greeks.

To intercalate four days in each year, as stated by the old lady of Hana mentioned above, or five days at the Makahiki festival, as suggested by Mr. Fornander, would have wholly disarranged their monthly calendar, so that the names of the several days would no longer have corresponded to the varying phases of the moon. Besides, the shortage of the so-called lunar year, which had to be made up, was not four or five but eleven days, so that neither of the above explanations meets the case.

The Polynesian year, as stated by Ellis, Fornander, Moerenhout and others, was regulated by the rising of the Pleiades, as the month of Makalii began when that constellation rose at sunset, *i.e.* about Nov. 20th. The approximate length of the solar year was also well known to the ancient Hawaiians.

The fact that they did intercalate a month about every third year, is well established, but we are still in the dark as to what rule was followed by their astronomers (*Kilo-hoku*) and priests, and what name was given to the intercalary month.

Mr. Dibble's statement is that the "twelve lunations being about eleven days less than the sidereal year, they discovered the discrepancy, and corrected their reckoning by the stars. In practice therefore the year varied, there being sometimes twelve and sometimes thirteen lunar months" (in a year).

The Tahitians had names for thirteen months, but, as Mr. Ellis states, "in order to adapt the moons to the same seasons, the moon generally answering to March, or the one occurring about July, is generally omitted."

The method referred to above of intercalating three moons in every eight years would cause an excess of one moon in 145 years.

By the Metonic cycle, however, according to which seven moons are intercalated in every nineteen years, the excess is only 2h. 4m. 33s. in a cycle, which would amount to one day in 220 years.

W. D. ALEXANDER

8. Sect. 7. I am informed (by O. K. Kapule of Kaluaaha, Molokai) that on the island of Molokai the year was divided into three seasons, *Maka-lii, Kau,* and *Hoo-ilo.* Maka-lii was so termed because the sun was then less visible, being obscured by clouds and the days were shortened. Kau was so named because then tapa could be spread out to dry with safety, *kau ke kapa,* and *kau ka hoe a ka lawaia.* Hoo-ilo meant changeable.

Makalii the period included the first month of the year *I-kuwa,* corresponding to January. It was so named from the frequent occurrence of thunder-storms. *Wa-wa* to reverberate, to stun the ear. *Hina-ia-eleele,* the second month of the year, corresponding to our February, so called from the frequent overcasting and darkening—*eleele*—of the heavens. 3rd. *Welo* (March), so named because the rays of the sun then began to shoot forth—*welo* more vigorously. 4th. *Maka-lii,* April, which ended the season.

Then came the season called *Kau,* made up of the 5th month *Ka-elo,* May, so named by the farmers because the potatoes burst out of the hill, or overflowed from the full basket (*ua piha ka hokeo a kaelo mawaho); Kau-lua,* the 6th month, corresponding to June, so called from coupling two canoes together—*kau-lua.* 7th, *Nana,* July, so called from the fact that a canoe then floated—*nana, lana*—quietly on the calm ocean. 8th, *Iki iki* (August) the hot month (*ikiki,* or *ikiiki,* hot and stuffy).

Then came *Hoo-ilo,* the changeable season, made up of *Kaa-ona* (Sept.) so called because then the sand-banks began to shift in the ocean. *Ona* is said to be another word for *one,* sand; *Hilinehu* or *Hili-na-ehu,* October, so named from the mists, *ehu,* that floated up from the sea.; *Hili-na-ma* (November) so called because it was necessary to keep the canoes well lashed (*hili*). Closing with *Welehu,* (December) so named from the abundance of ashes (*lehu*) that were to be found in the fireplaces at this time. Other variations might be mentioned. The names as given by Malo do not represent the usage on all the islands.

XIII

THE DOMESTIC AND WILD ANIMALS

1. It is not known by what means the animals found here in Hawaii reached these shores, whether the ancients brought them, whether the smaller animals were not indigenous, or where indeed the wild animals came from.

2. If they brought these little animals, the question arises why they did not also bring animals of a larger size.

3. Perhaps it was because of the small size of the canoes in which they made the voyage, or perhaps because they were panic-stricken with war at the time they embarked, or because they were in fear of impending slaughter, and for that reason they took with them only the smaller animals.

4. The hog[1] was the largest animal in Hawaii nei. Next in size was the dog; then came tame fowls, animals of much smaller size. But the wild fowls of the wilderness, how came they here? If this land was of volcanic origin, would they not have been destroyed by fire?

5. The most important animal then was the pig (*puaa*), of which there were many varieties. If the hair was entirely black, it was called *hiwa paa;* if entirely white, *haole;* if it was of a brindled color all over, it was *ehu;* if striped lengthwise, it was *olomea.*

6. If reddish about the hams the pig was a *hulu-iwi;* if whitish about its middle it was called a *hahei;* if the bristles were spotted, the term *kiko-kiko* was applied.

7. A shoat was called *poa* (robbed); if the tusks were long it was a *pu-ko'a.* A boar was termed *kca,*[2] a young pig was termed *ohi.*

8. Likewise in regard to dogs, they were classified according to the color of their hair; and so with fowls, they were classified and named according to the character of their feathers. There wre also wild fowl.

9. The names of the wild fowl are as follows, the *nene* (goose, *Bernicla Sandvicensis*). The nene, which differs from all other birds, is of the size of the (muscovy) duck, has spotted feathers, long legs and a long neck. In its moulting season, when it comes down from the mountains, is the time when the bird-catchers try to capture it in the uplands, the motive being to obtain the feathers, which are greatly valued for making kahilis. Its body is excellent eating.

10. The *alala* (*Coruus hawaiicnsis*) is another species, with a smaller body, about the size perhaps of the female of the domestic fowl. Its feathers are black, its beak large, its body is used for food. This bird will sometimes break open the shell of a water-gourd (*hue-wai*). Its feathers are useful in kahili-making. This bird is captured by means of the pole or of the snare.

11. The *pueo,* or owl, (*Brachyotus gallapagoensis*) and the *io* resemble each other; but the *pueo* has the larger head. Their bodies are smaller in size to that of the *alala.* Their plumage is variegated (striped), eyes large (and staring), claws sharp like those of a cat. They prey upon mice and small fowl. Their feathers are worked into kahilis of the choicest descriptions. The pueo is regarded as a deity and is worshipped by many. These birds are caught by menas of the bird-pole (*kia*), by the use of the covert,[3] or by means of the net.[4]

12. The *moho* is a bird that does not fly, but only moves about in thickets because its feathers are not ample enough (to give it the requisite wing-power). It has beautiful eyes. This bird is about the size of the *alala;* it is captured in its nesting-hole and its flesh is used as food. This bird does not visit (or swim in) the sea, but it lives only in the woods and coverts, because (if it went into the ocean), its feathers would become heavy and water-soaked.

13. I will not enumerate the small wild fowl, some of them of the size of young chickens, and some still smaller: the *o-u* is as large as a small chicken, with feathers of a greenish color; it is delicious eating and is captured by means of bird-lime.

14. Another bird is the *omao,* in size about like the *o-u.* Its feathers are black, it is good eating and is captured by means of bird-lime or with the snare.

The *o-o* and the *mamo* are birds that have a great resemblance to each other. They are smaller than the *o-u,* have black feathers, sharp beaks, and are used as food. Their feathers are made up into the large royal kahilis. Those in the axillae and about the tail are very choice, of a golden color, and are used in making the feather cloaks called *ahu-ula* which are worn by (the *aliis* as well as by) warriors as insignia in time of battle (and on state occasions of ceremony or display.—TRANSLATOR). They were also used in the making of *leis* (necklaces and wreaths) for the adornment of the female chiefs and women of rank, and for the decoration of the *makahiki*-idol. (See Chap. XXXVI). These birds have many uses, and they are captured by means of bird-lime and the pole.

15. The *i-i-wi*—the feathers of this bird are red, and used in making *ahu-ula.* Its beak is long and its flesh is good for food. It is taken by means of bird-lime. The *apa-pane* and the *akihi-polena* also have red feathers. The *ula* is a bird with black feathers, but its beak, eyes, and feet are red. It sits sidewise on its nest (*he punana moe aoao kona*). This bird is celebrated in song. While brooding over her eggs she covered them with her wings, but did not sit directly over them. The *u-a* is a bird that resembles the *o-u.* The *a-ko-he-kohe* is a bird that nests on the ground.

The *mu i*s a bird with yellow feathers.

The *ama-kihi* and *akihi-a-loa* have yellow plumage; they are taken by means of bird-lime. Their flesh is fine eating.

16. The *ele-paio*[5] (*chasiempis*): this bird was used as food.

The *i-ao* resembles the *moho;* in looking it directs its eyes backwards. In this list comes the *kaka-wahie* (the wood-splitter). The *ki* is the smallest of these birds. They all have their habitat in the woods and do not come down to the shore.

17. The following birds make their resort in the salt and fresh water-ponds. The *alae* (mud-hen, *Gallinula chloropus*) has blue-black feathers, yellow feet, red forehead,—but one species is white about the forehead (*Fulica alae*). This bird is regarded as a deity, and has many worshippers. Its size is nearly that of the domestic fowl, and its flesh is good eating (gamey, but very tough). Men capture it by running it down or by pelting it with stones.

18. The *koloa* (muscovy duck, *Anas superciliosa*), has spotted feathers, a bill broad and flat, and webbed feet. Hunters take it by pelting it with stones or clubbing it. It is fine eating. The *aukuu,* (heron, *Ardea sacra*), has bluish feathers and a long neck and beak. In size it is about the same as the *pueo,* or owl. This bird makes great depredations by preying upon the mullet (in ponds). The best chance of capturing it would be to pelt it with stones.

19. The *kukuluaeo* (stilts—one of the waders), has long legs and its flesh is sweet. It may be captured by pelting it with stones.

The *kioca* (one of the waders) is excellent eating.

The *kolea* (plover, *Charadrius fulvus*). It is delicious eating. In order to capture it, the hunter calls it to him by whistling with his fingers placed in his mouth, making a note in imitation of that of the bird itself.

20. The following birds are ocean-divers (*luu-kai*): The *ua-u* (*Procellaria alba*). Its breast is white, its back blue-black; it has a long bill

of which the upper mandible projects beyond the lower. It is delicious eating. Its size is that of the *io*. The *kiki*, the *ao* and the *lio-lio* resemble the *uau*, but their backs are bluish. Their flesh is used as food. They are captured with nets and lines.

21. The *o-u-o-u:* This bird is black all over; it is of a smaller size than the uau and is fair eating; it is caught by means of a line. The *puha-aka-kai-ea* is smaller than the o-u-o-u; its breast is white, its back black; it is caught with a net and is good for food.

22. The *koae* (tropic bird, "boatswain bird," "marlin spike," *Phaeton rubicauda*). This bird is white (with a pinkish tinge) all over; it has long tail-feathers which are made into kahilis; it is of the same size as the *u-a-u,* and is fit for food (very fishy). The *o-i-o* (*Anous stolidus*) has speckled feathers like the *ne-ne;* it is of the same size as the *u-a-u* and is good eating. All of these birds dwell in the mountains by night, but during the day they fly out to sea to fish for food.

23. I will now mention the birds that migrate (that are of the firmament, *mai ke lewa mai lakou*). The *ka-upu*: Its feathers are black throughout, its beak large, its size that of a turkey.

The *na-u-ke-wai* is as large as the *ka-upu*. Its front and wings are white, its back is black. The *a* is as large as the *ka-u-pu*, its feathers entirely white. The *moli* is a bird of about the size of the *ka-u-pu*. The *iwa* is a large bird of about the size of the *ka-u-pu;* its feathers, black mixed with gray, are used for making kahilis. The plumage of these birds is used in decorating the Makahiki idol. They are mostly taken at Kaula and Nihoa, being caught by hand and their flesh is eaten. The *noio* is a small bird of the size of the plover, its forehead is white. The *kala* (*Sterna panaya*) resemble the noio. These are all eatable, they are sea-birds.

24. The following are the flying things (birds, *manu*) that are not eatable: the *o-pea-pea* or bat, the *pinao* or dragon-fly, the *okai* (a butterfly), the *lepe-lepe-ahina* (a moth or butterfly), the *pu-lele-hua* (a butterfly), the *nalo* or common house-fly, the *nala-paka* or wasp. None of these creatures are fit to be eaten. The *uhini* or grasshopper, however, is used as food.

25. The following are wild creeping things: the mouse or rat, (*iole*), the *makaula* (a species of dark lizard), the *elelu*, or cockroach, the *poki-poki* (sow-bug), the *koe* (earth-worm), the *lo* (a species of long black bug, with sharp claws), the *aha* or ear-wig, the *puna-wele-wele* or spider, the *lalana* (a species of spider), the *nuhe* or caterpillar, the *poko* (a species of worm, or caterpillar), the *nao-nao* or ant, the *mu* (a brown-black bug or

beetle that bores into wood), the *kua-paa* (a worm that eats vegetables), the *uku-poo* or head-louse, the *uku-kapa* or body-louse.

26. Whence come these little creatures? From the soil no doubt; but who knows?

The recently imported animals from foreign lands, which came in during the time of Kamehameha I, and as late as the present time, that of Kamehameha III, are the following: the cow (*bipi*, from beef), a large animal, with horns on its head; its flesh and its milk are excellent food.

27. The horse (*lio*), a large animal. Men sit upon his back and ride; he has no horns on his head. The donkey (*hoki*), and the mule (*piula*); they carry people on their backs. The goat (*kao*), and the sheep (*hipa*), which make excellent food. The cat (*po-poki,* or *o-au*)[6] and the monkey (*keko*), the pig (*puaa*)[7] and the dog (*ilio*)[7]. These are animals imported from foreign countries.

28. Of birds brought from foreign lands are the turkey, or *palahu,* the *koloa*[8], or duck, the parrot or green-bird (*manu omaomao*), and the domestic fowl (*moa*), which makes excellent food.

29. There are also some flying things that are not good for food: such as the mosquito (*makika*), the small roach (*elelu liilii*), the large flat cock-roach (*elelu-papa*), the flea (*uku-lelc,* jumping louse). The following are things that crawl: the rabbit or *iole-lapaki,* which makes excellent food, the rat or *iole-nui,* the mouse or *iole-liilii,* the centipede (*kanapi*), and the *moo-niho-awa* (probably the scorpion, for there are no serpents in Hawaii). These things are late importations; the number of such things will doubtless increase in the future.

Notes on Chapter XIII

1. Sect. 4. *Kea-kca,* to tease, therefore literally a teaser.

2. Sect. 4. *Hawaii nei,* this Hawaii: literally Hawaii here. Its use is appropriate only to those who are at the time resident in the Hawaiian Islands.

3. Sect. 11. The covert was to ambush the hunter.

4. Sect. 11. A net with a wide mouth was laid in the track in which the birds walked to reach their nest.

5. Sect. 16. *Elepaio.* By its early morning song it was the fateful cause of interruption to many a heroic midnight enterprise in ancient song and legend.

6. Sect. 27. *Po-poki* is an imitative word from "poor pussy;" *oau* is imitated from the call made by the cat itself.

7. Sect. 27. The pig, *Puaa,* and the dog, *ilio,* were here in Hawaii long before the first white man landed on these shores; they are not modern importations.

The same is true of the domestic fowl. This can be proved by old prayers and *meles*. The word *moa* applied to the common fowl is the same as the Maori word.

8. Sect. 28. *Koloa* is the name generally applied to the wild muscovy duck. To the tame fowl which the white man did bring across the sea is generally given the name *ka-ka*.

XIV

Articles of Food and Drink in Hawaii

1. The food staple most desired in Hawaii nei was the taro (*kalo, Arum esculentum*). When beaten into *poi*, or made up into bundles of hard poi, called *pai-ai*, *omao*, or *holo-ai*,[1] it is a delicious food. Taro is raised by planting the stems The young and tender leaves are cooked and eaten as greens called *lu-au*, likewise the stems under the name of *ha-ha*. Poi is such an agreeable food that taro is in great demand. A full meal of poi, however, causes one to be heavy and sleepy.

2. There are many varieties of taro.[2] These are named according to color, black, white, red and yellow, besides which the natives have a great many other names. It is made into *kulolo* (by mixture with the tender meat of the cocoanut), also into a draught termed *apu* which is administered to the sick; indeed its uses are numerous.

3. The sweet potato (*uala*), (the Maori *kumara*), was an important article of food in Hawaii nei; it had many varieties[3] which were given names on the same principle as that used in naming taro, viz: white, black, red, yellow, etc.

4. The *uala* grows abundantly on the *kula* lands, or dry plains. It is made into a kind of poi or eaten dry. It is excellent when roasted, a food much to be desired. The body of one who makes his food of the sweet potato is plump and his flesh clean and fair, whereas the flesh of him who feeds on taro-poi is not so clear and wholesome.

5. The *u-ala* ripens quickly, say in four or five months after planting, whereas the taro takes twelve months to ripen. Animals fed on the sweet potato take on fat well; its leaves (when cooked) are eaten as greens and called *palula*. Sweet potato sours quickly when mixed into poi, whereas poi made from taro is slow to ferment. The sweet potato is the chief food-staple of the dry, upland plains. At the present time the potato is used in making swipes. The sweet potato is raised by planting the stems.

6. The yam, or *uhi* (*Dioscorea*) is an important article of food. In raising it, the body of the vegetable itself is planted. It does not soon spoil if uncooked. It is not made up into poi, but eaten while still warm from the oven, or after roasting. The yam is used in the preparation of a drink for the sick.

DAVID MALO

7. The *ulu* or bread-fruit is very much used as a food by the natives, after being oven-cooked or roasted; it is also pounded into a delicious poi, *pepeiee*. It is propagated (by planting shoots or scions).

8. The banana (*mai'a*) was an important article of food, honey-sweet, when fully ripe, and delicious when roasted on the coals or oven-cooked, but it does not satisfy. It was propagated from offshoots.

9. The *ohia*—or "mountain apple"—was a fruit that was much eaten raw. It was propagated from the seed.[4] The squash is eaten only after cooking.

10. The following articles were used as food in the time of famine: the *ha-pu-u* fern (the fleshy stem of the leaf-stalk); the *ma'u* and the *i-i-i* (the pithy flesh within the woody exterior). These (ferns) grow in that section of the mountain-forest called *wao-maukelc*. (See Chap VII. Sect. 12.) The outer woody shell is first chipped away with an ax, the soft interior is then baked in a large underground oven overnight until it is soft when it is ready for eating. But one is not really satisfied with such food.

11. The *ti*[5] (*Cordyline terminalis*) also furnishes another article of food. It grows wild in that section of the forest called *wao-akua* (Chap. VII. Sect. 12). The fleshy root is grubbed up, baked in a huge, underground oven overnight until cooked. The juice of the *ti*-root becomes very sweet by being cooked, but it is not a satisfying food.

12. The *pi-a*, in Hillebrand's Flora of the Hawaiian Islands called *piia* (a kind of yam, *Dioscorea pentaphylla*) is a good and satisfying food when cooked in the native oven. It is somewhat like the sweet-potato when cooked. The *ho-i* (*Helmia bulb-ifera*): this is a bitter fruit. After cooking and grating, it has to be washed in several waters, then strained through cocoanut-web (the cloth-like material that surrounds the young leaves.—Translator) until it is sweet. It is then a very satisfying food.

13. The *pala-fern* (*Marattia*) also furnished a food. The base of the leaf-stem was the part used; it was eaten after being oven-cooked. This fern grows wild in the woods.

14. The *pia* (*Tacca pinnatifida*) is another food-plant, of which the tubers are planted. When ripe the tubers are grated while yet raw by means of rough stones, mixed with water and then allowed to stand until it has turned sweet, after which it is roasted in bundles and eaten. The wild pea, *papapa,* the *nena,* the *koali*[6] (*Ipomoea tuberculata*) were all used as food in famine-times.

15. Among the kinds of food brought from foreign countries are flour, rice, Irish potatoes, beans, Indian corn, squashes and melons, of which the former are eaten after cooking and the latter raw.

16. In Hawaii nei people drink either the water from heaven, which is called real water (*wai maoli*), or the water that comes from beneath the earth, which is (often) brackish.

Awa was the intoxicating drink of the Hawaiians in old times; but in modern times many new intoxicants have been introduced from foreign lands, as rum, brandy, gin.

17. People also have learned to make intoxicating swipes from fermented potatoes, watermelon, or the fruit of the ohia.[7]

Notes on Chapter XIV

1. Sect. 1. Hard poi, that is, pounded taro unmixed with water, is made up into bundles, which on Oahu and Molokai were round and covered with the leaves of the *ti* plant. On Hawaii and on Maui they were long and cylindrical and were covered with banana stalks or the leaf of the pandanus, and were called *omao* or *holo–ai*.

2. Sect. 2. The names given to the different varieties of taro might be reckoned by the score. In spite of Mr. Malo's assertion, color seems to have had but little to do with the determination of the name. To mention a few representative names, the *ka–i*, which made the very best of poi, was of firm consistency, of a steel-blue color, and of an agreeable sweetish taste: the *hao–kea* of a light grey color, softer consistency and more neutral flavor; between these two, which may be taken as representing the extremes, are ranged a multitude of varieties representing all the intervening shades of blue and grey. The *ipu–o–lono* and *apu–wai* are of medium blue-grey color and consistency, representing a mean between the extremes mentioned. The *pii–alii* (king's desire) is of a pinky-purplish hue and makes a delicate poi that is regarded as the most choice of all varieties.

3. Sect. 3. This remark does not do justice to the facts. The names given to the different species of *uala* and of taro as well show accurate observation and good powers of description. One variety was named *lau–lii*, small leaf, another *piko nui*, big navel, another *hua–moa*, hen's egg, etc.

4. Sect. 9. By some mistake the author says that the ohia is propagated from branches or cuttings. Only the seed is used. One might as well expect a branch of oak to grow as a branch of ohia.

5. Sect. 11. The action of this famine-diet is well described in the following triplet:

> "*I ka wa wi, wi, wi,*
> *Ai ka ti, ti, ti,*
> *A hi, hi, hi.*"

6. Sect. 14. Koali. The juice of the leaves and stems of the koali was used as a cathartic in Hawaiian medicine. Its effects are powerful.

7. Sect. 17. *Okole-hao*—so called from the small round hole of the iron pipe from which the liquor dripped—is a liquor distilled from the fermented juice of the ti-root. It is said to be of excellent quality, resembling New England rum.

XV

The Fishes

1. There are many distinct species of fish in Hawaii. All products of the ocean, whether they move or do not move, are called fish (*i'a*).[1] There are also fish in the inland waters.

2. The mosses in fresh and salt water are classed with the fish (as regards food). There are many varieties of moss, which are named from their peculiarities, from color, red or black, or from their flavor. The *o-o-pu* (a small eel-like fish), and the shrimp (*opae*) are the fish of fresh water.

3. The fish from shoal and from deep water differ from each other. Some fish are provided with feet, some are beset with sharp bones and spines. Some fish crawl slowly along, clinging to the rocks, while others swim freely about, of which there are many different kinds, some small, some peaked (*o-e-o-e;* this is also the name of a fish); some flattened, some very flat, some long, some white, some red, many different species in the ocean.

5. The following fish have feet with prongs: the *hihiwai, elepi* (a four-footed sea-animal), *ele-mihi*[2] the *kukuma* (a whitish crab), the *kumimi* (a poisonous crab), the *papa*, the *pa-pai* (a wholesome crab), *papai-lanai*, the *lobster* or *ula*, the *alo*, the *popoki*, the *ounauna*, and the shrimp or *opae*. These are all good food save the *kumimi*. That is poisonous and is not eaten.

6. I will now mention some fish that are beset with spines: the *ina, hawae,* and *wana*,[3] the *ha-uke-uke*, and the *hakue*. These fish are all fit to be eaten; their flesh is within their shell. The *kokala, oopu-hue* and *keke* are also fish that are covered with spines; they move swiftly through the water and are eaten as food. Death is sometimes caused by eating the oopu-hue.[4]

7. The following fish are covered with heavy shells: the *pipipi* (one of the *Nerita*, which is excellent eating.—Translator), the *alea-alea*, the *aoa*, the *kuanaka*, the *pupu* (a generic name for all shells at the present time), the *kuoho*, the *pu-hookaui* or conch, the *pupu-awa*, the *olepe* (a bivalve), the *ole*, the *oaoaka*, the *nahana-wele*, the *uli*, the *pipi*, the *maha-moe*, the *opihi*, the cowry or *leho*, the *pana-pana-puhi;* the *pupu-loloa*. This is of course not the whole list of what are called fish.

8. The following are fish that move slowly: the *naka*, the *ku-alakai*, the *ku-nou-nou*, the *kona-lelewa*, the *loli* or beche de mer, the *mai-hole*,

the *kua-naka*, the *mini-ole*, the *lepe-lepe-ohina*. These are not fish of fine quality, though they are eaten.

9. The following small-fry are seen along shore—they are swift of motion: the young (*pua* or flowers) of the mullet or *anae* (when of medium size it is called *ama-ama*), of the *awa*, *aholehole*, *hinana*, *nehu*, *iao*, *piha*, *opuu-puu ohua-palemo*, *paoa*, *oluhe-luhe*, *ohune*, *moi-lii*, and the *akeke*. All of these fish are used as food. Doubtless I have omitted the mention of some.

10. The following fish have bodies with eminences or sharp protuberances (*kino oeoe*): the *paeaca*, *paniho-loa*, *olali*, *hinalea*, *aki-lolo*, *ami*, *mananalo*, *awela*, *maha-wela*, *hou*, *hilu*, *omalemale*, *o-niho-niho opule*, *lau-ia ulae*, *aoao-wela*, *upa-palu*, *uhu-elcele*, *lao*, *palao*, *oama*, and the *aawa*. No doubt I have omitted some of them. These fish are excellent eating.

11. The following fish have flattened bodies: the *aloi-loi*, *ku-pipi*, *ao-ao-nui*; *mai-i-i*, *kole*, *martini*, *mamamo*, *mao-mao*, *lau-hau*,[5] *laui-pala*, *mai-ko*, *maao*, *humu-humu*, *kihi-kihi*, *kika-kapu*, *ka-pu-hili*, *oili-lapa*, *pa-kii*, *paa-paa*, *uwi-wi*, *umauma-lei*, *walu*; and probably these are not all of them. These fish are good eating.

12. The following are fish with bodies greatly flattened: the *kala*, *palani*, *nanue*, *piha-weu-weu*, *pa-kukui*, and the *api*.

13. The following fish have bodies of a silvery color: the *ahole* (same as the *ahole-ahole*), *anae* (full grown *mullet*), *awa*, *uoa*, *o-io*, *opelu*, *mo-i*, *u-lua*, *ulua-mohai*, *a-ku*, *ahi*, *omaka*, *kawa-kawa*, *moku-le-ia*, *la-i*, and the *hoana*, all of which are good eating.

14. The following are fish with long bodies: the *ku-pou-pou*, *aha*, *nunu*, *a'u-a'u*, *wela*, *wolu*, *ono*, *aulepe*, *ha-uli-uli*; these fish are used as food.

15. The following fish have bodies of a red color: the *a-ala-ihi*, *u-u*, *moano*, *weke* (of a pink, salmon and fawn color, a fine fish), *a-we-o-we-o*,[6] *ku-mu*, *pa-ko-le-ko-le*, *uhu-ula*, *pa-ou-ou*, *o-pa-ka-pa-ka*, *ula-ula*, *ko-a-e*, *piha-weu-weu*, *o-ka-le-ka-le*, *muku-muku-waha-nui*. These fish are all wholesome food, though probably my list is not complete.

16. The following fish are furnished with rays or arms (*awe-awe*): the octopus (*he-e*), and the *mu-he-e* (squid?) which are eaten; also the *he-e-ma-ko-ko* which is bitter.

17. The following sea-animals have a great resemblance to each other: the sea-turtle or *honu*, from whose shell is made an instrument useful in scraping olona bark, also in making hair-combs in modern times; the *e-a*, a species of sea-turtle, whose shell was used in making fish-hooks. The *honu* is excellent eating, but the flesh of the *ea* is poisonous.

18. The *mono* or shark has one peculiarity, he is a man-eater. His skin is used in making drums for the worship of idols, also for the hula and the *ka-eke-eke* drum. The *ka-ha-la* and the *mahi-mahi* are quite unlike other fishes. Their flesh is excellent eating.

19. The following are fish that breathe on the surface of the ocean: the porpoise or *na-ia, nuao, pa-hu,* and the whale (*ko-ho-hi*). The *kohola* or whale was formerly called the *pa-lao-a.*[7] These fish, cast ashore by the sea, were held to be the property of the king. Both the *honu* and the *ea* come to the surface to breathe.

20. The following fish are provided with (long fins like) wings: the *lolo-au ma-lolo* (the flying-fish), the *puhi-kii* (*puhi-ki* is a mistaken orthography), *lupe, hihi-manu, haha-lua,* and the *hai-lepo.* These fishes are all used as food, but they are not of the finest flavor. No doubt many fish have failed of mention.

Notes on Chapter XV

1. Sect. 1. *I'a,* from this word the *k,* which still remains in its related form *i-ka* of the Maori language, has been dropped out; its grave is still marked, however, in the Hawaiian by a peculiar break, the result of a sudden glottic closure. It means primarily fish; also any kind of meat or animal food, and in the absence of these, any savory vegetable, which as a relish temporarily takes the place of animal food, is for the time spoken of as the *i-a for* that meal. Thus it is common to say, *luau* was our *i'a* on such an occasion. Even salt, *paa-kai,* is sometimes spoken of as the *i'a* for a particular meal or in time of want. In the Malay language the word for fish is *ikan.*

2. Sect. 5. *Alamihi.* A small crab, also called the *ala-mihi,* spoken of as the corpse-eating alamihi, *ka alamihi ai kupapau.* In spite of its scavenging propensities this crab is eaten, and it was undoubtedly one of the means of spreading cholera in Honolulu in 1895.

3. Sect. 6. All of these are *echini.* The spines of the *wana* are very long, fine and sharp as a needle.

4. Sect. 6. In the *oopu-hue* the poisonous part is the gall. By carefully dissecting out the gall-bladder without allowing the escape of any of its contents, the fish may be eaten with impunity. Its flavor is delicious.

5. Sect. 11. *Lau-han.* Its patches of gold and dark brown, resembling the ripe leaf of the *hau,* it give this name.

6. Sect. 15. *Aweowco,* also called *ala-lau-a.* The appearance of this fish in large numbers about the harbor of Honolulu was formerly regarded as an omen of death to some alii.

7. Sect. 19. The *palaoa* is the sperm whale.

XVI

THE TAPAS, MALOS, PAUS AND MATS
OF THE HAWAIIANS

1. Tapa was the fabric that formed the clothing of the Hawaiians. It was made from the bark of certain plants, *wauke, mamake, maaloa,* and *poulu,* the skin of young bread-fruit shoots.[1] Wauke (*Broussonetia papyrifera*) was extensively cultivated and the preparation and manufacture of it was as follows: It was the man's work to cut down the branches, after which the women peeled off (*uhole*) the bark and, having removed the cortex, put the inner bark to soak until it had become soft.

2. After this it was beaten on the log (*kua*) with a club called *i-e* (or *i-e kuku.* The round club, *hohoa,* was generally used in the early stage of preparation) until it was flattened out. This was continued for four days, or much longer sometimes, and when the sheet (being kept wet all the time) had been worked until it was broad and thin, it was spread out and often turned, and when dry this was the fabric used as blankets, loin-skirts (*pa-u*) for the women, and, when made into narrower pieces, as loin-cloths (*malos*) for the men.[2]

3. The *mamake* (*Pipturus albidus*) was another of the plants whose bark was made into tapa and used as blankets, malos and pa-us. This was a tree that grew wild in the woods. It was collected by the women who stripped off the bark and steamed it in the oven with *pala-a* (a fern that yielded a dark-red coloring matter). If not steamed and stained with *pala-a* the tapa made from it was called *kapa-kele-wai.*

4. Like *wauke,* it was first soaked until pulpy, when it was beaten on the tapa log with a club until it had been drawn out thin—this might require three or four days—after which it was spread out to dry in the sun, and was then used as sheets or blankets, clothing, *malos, paus.* The *mamake* made a very durable tapa and could be worn a long time.

5. The bark of the *maaloa* and *po-ulu,* the bark of tender bread-fruit shoots were also beaten into tapa. The method of manufacture was the same as that of *wauke* and *mamake.* There were many varieties of tapa, sheets, blankets, robes, *malos, pa-us,* etc., which the women decorated in different patterns with black, red, green, yellow and other colors.

6. If, after being stained with the juice of *kukui*-root, called *hili*, it was colored with an earth, the tapa was called *pu-lo'u;* another name for it was *o-u-holo-wai.*

7. If the tapa was colored with *ma'o* (*Gossypium tomento-sum*) *it* was called *ma'o-ma'o*, green. If stained with the *hoolei*, (*Ochrosia sandwicensis*) it took on a yellow color. If unstained the tapa was white. If red cloth was mixed with it in the beating, the tapa was called *pa'i-ula*, or red-print.[3]

8. There was a great variety of names derived from the colors (and patterns) stamped upon them by the women.

9. The loin-skirts (*pau*) of the women were colored in many different ways. If stained with turmeric, the *pau* was called *kama-lena*, if with cocoanut, it was called *hala-kea.*[4] Most of the names applied to the different varieties of *pau* were derived from the manner in which the women stained (and printed) them.[5]

10. In the same way most of the names applied to varieties of the malo were likewise derived from the manner of staining (and printing) them. If stained with the *noni* (*Morinda citrifolia*) it was a *kua-ula*, a red-back, or a *pu-kohu-kohu*, or a *pua-kai*, seaflower. A *pan* dyed with turmeric was soft, while some other kinds of *pau* were stiff. The names applied to *paus* were as diverse as the patterns imprinted on them; and the same was the case with the *malo*, of which one pattern was called *puali* and another *kupeke.*

12. These were the fabrics which the ancient Hawaiians used for their comfort, and in robing themselves withal, as loin-girdles for the men, and as loin-skirts for the women.

13. They braided mats[6] from the leaves of a tree called the *hala* (pandanus). The women beat down the leaves with sticks, wilted them over the fire, and then dried them in the sun. After the young leaves (*muo*) had been separated from the old ones (*laele*) the leaves were made up into rolls.

14. This done (and the leaves having been split up into strips of the requisite width) they were plaited into mats. The young leaves (*mu-o*)[7] made the best mats, and from them were made the sails for the canoes. Mats were also made from the *makaloa*, a fine rush, which were sometimes decorated with patterns in-wrought (*pawehe*). A mat of superior softness and fineness was made from the *naku*, or tule.

15. These things were articles of the greatest utility, being used to cover the floor, as clothing, and as robes. This work was done by the

women, and was a source of considerable profit; so that the women who engaged in it were held to be well off, and were praised for their skill. Such arts as these were useful to the ancient Hawaiians and brought them wealth.

16. From the time of Kamehameha I down to the present reign of Kamehameha III we have been supplied with cloth imported from foreign lands. These new stuffs we call *lole*[7] (to change). It has many names according to the pattern.

Notes on Chapter XVI

1. Sect. 1. Many other fibres not mentioned by Mr. Malo were used in making tapa, such as the *olona* and the hibiscus (*hau*), not to mention the mulberry since its introduction in modern times.

2. Sect. 2. The Hawaiians had no means of cutting their tapa corresponding to our shears. They knew nothing of the art of the tailor. As a piece of tapa was designed, so it remained to the end of its history, whether it were to serve as a cover at night—sheet or blanket—a toga-like robe of warmth and etiquette. *kihei*, or the democratic *malo* or *pau*. The *malo* was of more pliable material as a rule than the *kihei*; its width was generally nine to ten inches, its length from three to four yards. The patterns used on the *malo* were different from those used in decorating the *pau*; and the same remark applies to the *kihei*.

3. Sect. 7. In modern times foreign cloth, especially turkey-red has been used as a source from which to obtain dye. Red or yellow earths and ochre, as well as charcoal, were used in the make up of pigments. The Hawaiians did not use a glaze or varnish, after the manner of the Samoans, in finishing their tapas.

4. Sect. 9. The oily juice of the fully ripe cocoanut meat, mixed with turmeric and the juice of a fragrant mountain vine, *kupa-o-a*, was used to impart an agreeable odor to the malo of an alii. It also gave it a yellowish color. Mamake tapa was often treated in this way. Sandalwood and the fragrant *mokihana* berry were also used to impart an agreeable odor to tapa.

5. Sect. 9. No mention is made by the author of the art of printing tapa by means of stamps, which were generally made of bamboo. They were very extensively used and were in great variety of pattern. These printing blocks were named *laau-ka-pala-pala*.

6. Sect. 13. Mats were made from a dozen other things besides the hala-leaf. Niihau was famed for producing the most beautiful mats. The mats of the Micronesian and Gilbert islands, the people of which belong to the class of *weavers*, are superior to those of the Hawaiian archipelago.

7. Sect. 16. The Hawaiians distinctly belonged to that class of the Polynesians which may be called the *tapa-beaters*, in distinction from the weavers. When soiled or dirty, tapa was thrown away.

XVII

The Stone Ax and the New Ax

1. The ax of the Hawaiians was of stone. The art of making it was handed down from remote ages. Ax-makers were a greatly esteemed class in Hawaii nei. Through their craft was obtained the means of felling trees and of cutting and hewing all kinds of timber used in every sort of woodwork. The manner of making an ax was as follows:

2. The ax-makers (*poe ka-ko'i*) prospected through the mountains and other places in search of hard stones suitable for ax-making, carrying with them certain other pieces of hard stone, some of them angular and some of them round in shape, called *haku ka-koi*, to be used in chipping and forming the axes.

3. After splitting the rock and obtaining a long fragment, they placed it in a liquor made from vegetable juices (*wai-laau*)[1] which was supposed to make it softer, and this accomplished, they chipped it above and below, giving it the rude shape of an ax.

4. The lower part of the ax which is rounded (*e polipoli ana*) is termed the *pipi;* the upper part which forms an angle with it is termed the *hau-hana.* When the shape of the thing has been blocked out, they apply it to the grind-stone, *hoana,*[2] sprinkled with sand and water. The upper side and the lower side were ground down and then the edge was sharpened. The joiner's ax (*koi kapili*) had a handle of hau, or some other wood.

5. The next thing was to braid some string, to serve as a lashing, to fit the handle to the ax, to wrap a protecting cloth (*pale*) about it (in order to save the lashing from being cut by the chips), and lastly, to bind the ax firmly to the handle, which done, the ax was finished. The ax now became an object of barter with this one and that one, and thus came into the hands of the canoe-maker.

6. The shell called *o-le*[3] served as an ax for some purposes, also a hard wood called *ala-hee.* There were a few axes made from (scraps of) iron, but the amount of iron in their possession was small. It was with such tools as these that the Hawaiians hewed out their canoes, house-timber and did a great variety of woodwork. The ax was by the ancients reckoned an article of great value. How pitiful!

7. Now come new kinds of axes from the lands of the white man. But iron had reached Hawaii before the arrival of the foreigner, a jetsam iron which the chiefs declared sacred to the gods. (*He hao pae, ua hai na 'lii i na 'kua kii.*)

8. There was, however, very little iron here in those old times. But from the days of Kamehameha I down to those of Kamehameha III, iron has been abundant in this country.

9. Iron is plentiful now, and so are all kinds of iron tools, including the kitchen-ax, the hatchet, the adze, broad-ax, chisel, etc. These are the new tools which have been imported. The stone-ax (*koi-pohaku*) is laid aside.

Notes to Chapter XVII

1. Sect. 3. I am informed that this *wai-laau* was composed of the juice of the *pala'e* fern mixed with green kukui nuts. After keeping the stone in the liquor a few days it was thought to become softer and more easy to work.

2. Sect. 4. In spite of the resemblance of the word *hoana* to our word hone, it seems to be a genuine Hawaiian word of ancient origin. In N. Z it is *hoanga*, in *Raro-tonga oanga*.

3. Sect. 6.   "O *ka ole ke koi o kai,*
      O ke alahe'e ke koi o uka."

      The ole is the ax of the shore,
      The alahe'e is the ax of the inland.

The *ole* is a sea-shell, the *alahee* a hard wood found in the upland. The adzes made of these were not equal to the stone axes, but were useful in cutting soft woods, such as the wili-wili, kukui, etc.

N. B. On Mauna-kea—and probably such places have been found elsewhere—has been found a quarry, from which must have been taken in ancient times the material for stone axes. Judging from the quantity of chips and debris the amount of material removed from the place was very great. Broken axes and axes in various stages of finish and partial completion were also found. An ax-quarry anciently existed on Mauna Loa at the western end of Molokai, at a place named Ka-lua-ka ko'i.

The term *ala* is generally applied to the material, the kind of stone of which the Hawaiian ax was made, and the ax was often called *koi ala*. Ala is a dark, heavy, close-grained basalt.

XVIII

The Aliis and the Common People

1. The physical characteristics of the chiefs and the common people of Hawaii nei were the same; they were all of one race; alike in features and physique.[1] Commoners and aliis were all descended from the same ancestors, Wakea and Papa. The whole people were derived from that couple. There was no difference between king and plebeian as to origin. It must have been after the time of Wakea that the separation of the chiefs from the people took place.

2. It is probable that because it was impossible for all the people to act in concert in the government, in settling the difficulties, lifting the burdens, and disentangling the embarrassments of the people from one end of the land to the other that one was made king, with sole authority to conduct the government and to do all its business. This most likely was the reason why certain ones were selected to be chiefs. But we are not informed who was the first one chosen to be king; that is only a matter of conjecture.

3. The king was appointed (*hoonoho ia mai;* set up would be a more literal translation) that he might help the oppressed who appealed to him, that he might succor those in the right and punish severely those in the wrong. The king was over all the people; he was the supreme executive, so long, however, as he did right.

4. His executive duties in the government were to gather the people together in time of war, to decide all important questions of state, and questions touching the life and death of the common people as well as of the chiefs and his comrades in arms. It was his to look after the soldiery. To him belonged the property derived from the yearly taxes, and he was the one who had the power to dispossess commoners and chiefs of their lands.

5. It was his to assess the taxes both on commoner and on chiefs and to impose penalties in case the land-tax was not paid. He had the power to appropriate, reap or seize at pleasure, the goods of any man, to cut off the ear of another man's pig, (thus making it his own). It was his duty to consecrate the temples, to oversee the performance of religious rites in the temples of human sacrifice, (*na heiau poo-kanaka, oia hoi na luakini*)

that is, in the *luakini, lo* preside over the celebration of the *Makahiki*-festival, and such other ceremonies as he might be pleased to appoint.

6. From these things will be apparent the supremacy of the king over the people and chiefs. The soldiery were a factor that added to the king's pre-eminence.

It was the policy of the government to place the chiefs who were destined to rule, while they were still young, with wise persons, that they might be instructed by skilled teachers in the principles of government, be taught the art of war, and be made to acquire personal skill and bravery.

7. The young man had first to be subject to another chief, that he might be disciplined and have experience of poverty, hunger, want and hardship, and by reflecting on these things learn to care for the people with gentleness and patience, with a feeling of sympathy for the common people, and at the same time to pay due respect to the ceremonies of religion and the worship of the gods, to live temperately, not violating virgins (*aole lima koko kohe*),[2] conducting the government kindly to all.

8. This is the way for a king to prolong his reign and cause his dynasty to be perpetuated, so that his government shall not be overthrown. Kings that behave themselves and govern with honesty,—their annals and genealogies will be preserved and treasured by the thoughtful and the good.

9. Special care was taken in regard to chiefs of high rank to secure from them noble offspring, by not allowing them to form a first union with a woman of lower rank than themselves, and especially not to have them form a first union with a common or plebeian woman (*wahine noa*).

10. To this end diligent search was first made by the genealogists into the pedigree of the woman, if it concerned a high born prince, or into the pedigree of the man, if it concerned a princess of high birth, to find a partner of unimpeachable pedigree; and only when such was found and the parentage and lines of ancestry clearly established, was the young man (or young woman) allowed to form his first union, in order that the offspring might be a great chief.

11. When it was clearly made out that there was a close connection, or identity, of ancestry between the two parties, that was the woman with whom the prince was first to pair. If the union was fruitful, the child would be considered a high chief, but not of the highest rank or tabu. His would be a *kapu a noho,* that is the people and chiefs of rank inferior to his must *sit* in his presence.

12. A suitable partner for a chief of the highest rank was his own sister, begotten by the same father and mother as himself. Such a pairing was called a *pi'o* (a bow, a loop, a thing bent on itself); and if the union bore fruit, the child would be a chief of the highest rank, a *ninau pi'o*, so sacred that all who came into his presence must prostrate themselves. He was called divine, *akua*. Such an alii would not go abroad by day but only at night, because if he went abroad in open day (when people were about their usual avocations), every one had to fall to the ground in an attitude of worship.

13. Another suitable partner for a great chief was his half-sister, born, it might be of the same mother, but of a different father, or of the same father but of a different mother. Such a union was called a *naha*. The child would be a great chief, *niau-pio;* but it would have only the *kapu-a-noho* (sitting tabu).

14. If such unions as these could not be obtained for a great chief, he would then be paired with the daughter of an elder or younger brother, or of a sister. Such a union was called a *hoi* (return). The child would be called a *niau-pio,* and be possessed of the *kapu-moe.*

15. This was the practice of the highest chiefs that their first born might be chiefs of the highest rank, fit to succeed to the throne.

16. It was for this reason that the genealogies of the kings were always preserved by their descendants, that the ancestral lines of the great chiefs might not be forgotten; so that all the people might see clearly that the ancestors on the mother's side were all great chiefs, with no small names among them; also that the father's line was pure and direct. Thus the chief became peerless, without blemish, sacred (*kuhau-lua, ila-ole, hemolele*).

17. In consequence of this rule of practice, it was not considered a thing to be tolerated that other chiefs should associate on familiar terms with a high chief, or that one's claim of relationship with him should be recognized until the ancestral lines of the claimant had been found to be of equal strength (*manoanoa*, thickness) with those of the chief; only then was it proper for them to call the chief a *maka-maka* (friend, or intimate—*maka* means eye).

18. Afterwards, when the couple had begotten children of their own, if the man wished to take another woman—or the woman another man—even though this second partner were not of such choice blood as the first, it was permitted them to do so. And if children were thus begotten they were called *kaikaina,* younger brothers or sisters of the great chief, and would become the backbone (*iwi-kua-moo*), executive officers (*ila-muku*) of the chief, the ministers (*kuhina*) of his government.

19. The practice with certain chiefs was as follows: if the mother was a high chief, but the father not a chief, the child would rank somewhat high as a chief and would be called an *alii papa* (a chief with a pedigree) on account of the mother's high rank.

20. If the father was a high chief, and the mother of low rank, but a chiefess, the child would be called a *kau-kau-alii*. In case the father was a chief and the mother of no rank whatever, the child would be called a *kulu*, a drop; another name was *ua-iki*, a slight shower; still another name was *kukae-popolo*. (I will not translate this.) The purport of these appellatives is that chiefish rank is not clearly established.

21. If a woman who was a *kaukau-alii*, living with her own husband, should have a child by him and should then give it away in adoption to another man, who was a chief, the child would be an *alii-poo-lua*, a two-headed chief.

22. Women very often gave away their children to men with whom they had illicit relations.[4] It was a common thing for a chief to have children by this and that woman with whom he had enjoyed secret amours. Some of these children were recognized and some were not recognized.

23. One of these illegitimates would be informed of the fact of his chiefish ancestry, though it might not be generally known to the public. The child in such case, was called an *alii kuauhau* (chief with an ancestry), from the fact that he knew his pedigree and could thus prove himself an *alii*.

24. Another one would merely know that he had *alii* blood in his veins, and on that account perhaps he would not suffer his clothing to be put on the same frame or shelf as that of another person. Such an one was styled a clothes-rack-chief (*alii-kau-holo-papa*), because it was in his solicitude about his clothes-rack that he distinguished himself as an alii.

25. If a man through having become a favorite (*punahele*) or an intimate (*aikane*) of an *alii*, afterwards married a woman of *alii* rank, his child by her would be called a *kau-kau-alii*[5], or an *alii maoli* (real *alii*).

26. A man who was enriched by a chief with a gift of land or other property was called an *alii lalo-lalo*, a low down chief. Persons were sometimes called *alii* by reason of their skill or strength. Such ones were *alii* only by brevet title.

27. The great chiefs were entirely exclusive, being hedged about with many tabus, and a large number of people were slain for breaking, or infringing upon, these tabus. The tabus that hedged about an *alii* were

exceedingly strict and severe. Tradition does not inform us what king established these tabus. In my opinion the establishment of the tabu-system is not of very ancient date, but comparatively modern in origin.

28. If the shadow of a man fell upon the house of a tabu-chief, that man must be put to death, and so with any one whose shadow fell upon the back of the chief, or upon his robe or malo, or upon anything that belonged to the chief. If any one passed through the private doorway of a tabu-chief, or climbed over the stockade about his residence, he was put to death.[6]

29. If a man entered the *alii's* house without changing his wet malo, or with his head smeared with mud, he was put to death. Even if there were no fence surrounding the *alii's* residence, only a mark, or faint scratch in the ground hidden by the grass, and a man were to overstep this line unwittingly, not seeing it, he would be put to death.

30. When a tabu-chief ate, the people in his presence must kneel, and if any one raised his knee from the ground, he was put to death. If any man put forth in a *kio-loa*[7] canoe at the same time as the tabu-chief, the penalty was death.

31. If any one girded himself with the king's malo, or put on the king's robe, he was put to death. There were many other tabus, some of them relating to the man himself and some to the king, for violating which any one would be put to death.

32. A chief who had the *kapu-moe*—as a rule—went abroad only at night; but if he travelled in daytime a man went before him with a flag calling out "kapu! moe!" whereupon all the people prostrated themselves. When the containers holding the water for his bath, or when his clothing, his malo, his food, or anything that belonged to him, was carried along, every one must prostrate himself; and if any remained standing, he was put to death. Kiwalao was one of those who had this *kapu-moe*.

33. An *alii* who had the *kapu-wohi*[8] and his *kahili*-bearer, who accompanied him, did not prostrate himself when the *alii* with the *kapu-wohi* came along; he just kept on his way without removing his *lei* or his garment.

34. Likewise with the chief who possessed the *kapu-a-noho*, when his food-calabashes, bathing water, clothing, malo, or anything that belonged to him, was carried along the road, the person who at such a time remained standing was put to death in accordance with the law of the tabu relative to the chiefs.

35. The punishment inflicted on those who violated the tabu of the chiefs was to be burned with fire until their bodies were reduced to ashes, or to be strangled, or stoned to death. Thus it was that the tabus of the chiefs oppressed the whole people.

36. The edicts of the king had power over life and death. If the king had a mind to put some one to death, it might be a chief or a commoner, he uttered the word and death it was.

37. But if the king chose to utter the word of life, the man's life was spared.

38. The king, however, had no laws regulating property, or land, regarding the payment or collection of debts, regulating affairs and transactions among the common people, not to mention a great many other things.

39. Every thing went according to the will or whim of the king, whether it concerned land, or people, or anything else—not according to law.

40. All the chiefs under the king, including the *konohikis* who managed their lands for them, regulated land-matters and everything else according to their own notions.

41. There was no judge, nor any court of justice, to sit in judgment on wrong-doers of any sort. Retaliation with violence or murder was the rule in ancient times.

42. To run away and hide one's self was the only resource for an offender in those days, not a trial in a court of justice as at the present time.

43. If a man's wife was abducted from him he would go to the king with a dog as a gift, appealing to him to cause the return of his wife—or the woman for the return of her husband—but the return of the wife, or of the husband, if brought about, was caused by the gift of the dog, not in pursuance of any law. If any one had suffered from a great robbery, or had a large debt owing him, it was only by the good will of the debtor, not by the operation of any law regulating such matters that he could recover or obtain justice. Men and chiefs acted strangely in those days.

44. There was a great difference between chiefs. Some were given to robbery, spoliation, murder, extortion, ravishing. There were few kings who conducted themselves properly as Kamehameha I did. He looked well after the peace of the land.

45. On account of the rascality (*kolohe*) of some of the chiefs to the common people, warlike contests frequently broke out between certain chiefs and the people, and many of the former were killed in battle by the commoners. The people made war against bad kings in old times.

46. The amount of property which the chiefs obtained from the people was very great. Some of it was given in the shape of taxes, some was the fruit of robbery and extortion.

Now the people in the out-districts (*kua-aina*) were—as a rule—industrious, while those about court or who lived with the chiefs—were indolent, merely living on the income of the land. Some of the chiefs carried themselves haughtily and arrogantly, being supported by contributions from others without labor of their own. As was the chief, so were his retainers (*kanaka*).

47. On this account the number of retainers, servants and hangers-on about the courts and residences of the kings and high chiefs was very great. The court of a king offered great attractions to the lazy and shiftless.

48. These people about court were called *pu-ali*[9] or *ai-alo* (those who eat in the presence), besides which there were many other names given them. One whom the *alii* took as an intimate was called *ai-kane*. An adopted child was called *keiki hookama*.

49. The person who brought up an alii and was his guardian was called a *kahu;* he who managed the distribution of his property was called a *puu-ku.* The house where the property of the *alii* was stored was called a *hale, pa-paa* (house with strong fence). The keeper of the king's apparel (master of the king's robes), or the place where they were stored, was called *hale opeope,* the folding house.

50. The steward who had charge of the king's food was called an 'a- i-puu-puu, calloused-neck. He who presided over the king's *pot de chambre* was called a *lomi-lomi,* i.e., a masseur. He who watched over the king during sleep was called *kiai-poo,* keeper of the head. The keeper of the king's idol was called *kahu-akua.*

51. The priest who conducted the religious ceremonies in the king's *heiau* was a *kahuna pule.* He who selected the site for building a heiau and designed the plan of it was called a *kuhi-kuhi puu-one.*[10] He who observed and interpreted the auguries of the heavens was called a *kilo-lam.* A person skilled in strategy and war was called a *kaa-kaua.* A counselor, skilled in statecraft, was called a *kalai-moku* (*kalai,* to hew; *moku,* island). Those who farmed the lands of the king or chiefs were *kono-hiki.*

52. The man who had no land was called a *kaa-owe.*[11] The temporary hanger-on was called a *kua-lana* (*lana,* to float. After hanging about the alii's residence for a time, he shifted to some other *alii.*—Translator);

another name for such a vagrant was *kuewa* (a genuine tramp, who wheedled his way from place to place). The servants who handled the fly-brushes *kahili,* about the king's sleeping place were called *haa-kue;* another name for them was *kua-lana-puhi;* or they were called *olu-eke-loa-hoo-kaa-moena.*[12]

53. Beggars were termed *auhau-puka,*[13] or *noi* (a vociferous beggar), or *makilo* (a silent beggar), or *apiki.*[14]

54. One who was born at the residence of the king or of a chief was termed a *kanaka no-hii-alo,* or if a chief, *alii no-hii-alo* (*noho i ke alo*). A chief who cared for the people was said to be a chief of *aau-loa*[15] or of *mahu-kai-loa.* A man who stuck to the service of a chief through thick and thin and did not desert him in time of war, was called a *kanaka no kahi kaua,* a man for the battle-field. This epithet was applied also to chiefs who acted in the same way.

55. People who were clever in speech and at the same time skillful workmen were said to be *noeau* or *noiau.* There are many terms applicable to the court, expressive of relations between king and chiefs and people, which will necessarily escape mention.

56. As to why in ancient times a certain class of people were ennobled and made into *aliis,* and another class into subjects (*kanaka*), why a separation was made betweeen chiefs and commoners, has never been explained.

57–58. Perhaps in the earliest times all the people were *alii*[16] and it was only after the lapse of several generations that a division was made into commoners and chiefs; the reason for this division being that men in the pursuit of their own gratification and pleasure wandered off in one direction and another until they were lost sight of and forgotten.

59. Perhaps this theory will in part account for it: a handsome, but worthless, chief takes up with a woman of the same sort, and, their relatives having cast them out in disgust, they retire to some out of the way place; and their children, born in the back-woods amid rude surroundings, are forgotten.[17]

60. Another possible explanation is that on account of lawlessness, rascality, dishonorable conduct, theft, impiousness and all sorts of criminal actions that one had committed, his fellow chiefs banished him, and after long residence in some out of the way place, all recollection of him and his pedigree was lost.[18]

61. Another reason no doubt was that certain ones leading a vagabond life roamed from place to place until their ancestral genealogies came

to be despised, (*wahawaha ia*) and were finally lost by those whose business it was to preserve them. This cause no doubt helped the split into chiefs and commoners.

62. The commoners were the most numerous class of people in the nation, and were known as the *ma-ka-aina-na;* another name by which they were called was *hu*. (*Hu,* to swell, multiply, increase like yeast.) The people who lived on the windward, that was the back, or *koolau* side of any island, were called *kua-aina* or back-country folks, a term of depreciation, however.

63. The condition of the common people was that of subjection to the chiefs, compelled to do their heavy tasks, burdened and oppressed, some even to death. The life of the people was one of patient endurance, of yielding to the chiefs to purchase their favor. The plain man (*kanaka*) must not complain.

64. If the people were slack in doing the chief's work they were expelled from their lands, or even put to death. For such reasons as this and because of the oppressive exactions made upon them, the people held the chiefs in great dread and looked upon them as gods.

65. Only a small portion of the kings and chiefs ruled with kindness; the large majority simply lorded it over the people.

66. It was from the common people, however, that the chiefs received their food and their apparel for men and women, also their houses and many other things. When the chiefs went forth to war some of the commoners also went out to fight on the same side with them.

67. The *makaainana* were the fixed residents of the land; the chiefs were the ones who moved about from place to place. It was the makaainanas also who did all the work on the land; yet all they produced from the soil belonged to the chiefs; and the power to expel a man from the land and rob him of his possessions lay with the chief.

68. There were many names descriptive of the *makaainanas*. Those who were born in the back-districts were called *kanaka no–hii-kua* (*noho-i-kua*), people of the back. The man who lived with the chief and did not desert him when war came, was called a *kanaka no lua-kaua,* a man for the pit of battle.

69–70. The people were divided into farmers, fishermen, house-builders, canoe-makers (*kalai-waa*), etc. They were called by many different appellations according to the trades they followed.

71. The (country) people generally lived in a state of chronic fear and apprehension of the chiefs; those of them, however, who

lived immediately with the chief were (to an extent) relieved of this apprehension.[19]

72. After sunset the candles of *kukui*-nuts were lighted and the chief sat at meat. The people who came in at that time were called the people of *lani-ka-e*.[20] Those who came in when the midnight lamp was burning (*ma ke kui au-moe*) were called the people of *pohokano*. This lamp was merely to talk by, there was no eating being done at that time.

73. The people who sat up with the chief until day-break (to carry-on, tell stories, gossip, or perhaps play some game, like *konane*.— TRANSLATOR) were called *ma-ko'u*[21] because that was the name of the flambeau generally kept burning at that hour.

74. There were three designations applied to the *kalai-moku*, or counselors of state. The *kalaimoku* who had served under but one king was called *lani-ka'e*. He who had served under two kings was called a *pohokano*, and if one had served three kings he was tremed a *ma-ko'u*. This last class were regarded as being most profoundly skilled in state-craft, from the fact that they had had experience with many kings and knew wherein one king had failed and wherein another had succeeded.

74. It was in this way that these statesmen had learned—by experience—that one king by pursuing a certain policy had met with disaster, and how another king, through following a different policy had been successful. The best course for the king would have been to submit to the will of the people.

Notes on Chapter XVIII

1. Sect. 1. Much has been said about the physique of the Hawaiian *alii* class, its quality, the probability that they were of a different and superior stock, &c., &c. Such talk is a mixture of flattery and of bosh. One might as well talk of the superiority of the breed of aldermen. When one considers to what extent the blood of the lower classes found its way into the veins of the *alii*-class, in spite of all tabus and precautions, and *vice versa,* all attempts to account for the rotund athleticism of the Hawaiian *alii* by any such theory are off the track. Feeding and grooming are sufficient to account for all the facts.

2. Sect. 7. *Aole lima koko kohe.* The literal translation of this would be *non manibus sanguine vaginae pollutis.* To lie with a woman at the time of her infirmity was a greater offense than to commit a rape.

3. Sect. 22. *Kau-kau-alii*: A Hawaiian explains the use of this phrase as meaning a step, stepping up to be an alii. Kau means a stepping place, or a foot-rest.

4. Sect. 22. Such relations might be known and approved by the husband. The unfruitfulness of a marriage relation was a frequent cause of this practice.

5. Sect. 25. The figure in this appellation is that of a flight of steps, *kau, kau,* step, step. Such is the explanation given of it by an intelligent Hawaiian.

6. Sect. 28. When Umi went to the court of Liloa to claim that king as his father, following his mother's instructions, he climbed the outside *pa* and then entered into the king's presence by the king's private entrance, thus by his defiance of tabu asserting his rank. See Chap. XLIX.

7. Sect. 30. The *kioloa* was a long, elegant, swift canoe, used for display and for racing. If any one were to show himself in one of these while the chief or king was also on the water, he would be chargeable with arrogance, *lese majeste,* in vying with him in display and thus detracting from the honor due the chief. This tabu did not apply to an ordinary fishing craft. It was in force until the chief had returned to his residence.

8. Sect. 33. One informant says the *kapu-wohi* was possessed by a young chief who had not yet known carnal intercourse. I do not trust this statement. Kanipahu, a king of Puna, is said to have been a very kapu-chief, to have combined in his own person *kapu-moe, kapu ku* and *kapu-helc* at the same time. How this could be I cannot see. His son, Kalapana, is said to have had the same range of *kapu.*

9. Sect. 48. In the original the word is *pualii,* but that is evidently a mistake and it should be *puali,* the literal meaning of which is band or cohort or company. Pualii is a term specially applied to orphans who were adopted by a chief or the king.

10. Sect. 51. *Kuhikuhi-puu-one.* One who pointed out the sand-heaps. The design for a heiau was first shown rudely in sand.

11. Sect. 52. An allusion to the rustling of his paper-like robe or blanket of tapa as he turned from side to side while lounging on his riat.

12. Sect. 52. The author has not mentioned the class to whom was given the expressive name *hoopili-mea-ai,* hangers-on-for-something-to-eat.

13. Sect. 53. Full form *auhau-puka-a-pae,* a slang phrase meaning to send one on a fool's errand, that being the way in which some of these gentry were treated.

14. Sect. 53. *Apiki.* Tricky; one, for instance, who, on receiving food, perhaps from several places, instead of taking it to his family, shared it with his pals.

15. Sect. 54. *Aau-loa,* literal meaning long shanks, derivative long-suffering.

16. Sect. 57. The development of this thought would have explained the whole mystery of why one became a king and the others remained commoners, *karaka* or *makaainana.*

17. Sect. 59. The tacit theory on which this explanation rests is that the passport to recognition as having a standing in the *papa alii,* or as being entitled to recognition as of the *alii* class, was that one's pedigree should be vouched for by the genealogist. One's pedigree being forgotten he must fall to the rank of the commoner.

18. Sect. 60, 61. It seems impossible to suppose that in the narrow limits of any of the Hawaiian islands any one could have wandered far enough to have become lost to the knowledge of the genealogists.

19. Sect. 71. That may have been because they had nothing to lose. The terror of death was passed perhaps. The people in the out-districts also were more timid and retiring in their manners.

20. Sect. 72. *Lani-ka'e,* or *lani-ka'e'e'e.* Later and towards the middle of the night, light was given by the *pohokano,* which was simply a hollowed stone containing oil and a wick.

21. Sect. 73. *Ma-ko'-u.* This flambeau was for the accommodation of the fishermen who returned from the sea at this early hour in the morning. The *ma-ko'u* was generally a torch of three strings of kukui-nuts. *ihoiho. Ma-ko-u* is the name also given to the castor oil bush, whose seed was sometimes in later times used as lamp-oil.

XIX

Life in the Out-Districts and at the King's Residence

1. The manner of life in the out-districts was not the same as that about the residence of the chief. In the former the people were cowed in spirit, the prey of alarm and apprehension, in dread of the chief's man.

2. They were comfortably off, however, well supplied with everything. Vegetable and animal food, tapa for coverings, girdles and loin-cloths and other comforts were in abundance.

3. To eat abundantly until one was sated and then to sleep and take one's comfort, that was the rule of the country. Sometimes, however, they did suffer hunger and feel the pinch of want The thrifty, however, felt its touch but lightly; as a rule they were supplied with all the comforts of life.

4. The country people were well off for domestic animals. It was principally in the country that pigs, dogs and fowls were raised, and thence came the supply for the king and chiefs.

5. The number of articles which the country (*kua-aina*) furnished the establishments of the kings and chiefs was very great.

The country people were strongly attached to their own homelands, the full calabash,[1] the roasted potatoes, the warm food, to live in the midst of abundance. Their hearts went out to the land of their birth.

6. It was a life of weariness, however; they were compelled at frequent intervals to go here and there, to do this and that work for the lord of the land, constantly burdened with one exaction or another.

7. The country people[2] were humble and abject; those about the chiefs overbearing, loud-mouthed, contentious.

8. The wives of the country people were sometimes appropriated by the men about court, even the men were sometimes separated from their country wives by the women of the court, and this violence was endured with little or no resistance, because these people feared that the king might take sides against them. In such ways as these the people of the *kuaaina* were heavily oppressed by the people who lived about court.[3]

9. Some of the country people were very industrious and engaged in farming or fishing, while others were lazy and shiftless, without

occupation. A few were clever, but the great majority were inefficient. There was a deal of blank stupidity among them.

10. These country people were much given to gathering together for some profitless occupation or pastime for talk's sake (*hoolua nui*), playing the braggadocio (*hoo-pehu-pehu*), when there was nothing to back up their boasts (*oheke wale*). The games played by the country people were rather different from those in vogue at court or at the chief's residence. Some people preferred the country to the court.

11. Many people, however, left the country and by preference came to live near the chiefs. These country people were often oppressive toward each other, but there was a difference between one country district and another.

12. The bulk of the supplies of food and of goods for chiefs and people was produced in the country districts. These people were active and alert in the interests of the chiefs.

13. The brunt of the hard work, whether it was buliding a temple, hauling a canoe-log out of the mountains, thatching a house, building a stone-wall, or whatever hard work it might be, fell chiefly upon the *kua-ainas*.

14. Life about court was very different from that in the country. At court the people were indolent and slack, given to making excuses (making a pretense of) doing some work, but never working hard.

15. People would stay with one chief awhile and then move on to another (*pakaulei*). There was no thrift; people were often hungry and they would go without their regular food for several days. At times there was great distress and want, followed by a period of plenty, if a supply of food was brought in from the country.

16. When poi and fish were plentiful at court the people ate with prodigality, but when food became scarce one would satisfy his hunger only at long intervals (*maona kalawalawa. Kawalawala* is the received orthography). At times also tapa-cloth for coverings and girdles, all of which came from the country, were in abundance at court.

17. At other times people about court, on account of the scarcity of cloth, were compelled to hide their nakedness with malos improvised from the narrow strips of tapa (*hipuupuu*)[4] that came tied about the bundles of tapa-cloth. A man would sometimes be compelled to make the *kihei* which was his garment during the day, serve him for a blanket by night, or sometimes a man would sleep under the same covering with another man. Some of the people about court were well furnished with all these things, but they were such ones as the *alii* had supplied.

18. Of the people about court there were few who lived in marriage. The number of those who had no legitimate relations with women was greatly in the majority. Sodomy[5] and other unnatural vices[6] in which men were the correspondents, fornication and hired prostitution[7] were practiced about court.

19. Some of the sports and games indulged in by the people about court were peculiar to them, and those who lived there became fascinated by the life. The crowd of people who lived about court was a medley of the clever and the stupid, a few industrious workers in a multitude of drones.

20. Among those about court there were those who were expert in all soldierly accomplishments, and the arts of combat were very much taught. Many took lessons in spear-throwing (*lono-maka-ihe*[8]), spear-thrusting, pole-vaulting (*ku-pololu*[9]), single-stick (*kaka-laau*)[10], rough-and-tumble wrestling (*kaala*),[11] and in boxing (*kui-alua*).[12] All of these arts were greatly practiced about court.

21. In the cool of the afternoon sham fights were frequently indulged in; the party of one chief being pitted against the party of another chief, the chiefs themselves taking part.

22. These engagements were only sham fights and being merely for sport were conducted with blunted spears, (*kaua kio*) or if sharp spears were used it was termed *kaua pahu-kala*. These exercises were useful in training the men for war.

23. In spite of all precautions many of the people, even of the chiefs, were killed in these mock battles. These contests were practiced in every period in the different islands to show the chiefs beforehand who among the people were warriors, so that these might be trained and brought up as soldiers, able to defend the country at such time as the enemy made war upon it. Some of the soldiers, however, were country people.

24. One of the games practiced among the people about court was called *honuhonu*.[13] Another sport was *lou-lou*.[14] Another sport was *uma*.[15] *Hakoko,* wrestling; *kahau,*[16] *lua*[17]. The people who attended the chiefs at court were more polite in their manners than the country people, and they looked disdainfully upon country ways. When a chief was given a land to manage and retired into the country to live, he attempted to keep up the same style as at court.

25. The people about court were not timid nor easily abashed; they were not rough and muscular in physique, but they were bold and impudent in speech. Some of the country people were quite up to them, however, and could swagger and boast as if they had been brought up at court.

DAVID MALO

26. There was hardly anybody about court who did not practice robbery, and who was not a thief, embezzler, extortionist and a shameless beggar. Nearly every one did these things.

27. As to the women there was also a great difference between them. Those who lived in the country were a hard-working set, whereas those about court were indolent.

28. The women assisted their husbands; they went with them into the mountains to collect and prepare the bark of the *wauke, mamake, maaloa* and bread-fruit, and the flesh of the fern-shoot (*pala-holo*)[18] to be made into tapa. She beat out these fibres into tapa and stamped the fabrics for *paus* and *malos,* that she and her husband might have the means with which to barter for the supply of their wants.

29. The country women nursed their children with the milk of their own breasts, and when they went to any work they took them along with them. But this was not always the case; for if a woman had many relations, one of them, perhaps her mother (or aunt), would hold the child. Also if her husband was rich she would not tend the child herself; it would be done for her by some one hired for the purpose, or by a friend.

30. The indolent women in the country were very eager to have a husband who was well off, that they might live without work. Some women offered worship and prayers to the idol-gods that they might obtain a wealthy man, or an *alii* for a husband. In the same way, if they had a son, they prayed to the idols that he might obtain a rich woman or a woman of rank for his wife, so that they might live without work.

31. It was not the nature of the women about court to beat tapa or to print it for *paus* and *malos.* They only made such articles as the *alii* specially desired them to make.

32. All the articles for the use of the people about court, the robes, *malos, paus,* and other necessaries (*mea e pono ai*) were what the chiefs received from the people of the country.

33. One of the chief employments of the women about court was to compose meles in honor of the *alii,*[19] which they recited by night as well as by day.

Notes on Chapter XIX

1. Sect. 5. *"Ipu ka eo,* or *umeke ka eo"* was an epithet applied to the full calabash. An empty calabash was *"umeke pala ole,"* i.e., an unripe calabash.

2. Sect. 7. This remark does not apply to the people of the Kau district on Hawaii. They had a reputation for being quick to assert their rights. Kau was called the rebellious district.

3. Sect. 8. If an insolent courtier were to see that a country clown had a beautiful woman for a wife he would say to her, "You come along with me," and the country clown would be too spiritless to make any resistance. Or one of the women about court, meeting a handsome young countryman whom she fancied, would turn his head with flattery and try to win him to herself, saying, "Why does such a fine fellow as you condescend to live with such a fright of a creature as that wife of yours? You'd better come along with me."

4. Sect. 17. These *hipuu puu* were only two or three inches wide, and it took several of them knotted together to go about a man and cover his nakedness.

5. Sect. 18. *Aikane,* now used to mean an honest and laudable friendship between two males, originally meant the vice of that burnt-up city.

6. Sect. 18. *Hoo-ka-maka,* a bestial form of vice in which man confronted man.

7. Sect. 18. *Moe hoo kuli-hoo-kuli,* to shut one's mouth with a bribe.

8. Sect. 20. *Lono-maka-ihe*—In this the spear was discharged from the hand.

9. Sect. 20. *Ku-pololu*—In this the assailant used the long spear, pololu, as a vaulting-pole with which to pursue his opponent. The same weapon served him both offensively and defensively.

10. Sect. 20. In *Kaka-laau* a short staff or sword-like stick was used to strike, thrust, and parry, as in single-stick.

11. Sect. 20. *Kaala* was a rough and tumble form of wrestling, in which each man sought to down the other.

12. Sect. 20. *Kui-alua* was a most savage form of combat, combining, in addition to wrestling and boxing, bone-breaking and maiming.

13. Sect. 24. *Honuhonu.* Two men sat *a la Ture* facing each other, the hands of each resting on the shoulders of his opposite, knees touching. The game consisted in rocking alternately backward and forward, thus causing each player in turn to be placed now above and now below the other.

14. Sect. 24. *Loulou.* Two men sat facing each other with legs intertwined and attempted to tip each other over sideways.

15. Sect. 24. *Uma.* Also called *kulakula'i.* The two players kneeled facing each other, right hands grasped elbows of the same side firmly planted on the ground. Each one now strove to tip the fore-arm of his opponent over and bring the back of his hand onto the ground.

16. Sect. 24. *Kahau.* A wrestling contest between two persons mounted on stilts.

17. Sect. 24. *Lua.* A famous style of contest which combined boxing wrestling, rough-and-tumble tossing and gripping, maiming and bone-breaking.

18. Sect. 28. *Palaholo* was mixed with the fibre of mamake in making tapa after being steamed in the oven.

N. B. The language of this as well as the preceding chapter is full of technical expressions which few Hawaiians of the present day know the meaning of.

19. Sect. 33. The *mele inoa* was a mele in adulation of a prince or king, reciting the glories of his ancestry.

* The title of this chapter might have been translated with no breach of fairness, LIFE IN THE COUNTRY CONTRASTED WITH LIFE AT COURT. Any one who wishes is at liberty to make the substitution. If it were true that the place where the king lives is always to be called *court,* then by all means let us make this verbal substitution; and not only that, but also the necessary mental and imaginative substitution which shall make the thing fit the name.

XX

Concerning Kauwa[1]

1. There was a class of people in the Hawaiian Islands who were called *kauwa*, slaves. This word *kauwa* had several meanings. It was applied to those who were *kauwa* by birth as well as those who were *alii* by birth.

2. *Kauwa* was a term of degradation and great reproach. But some were *kauwa* only in name; because the younger brother has always been spoken of as the *kauwa* of the elder brother. But he was not his *kauwa* in fact. It was only a way of indicating that the younger was subject to the older brother.

3. So it was with all younger brothers or younger sisters in relation to their elder brothers or elder sisters, whether chiefs or commoners.

4. Those who had charge of the chief's goods or who looked after his food were called *kauwa*. Their real name was *'a-'i-pu'u-pu'u* and they were also called *kauwa;* but they were *kauwa* only in name, they were not really slaves.

5. There were people who made themselves *kauwa*, those who went before the king, or chief, for instance, and to make a show of humbling themselves before him said, "We are your *kauwa*." But that was only a form of speech.

6. Again people who lived with the rich were sometimes spoken of as their *kauwa*. But they were not really *kauwa;* that term was applied to them on account of their inferior position.

7. Mischievous, lawless people (*poe kolohe*) were among those who were sometimes called *kauwa*, and it was the same with the poor. But they were not the real *kauwa;* it was only an epithet applied to them.

8. When one person quarreled with another he would sometimes revile him and call him a *kauwa;* but that did not make him a real *kauwa*, it was only an epithet for the day of his wrath, anger and reviling.

9. The marshals or constables (*ilamuku*) of the king were spoken of as his *kauwa*, but they were not really *kauwa*. There were then many classes of people called or spoken of as *kauwa*, but they were *kauwa* only in name, to indicate their inferior rank; they were not really and in fact *kauwa*.

The people who were really and in fact *kauwa* were those who were born to that condition and whose ancestors were such before them. The ancestral line of the people (properly to be) called *kauwa* from Papa down is as follows:

10. Wakea had a *kauwa* named *Ha'akauilana*. We are not informed in what way Ha'akauilana became a *kauwa* to Wakea. He may have been obtained by purchase—we don't know how it came about. After Wakea deserted his wife Papa, she lived with their *kauwa* Ha'akauilana.

11. In time there was born to the couple a son named *Kekeu*.

Kekeu lived with *Lumilani* and they begot *Noa*.

Noa lived with *Papa* the second and they begot *Pueo-nui-welu-welu*.

Pueo-nui-welu-welu lived with *Noni*. Their first born was *Maka-noni*, their last K——, and these were the ancestors of the actual and real *kauwa* in the Hawaiian Islands.

12. The descendants of Makanoni and of K—— were the real *kauwa* in Hawaii nei. If persons of another class, a chief perhaps, married one of these people and had children, the children were real *kauwa*.

13. The name *kauwa* was an appellation very much feared and dreaded. If a contention broke out between the chiefs and the people and there was a fracas, pelting with stones and clubbing with sticks, but they did not exchange reviling epithets and call each other *kauwa*, the affair would not be regarded as much of a quarrel.

14. But if a man or a chief contended with his fellow or with any one, and they abused each other roundly, calling one another *kauwa;* that was a quarrel worth talking about, not to be forgotten for generations.

15. The epithet *kauwa maoli*, real slave, was one of great offense. If a man formed an alliance with a woman, or a woman with a man, and it afterwards came out that that woman or that man was a *kauwa*, that person would be snatched away from the *kauwa* by his friends or relatives without pity.

16. If a chief or a chiefess lay with one who was a *kauwa*, not knowing such to be the fact, and afterwards should learn that the person was a *kauwa*, the child, if any should be born, would be dashed to death against a rock. Such was the death dealt out to one who was abhorred as a *kauwa*.

17. The *kauwa* class were so greatly dreaded and abhorred that they were not allowed to enter any house but that of their master, because they were spoken of as the *aumakua* of their master.

18. Those who were *kauwa* to their chiefs and kings in the old times continued to be *kauwa*, and their descendants after them to the latest generations; also the descendants of the kings and chiefs, their masters, retained to the latest generation their position as masters. It was for this reason they were called *au-makua*, the meaning of which is ancient servant (*kauwa kahiko*). They were also called *akua. i.e.*, superhuman or godlike (from some superstitious notion regarding their power). Another name applied to them was *kauwa lepo*, base-born slave (*lepo*, dirt. "Mud-sill"); or an outcast slave, *kauwa haalele loa*, which means a most despised thing.

19. Those *kauwa* who were tattooed on the forehead were termed *kauwa lae-puni*, slaves with bound foreheads; or they were called *kauwa kikoni*, the pricked slave; or *kauwa makawela*, red-eyed slave. These were most opprobrious epithets.

20. If a person of another class had a child by one of these *au-makuas* or *kauwas*, the term *no'u* was applied to it, which meant that it also was a kauwa to the same master.

21. Some people of other classes, and of the *alii* class as well, formed connections with *kauwas*, either through ignorance or through concupiscence, or because they happened to have met a fine-looking woman or man of the *kauwa* class. In this way some *aliis*, as well as others, became entangled (*hihia*). Children begotten of such a union were termed *ula-ula-ili*, red skin (from the sun-burn acquired by exposure through neglect and nakedness).

22. Men and women who were *kauwa* were said to be people from the wild woods (*nahelehele*), from the lowest depths (*no lalo liio loa*).

23. It was for this reason that the rank of the first woman or man with whom a great chief or chiefess was paired, was so carefully considered beforehand by those skilled in genealogies (*kuauhau*), who knew the standing of the woman or man in question, whether an *alii* or a *kauwa*.

24. For the same reason great chiefs were—sometimes—paired with their elder sisters (or elder brothers, as the case might be), or with some member of their own family, lest by any chance they might unite with a *kauwa*.

25. It was for this reason also that the genealogies of the *aliis* were always carefully preserved, that it might be clear who were free from the taint of *kauwa* blood, that such only might be paired with those of *alii* rank.

26. It was a matter likely to cause the death of a high chief to have it said of him that he was an *alii kauwa*. In such a case the most expert genealogists would be summoned to search the matter to the bottom.

Genealogists were called the wash-basins of the *aliis*, in which to cleanse them. The *kauwa* class were regarded as a defilement and a stench.

27. A female *kauwa* was an outcast and was not allowed to enter the eating house of a female chief.

Notes on Chapter XX

1. The word *Kauwa* in the title as it stands in the original has been deliberately mutilated and an unsuccessful attempt made to make it illegible with pen-strokes. In its place, *i.e.,* following it, has been inserted the word *kanaka.* The same crude and unsuccessful attempt to cover up the word has been made in sections 9, 10, 11, 12, and 13, and in some places there has been substituted for it the word *ai-kane.* The same thing has also been done to the proper names *Haakauilana, Makanoni* and one other name, the initial letter of which, K——, is all that can be made out.

This attempt to obliterate these words was evidently not done by the author himself. What motive could the author have had to undo his own darker tint. What motive could the author have had to undo his own work? The theory that seems to me most probable is that the culprit did it from shame, being himself a *kauw'a.*

I am informed by an intelligent Hawaiian that he once knew in Kipahulu, Maui, a man named Moo, who had in the center of his forehead a small, round tattooed spot as large as the tip of one's finger. He now believes him to have been a *kauwa.* "I am strongly of the opinion that he was undoubtedly such. He lived on friendly terms with the people about him, apparently creating no aversion or fear. He had a wife who had no signs of being a *kauwa.* He died at Kipahulu some time in the sixties. He was a fine-looking, well made man, intelligent and self-respecting, able and ready to stand up for his own rights. I did not know anything about this man's history, but I believe him to have been a *kauwa.* I would have been ashamed to have questioned him on the subject, or to have gone about seeking information from others in regard to him." said my informant.

The Hawaiians are still very sensitive about this matter of the *kauw'a.* To this day people in reviling each other will occasionally fling out the epithet *kauw'a.* The institution itself, however, has gone by.

2. Sect. 19. I am informed that *kauw'a* were marked by means of the tattoo on the parts of the face about the eyes and on the forehead, as indicated in the accompanying cuts.

1   **2**   **3**

No. 1 is a round spot in the middle of the forehead.

No. 2 is a curved figure arched over the root of the nose from one eye to the other.

No. 3 represents two curved figures which are placed like two halves of a bracket-mark outside of and so as to include the eyes.

Kapule of Molokai informs me that in his childhood he knew a family on Molokai in which there were several fine girls, but as they were said to be *kauw'a* no one wanted to marry them, and they were neglected in the matrimonial market, in spite of their attractions. His grandmother explained to him the reason for their being so much avoided and despised. He said that he used to be informed that a *kauw'a* was thought to be the offspring of a bestial alliance. The same informant said he never had heard of such a thing as a *kauw'a's* being marked or tattooed in any way.

XXI

Wrong Conduct and Right Conduct
(na hewa me na pono)

The Ancient Idea of Morality

1. There are many kinds of wrong committed by men, if their number were all told; but a single stem gives birth to them all. The thought that proceeds from the mind is the parent that begets a multitude of sins.[1]

2. When the heart proposes to do wrong then doubtless it will commit a sin; and when it purposes to do right, then no doubt it will do right; because from the heart (*naau,* bowels) comes good and from the heart also comes evil. But some evils light down of themselves (*lele wale mai*), and so do some good things.

3. If the eye sees a thing, but the heart does not covet it, no wrong is done. But if the eye observes and the heart covets a certain thing, a great many thoughts will arise within having inordinate desire (*kuko*) as the root, a restless yearning (*lia*), a vehement desire (*uluku*), and a seizing (*hookaha*); or duplicity (*hoo-makauli'i*) and covetousness (*iini*), which make one look upon a thing with deep longing and the purpose to take it secretly and appropriate it to one self. These faults are to be classed with theft.

4. Coveting the property of another has many aspects to it, a spying upon another, lying in ambush on his trail, plotting, treachery, deceit, trickery with the intent to murder secretly in order to get someone's goods. All of these things come under the head of robbery and are of the nature of murder (*pepehi wale*).

5. If one has determined to enrich himself at another's expense the evil has many shapes. The first thing is covetousness (*pakaha*), filching, thrusting one's self on the hospitality of one's neighbor (*kipa wale*), stripping another of his property (*hao wale*), appropriating his crops (*uhuki wale*), theft, robbery and other wrong deeds of that nature.

6. If a man wishes to deal truthfully with another and afterwards finds that things have been misrepresented to him, there are many things involved in that. In the first place there is deceit (*hoo-punipuni*), lying (*waha-he'e*), slander (*alapahi*), falsehood (*palau*), the lie jestful (*ku-kahe-kahe*), the lie

fluent (*palolo*), the lie unclothed (*kokahe*), the lie direct (*pahilau*), and many other things of like sort.

7. If a person seeks to find fault with another there are many ways of doing it, the chief of which is slander (*aki*, biting), defamation (*ahiahi*), making false accusations (*niania*), circulating slanders (*holoholo oleo*), vilifying (*makauli'i*), detraction (*kaamehai*, belittling (*kuene*), tale-bearing (*poupou-noho-ino*), ensnaring (*hoowalewale*), misleading (*luahele*), treachery (*kumakaia*), fault-finding (*hoolawehala*), malice (*opu-inoino*), scandal-mongering (*lawe-olelo-wale*), reviling (*paonioni*), and a host of other things of the same sort.

8. If one has evil thoughts against another there are a great many ways in which they may express themselves. The first is anger (*huhu*), indignation (*inaina*), sarcasm (*a-aka*), scolding (*keke*), fault-finding (*nana*), sourness (*kukona*), bitterness (*nahoa*), fretfulness (*makona*), rudeness (*kalaca*), jealousy (*hoolili*), scowling (*hoomakue*), harshness (*hookoikoi*), intimidation (*hooweliweli*), and many other ways.

9. If a man wished to kill an innocent person there are many ways in which he can do it, first to simply beat him to death (*pepehi wale*), by stoning (*hailuku*), whipping (*hahau*), knocking him down (*kulai*), garroting (*umiwale*), pounding with his fists (*kuku'i wale*), smiting (*papa'i*), wrestling (*hako'oko'o*), stirring up a fight (*hookonokono*), and many other similar ways.

10. These were all sins, clearly understood to be very wrong, but those who did these things were not suitably punished in the old times. If any one killed another, nothing was done about it—there was no law. It was a rare thing for any one to be punished as at the present time.[2]

11. It should be remarked here that in ancient times indiscriminate sexual relations between unmarried persons (*moe o na mea kaawale*), fornication, keeping a lover (*moe ipo*), hired prostitution (*moe kookuli*), bigamy, polyandry, whoredom (*moe hoo-kama-kama*), sodomy (*moe aikane*), and masturbation were not considered wrong, nor were foeticide and idol-worship regarded as evils.

12. The following things were held to be wrong, *hewa*, both in men and women, to change husband or wife frequently (*koaka*), go about eating from place to place (*pakela ai*), to be a shift, to be a glutton or to in men and women: to change husband or wife frequently (*ko*-less gossip (*palau-alclo*), to be indolent and lazy, to be an improvident vagabond (*aca, kuonoono-ole*), to be utterly shiftless (*lima-lima-pilan*) *to* go about getting food at other people's houses (*koalaala-make-hewa*)—these and other like actions were really wrong, *hewa*.

13. The following practices were considered *hewa* by the landlord, that one should give himself up to the fascinations of sport and squander his property in *puhenehene,* sliding the stick (*pahee*), bowling the *ulu-maika,* racing with the canoe, on the surf-board or on the *holua*-sled, that one should build a large house, have a woman of great beauty for his wife, sport a fine tapa, or gird one's self with a fine malo.

13. All of these things were regarded as showing pride, and were considered valid reasons for depriving a man of his lands, because such practices were tantamount to secreting wealth.

14. If a landlord, or land agent, who farmed the land for an *alii* (*kono-hiki*) had to wife a woman who did no work, neither beating out or printing tapa, doing nothing in fact, but merely depending on what her husband produced, such a non-producer was called a *polo-hana-ole,* and it would be counted a *hewa,* and a sufficient reason why the man should be turned out of his lands.

15. Mere complaining and grumbling, with some other misfortunes are evils that come of themselves. There are other ills of the same sort which I have not mentioned.

16. There was a large number of actions that were considered essentially good (*pono maoli*), and the number of persons who did them was very considerable, in spite of which there lighted down upon them the misfortune that when they looked upon the things belonging to another their heart lusted after them. The right course in such a case is to resist the temptation, not to pursue the object of one's desire, to cease thinking about it and touch it not.

17. To act justly without trespassing or deceiving, not frequenting another's house, not gazing wistfully upon your neighbor's goods nor begging for anything that belongs to him—that is the prudent course.

18. The following actions were considered worthy of approbation; to live thriftily, not to be a vagabond, not to keep changing wives, not to be always shifting from one chief to another, not to run in debt.

19. It was reckoned a virtue for a man to take a wife, to bring up his children properly, to deal squarely with his neighbors and his landlord, to engage in some industry, such as farming, fishing, house-building, canoe-making, or to raise swine, dogs and fowls.

20. It was also deemed virtuous not to indulge in sports, to abstain from such games as *puhenehene, pahee,* bowling the *maika,* running races, canoe-racing, surf-riding, racing on the *holua*-sled, and to abstain from the tug-of-war and all other games of such sort.

21. The practice of these virtues was a great means of bettering one's self in this life and was of great service.

22. The farmer and the fisherman acquired many servants and accumulated property by their labors. For this reason the practice of these callings was regarded as most commendable.

23. The worship of idols was regarded as a virtue by the ancients, because they sincerely believed them to be real gods. The consequence was that people desired their chiefs and kings to be religious (*haipule*). The people had a strong conviction that if the king was devout, his government would abide.

24. Canoe-building was a useful art. The canoe was of service in enabling one to sail to other islands and carry on war against them, and the canoe had many other uses.

25. The priestly office was regarded with great favor, and great faith was reposed in the power of the priests to propitiate the idol-deities, and obtain from them benefits that were prayed for.

26. The astrologers, or *kilo-lani*, whose office it was to observe the heavens and declare the day that would bring victory in battle, were a class of men highly esteemed. So also were the *kuhi-kuhi-puu-one*, a class of priests who designated the site where a *heiau* should be built in order to insure the defeat of the enemy.

27. The *kaka-olelo*, or counsellors who advised the alii in matters of government, were a class much thought of; so also were the warriors who formed the strength of the army in time of battle and helped to rout the enemy.

28. Net-makers (*poe ka-upena*) and those who made fishing-lines (*hilo-aha*) were esteemed as pursuing a useful occupation. The mechanics who hewed and fashioned the tapa log, on which was beaten out tapa for sheets, girdles and loin-cloths for men and women were a class highly esteemed. There were a great many other actions that were esteemed as virtuous whether done by men and women or by the chiefs; all of them have not been mentioned.

Notes on Chapter XXI

1. Sect. 1. What did the ancient Hawaiians seriously regard as wrong?
First—Any breach of tabu or of ceremonious observance.
Second—Failure to fulfill a vow to the gods or to make good any religious obligation.

Third—Any failure in duty towards an *alii,* especially an *alii kapu.*

Fourth—For the *kahu* of an idol to have neglected any part of his duties, as feeding it or sacrificing to it. Under this same head should be put the duties of the keeper of the bones of the dead king; to have neglected such a duty would put a terrible load on the conscience. It is owing to the fidelity of the *kahu* that the hiding place of the great Kamehameha's bones is to this day a profound secret. The fidelity with which such obligations as these were kept is proof enough that this people had all the material of conscience in their make up. It will be seen that the duties and faults that weighed most heavily on the conscience of the Hawaiian were mostly artificial matters, and such as in our eyes do not touch the essense of morality. But that is true of all consciences to a large extent. It should be remarked that the Hawaiian was a believer in the doctrine of the divine right of kings to the extremest degree. His duties to his *alii, or lani,* as the poets always styled him, was, therefore, on the same footing with those due to the *akuas.*

Fifth—I believe that the Hawaiian conscience would have been seriously troubled by any breach of the duties of hospitality.

2. Sect. 10. The *lex talionis* was the rule. Friends often took up the matter and enacted something like a vendetta.

XXII

The Valuables and Possessions of the Ancient Hawaiians

1. The feathers of birds were the most valued possessions of the ancient Hawaiians. The feathers of the *mamo* were more choice than those of the *oo* because of their superior magnificence when wrought into cloaks (*ahu*). The plumage of the *i'iwi, apapane* and *amakihi* were made into *ahu-ula*, cloaks and capes, and into *mahi-ole*, helmets.

2. The *ahu-ula* was a possession most costly and precious (*makamae*), not obtainable by the common people, only by the alii. It was much worn by them as an insignia in time of war and when they went into battle. The *ahu-ula* was also conferred upon warriors, but only upon those who had distinguished themselves and had merit, and it was an object of plunder in every battle.

3. Unless one were a warrior in something more than name he would not succeed in capturing his prisoner nor in getting possession of the *ahu-ula* and feathered helmet of a warrior. These feathers had a notable use in the making of the royal battle-gods.[1] They were also frequently used by the female chiefs in making or decorating a comb called *huli-kua*, which was used as an ornament in the hair.

The lands that produced feathers were heavily taxed at the *Makahiki* time, feathers being the most acceptable offering to the *Makahiki*-idol. If any land failed to furnish the full tale of feathers due for the tax, the landlord was turned off (*hemo*). So greedy were the *alii* after fathers that there was a standing order (*palala*) directing their collection.

4. An *ahu-ula* made only of *mamo* feathers was called an *alaneo* and was reserved exclusively for the king of a whole island, *alii ai moku*; it was his *kapa wai-kaua* or battle-cloak. Abu-ulas were used as the regalia of great chiefs and those of high rank, also for warriors of distinction who had displayed great prowess. It was not to be obtained by chiefs of low rank, nor by warriors of small prowess.

5. The carved whale-tooth, or *niho-palaoa*, was a decoration worn by high chiefs who alone were allowed to possess this ornament. They were not common in the ancient times, and it is only since the reign of Kamehameha[2] I that they have become somewhat more numerous.

In battle or on occasions of ceremony and display (*hookahakaha*) an *alii* wore his *niho-palaoa*. The *lei-palaoa* (same as the *niho-palaoa*) was regarded as the exclusive property of the *alii*.

6. The *kahili*,—a fly-brush or plumed staff of state—was the emblem and embellishment of royalty. Where the king went there went his *kahili*-bearer (*paa-kahili*), and where he stopped there stopped also the *kahili*-bearer. When the king slept the *kahili* was waved over him as a fly-brush. The *kahili* was the possession solely of the *alii*.

7. The canoe with its furniture was considered a valuable possession, of service both to the people and to the chiefs. By means of it they could go on trading voyages to other lands, engage in fishing, and perform many other errands.

8. The canoe was used by the kings and chiefs as a means of ostentation and display. On a voyage the *alii* occupied the raised and sheltered platform in the waist of the canoe which was called the *pola*, while the paddle-men sat in the spaces fore and aft, their number showing the strength of the king's following.

9. Cordage and rope of all sorts (*na kaula*), were articles of great value, serviceable in all sorts of work. Of *kaula* there were many kinds. The bark of the *hau* tree was used for making lines or cables with which to haul canoes[3] down from the mountains as well as for other purposes. Cord—*aha*—made from cocoanut fibre was used in sewing and binding together the parts of a canoe and in rigging it as well as for other purposes. Olona fibre was braided into (a four or six-strand cord called) *lino*, besides being made into many other things. There were many other kinds of rope (*kaula*).

10. Fishing nets (*upena*) and fishing lines (*aho*) were valued possessions. One kind was the *papa-waha*, which had a broad mouth; another was the *aei* (net with small meshes to take the opelu); the *kawaa* net (twenty to thirty fathoms long and four to eight deep, for deep sea fishing); the *kuu* net (a long net, operated by two canoes); and many other varieties.

11. Fish-lines, *aho*, were used in fishing for all sorts of fish, but especially for such fine large fish as the *ahi* and the *kahala*. The *aho* was also used in stitching together the sails (of matting) and for other similar purposes.

12. The *ko'i*, or stone ax, was a possession of value. It was used in hewing and hollowing canoes, shaping house-timbers and in fashioning the agriculture spade, the *oo*, and it had many other uses.

13. The house was esteemed a possession of great value. It was the place where husband and wife slept, where their children and friends met, where the household goods of all sorts were stored.

14. There were many kinds of houses: the *mua* for men alone, the *noa*, where men and women met, the *halau* for the shelter of long things, like canoes, fishing poles, etc., and there were houses for many other purposes.

15. Tapa was a thing of value. It was used to clothe the body, or to protect the body from cold during sleep at night. The *malo* also was a thing of great service, girded about the loins and knotted behind, like a cord, it was used by the men as a covering for the immodest parts.

16. Another article of value was the *pau;* wrapped about the loins and reaching nearly to the knees it shielded the modesty of the women.

17. Pigs, dogs and fowls were sources of wealth. They were in great demand as food both for chiefs and common people, and those who raised them made a good profit.

18. Any one who was active as a farmer or fisherman was deemed a man of great wealth. If one but engaged in any industry he was looked upon as well off.

19. The man who was skilled in the art of making fish-hooks (*ka-makau*) was regarded as fore-handed. The fish-hooks of the Hawaiians were made of human bones, tortoise shell and the bones of pigs and dogs.

20. The names of the different kinds of hooks used in the ancient times would make a long list. The *hoonoho*[4] was an arrangement of hooks made by lashing two bone hooks to one shank (they were sometimes placed facing each other and then again back to back).

21. The *kikii* (in which the bend of the hook followed a spiral); the *lua-loa* (sometimes used for catching the *aku); the *nuku* (also called the *kakaka.* It consisted of a series of hooks attached to one line), the *keaa-wai-leia* (for *ulua.* The bait was strewn in the water and the naked hook was moved about on the surface); the *au-ku'u* (a troll-hook, having two barbs, used to take the *ulua); the *maka-puhi* (about the same as the *au-ku'u,* but with only one barb); the *kai-anoa* (used in the deep sea—composed of two small hooks, without barbs, arranged as in fig. 4); the *omau* (about the same as the *kea'a-wai-leia* but more open, with no barb, for the deep sea); the *mana* (a hook for the eel); the *kohe-lua* (also called *kohe-lua-a-pa'a,* a hook with two barbs); the *hulu* (having a barb on the outside); the *kue* (a very much incurved hook, used to take the *oio,* etc.); the *hui-kala* (a large hook with two barbs, one without and one within);

the *hio-hio* (a minute hook of mother o' pearl, for the opelu): the *lawa* which was used for sharks.

22. Such were the names of the fish-hooks of the ancients, whether made of bone or of tortoise shell (*ea*). In helping to shape them the hard wood of the *pua* and the rough pahoehoe lava rock were used as rasps.

23. The *oo* (shaped like a whale-spade) was an instrument useful in husbandry. It was made of the wood of the *ulei, ma-mane, omolemole, lapalapa* (and numerous other woods including the alahe'e).

24. Dishes, *ipu,* to hold articles of food, formed part of the wealth, made of wood and of the gourd; *umeke* to receive poi and vegetable food; *ipu-kai,* bowls or soup-dishes, to hold meats and fish, cooked or raw, with gravies and sauces; *pa-laau*—platters or deep plates for meats, fish, or other kinds of food; *hue-wai*—bottle-gourds, used to hold water for drinking. Salt was reckoned an article of value.

25. A high value was set upon the cowry shell, *leho,*[5] and the mother o' pearl, *pa,*[6] by the fishermen, because through the fascination exercised by these articles the octopus and the bonito were captured.

26. Mats, *moena* (*moe-na*), constituted articles of wealth, being used to bedeck the floors of the houses and to give comfort to the bed.

27. A great variety of articles were manufactured by different persons which were esteemed wealth.

28. At the present time many new things have been imported from foreign countries which are of great value and constitute wealth, such as neat cattle, horses, the mule, the donkey, the goat, sheep, swine, dogs, and fowls.

29. New species of birds have been introduced, also new kinds of cloth, so that the former tapa-cloth has almost entirely gone out of use. There are also new tools, books, and laws, many new things.

30. But the book that contains the word of Jehovah is of a value above every other treasure because it contains salvation for the soul.

Notes on Chapter XXII

The Hawaiians had no money, nor anything that stood as an accepted representative of value to take its place. In the barter carried on between them and the ships in the early days of intercourse with the foreigner, the value of the pig was reckoned by the Hawaiian in proportion to his length, so much for the pigling of the length of the forearm, so much hoop-iron for the three-foot porker, and so much for the full-grown, fathom long (*anana*) hog. (N. Z., *whanganga*).

The one barrier that stood in the way of the invention and adoption of some tangible representative of value was the selfish and exclusive policy of the chiefs, which allowed the poor *kanaka* to possess nothing he might call his own, not even his *malo* or his wife.

1. Sect. 3. *Akua kaai*, literally a god with a sash. This was a carved staff with a tuft of feathers at the top. The color-bearer who carried this emblem into battle was called its *kahu*. The image, or staff already mentioned, was bound to the body of the *kahu* by this *kaai*, or sash, and the *kahu* wore upon his own head the *mahiole* or helmet which was said to be worn by the idol. This substitution of the *kahu*, or man who carried the idol, for the idol itself, was not an uncommon thing in Hawaiian cult. It was looked upon as an act of infamy to take the life of the *kahu* of an *akua-kaai* in battle.

Ku-kaili-moku, the war god of Kamehameha, was a feather god, *akua-hulu-manu*.

2. Sect. 5. Kamehameha in his wars of conquest took a large number of these things as spoils of war, thus causing them to seem more plentiful. But it was merely that they were brought out of their hiding places. It cannot be that they were manufactured in any number during the troublous times of his reign.

3. Sect. 9. The *koa* tree, felled in the depths of the forest, after being rudely shaped, was hauled up hill and down dale to the ocean, its real home, by means of strong lines of *hau* bark. This hauling was termed *ko waa*. See Chap. XXXIV.

4. Sect. 20. *Hoonoho;* there seem to have been two varieties of this kind of arrangement as represented in the two cuts.

5. Sect. 25. A stone-sinker, carved in the shape of the cowry, was lashed with the shell to a straight staff to which was attached a hook. When this apparatus was let down into the ocean the squid, attracted by the rich color of the shell, wrapped his arms about it and was drawn up.

6. Sect. 25. The *pa* was a plate of mother o' pearl with a hook of bone attached. It was used as a troll for the aku. The color and sheen of the pearl seemed to have some sort of fascination for the fish.

XXIII

The Worship of Idols

1. There was a great diversity as to cult among those who worshipped idols in Hawaii nei, for the reason that one man had one god and another had an entirely different god. The gods of the *aliis* also differed one from another.

2. The women were a further source of disagreement; they addressed their worship to female deities, and the god of one was different from the god of another. Then too the gods of the female chiefs of a high rank were different from the gods of those of a lower rank.

3. Again the days observed by one man differed from those observed by another man, and the things that were tabued by one god differed from those tabued by another god. As to the nights observed by the alii for worship they were identical, though the things tabued were different with the different *alii*. The same was true in regard to the female chiefs.

4. The names of the male deities worshipped by the Hawaiians, whether chiefs or common people, were *Ku, Lono, Kane,* and *Kanaloa;* and the various gods worshipped by the people and the *alii* were named after them. But the names of the female deities were entirely different.

5. Each man worshipped the *akua* that presided over the occupation or profession he followed, because it was generally believed that the *akua* could prosper any man in his calling. In the same way the women believed that the deity was the one to bring good luck to them in any work.

6. So also with the kings and chiefs, they addressed their worship to the gods who were active in the affairs that concerned them; for they firmly believed that their god could destroy the king's enemies, safeguard him and prosper him with land and all sorts of blessings.

7. The manner of worship of the kings and chiefs was different from that of the common people. When the commoners performed religious services they uttered their prayers themselves, without the assistance of a priest or of a *kahu-akua.* But when the king or an *alii* worshipped, the priest or the keeper of the idol uttered the prayers, while the *alii* only moved his lips and did not say a word. The same was true of the female chiefs; they did not utter the prayers to their gods.[1]

8. Of gods that were worshipped by the people and not by the chiefs the following are such as were worshipped by those who went up into the mountains to hew out canoes and timber: *Ku-pulupulu*,[2] *Ku-ala-na-wao*,[3] *Ku-moku-halii*,[4] *Ku-pepeiao-loa*, *Ku-pepeiao-poko*, *Ku-ka-ieie*, *Ku-palala-ke*, *Ku-ka-ohia-laka*.[5] *Lea*,[6] though a female deity, was worshipped alike by women and canoe-makers.

9. *Ku-huluhulu-manu* was the god of bird-catchers, bird-snares (*poe-ka-manu*),[7] birds limers and of all who did feather-work.

10. *Ku-ka-oo* was the god of husbandmen.

11. Fishermen worshipped *Ku-ula*,[8] also quite a number of other fishing-gods. *Hina-hele* was a female deity worshipped both by women and fishermen.

12. Those who practiced sorcery and praying to death or *anaana* worshipped *Ku-koae, Uli* and *Ka-alae-nui-a-Hina*.[9]

Those who nourished a god—an *unihi-pili*[8] for instance—or one who was acted upon by a deity, worshipped *Kalai-pahoa*.

13. Those who practiced medicine prayed to *Mai-ola*. *Kapualakai* and *Kau-ka-hoola-mai* were female deities worshipped by women and practitioners of medicine.

14. Hula-dancers worshipped *Laka;* thieves *Makua-aihue;* those who watched fish-ponds *Hau-maka-pu'u;* warriors worshipped *Lono-maka-ihe;* soothsayers and those who studied the signs of the heavens (*kilokilo*) worshipped the god *Kuhimana*.

15. Robbers worshipped the god *Kui-alua;* those who went to sea in the canoe worshipped *Ka-maha-alii*. There were a great many other deities regarded by the people, but it is not certain that they were worshipped. Worship was paid, however, to sharks, to dead persons, to objects celestial and objects terrestrial. But there were people who had no god, and who worshipped nothing; these atheists were called *aia*.

16. The following deities were objects of definite special worship by women: *Lau-huki* was the object of worship by the women who beat out tapa. *La'a-hana* was the patron deity of the women who printed tapa cloth. *Pele* and *Hiiaka* were the deities of certain women. *Papa* and *Hoohoku*,[11] our ancestors were worshipped by some as deities. *Kapo* and *Pua* had their worshippers. The majority of women, however, had no deity and just worshipped nothing.

17. The female chiefs worshipped as gods *Kiha-wahine, Waka, Kalamaimu, Ahimu* (or *Wahimu*), and *Alimanoano*. These deities were reptiles or *Moo*.

18. The deities worshipped by the male chiefs were *Ku, Lono, Kane, Kana-loa, Kumaikaiki, Ku-maka-nui, Ku-makela, Ku-maka'aka'a, Ku-holoholo-i-kaua, Ku-koa, Ku-nui-akea, Ku-kaili-moku,*[12] *Ku-waha-ilo-o-ka-puni, Ulu, Lo-lupe*—this last was a deity commonly worshipped by many kings. Besides these there was that countless rout of (woodland) deities, *kini-akua, lehu-akua,* and *mano-akua*[13] whose shouts were at times distinctly to be heard. They also worshipped the stars, things in the air and on the earth, also the bodies of dead men. Such were the objects of worship of the kings and chiefs.

19. The following gods were supposed to preside over different regions: *Kane-hoa-lani* (or *Kane-wahi-lani*) ruled over the heavens; the god who ruled over the earth was *Kane-lu-honua;* the god of the mountains was *Ka-haku-o;* of the ocean *Kane-huli-ko'a.*

20. The god of the East was *Ke-ao-kiai,* of the West *Ke-ao-halo,* of the North *Ke-ao-loa,* of the South *Ke-ao-hoopua.* The god of winds and storms was *Laa-mao-mao.*

21. The god of precipices (*pali*) was *Kane-holo-pali,* of stones *Kane-pohaku,* of hard—basaltic—stone *Kane-moe-ala,* of the house *Kane-ilok'a-hale*[14] (or *Kane-iloko-o*), of the fire-place *Kane-moe-lehu,*[15] of fresh water *Kane-wai-ola.*

22. The god of the doorway or doorstep was *Kane-hohoio*[16] (*Kane-noio* according to some). The number of the gods who were supposed to preside over one place or another was countless.

23. All of these gods, whether worshipped by the common people or by the alii, were thought to reside in the heavens. Neither commoner nor chief had ever discerned their nature; their coming and their going was unseen; their breadth, their length and all their dimensions were unknown.

24. The only gods the people ever saw with their eyes were the images of wood and of stone which they had carved with their own hands after the fashion of what they conceived the gods of heaven to be. If their gods were celestial beings, their idols should have been made to resemble the heavenly.

25. If the gods were supposed to resemble beings in the firmament, birds perhaps, then the idols were patterned after birds, and if beings on the earth, they were made to resemble the earthly.

26. If the deity was of the water, the idol was made to resemble a creature of the water, whether male or female.[17] Thus it was that an idol was carved to resemble the description of an imaginary being, and not to give the actual likeness of a deity that had been seen.

27. And when they worshipped, these images, made after the likeness of various things, were set up before the assembly of the people; and if then prayer and adoration had been offered to the true god in heaven, there would have been a resemblance to the popish manner of worship. Such was the ancient worship in Hawaii nei, whether by the common people or by the kings and chiefs. There was a difference, however, between the ceremonies performed by the common people at the weaning of a child and those performed by a king or chief on a similar occasion.

Notes on Chapter XXIII

1. Sect. 7. There were important exceptions to this general statement by Mr. Malo which should be noted. The prayers offered in the *Hula* were, as a rule, uttered by persons, *kahunas,* specially consecrated or appointed for that office. The consecration of a house or of a *wa'a,* canoe, was done with the aid of a *kahuna;* and the common people did resort to *kahunas* of different classes. As regards their private worship and devotions, however, the statement of Malo as regards the common people is undoubtedly correct.

2. Sect. 8. These are all different forms of the god *Ku. Pulupulu* is a name applied to anything cottony; derived from the fibres that cover the fern; applied to any vegetable wool.

3. Sect. 8. It seems as if there were a play on the word *ku,* which primarily means to stand. *Ku-ala-na-wao* may be translated, there stand the wildernesses.

4. Sect. 8. *Ku-moku-halii,* Ku is here personified as the one who "clothes the island."

5. Sect. 8. *Ku-ka-ohia-laka.* The epithet *laka* is the part of the name that is difficult of explanation. The epithet *ohia* is evidently from the tree of that name. The tree was said to have a human voice, and a groan was audible when it was cut into. Mr. S. Percy Smith informs me (Dec., 1897) that *Rata,* the same as *Laka,* was the Tahiti, Rarotonga and N. Z. name of the *ohia* (*Metrosideros lutea*). The whole mystery is thus explained.

6. Sect. 8. *Lea* was said to present herself at times in the form of the *elepaio* bird, a deity that greatly concerned canoe-makers.

7. Sect. 9. *Poe ka-manu;* the word *ka* is used in a great many meanings, to catch, smite, etc., as in the following, "He uahi ke kapeku e hei ai ka ia-manu o Puoalii." The reference is to the fact that the people of Puoalii, Hamakau, Hawaii, were wont to make a smudgy fire at night on the coast, and as the birds flew in from the sea, coming into the reek of the smoke they became bewildered and were easily caught in scoop-nets.

8. Sect. 11. The idols of Kuula were numerous, most of them being uncarved stones.

9. Sect. 12. *Hina* was the mother of the mythical hero Maui, who, according to one legend, learned the art of making fire from the red-headed mud-hen, *alae,* who was a brother to himself.

10. Sect. 12. An *unihi pili* was a familiar spirit, or infernal deity, which was made resident in some object, very often the bones of an infant, through the agency of the persistent prayers and offerings of a sorcerer, who became its *kahu,* keeper or patron, and to whom the *unihi pili* held the relation of a benefactor, protector and infernal agent, ready when called upon to do any errand of vengeance, murder of body or soul, to which his kahu might commission him. (For the full explanation of this subject see Papers of the Hawaiian Historical Society, No. 2. "The Lesser Hawaiian Gods," by J. S. Emerson: read before the Hawn. Hist Sec. April 7, 1892: Honolulu, H. I.)

11. Sect. 16. *Papa* was the wife of *Wakea,* and *Hoohokukalani* their daughter. With the latter he committed incest and broke up the peace of the family.

12. Sect. 18. *Ku-kaili-moku*—Ku-the-land-grabber; this most appropriately, was the war god and favorite deity of Kamehameha I, the one who aided him in his expeditions of war and conquest, plunder and murder.

13. Sect. 18. *Kini, lehu* and *mano* meant respectively 40,000 and 400,000, and 4,000, this being a set phrase used to indicate that countless multitudes of elves, sprites, gnomes and fairies with which the imagination of the Hawaiian peopled the wilderness. They were full of mischief and had their hands in every pie. See the story of *Laka* of Kipahulu, son of Wahieloa, the canoe-builder. In addition to these must be mentioned *"Ka puku'i o ke akua, o ka pohai o ke akua. o ke kokoolua o ke akua, o ke kokookolu o ke akua, o ka ikuwa o ke akua."* It may be difficult to describe the different notions expressed by these words, but the *ikuwa,* the mysterous voices and murmurings of the gods in the wilderness—these can be heard at almost any time in the woodlands.

14. Sect. 21. *Kane-ilok'a-hale* is no doubt a contraction from *Kane-iloko-o-ka-hale.* The man who built a house did well to make an offering to him.

15. Sect. 21. Kane who lies in the ashes: *Kane-moe-lehu.*

16. Sect. 22. The door-step was a very *tabu* place and it was looked upon as highly improper to sit or stand on it. This is also an Asiatic superstition.

Apropos of the title placed at the head of the chapter, the question arises, did the Hawaiians worship the idol? or did they rather use it as an emblem of the spiritual being back of it? Does the communicant believe that the bread, or wafer, placed on his tongue is the real body of his Saviour? Does the pietist believe that power, virtue, reside in the consecrated image and rosary that hang from his neck? Human nature is much the same at all times; answer the one question and you answer the other. I do not share with Mr. Malo the belief that the imagination and thoughts of the ancient worshipper went no higher than the image before which he bowed. Very naturally in the enthusiasm of deliverance from idolatrous superstition, Mr. M. was unable to do justice to the system from which he had escaped. The influences that moulded his opinions were not favorable to a philosophic view of the whole question. In spite of everything, however, the fact that the ancient Hawaiians kept in view a spiritual being back of the idol makes itself manifest in Mr. Malo's account, cropping up from time to time in his statement of their worship and beliefs. Consider, for instance, the account of Wakea's deliverance from the perils of the ocean, and the manner in which his *kahuna* directed him to build a heiau and perform a sacrifice to the deity, while swimming in the ocean. (See the story of Wakea, pp. 247–8). The Hawaiians spoke of *akua-kii, akua maoli, akua-kino-ole,* etc. What was an *akua maoli,* if not a spirit?

REMARKS.—"The Hawaiians usually worshipped their gods by means of idols, believing that by the performance of certain rites power, *mana,* was imparted to the idols, so that they became a means of communication with unseen divinities. They imagined that a spirit resided in or conveyed influence through the image representing it."—Alexander's Haw. Hist., p 41.

The above is probably true of all idolaters, of whatever race or name.

W. D. A.

The Legend of Kaua Kahi-A-Kawau

17. Sect. 26. The following legend has been related to me apropos of the statement made by Mr. Malo:

Kauakahi-a-kawau was an ancient king on Kauai who had his home in the mountains. One time when down at the coast he saw a deity in the form of a woman who, after disporting herself in the ocean, climbed upon a rock and began to braid and comb her hair. The charms of her person made such a vivid impression on him that on returning to his home in the mountains, he laboriously carved a figure in stone portraying the person of his goddess whom he called *Ono'ilele.* The real name of the woman, who was a *kupua,* creature of supernatural power, was *Uli-poai-o-ka-moku.* The woman was most beautiful and voluptuous, so that Kaua-kahi fell dead in love with her. He devoted himself with great attention to carving the figure, and succeded in making a very perfect representation of the human body, even to the hair on the head, the figure being that of a woman.

When the work was done he brought the image down to the shore, and at the time of day when he thought she would be likely to appear he carried it down and placed it at the water's edge in a sitting position on a rock, the attitude being that which a woman would assume in making her toilet after the bath, Kauakahi himself crouched behind the figure and awaited the appearance of the goddess. She soon showed herself in the midst of the waves, and climbing upon a large rock, busied herself in combing the sea-weed out of her long hair with her fingers. Kauakani immediately imitated her motions, passing his own fingers through the hair of the image in front of him. "It's nothing but a sham, an image," said the goddess disdainfully. Kauakahi at once shifted the position of the graven figure before him, and in a manner so lifelike, that the goddess, thinking she had been mistaken, said, "It is a woman after all." "Come over here and give me your company," said Kauakahi, and she, thinking it was the woman who addressed her, swam over and climbed upon the rock on which Kauakahi and the image were sitting.

As she came up out of the water, Kauakahi, using his magic power, caused the image to disappear and standing before her, a man, put his arms about her, and made hot love to her, saying. "Come with me and be my wife." The goddess consented to his proposition, and allowed him to lead her up into the mountains to the mystic region of *Piha'na-ka-lani*. Entering the house they found the place full of beautiful birds of gay plumage, one bird standing uopn another four tiers in height all about the apartment. In wonder *Uli-poai* turned to her lover for an explanation of the bewildering sight, but he had disappeared, having assumed the shape of an image. Thereupon the goddess, true to the woman in her, burst into tears and was in great distress. Presently an old woman came in and kindly asked her what was the matter, and she told her story from the beginning. "I will find your husband for you," said the old dame, and she took her into an adjoining house and showed her a large number of images ranged along the side of the apartment. "Which of these images would you choose for a husband, if you were to take one?" asked the old witch. After looking at them all she selected the one that pleased her and going up to it found it very heavy to lift. She then kissed it affectionately, and that which had been but an image smiled upon her—it was a human being, her husband. "Who was it directed you to my place of hiding?" asked Kauakahi; "it was probably a *kamaaina*, was it not?" "Yes," said she, "it was an old woman named *Kahi-hi-kolo.*" "An ancestor of mine," said Kauakahi, "but now let us return to the house." Their bed that night was quilted with bird's feathers.

Soon after this Kilioe, the god of precipices, *na pali*, sent an invitation to Kauakahi to come and visit him at Haena. Having accepted the invitation, Kauakahi and his bride were conveyed thither by the multitude of birds. Their stay at Haena was prolonged to the end of the *anahulu*, a period of ten days, after which taking their departure, they essayed to return by way of the region of Wailua, following the precipitous trails that go inland to Kalalau. Now Kilioe had warned his friend Kauakahi, saying, "See to it that you keep your image at hand; for you must know that this wife of yours belongs to the ocean, and will ere long return thither; and when she does so she will seek to take you with her, in which case you will of course be drowned." By and by having reached the Wailua river, while they were sitting on the bank of the stream talking together, of a sudden the woman seized him and plunged into the depths of the river. But Kauakahi, mindful of his friend's advice, succeeded in substituting the image in place of himself, and escaped from her embrace, half dead from his prolonged stay under water.

No sooner did the birds from the mountain note his disappearance, than they flew to his aid, reaching him just in time to pluck him out of the water as he rose exhausted to the surface. They bore him on their wings back to his mountain home, where Kauakahi was content to remain, enjoying the society of his good friend, Kilioe.

XXIV

Religious Observances Relating to Children

1. Here is another occasion on which worship was paid to the gods. After the birth of a child it was kept by the mother at the common house, called *noa*, and was nursed with her milk, besides being fed with ordinary food.

2. When it came time for the child to be weaned, it was provided with ordinary food only, and was then taken from the mother and installed at the *mua*, or men's eating house. In regard to this removal of the child to the *mua* the expression was *ua ka ia i mua*. The eating tabu was now laid upon the child, and it was no longer allowed to take its food in the company of the women.

3. When the child was separated from its mother, a pig was offered up by the father to the deity as a ranson (*mohai pana'i*) for the child, in order to propitiate the favor of the deity for the little one. The pig that was used as an offering was baked in an oven in the presence of the worshipping assembly, and being sacred, only those who went in to take part in the ceremony ate of it.

4. When the pig had been consecrated, its head was cut off and set apart for the deity,—though still it was eaten by the people—being placed on the altar or *kua-ahu*,[1] (*kuahu* is the accepted orthography at the present time) where always stood images in the likeness of the gods.

5. This image had suspended from its neck a gourd, *ipu*, which was perforated to receive a wooden bail. This was called *ipu o Lono*,[2] or Lono's gourd.

6. The ear of the pig was now cut off and placed in the gourd that hung from the neck of the image, and at the same time a prayer was recited.

7. This prayer, however, was not an extemporaneous supplication, dictated by the feelings and intelligence of the man, as in the case of a prayer addressed to Jehovah, but was committed to memory, as if it had been a *mele*, a song or poem. Such was the nature of the prayers offered to their deities by the *aliis* as well as by the people.

8. When all was ready for the recital of the prayer, bananas, cocoanuts, awa-root, and awa prepared for drinking were set before the image. The

father then took the awa-bowl and offered it to the idol with these words, "Here is the pig, the cocoa-nuts, the awa, O ye gods, *Ku, Lono, Kane* and *Kanaloa,* and ye *Au-makuas.*" At the close of this address he offered the prayer called

PULE IPU

9. *Ala mai, e Lono, i kou haina[3] awa, haina awa nui nou, e Lono.*

He[4] ulu mai, e Kea,[5] he pepeiao puaa, he pepeiao[6] ilio, he pepeiao aina nui—nou, e Lono!

Halapa i ke mauli! Kukala[7] ia hale-hau! mau, malewa i ka po; molia ia hai ka po.

O ku'u kaipu[8]; o ku'u hua i ka-ipu; hua i kakala[9] ka ipu kakala; he kalana[10] ipu.

O hua i na mo'o a[11] Hi'i! I au i'a ko[12] ia.

Ahia la anoano a ke ahi-kanu,[13] a kanu la, i pua i Hawaii?

A kanu la o ka ipu nei; a ulu; a lau; a pua; a hua la o ka ipu nei.

Hoonoho[14] la o ka ipu nei. Kekela o ka ipu nei.

O uha'i o ka ipu nei. Kalai la o ka ipu nei.

O oki, o kua i o ka piha o ka ipu.

O ka ipu ka honua[15] nui nei; o po'i o ka lani o Kuakini.

A hou i ka hakaokao;[16] kakai i ke anuenue.[17]

O uhao[18] i ka lili; o uhao i ka hala; o uhao i ka la manolele[19] i ona!

O ka ipu o ka lua mu-a-Iku,[20] o ka ipu a makani koha, a kau ka hoku[21] a'ia'i.

Owahi![22] o kani mai, a hea o ka uka manu![22½]

Ka lalau a ha'a[23] ka manu; ka lalau kuli'a i Wawau.[24]

He malino[25] a po, e Lono, i ka haunaele;

Na lili la i ka haunaele, na hala la i ka haunaele o mau kahuna[26] o ke makala ulua[27]

Ulua[28] mai, o Lono, ulua kolea ino o Ma'a-ku-newa[29] awa lilelile!

O makia, Lono, a hano, a hano wale no!

Kila i nei; muli o hala, muli ke kani o Waioha!

Arise, O Lono, eat of the sacrificial feast of awa set for you, an abundant feast for you, O Lono!

Provide, O Kea, swine and dogs in abundance! and of land a large territory—for you, O Lono!

Make propitious the cloud-omens! Make proclamation for the building of a prayer-shrine! Peaceful, transparent is the night, night sacred to the gods.

My vine-branch this; and this the fruit on my vine-branch. Thick set with fruit are the shooting branches, a plantation of gourds.

Be fruitful in the heaped up rows! fruit bitter as fish-gall.

How many seeds from this gourd, pray, have been planted in this land cleared-by-fire? have been planted and flowered out in Hawaii?

Planted is this seed. It grows; it leafs; it flowers; lo! it fruits—this gourd-vine.

The gourd is placed in position; a shapely gourd it is.

Plucked is the gourd; it is cut open.

The core within is cut up and emptied out.

The gourd is this great world; its cover the heavens of Kuakini.

Thrust it into the netting! Attach to it the rainbow for a handle!

Imprison within it the jealousies, the sins, the monsters of iniquity!

Within this gourd from the cavern of *Mu-a-Iku,* calabash of explosive wind-squalls,—till the serene star shines down.

Make haste! lest the calabash sound, and the mountain bird utter its call!

Take hold of it and it crouches; take hold of it and it displays itself at Vavau.

It has been calm and free from disturbances into the night, O Lono, free from the turbulent enmities and bickerings of the kahunas, hunters after men.

Arrest them, O Lono! arrest the malicious sea-birds of *Maa-ku-newa,* with their flashing wings!

Confirm this and make it sacred, wholly sacred, O Lono!

Bind it securely here! The faults will be put in the background; the babbling waters of Waioha will take a second place.

10. The reference in this *pule-ipu* are to the gourd suspended from the neck of the idol and to the articles which had been put therein.

11. On the completion of this prayer the father took the dry awa-root and sucked it in his mouth. This was said to be the idol's drinking of it. It was not really imbibed (by the idol). Then he took the strong awa (*awa wai anu*), and, mixing it with water, drank of it and ate of the vegetables and meats until he was satisfied; and, this done, he declared the ceremony *noa,* no longer burdened with a tabu, using these words:

"Installed is the child, the awa smitten against the brain. Free is the awa; there is freedom to come and go; the tabu is entirely lifted. One is free to travel to the ends of the earth."

12. Then those who had taken part in the service ate the pork and the vegetables until they had satisfied their hunger, and thus the ceremony was accomplished. In this it was shown that the child had come under the eating-tabu, and would no longer be allowed to eat with the women. Such was the meaning of this service.

Notes on Chapter XXIV

1. Sect. 4. This *kua-ahu*, or *ku-ahu* was a rustic framework of wood, decorated with flowers and leaves.

2. Sect. 5. *Ipu-o-lono* is also the name applied to a variety or species of taro.

3. Sect. 9. *Haina awa*: There have been numerous conjectures as to the meaning of the word *haina*. After considering them all, I have come to the conclusion that it means the feast (*aha-aina*), or what amounts to almost the same thing, the assembly gathered to sacrifice and do honor to the god. (It has been suggested that it might have its origin in the Maori *"wahainga kawa,"* the act of repeating certain prayers, called *kawa,* connected originally with offerings of awa; hence *haina* might mean "the offering." The Maori expression *"whai i te kawa"* means to recite the *kawa* (prayer). *Whai* is itself a noun-form of prayer, also used in taking the *kapu* off houses, healing a burn, &c). This suggestion serves to mark to what an extent meanings of words in Hawaii have drifted away from that of their originals in southern Polynesia.

4. Sect. 9. *He ulu mai*: *He* is the equivalent of the causatives, *ho, ho'o, ha, ha'a,* all of which forms are found in the Hawaiian, or it may be an unusual, archaic, form of the imperative prefix, which is usually *e*.

5. Sect. 9. *Kea*: This is probably the same beneficent goddess, or *kupua,* whose full name was *Nua kea*. She was the goddess of lactation. The name was also applied to the woman who acted as wet-nurse to a young prince or princess, and whose breasts were therefore sacred to that duty, *kapu* to others. I am told that when the time came for a woman to wean her nursling, she would some times call upon Nua-kea to staunch the flow of milk in her breasts, using perhaps the following prayer:

E Lono, e Kane, e Nua-kea, ka wahine iaia ka poli-waiu o ke keiki.
Eia ke ukuhi nei o Mea.
E lawe aku oe i ka waiu o ka makuahine.
Ia oe e ka la, ka mahina, ka hoku;
E lawe oe a kukulu o Kahiki!
Haalele aku i ka omimo, ka uwe wale o Mea,
A e hauai oe i ka i'a kapu a Kane,

Oia ka hilu, ka noho malie,*
Ke ola ia oe, Kane!
  Amama. Ua noa.

O Lono, O Kane, O Nua-kea, the woman with a breast of milk for
   the child.
We are about to wean Mea.
Staunch the flow of milk in his mother.
Yours are the sun, the moon, the stars.
Carry away to the pillars of Kahiki
And there leave the emaciation, peevishness and wailing of the child;
Feed him with the sacred fish of Kane,

That is repose (*hilu*) and quiet.
This is your blessing, O Kane.
   Amen. The prayer is ended.

* *Hilu*: This word is used in a double sense. It is the name of a fish that is variegated with bright colored spots, and also means quiet, reserved, dignified in a commendable sense.

6. Sect. 9. *Pepeiao, puaa, pepeiao ilio,* etc.: The reference is to the ear, or ears put into the gourd, which was suspended about the neck of the image. The ear is used as a symbol of ownership, as well perhaps as of abundance. When an alii cut off a pig's ear he marked it as his own. The petition is that an abundance of this world's goods be granted to the child.

7. Sect. 9. . . . *kukala ia hale-hau*: *kukala* seems to be used in the sense of making proclamation ordering a thing to be done. Such was the custom even after the coming of the white man. *Ia* should probably be *i*. . . *hale-hau*: It has been a long hunt to trace this word to its burrow. I am informed that it means a house thatched with the leaves of the hau tree, the well known *hibiscus* of Polynesia. The house was of a temporary character and was used by the king and high chief for religious purposes. I am informed on the best of authority that the *hale-hau* of New Zealand—cf. *fare-hau* of Tahiti—was a council chamber, the house of the *hau*, or government. In Polynesia *hau* or *sau* means the powers that be. This is another instance aof Hawaiian departure, drifting, from what was probably the original meaning.

8. Sect. 9. *Ka-ipu*: The stem or stalk of a gourd-vine.

9. Sect. 9. *Kakala*: From the same root doubtless as *kala*, or *kala-kala*, rough, bristling, in this case meaning beset with shoots.

10. Sect. 9. *Kalana*, a small division of land; *kalana ipu*, therefore a field of gourd-vines.

11. Sect. 9. *O hua i na moo a Hi'i*: The expression *moo a Hi'i* seems to have almost the vogue of a proverb. Who this man, hero or god *Hi'i* was is more than I have been able to discover. I am informed that there was a god *Hiki*—something in the Maori pantheon. The best explanation I can give of the

passage is that the reference here is to the snake-like ridges in which the earth is heaped up about the vines.

12. Sect. 9. *Au i'a;* fish-gall. The best calabashes were from gourds that were exceedingly bitter.

13. Sect. 9. *Ahi-kanu,* a probable reference to the use of fire to clear land for planting. There is probably a reference in the expression to the ravages of war, a war of conquest.

14. Sect. 9. *Hoonoho,* to place, to put the immature gourd in a position favorable to symmetry.

15. Sect. 9. *O ka ipu ka honua,* etc.: This comparison of the world and the sky to the body and cover of a calabash is a piece right out of Polynesian cosmogony. The seeds of the gourd, when scattered through the sky, become stars, and the pulpy mass inside the clouds, the cover belikened to the solid dome of heaven, ka lani. As to who was *Kua-kini* I have not been able to discover.

16. Sect. 9. *A hou i ka hakaokao*: I am told that *hakaokao* is the name applied to the net that enclosed a calabash that was used as a kind of clothes trunk. The name is said to also have been applied to the net itself. Exactly how this kind of calabash differed from the ipu *holo-holo-na,* in which the fisherman was wont to stow his hooks, lines and small appurtenances, I am unable to say.

17. Sect. 9. *Kakai i ke annenue*: This might be more literally translated, make the rainbow a handle. By a bold and beautiful figure the poet compares the arched bail or handle of the net about the calabash to the rainbow.

18. Sect. 9. *O uhao i ka lili. O* in this is the prefix of the imperative mood. *Ka* in the phrase *ka lili* is the singular form of the article which is here used instead of the plural. Such practice was specially common in archaic Hawaiian.

19. Sect. 9. . . . *mono lele i ona*: In the text the words are fused into one continuous length *manoleleiona* much to the perplexity of the translator. Disentangled they array themselves thus. The *mano lele,* literally a flying shark, is doubtless figurative of a big sinner.

20. Sect. 9. . . . *ka lua mu a Iku*: This would probably be a more correct reading than *ka lua Mu-a-Iku.* In the original the words are run together *kaluamuwaiku,* with the addition of a *w.* It is impossible to make sense out of such a formless string of letters. Obedient to the duty of an editor, as well as of a translator, I have arranged the letters into words in such manner as to make the sense best agree with the context. The literal interpretation of *ka lua mu a Iku* would be something like *the haunted cave of Iku.* There is an interesting story hidden under this allusion to Iku's cave, which I have only partially uncovered. Iku was a *ku-pua* who lived at *Kuai-he-lani* in the southern region called *Kululu-o Kahiki,* having for wife *Ka-papa-ia-kea,* by whom he had twelve children who were always designated as So-and-So-a-Iku (*a-Iku* means the child of Iku). Iku inhabited an under ground cavern, in which grew famous gourds. These gourds, or some of them, are said to have had a voice, capable of emitting an explosive sound, "an explosive wind-squall" as put in the translation. It is useless to inquire or conjecture what natural phenomenon gave rise to this peculiar legend, of

which I have been able to obtain only a fragment. There is, I think, no reference in this legend to the famous *ipu a Laa-mao-mao.*

21. Sect. 9. . . . *a kau ka hoku aiai:* It seems as if the shining of the star was so as to look into the mouth of the cave. The meaning is not evident.

22. Sect. 9. *Owahi,* a word not to be found in the dictionary, and which I had never met until by inquiry I learned that it meant to hasten, be in a hurry, bestir one's self.

22½. *Ka uka manu*: A possible reference to the call of the sacred elepaio, a bird whose early note is often interrupting the works of heroes.

23. Sect. 9. *Ka lalau, a haa manu;* &c. The figure is that of the hunter putting his hand on a bird—probably in this case the *uau,* a fat bird, which, though frequenting the sea, nested in the mountains—on which the bird instantly squats down, crouches; again he puts his hand on the bird and it stands forth, shows itself, (*kuli'a*) in. . .

24. Sect. 9. *Wawau,* the same as *Vavau,* an island in the northern part of the *Tongan* group. (In the Hawaiian *W* represents both the sound *way* and the sound *vay.*) Mr. S. Percy Smith, than whom there is no better authority on such points, says: "In his prayer *Wawau (Vavau): Porapora = Polapola—Hawaii = Lani-akea.*" In his opinion *Wawau i.e.,* Vavau, is a sacred name for *Havaii* or *Lani-akea,* the proof on this point is round about and cumulative.

25. Sect. 9. *Malino*: A clear sky was an omen of favorable significance in connection with the performance of any religious rite, or the utterance of any prayer.

26. Sect. 9. . . . *haunaele o mau kahuna*: We have here an interior view of the wranglings and bickerings that went on among the body of kahunas.

27. Sect. 9. *Makala ulua*: *Makala,* a trail made by wild animals; *makala ulua,* a place frequented by those who fished for *ulua*: *ulua,* the name of a fish, was also a euphemism for a human body used in sacrifice. (See the account in Chap. XXXVII. p. 173.)

28. Sect. 9 *Ulua mai, e Lono.* This repetitious use of the word *ulua* in an entirely new sense, of which the present example forms a capital instance, is one of the artifices that marks Hawaiian poetry.

29. Sect. 9. . . . *kolea ino o Maa-ku-newa*: *Mo-i,* a *kupua,* or king of Molokai, sent *Maka-ulili,* the ruler of the *ko-leas,* to Vavau to bring an assortment of those birds, *i.e.,* the plover. He returned with one *lau* (400) *kolea ulili,* one *lau* of mischievous *kolea,* and one *lau* of good *kolea.* The birds were located on the hill *Ha-upu,* near *Pele-kunu* valley. It was then noticed that the hill at times sank below the surface of the ocean, and then as mysteriously rose from beneath waves. *Mo'i* sent a flight of the plover to learn the cause of this unusual phenomenon. They returned and reported that it was caused by the uneasy motions of a huge turtle, on which the hill was based, and they urged him to put an end to the disturbance by killing the turtle. Mo'i declined their advice and in revenge the *kolea ino* stole upon him while asleep, and tore his face with their talons; the hero, or wizard, Mo'i, then had all the mischievous birds, kolea

ino, who had sought to tear his eyes out, banished to the barren hill of *Maa-ku-newa*.

In a pule *anaana*, i.e., an incantation to cause the death of some one, occurs the following passage:

> *Kela kolea ino ulili o Ma'a-ku-newa;*
> *Newa i ka ulu kai o Kahiki, c Lono!*

> That teetering plover of Ma'aku-newa that portends foul weather;
> Ruffling the sea on its way from Tahiti, O Lono!

It is a common saying that the seesawing of the plover on the shore is a sign of coming storm.

As an instance of the mention of the *kolea* in ancient poetry, I quote from an old mele, as repeated to me:

> *A luna au o Akani-kolea,*
> *A nele i ka hokahoka.*

> I stood on Akani-kolea,
> My hopes entirely bankrupt.

The allusion in this fragment is to the story of *Hii-aka* (*i-ka-poli-o-Pele*).

XXV

Concerning the Circumcision of Children

1. After installation in the *mua,* when the boy had increased somewhat in size, was the time suitable for his circumcision. It was a religious rite and the ceremony resembled that of installation in the mua (*ke ka ana i mua*).

2. This rite of circumcising the foreskin was conducted in the following manner: A pig was offered to propitiate the deity and the friends of the child's parents were gathered in a religious assembly to celebrate the event.

3. When the pig that was used as an offering was baked to a turn, the operation of circumcision took place, and the manner of performing it was as follows:

4. Four men held the child fast. One was at the back of the child with the child held against his breast; at the same time the man held the little one's arms folded against his neck so that it could not move.

5. The length of the foreskin was measured from the extremity of the prepuce to its junction within, and at this point a black line was marked with charcoal. The length was also measured within to the point where the prepuce was reflected, and compared with the length indicated by the black mark made on the back of the penis.

6. Then one man held a thigh of the child with his left hand, and with his (right) hand seized one side of the preputial skin, and another man on the other side of the child did likewise, pulling the stretched prepuce taut.

7. Then the kahuna stood forth with his bamboo (*ohe* in place of a knife), and uttered the following *hoohiki,* prayer or blessing:

E kii ka ohe, i ho mai ka ohe, he ia ka ohe laulii a Kane, o kia i ke maka o ka mai; ua moku.[1]

(*E kii ka ohe i Homaikaohe. Eia ka ohe lauliia Kane*).[2]
(*Oki a i ka make o ka mai Ua moku*).

Bring the bamboo from Ho-mai-ka-ohe. Here is the small-leafed bamboo of Kane. Cut now the foreskin—It is divided.

8. Then the kahuna gave the bamboo to the one who was to perform the operation, and he thrust the bamboo into the preputial orifice until it reached the head of the penis, as far as had been measured with the bamboo within, and had been marked with the charcoal on the outside.

9. Then the foreskin was separated from its adhesions to the gland below and split lengthwise.[3] The blood was now removed by sucking, the foreskin was dressed with a medicinal leaf, and the child was arrayed in a white malo.

10. After this, a pig having been baked, worship was performed in a manner similar to that performed when the child was taken to the *mua*. Such was the worship and the prayer.

11. This was the way in which were treated the sons of the religionists, of the solid people, people of distinction, of the kahuna-class, and the sons of the lower ranks of chiefs.

The rite was different (more elaborate) when it touched the sons of high chiefs; there were also certain people who had no such ceremony performed at the circumcision of their sons—they were merely taken to the *mua* and circumcised with no religious ceremony whatever.

12. The children of *kahunas* and of *aliis* were not allowed, however, to partake of common food (*ai noa*) while they were being nourished on (their mother's) milk in the *noa* house. After being installed at the *mua* house they were allowed this common food, but while still at the *noa* they were fed only on (breast) milk. It was after this manner that some people acted towards their children.

Notes on Chapter XXV

1. Sect. 7. The text of this ancient prayer, like that of several others reported by Mr. Malo, is in a very unsatisfactory state. In the identical form reported by him it is impossible to make sense out of it, and in the translation I have followed an amendment proposed by an eminent Hawaiian scholar (J. K. K.). I am not altogether satisfied with the amendment, which is that enclosed in the brackets and numbered (2). In place of this I would propose what seems to me a simpler way out of the difficulty, namely, that shown in the following:

> *E kii ka ohe! Homai ke ohe! Eia ka ohe laulii a Kane.*
> *Oki'a i ka maka o ka mai! Ua moku.*

The translation of this will differ but little from that given.

Bring the bamboo! Give me the bamboo! Here is the small-leafed
bamboo of Kane.
Cut now the foreskin! It is cut.

3. Sect. 9. The Hawaiian operation is, strictly speaking, not circumcision at all. The prepuce is merely slit up from its free edge or lip to the line of its attachment to the penis. The operation is still occasionally practiced by the Hawaiians.

XXVI

Religious Worship for Healing
of the Sick

1. When a husband, a wife, a child, or a beloved friend became ill it was an occasion that called for religious ceremonies (*hoomana*).

2. The offering—*mohai*—of the sick person—it might be a pig, a fowl, or set of tapa sheets (*kuina kapa*) was laid before the gods.

3. It was some friend of the sick man who took the offering and presented it to the gods and at the same time he uttered this petition:

4. "O God, be kind to the one who is afflicted with illness; freely pardon his sins and impurities, his ceremonial faults, his faults of the heart, his faults of speech and his non-fulfillment of vows to thee.

5. "Let your anger be appeased by these offerings. Look with favor upon him and prosper him all the days of his life. Keep in health his body, until he shall have passed the age of walking upright, until he shall crawl or shall walk bent over a staff, until he shall be blinked-eyed (*hau-maka-iole*), and then bed-ridden (*pala-lau-hala*). Keep him in health until the last trance-vision (*a kau i ka pua-ane-ane*). That is thy benefit to us, O God, and thus do I worship thee."[1]

6. Now this was because there was a strong belief that animal sacrifices were the right means with which to propitiate the deity and obtain his forgiveness for the sins of men, and healing for men's bodies—not for their souls.

7. If the malady did not abate, a house was erected to the deity and a pig was sacrificed and exposed as an offering on a frame-work, called a *lele*, where it was allowed to remain (untill it mouldered away). Another pig also was oven-baked and its head offered in sacrifice, but the body of this one was eaten.

8. Supplication was again made to the deity to heal the sick one, and if he recovered that ended the ceremonies and the worship addressed to the deity, and if he died, then also was there an end to the praying and worshipping.

Notes on Chapter XXVI

1. Sect. 5. *E ke Akua, e aloha mai oe i ka mea i mai ia. E kala wale mai oe i kona hewa ana, a me kona haumia, a me kona ai-ku, a me kona ai-a, a me kona waha-hcwa, a me kona hoohiki ino ana ia oe.*

E na mai kou lili ma keia mau mohai. E maliu mai oe; c hoola mai iaia ma ke kino a hele ku, a hele kolo, a hele nee, a kolo pupu, a hau-maka-iole, a pala-lau-hala, a ola loa a ka pua-ane-ane. Kau ola ia, e ke Akua. Pela ka'u waiha aku a me ka'u waipa aku ia oe, e ke Akua. Pela ka'u hoomana ia oe.

N. B.—Kane and Lono were the deities most commonly addressed by those who offered prayers for the restoration of any one to health. The practice of medicine—and the Hawaiians had some proficiency in certain branches of the healing art—was always accompanied by religious ceremonies of some kind.

XXVII

Concerning Dead Bodies

1. A corpse was a very tabu thing in Hawaii nei. It was the ancients themselves who imposed this tabu; but the reason for it and the author of it have not been made known. The mere fact of the tabu was all that was known in Hawaii nei.

2. The tabu that applied to the dead body of an *alii* continued in force longer than that which concerned the dead bodies of others; it might be ten days or even longer before the ban of uncleanness would be removed. If it concerned the body of a person of more than ordinary distinction, perhaps it would be three days before the ban of uncleanness would be removed; but if it were a person of low class it would be only a day or two before the tabu would be lifted (*noa*). When the corpse was buried out of sight then the period of tabu came to an end.

The *modus operandi* of the tabu that concerned corpses was as follows:

3. On the death of a person in a house in which other people were living, those who were not blood-relatives of the deceased were driven out (*kipaku ia*), but relatives were allowed to remain with the body.

4. Those who remained with the corpse were considered defiled, *haumia,* and must not on any account enter another house, eat of the food of other people, touch any one else, or do any work, during the days of their defilement.

5. If the deceased had other friends outside, they were permitted to come and mourn, but other people might not enter the house in which was the dead body, nor eat of the food, nor touch any one within, lest they should be defiled.

6. The ceremonies for the dead were as follows: If the dead person was much beloved, or had died in full vigor and health, *i.e.* suddenly, the ceremony of *kuni*[1] would be performed on the body by the *kahuna anaana,* on the supposition that (in such a case) the death was from natural causes (*make maoli no*).

7. Again if the body was that of a person much beloved, husband, or wife, it was the custom to keep it a good many days before burial.

8. The body was first cut open[2] and the inner parts removed, and it was then filled with salt to preserve it. A body treated in this manner was termed *i'a loa*, long fish. It was a common thing to treat dead bodies in this way.

9. The manner of arranging a corpse for burial I will describe. A rope was attached to the joints of the legs and then being passed about the neck was drawn taut until the knees touched the chest. The body was then done up in a rounded shape and at once closely wrapped in tapa and made ready for burial.

10. Sepulture was done at night, so that by morning the burial was accomplished. Then in the early morning all who had taken part in the burial went and bathed themselves in water, and on their return from the bath seated themselves in a row before the house where the corpse had been.

11. The priest was then sent for to perform the ceremony of *huikala*, or purification. A sorcerer or *kahuna anaana*,[3] could not officiate at this service of purification. It was only a temple-priest, *kahuna pule heiau*, who could purify one from the uncleanness of a corpse or any other source of defilement.

12. The kahuna brought with him a dish filled with sea-water, which also contained a sea-moss called *limu-kala* and turmeric; and standing before the people who sat in a row, he prayed as follows:

13.   *Lele Uli e! Lele wai e!*
       He Uli, he Uli, he wai, he wai!
       Lele au i ke ahua e Kane me' hani.
    O Nehelani, nehe ia pika'na ka lani.
    A lama. He mu oia.[5]

       Hasten, O Uli; hasten, O water.
       Here is Uli, Uli; here is water, water.
       I fly to thy shrine, O Kane, the approachable one.
       A rustling in heaven—it rustles with the sprinkling.
       Light appears. The deity is silent.

Then the people respond:

                He mu.
                The deity is silent.

The Kahuna resumes:

> *He-mu ka aiku*
> *He-mu ka aia,*
> *He-mu ka ahula,*
> *He-mu ka paani,*
> *He-mu koko lana,*
> *I koko pua'a!*
> *I koko ilio!*
> *I koko kanaka make!*
> *He mu oia!*

Silent and attentive are the rude and unceremonious,
Silent are the wicked and unbelievers,
Silent are the hula-dancers,
Silent are those given to sports and games,
Silent are the hot-blooded ones.
Give us now the blood of swine!
Give us now the blood of dogs!
The blood of the human sacrifice!
The deity is silent.

The people respond:

> *He mu.*
> The deity is silent.

The kahuna says:

> *Elieli.*
> Profoundly.

The people respond:

> *Kapu.*
> Tabu.

The kahuna says:

Elieli.
Entirely, profoundly.

The people

Noa.
Free.

The kahuna

Ia e!
O Ia!

The people

Noa honua.
Freedom instant and complete.

The kahuna then sprinkled the water mixed with turmeric on all the people, and the purification was accomplished, the defilement removed.

14. After this each one departed and returned to his own house. When a corpse was buried in such a secret place that it could not be discovered it was said to be *huna-kele.*

15. Sometimes a person would secretely exhume the body of a beloved husband or wife, and remove the four leg-bones and the skull, washing them in water until they were clean.

16. They were then wrapped up and enclosed within the pillow, and the friend took them to bed with him and slept with them every night. The number of corpses treated in this way was considerable among those who were fond of each other.

17. Instead of the bones just mentioned, perhaps the palm of the hand would be cut off, dried in the sun and taken to bed with one. Or, if not the hand, the hair of the head, the teeth, or the finger nails.

18. These parts of the corpse were preserved by the fond lover until such time as the love came to an end, when they were neglected.

Notes to Chapter XXVII

1. Sect. 6. *Kuni,* an incantation and sorcery for the purpose of revealing and bringing to punishment him who prayed to death (*anaana*) the person concerned. For full description see Chap. XXVIII.

2. Sect. 8. Access to the cavities of the body was gained through a transverse cut made just below the ribs.

3. Sect. 11. The *kahuna anaana* was feared and shunned as an assassin would have been. He was from the nature of the case disqualified for performing such a beneficent ceremony. It would have been like setting the wolves to guard the sheep.

4. Sect. 14. This was the favorite way of dealing with the bones of a very high chief—by sepulture in caves and secret places. These were known only to the *kahu,* and it was an act of perfidy for him to betray the secret.

5. Sect. 13. *Mu.* I am not sure that I have found and expressed the true meaning of the word *mu.* As ordinarily used it means either a bug that lives in wood or an odious official whose duty it was to procure human victims to be used as sacrifices in the dedication of a *heiau* or other important building. Neither of those uses will suit the meaning in this case. The language is evidently quite archaic, and it seems probable that the word is no longer used in the same meaning. Such was my conclusion after much searching for a clue as to the probable meaning of this term. On referring the matter to a learned Hawaiian, one who had giver me many useful points, he expressed it as his opinion that the word meant to be silent. The generic meaning of the word agrees well with my friend's opinion. *Mumule* is to sulk in silence; *Kamumu* is to murmur, the gentle, breezy inarticulate sound that comes from a multitude. *Mumu* is to hum, to make an indistinct sound; to be silent; etc., etc. In an ancient story I find the word *mu* to be applied to the buzzing of the flies about, a dead body.

The meaning of the verse *"He-mu ka aiku',"* is that the one who had been unruly, eating in an unceremonious manner, had now become quiet, i.e., the assembly is now in order, attentive to the service in hand.

In Maori *mu-hore* means unlucky; *mu-tie* silence. (S. P. S.)

In Hawaiian *mu-ki'* expresses the action of kissing, and is used to signify the act of sucking a tobacco pipe.

See also p. 141, 2nd line. (W. D. A.)

XXVIII

Concerning the Ceremony of Kuni[1]

1. On the death of a rich or distinguished person, or of one greatly beloved, it would (very frequently) be said that he came to his death through *anaana,* that is through being prayed to death, for the reason that he was envied for his property, or hated on account of his distinction. Under such circumstances the ceremony of *kuni* would be performed on the body of the dead person.

2. The affair, was conducted in the following manner: The friend or interested party, having provided himself with a pig, went before the *kahuna kuni* and offered it to the deity with these words:

3. "Here is the pig, o Uli[2] in the heavens. This pig is offered to purchase the death of him who prayed to death my friend. It devolves upon you, o *Uli* and upon *Maka-ku-koae,*[3] and upon *Ka-alae a-hina*[4] to perform the funeral of this man."

4. "Is this the pig to procure *anaana?*" asks the kahuna. "Yes."

5. "Then let him go, and observe in what direction he moves." The pig was then released, and if he went to rooting in the earth, the kahuna declared that the one who had *anaanaed* the man was himself a doomed one, and it would not be long before he would meet with his death; "because the pig roots in the earth."

6. If it did not act in this way, but went to the left side of the kahuna, he would declare, "it seems the death was caused by your wife's relatives;" and if the pig went to the right of the kahuna, he would declare, "so it seems the death was due to the younger brother's people."

7. If, again the pig passed behind the kahuna he declared the deceased came to his death through the agency of some outside party, or, if the pig raised his snout in the air, the kahuna declared that the death was chargeable to some *alii;* and if the pig came and stood before the man who brought him, he declared the responsibility for the man's death lay with the man's *hoa ai,* his table-companions. This was the gist of the remarks made by the kahuna.

The kahuna thereupon instructed the man to prepare the kukui nuts, gourds, and all the other paraphernalia of *kuni.*

8. Then the man who took the offering returned and reported the prediction of the *kahuna kuni,* that the one who had caused the death of the victim by *anaana* would soon die himself.

9. The friends of the deceased rejoiced greatly when they heard that the one who had *anaanaed* their friend was himself soon to die, and they went to work with alacrity to execute the commands of the *kahuna kuni,* so as to have everything ready to hand before his arrival. By the time the kahuna arrived, everything was in readiness.

10. The kahuna conducted his operations as follows:

A stone, wrapped in a tapa of the kind called *ae-o-kaha-loa,*[5] having been set before him, the dead body was laid with its head close to the stone.

11. The kahuna then stood up with the cluster of kukui nuts and the gourd in his hands and repeated an incantation called the *pule hui* which runs thus:

'Tis cluster, sacred cluster, utters its meaning, and it is this: the cluster this with which the *aumakua* invokes death upon him who *anaanaed* this one, praying that his destruction be turned back upon himself. Behold this cluster breaks up and scatters, and so it symbolizes its meaning. This is the compact of Uli, Kaalae-a-Hina, and Ku-koa'e; it pledges death to the one who *anaanaed* him; his incantation shall be turned back upon himself.

"Behold the cluster breaks up and utters its meaning thus—the sacred cluster!"

12. Then the kahuna struck the bunch of kukui nuts against the table of stone which was called the *papa ka hui,* and the kukui nuts and gourd were broken and scattered in all directions.

13. From the direction in which the kukui nuts flew the kahuna again pointed out the locality of those who caused the death, it being indicated by the direction taken by the nuts. Thus ended this office of the *kahuna kuni.*

14. Then a fire-place for the *kuni* ceremony, called a *kapuahi kuni,* was constructed. It was of large size and when built was wreathed with *auhuhu*[7] and gourds and a flag[6] was displayed at each corner of it, after which a fire was lighted in the fire-place.

15. Then a number of fowls and dogs were brought as *kuni* offerings. Men, probably two in number, selected and detailed for the purpose, then opened the dead body and having cut the liver into small pieces,

stuffed them into each fowl and dog as a *manu-kuni*,[8] that is a charm to bring the victim under the spell of the incantation.

16. The two men who dissected the dead body were (of course) utterly defiled, anl were therefore not permitted to touch food with their hands, so that it was necessary for others to feed them.

17. As soon as the body of a fowl or dog had been charged with its portion of liver it was thrown into the fire in the fire-place; at the same time the man called aloud, "Here comes John Doe,[9] seeking the one who caused his death by *anaana*."

18. After that the kahuna stood up and offered his *kuni* prayer, using great fervor and continuing until sunset without eating or drinking. The prayer might come to and end only when the sacrifices were reduced to ashes.

19. While the fire burned the kahuna prayed and his prayer ran thus:

> *A-a ke ahi, ke ahi a ka po o Lani-pili.*[10]
> *A i hea ke ahi, ke ahi a ka po a Lani-pili?*
> *A i ka lani; make i ka lani;*
> *Popo i ka lani; ilo i ka lani;*
> *Punahelu i ka lani.*
> *Hoolehua i ka lani ka make o kahuna anaana.*
> *Me ka lawe-maunu, e Kane.*
> *Ahi a Ku o ke ahi.*
> *Kupu malamalama o ke ahi o ka po a,*
> *Ahi a Kulu-alani e a ana.*
> *Ku o Wakea, a ke ahi, he ahi no keia pule.*

The fire burns, fire of the night of Lani-pili.
Where burns the fire, fire of the night of Lani-pili?
It burns in the heavens.
Death in the heavens; corruption in the heavens;
Maggots in the heavens; mildew in the heavens.
Heaven speed the death of the kahuna anaana,
And of the one who got for him the *maunu,* o Kane.
It is the fires of Ku that burn.
Flash forth light of the burning night,
The fires of Kulu-a-lani are burning.
Wakea stands up and the fire burns, fire for this prayer.

DAVID MALO

20. By the time the *kuni* offerings were reduced to ashes it was night. The ashes were then carried down to the ocean and thrown into a spout-hole together with all the appurtenances of the fire-place; the fire-place itself was buried.

21. The next morning a boy and a girl were made to walk naked about the fire-place, not covering their parts of shame as they walked.

22. As they made their round about the fire place the kahuna kuni stood and prayed, and when the kahuna had finished his prayer the ceremony of *kuni* was completed. Then it was that the kahuna declared the name of the one who had *anaanaed* the deceased one.

23. "I have seen," said he, "the wraith or *kahoaka* of him who *anaanaed* this man coming this way, his head down, his eyes closed, as good as dead. And it will not be long before this one also shall die."

24. "The death to which I consign him is a swelling, a dropsy, a bloody flux, a vomiting of blood, a broken back. That is the manner of death I predict for him. Take you note of this."

25. The body was then buried and a different kahuna came—the one previously spoken of to whom belonged the ceremony of purification. After this the kahuna kuni received his pay, and it was a large amount.

26. If after this, any one died of one of the diseases mentioned by the kahuna, the kahuna in question would be in great demand and at the same time much feared for his power (*mana*).

The number of *alii* that were prayed to death was about the same as of the common people. As to *kuni* sacrifices, the number of those that were required of an *alii* was greater than what was required of an ordinary person, because this function of *kuni*, (*anaana* in the text) was a ceremony of worship (*hoo-mana*). Ordinarily the number of dogs required for a sacrifice was forty, with double that number of fowls, but an *alii* was required to offer a *lau*, four hundred dogs, and of fowls an immense number.

Notes on Chapter XXVIII

1. Sect. 1. The subject of this chapter is *kuni*, not *anaana*, and I have accordingly substituted the word *kuni* for that of *anaana* in the title, and the same has been done as necessary throughout the chapter, as for instance in Sect. 2, where *kahuna kuni* has been substituted for *kahuna anaana*. It goes almost without saying that a *kahuna anaana* would not be the one to avenge the foul work of his own craft.

2. Sect. 2. . . . *e Uli i ka hoolewa,* which is the reading in the text, I have ventured to amend so as to read *e Uli ke aolewa,* or *olewa. Aolewa* is the atmosphere, the space beneath the solid dome (*ao paa*) of heaven. *Uli* may be described as the judicial spirit, as well as the detective one, fitted therefore to discover the one whose incantations had *anaanaed* and brought death to the deceased. *Uli* was addressed in prayer:

> *E Uli nana pono,*   O *Uli* that discerns the right,
> *E Uli nana hewa. . .* O *Uli* that discerns the wrong. . .

3. Sect. 3. *Maka-ku-koae,* or *Ka-maka-ku-koae* as it is in the text, was a male deity who induced craziness (*pupule*), raving insanity (*hehena*), or palsy and imbecility (*lolo*), he was therefore a very appropriate being to call upon for aid in such an emergency as this.

4. Sect. 3. *Ka-alae-a-Hina,* the mud-hen of Hina, a deity who induced sudden death. Hina had a numerous family of sons, all of them *kupuas,* i.e., supernatural beings. Maui, the discoverer of fire, was one of them. So also was the mud-hen, from whom Maui forced the secret of fire.

5. Sect. 10. *A'e-o-kaha-loa,* a *wauke tapa* of pinkish color.

6. Sect. 14. These were of white *tapa.*

7. Sect. 14. *Auhuhu,* Tephrosia piscatoria, a small shrubby plant which is used as a fish-poison.

8. Sect. 15. *Maunu-kuni*: this might be a shred of clothing, a bit of hair, finger—or toe-nail, or any exuviae from the victim's body. *Maunu* literally means bait, but originally it meant something moulted or sloughed off, like feathers, etc.

9. Sect. 17. In the original prayer of the kahuna the name of the postulant would be given.

10. Sect. 19. *Lani-pili* was the name of a deity; it meant literally a close, dark, night, a night when the heavens shut down close over the earth as before they were lilted up and separated from the earth, a clear reference to the ancient mythology.

The following is communicated to me as a *kuni pule* used by Wailiilii, a distinguished *kahuna* in the old times on the Island of Molokai:

> *Ia Awaiku* ka ua i Lanikeha,†*
> *Ka ua maawe au e Kane,*
> *E Kane pakanaka,*
> *Kane pamahana,*
> *Mahana kaua ia oe, e Kane.*
> *E make ka mea nana i kolohe i ku'u keiki,*
> *Make emoole, naha ke kua, eu ka ilo,*
> *Popopo a helelei,*
> *Kau make, e Kane.*

The spirits Awaikau send rain from the heavens of Lanikeha,
The fine rain of you, o Kane,
Kane who touches humanity,
Who warms us by his presence.
You and I warm to each other Kane.
Send death to him who dealt mischievously with my boy.
Let his be a speedy death, a broken back with rapid decay,
Rotting and falling to pieces.
This is the death I ask you to inflict, o Kane.

* *Awa-iku*: These were spirits that acted as the messengers, spies, and agents to do the bidding of Kane. They were also guardian spirits, shielding and warding off from people the malign influences of the *mu*, who were a mischievous set of sprites, up to all kinds of minor deviltries according to their power. These *Awa-iku* managed the rain, the winds and the weather and a great many other things, and were beneficent in their conduct.

† *Lani-keha*: an epithet applied to some part or district of heaven, the solid heaven. The residence of Kamehameha III at Lahaina was called *Lanikeha*.

N.B. The first part of this prayer has the marks of greater age than the remainder of the prayer. It was a common trick of the kahuna to impose on people as well by high—sounding phrases as by other tricks.

XXIX

CONCERNING THE CEREMONIES ON THE DEATH OF A KING

1. On the death of a king, one who was at the head of the government, the ceremonies were entirely different from those performed on the death or any other *alii* whatsoever.

2. When the king was dead his heir was removed to another district, because that in which his death took place was polluted by the corpse.

3. The *kuni*[1] priests took a part of the flesh of the dead king's body to be used as *maunu* in their incantations against those who had prayed him to death. The body was then taken to the *mua*[2] house in the presence of the multitude and laid in the *heiau*, that it might be deified and transformed into an *au-makua*.

4. The ceremony was performed by the *kahuna hui* working under the rite of *Lolupe*,[3] who was the god of the *kahuna hui*. It was believed that *Lolupe* was the deity who took charge of those who spoke ill of the king, consigning them to death, while the souls of those who were not guilty of such defamation he conducted to a place of safety (*ola*, life).

5. The service of the deity *Lolupe* was in one branch similar to the ceremony of *kuni* (*or anaana*). The deification of the corpse and imparting godlike power to it was another branch of the priests' work, and was accomplished in the following manner.

6. The dead body was first wrapped in leaves of banana, *wauke* and taro, a rite which was called *kapa lau*, garment of leaves.

7. The body being thus completely enveloped, a shallow pit was dug and the body was buried therein about a foot below the surface, after which a fire was made on the ground the whole length of the grave.

8. This was kept constantly burning for about ten days, during which time the prayer called *pule hui* was continually recited. By that time the body had gone into decay and that night the bones were separated from the flesh and worship was performed to secure their deification after the following manner.[4]

9. After disinterment the bones were dissected out and arranged in order, those of the right side in one place, those of the left side in

another, and, the skull-bones being placed on top, they were all made up into a bundle and wrapped in tapa.

10. The flesh which had gone to decay (*pala-kahuki*) and all the corruptible parts were called *pela* (*pelapela*, foul, unclean) and were cast into the ocean.

11. It was by night that this *pela* was thrown into the ocean, on a tabu night. On that night no one from the village must go abroad or he might be killed by the men who were carrying forth the *pela* to consign it to the ocean.

12. After this was accomplished, the bones were put in position and arranged to resemble the shape of a man, being seated in the house until the day of prayer, when their deification would take place and they would be addressed in prayer by the *kahunas* of the *mua*. The period of defilement was then at an end; consequently the king's successor was permitted to return, and the apotheosis of the dead king being accomplished, he was worshipped as a real god[6] (*akua maoli*).

13. His successor then built for the reception of the bones a new *heiau*, which was called a *hale poki*, for the reason that in it was constructed a network to contain the bones, which, being placed in an upright position, as if they had been a man, were enshrined in the *heiau* as a god.

14. After this these bones continued to be a god demanding worship, and such a deity was called an *au-makua*. Common people were sometimes deified,[5] but not in the same manner as were kings.

It was believed that it was the gods who led and influenced the souls of men. This was the reason why a real god, an *akua maoli*,[6] was deemed to be a spirit, an *uhane*—(or) this is the reason why it was said that the soul of the king was changed into a real god (*oia ka mea e olelo ai ka uhane i akua maoli*).

Notes on Chapter XXIX

1. Sect. 3. The functions of the *kahuna kuni* and *kahuna anaana* bore a strong outward resemblance to each other, but the purpose was different. The meaning of this passage is that the ceremony of *kuni* was performed on the king's body in order to find out who had compassed his death by sorcery (*anaana*).

2. Sect. 3. David Malo uses the terms *mua* and *heiau* almost as if they were interchangeable, and meant the same thing. The *mua* was the men's eating house, tabu to women. The family idols were probably kept there, and it seems as if some part of it was set apart as a shrine or *heiau*.

3. Sect. 4. *Lolupe,* seems to have been rather a *kupua* than a full fledged deity. This deity was represented by a kite made in the shape of a fish, with wings, tail, etc.; when made the figure was sent up the same as any kite. Its special function was to go in search of the spirits of the dead and bring them before the *kahunas* for identification, interrogation and judgment. Prayer and offerings were used at the time of its being sent up. The errands committed to it were never of a criminal nature. A suitable errand to commit to *Lolupe* would have been the recovery of the soul of a dear one from the land of shades, as Hiku brought back the soul of his bride or sister, Kawelu, after it had gone into the shades of Milu. If a man wanted a big piece of land, he might pray to *Lolupe* and commit the job to him.

Apropos of Hiku, the following beautiful *kanaenae** has been told me which comes in not inappropriately at this time. Hiku is represented as climbing the mountain side in search of the shade of his bride:

> *Pi'i ana Hiku i ke kualono,*
> *Pi'i ana Hiku i ke kualono,*
> *E ka lala e kaukolo ana,*
> *Ua ke'eke'ehi ia e Lolupe ka pua, ua haule ilalo.*
> *Ka pua kui lei au, e Malaikanaloa.*
> *Homai ana kahi pua, e Lolupe,*
> *I hoolawa ae no ko'u lei.*

Hiku is climbing the mountain ridge,
Climbing the mountain ridge,
The branch hangs straggling down,
Its blossoms, kicked off by Lolupe, lie on the ground,
Blossoms to be strung into a *lei* by Malaikanaloa.
Give me also a flower, o Lolupe,
That I may piece out my wreath.

Long before Franklin made use of the kite to draw electricity from the clouds the Hawaiian *kahuna,* following the rite of Lolupe, used it to ensnare ghosts in the heavens.

* A *kanaenae* is a complimentary address which stands as a prelude to the more serious matter of a prayer or *mele.* (In Maori *tangaengae* is the prayer used at the cutting of the umbilical cord. S. P. S.)

4. Sect. 13. *Hoaha ia a pa'a i ka aha,* as it is in the text, would be better expressed *hoa ia a pa'a i ka aha.* I am informed that when, as in this case, the bones were those of a king, or chief of high rank the fitting expression was *kama ia a pa'a i ka aha,* the meaning being in each case the same. Each limb and the trunk, neck and head were separately bound with sinnet, and the parts being then placed in position were joined together to resemble the shape and appearance of a human figure.

5. Sect. 14. The deification of a common person could be accomplished, but it was more burdensome and took longer time to accomplish than that of a king.

6. Sect. 14. *Akua maoli*: The gods Ku, Kane, Kanaloa and Lono, though making themselves visible to men occasionally in human form perhaps, were conceived of as spirits, *uhane*, and as such were spoken of as *akua maoli*. Mr. Malo unwittingly, probably as the result of the new theology which had come for the enlightenment of him and his people, was inclined to do scant justice to the discarded ideas of his heathen ancesteor. An *akua maoli* was, as he says, an *uhane*. The person of the dead king was by *hoomana*, prayer and incantation made into an *akua maoli*. Theologic disapproval of the use of images, eikons and relics as aids to a devotional frame of mind must not blind us to the fact that while the culture of the ancient Hawaiians had advanced so far as to have attained the idea of a spiritual deity, it had not gone far enough to be able to dispense with that old time crutch of superstition, the image and the effigy. It is one thing for a people in the natural course of religious evolution to make use of the image, as an aid to the imagination, in the attempt to form a definite concept of the unseen, but quite another thing to relapse from a higher plane of religious evolution and take up again with the defunct and discarded emblem. Such a retrogression is a sure sign of mental and moral degeneracy.

XXX

THE MEDICAL TREATMENT OF THE SICK

1. The medical treatment of the sick was a matter that belonged to the worship of the gods. When any one was seized with an illness a messenger was despatched to the *kahuna* who practiced medicine, *kahuna lapaau*, taking with him an offering for *mai-ola*,[1] the god of medicine.

2. When the messenger came before the *kahuna* the latter inquired regarding the disease, and having learned about it, before beginning the treatment, he forbade certain articles of food to the sick man.

3. The sick man must not eat the squid, moss, bêche de mer, *loli*, a certain fish called *kualaka'i*, nor the *ina, wana,* or *haukeke*, echini, nor the *pipipi*,[2]—the small sea-shell, *Nerita*, which is much eaten; all of these were forbidden, together with such other fish as the *kahuna* saw fit.

4. When the sick man had agreed to these restrictions, the *kahuna* began his treatment by administering some sort of potion.

5. After the treatment had continued a while, if the *kahuna* saw that the disease was about to let up he went and slept for a night in the *mua*,[3] that he might worship the god of medicine and so he might obtain a sign from the deity whether the sick man would recover or die.

6. He took with him to the *mua* a certain kind of moss (*limu kala* probably), also some *pipipi* shells, such things in fact as he had forbidden the man to partake of. If rain fell during the night, he regarded it as an unpropitious omen, in which case he spent another night there.

7. If, however, there was no rain that night the *kahuna* accepted the omen as favorable, and at daybreak he lighted a fire and performed the ceremony called *pu-limu*.[4] He also baked a fowl, as an offering to the *au-makua*, of which only the *kahuna* ate. Two dogs also were baked, one for the *mua*, or men's house, and one for the *noa* or common sleeping house. Five sheets of tapa-cloth were used to cover the oven[5] for the *mua*, and five to cover the oven for the *noa*. When the animals were baked, the men assembled at the *mua* and ate their portion of the sacrifice in company with the sick man, at the same time paying their worship to the god of medicine. Likewise the women in the *noa* house at the same

time worshipped the female god of medicine. (On Molokai this was *La'a-uli.*)

8. After the ceremony of the *pu-limu* fire was over, the medical treatment of the patient was resumed. For a cathartic the juice of the *koali* (a convolvulus) was used; as an emetic was administered a vegetable juice called *pi'i-ku* (obtained from the fresh green stems of the *ku-kui nut*). The enema was sometimes employed. Another remedy was the *popo kapai.*[6] To reduce fever a draught of raw taro-juice or yam-juice, called *apu-kalo* or *apu uhi,*[7] was found to be of service.

9. The next thing was to make a hut called *hale hau,* which was done with sticks of *hau wood* and was arched on top. The sick man was removed to this little hut and given a steam-bath, after which he was bathed in sea-water and then nourishment was administered. After this the ceremony of the *pipipi* fire was performed which was very similar to the *pu-limu* fire. A fowl was then sacrificed to the *aumakua;* a dog was baked for the *mua* and another for the *noa.* Five tapas were used in covering the oven for the *mua* and five to cover that for the *noa.* When all this had been done the prognosis of the sick one was again considered.

10. If it was seen that the patient was somewhat relieved (*maha*), the *kahuna* took the next step, which was to put the patient to bed and perform the ceremony called *hee mahola.*[8] If rain fell that night it was a bad omen and the *kahuna* then informed the sick man that he must die, because the omens derived from the *hee mahola* ceremony were adverse.

11. If, on the other hand, no rain fell that night the *kahuna* assured the man he would live. "The *hee mahola* has been attended with favorable omens. You will surely recover."

12. The following morning a fire, called *ahi mahola,* was lighted, the squid was cooked, and the prayer called *pule hee,* having been offered by the *kahuna,* the patient ate of the squid and thus ended the medical treatment and the incantations (*hoomana*).

13. The treatment of a sick *alii* was different from that described above. Every time the *alii* took his medicine the *kahuna* offered prayer.

> *E Kii, e Kii ma Kalapua,*
> *E lapu ke kii aku.*
> *Oioi o ka maau akua,*
> *Lana'i au i ke anaana,*
> *A ka la papa i ke akua i laau waiola.*

O image, o image at Kalapua,
What if the god-image plays the ghost?
What if the vagrant ghosts act with insolence?
I am secure from the *anaana,*
By the day which the deity has made clear,
Deity with the water of life.

Only after the repetition of this prayer did the *alii* swallow his medicine.

14. The *hee mahola*[9] ceremony was thought to be the thing to disperse (*hehee*) disease and bring healing to the body. When an *alii* had recovered from a malady he built a *heiau,* which was called either a *Lono-puha*[10] or a *kolea-muku.*[11]

Such were the incantations in connection with the treatment of disease. When the work of the *kahuna* was done he was rewarded for his professional services.

Notes on Chapter XXX

1. Sect. 1. I can gain no information about *Mai-ola.* Among the several deities that are represented as presiding over the healing art is *Mauli-ola.* *Mauli-ola* seems to have been an *akua maoli* and not to have had any visible representation, so far as can be learned. The word had a considerable variety of applications. As, for instance, the breath of life, or the first inspiration, after the close call of death, were called *mauli-ola.* A physician, or his art, when successful in prolonging life was called *mauli-ola;* also a prayer or vow which brought life was called *mauli-ola.* The above statement is in accordance with the views of an expert in such matters from the island of Molokai. He also communicates to me the following:

Prayer to Mauli-ola

I Hiiaka[a] paha oe, i Hiialo,[b] i kakahiaka nei.
I ka laau a ke kaukau alii, i nui ke aho,
A hiki ia Mauli-ola, i ka heiau i Mahina-uli,
I ola ia Mauli-ola.

Perhaps thou are in Hiikua, perhaps in Hiialo, this morning.
Give virtue to the chief's medicine;
Grant him great vigor, and let him attain health,
To worship at the *heiau* of Mahina-uli.[c]

Life through Mauli-ola! (The Maori mother says to her child, when it sneezes, "Tihe mauri ora!" sneeze, living heart!)

a b. *Hiiaka, Hiialo,* unknown places, remote and mystical. There is a suggestion in this of the ironical speech of Elijah to the priests of Baal.

c. *Mahina-uli,* a *heiau* in Kohala, at Kipahulu.

2. Sect. 3. The list of things forbidden is, I am told, such as in accordance with Molokai practice would be denied to children and young persons. If it were an adult male the red fish, *kumu,* and the *i'a kea,* mullet, would be denied to the patient. If it concerned a woman the things denied would include such articles as *ananalo* and *olali.*

3. Sect. 5. The *mua* must have been the place where the family idols were kept, where was the family shrine.

4. Sect. 7. *Pu limu*: Into the fire were thrust a number of the forbidden articles of food, and while these were burning, two men, with bunches of twigs, fanned away the smoke and flames, and then the ashes and coals, until the hearth was clean and bare. This was done as a symbol of physical and spiritual cleansing and pardon.

5. Sect. 7. The Hawaiian *imu,* oven, was a hollow in the ground lined and arched over with stones. Live steam was the cooking agent. To retain this the food was covered with leaves, mats and earth. In the case of this particular oven, *tapa* was substituted for leaves.

6. Sect. 8. *Popo kapai*: The bruised leaves of the *popolo* were made into a ball and rubbed over the abdomen of the sick man. The juice of *popolo* was also effective as a laxative.

7. Sect. 8. *Apu kalo*—The juice of the taro, being very irritant in its raw state, was mixed with the milk and juice of the cocoanut, and with sugar cane juice to make it more agreeable. The juice of *ahuawa* was sometimes added as a corroborant. It was given to relieve the malaise and distress which accompany fever.

7. Sect. 8. *Apu hui.* This was given as a febrifuge and mild laxative.

8. Sect. 10. *Hee makola. Hoomoe hou i ka hee mahola.* In this peculiar ceremony a squid, which was taken while lying spread out on the ocean bottom, was offered to the deity in the same attitude.

9. Sect. 14. *Hee mahola.* This is an instance of that confusion which prevails in the savage mind by which the name of a thing is accredited with the powers and attributes of the thing itself. Thus *hee* means squid (*i.e.,* octopus) and it also means to dissolve, disperse, put to flight. Hence its use to put to flight a disease. We find the same process of thought in enlightened minds.

10. Sect. 14. *Lono-puha,* an ancient god of healing. To him belonged particularly chronic diseases. *Puha* was an ulcer or abcess.

The following story is told me of the origin of Lono's power in medicine: In remote antiquity, Lono took upon him the human form and was a great farmer. One day while Lono was busy with his *oo* in his cultivated fields, Kane called to him, "Oh, Lono, what are you doing?" Lono stood up and, looking at Kane, thought to strike the *oo* into the ground, but instead wounded his own foot. "I have hurt my foot," said Lono. "Take of the leaves of the *popolo*," said Kane, "which you will find growing at hand and apply them as a remedy." He did so and his foot was at once made whole. From that time Lono became a skilled physician. He knew at once that the one with whom he was talking was Kane. "Yes, I am Kane, to whom you have prayed," said he in answer to the question of Lono. Kane then taught Lono the properties of medicinal plants. Lono then became the great patron of *kahuna lapaau.* Kane went away; but there were set up the *pohaku o Kane,* monoliths, which are still found from one end of the group to the other.

11. Sect. 14. *Kolea muku,* a god who healed acute diseases.

12. Sect. 10. Whatever concerns the treatment of the sick by means of sorcery, prayers to supernatural beings, and all the mystic paraphernalia of savagedom, is of such interest that I feel compelled to add the following note regarding *he'e mahola,* apropos of the Hawaiian text, *ala-ila hoomoe hou ke kahuna i ka he'e mahola,* found in section 10. This note is based on fuller information (gained from O. K. K. of Molokai).

The patient is put to bed without medicine and that night towards morning the fishermen seek to obtain a *he'e mahola.* That is an octopus which is lying on the sand, outside of its hole, with its legs extended on the ocean floor. While letting down his *leho* for the creature, the fisherman repeats the following prayer. The same prayer is likewise used by the *kahuna* when he puts the sick man to bed:

Pule Hee

E Kanaloa, ke akua o ka he'e!
Eia kau ma'i o Kalua.
E ka he'e o kai uli,
Ka he'e o ka lua one,
Ka he'e i ka papa
Ka he'e pio!
Eia ka oukou ma'i, o Kalua,
He ma'i hoomoe ia no ka he'e palaha.
Eia ka leho,
He leho ula no ka he'e-hoopai.
Eia ke kao, he laau,
He lama no ka he'e-mahola, no ka he'e-palaha.
E Kanaloa i ke ku!
Kuli'a i ke papa,
Kuli'a i ke papa he'e,
Kuli'a i ka he'e o kai uli!
E ala, e Kanaloa!
Hoeu! hoala! e ala ka he'e!
E ala ka he'e-palaha! E ala ka he'e-mahola!

O Kanaloa, god of the squid!
Here is your patient, Kalua.
O squid of the deep blue sea,
Squid that burrows in the sand,
Squid that inhabits the coral reef,
Squid that squirts water from its sack,
Here is a sick man for you to heal, Kalua by name,
A patient put to bed for treatment by the squid that lies flat.
Here is the cowry,
A red cowry to attract the squid to his death.
Here is the spear, a mere stick,
A spear of lama wood for the squid that lies flat.
O Kanaloa of the tabu nights,
Stand upright on the solid floor!
Stand upon the floor where lies the squid!
Stand up to take the squid of the deep sea!
Rise up, O Kanaloa!
Stir up! agitate! let the squid awake!
Let the squid that lies flat awake, the squid that lies spread out.

The former part of this *pule* is evidently that which is repeated over the sick man, the second part is that which is repeated when the cowry is let down into the ocean for the squid.

XXXI

Necromancy

1. Necromancy, *kilokilo uhane,* was a superstitious ceremony very much practiced in Hawaii nei. It was a system in which bare-faced lying and deceit were combined with shrewd conjecture, in which the principal extorted wealth from his victims by a process of terrorizing, averring, for instance, that he had seen the wraith of the victim, and that it was undoubtedly ominous of his impending death. By means of this sort great terror and brooding horror were made to settle on the minds of certain persons.

2. The sorcerer, *kahuna kilokilo,* would announce that the wraith or astral body of a certain one had appeared to him in spectral form, in a sudden apparition, in a vision by day, or in a dream by night.

3. Thereupon he called upon the person whose wraith he had seen and

4. Stated the case, saying, "Today, at noon, while at my place, I saw your wraith. It was clearly yourself I saw, though you were screening your eyes.

5. You were entirely naked, without even a *malo* about your loins. Your tongue was hanging out, you eyes staring wildly at me. You rushed at me and clubbed me with a stick until I was senseless. I was lucky to escape from you with my life.

6. Your *au-makua* is wroth with you on this account. Perhaps he has taken your measure and found you out, and it is probably he who is rushing you on, and has led you to this action which you were seen to commit just now.

7. Now is the proper time, if you see fit, to make peace with me, whilst your soul still tarries at the resting place of *Pu'u-kuakahi.*[1] Don't delay until your soul arrives at the brink of *Kua-ke-ahu.*[2] There is no pardon there. Thence it will plunge into *Ka-paaheo,*[2] the place of endless misery."

8. At this speech of the *kahuna kilokilo,* the man whose soul was concerned became greatly alarmed and cast down in spirit, and he consented to have the *kahuna* perform the ceremony of *kala,* atonement, for him.

9. The *kahuna* then directed the man whose soul was in danger first to procure some fish as an offering at the fire-lighting (*hoa ahi ana*). The fish to be procured were the *kala,* the *weke,* the *he'e* or octopus, the

maomao, the *palani,* also a white dog, a white fowl, awa, and ten sheets of tapa to be used as a covering for the oven.

10. When these things had been made ready the *kahuna* proceeded to perform the ceremony of lighting the fire (for the offering) that was to obtain pardon for the man's sin (*hula*).

11. The priest kept up the utterance of the incantation so long as the fire-sticks were being rubbed together; only when the fire was lighted did the incantation come to an end. The articles to be cooked were then laid in the oven, and it was covered over with the tapa.

12. When the contents of the oven were cooked and the food ready for eating, the *kahuna kilokilo* stood up and repeated the *pule kala,* or prayer for forgiveness:

> *E Ku i ke kala,*
> *E lono i kau weke kala,*
> *Weke puha ia,*
> *Kalakala i Ahuena.*
> *Kapu ka aha o ke makala au e Kane,*
> *Kala weke puha ia.*

Oh Ku, the forgiving,
Oh Lono who grants pardon,
Giving full pardon,
Undo the knot of our sins at Ahuena.
Tabu is the ceremony presided over by you Kane.
Pardon is wide and free.

13. After this prayer the one in trouble about his soul ate of the food and so did the whole assembly. This done, the *kahuna* said, "I declare the fire a good one (the ceremony perfect), consequently your sins are condoned, and your life is spared, you will not die." The *kahuna* then received his pay.

If one of the chiefs found himself to be the victim of *kilokilo,* he pursued the same plan.

14. House-building was a matter that was largely decided by incantation (*hooiloilo ia*), there were also many other matters that were controlled by the same superstition, enterprises that could not succeed without the approval of *kilokilo.*

15. The *makaula,* or prophet, was one who was reputed to be able to see a spirit, to seize[3] and hold it in his hand and then squeeze it to death.

It was claimed that a *makaula* could discern the ghost of any person, even of one whose body was buried in the most secret place.

16. The *makaula* made a spirit visible by catching it with his hands; he then put it into food and fed it to others. Any one who ate of that food would see the spirit of that person, be it of the dead or of the living. The *makaula* did not deal so extortionately with his patrons as did the *kilokilo uhane*.

17. The *makaulas* termed the spirits of living people *oio*.[4] The *oio* comprised a great number (or procession) of spirits. A single spirit was a *kakaola*. The spirit of a person already dead was termed a *kino-wailua*.

18. The *kaula*,[5] prophets or foretellers of fututre events, were supposed to possess more power than other class of *kahunas*. It was said that *Kane-nui-akea* was the deity who forewarned the *kaulas* of such important events as the death of a king (*alii ai au-puni*), or of the overthrow of a government. These prophesies were called *wanana*.

19. The *kaulas*[6] were a very eccentric class of people. They lived apart in desert places, and did not associate with people or fraternize with any one. Their thoughts were much taken up with the deity.

20. It was thought that people in delirium, frenzy, trance, or those in ecstacy (*poe hewahewa*) were inspired and that they could perceive the souls or spirits of men the same as did the *kaulas* or the *makaulas*, i.e., prophets and soothsayers. Their utterances also were taken for prophesies the same as were those of the *kaula*.

It was different, however, with crazy folks (*pupule*) and maniacs (*hehena*): they were not like prophets, soothsayers and those in a state of exaltation, i.e., the *hewahewa*. Crazy people and maniacs ate filth, and made an indecent exposure of themselves. Those in a state of exaltation, prophets and soothsayers did not act in this manner. There were many classes of people who were regarded as *hewahewa* (i.e., cranky or eccentric). This was also the case with all those who centered their thoughts on some fad or specialty—(some of them were perhaps monomaniacs)—some of them were *hewahewa* and some were not.

Notes to Chapter XXXI

1. Sect. 7. *A lele aku kou uhane ma Ka-paaheo, ma kahi make mau loa.* The notion implied in the expression, *make mau loa,* everlasting death, would seem to be an imported thought, not at all native to the Polynesian mind. It seems as if Malo had allowed his new theology to creep in and influence his statement at this place.

2. Sect. 7. Apropos of *Puu-ku-akahi, Ku-a-ke-ahu,* and *Ka-paa-heo*: If, on account of some fault or sin (*hala*), the *uhane hele*, wandering soul, became at variance with its *aumakua*, the aumakua would conduct it to the resting place or tarrying place of souls called *Puu-ku-akahi*, at which reconciliation and pardon were still possible, and if this were obtained the *aumakua* conducted it back to the body and restored it to the joys of earth. Souls frequently wandered away from the body during sleep or unconsciousness. If reconciliation was not made, it travelled on to *Ku-a-ke-ahu*, the brink of the nether world of spirits (Hades, Sheol), whence it plunged (*leina uhane*) into *Ka-paa-heo*. This was an insubstantial land of twilight and shades, a barren and waterless waste, unblest by grass, or flower, or tree, or growing herb. Here the famished ghosts of men, who fled each other's presence in fear and suspicion, strove to appease their hunger by eating butterflies, moths and lizards. This region was under the sway of *Milu*, and hence was called *ka lua o Milu*. It was from this place that Hiku rescued the ghost of his sister or bride, Kawelu (Legend of Hiku and Kawelu). Entrance to *Milu* was supposed to be gained through a pit situated in the mouth of Waipio valley, on Hawaii, also in some other places.

3. Sect. 15. The art or action of soul-catching is generally spoken of as *po'i-uhane.*

4. Sect. 17. *Oio*—this is generally used to mean a procession of the souls of the dead. Such processions are claimed to have been seen by persons now living on the road between Waimea and Hamakua ("mudlane"), on Hawaii. Apropos of the spirits of the night and of ghosts, it is said that if luau be cooked after dark it is liable to be eaten, or defiled by the touch of the foul spirits of the night, *lapu o ka po*. To guard against this it was the custom to wave a lighted candle about the dish to drive them away. The term *kino-wailua* was also applied to the second soul, which, it was alleged, sometimes wandered away from the body during sleep and got into trouble to the peril of its owner.

5. Sect. 18. *Kaula.* There seems to be some doubt whether this word is of equal antiquity with the word *makaula.** Kapihe was a noted kaula of the last century, living in Kona, Hawaii, at the time when Kamehameha was a general under Kalaniopuu. To Kapihe was ascribed the following oracular utterance (*wanana*) which is of the nature of a prophecy:

> *E iho ana o luna; e pii ana o lalo;*
> *E hui ana na moku; e ku ana ka paia.*
> That which is above shall be brought down;
> That which is below shall be lifted up;
> The islands shall be united;
> The walls shall stand upright.

Opulupulu of Waianae was another famous prophet or *makaula*. He uttered this oracular expression, *I nui ka mama, a pa i ke kai. No ke kai ka aina.* This prophecy, if so it may be called, was uttered in the time of Kahahana, and referred, perhaps, to invasion from abroad.

According to another account, or version of this same prophesy it was as follows: "E hoomanawanui a pa ka ili i ke kai; no ke kai ka aina." Like an utterance of the Delphic or Pythian oracle the meaning of this saying is not apparent.[†]

[*] By some scholars the word *maka'ula* is compounded from *maka* = eye, and *ula* = red.

[†] The term *Kaula* was used by the scholars who made the Hawaiian translation of the Bible to signify prophet.

XXXII

Concerning Obsession

(*Akua Noho*[1])

1. A spirit that enters into a person and then gives forth utterances is called an *akua noho*, that is an obsident deity, because it is believed that it takes possession of (*noho maluna*) the individual.

2. If, after death a man's bones were set in position along with an idol, and then his spirit came and made its residence with the bones, that was an *akua noho*, though specifically termed an *unihipili*[2] or an *aumakua*.[2]

3. There was a large number of deities that took possession of people and through them made utterances. *Pua* and *Kapo* were deities of this sort. What they said was not true, but some persons were deceived by the speeches they made, but not everyone.

4. *Kiha-wahine, Keawe-nui-kauo-hilo, Hia,* and *Keolo-ewa* were *akua noho* who talked.

5. *Pele* and *Hiiaka* also were *akua noho,* as well as many other deities. But the whole thing was a piece of nonsense.

6. There were many who thought the *akua noho* a fraud, but a large number were persuaded of its truth. A great many people were taken in by the trickeries of the *kahus* of these obsident gods, but not everybody.

7. The *kahus* of the shark-gods would daub themselves with something like *ihee-kai* (turmeric or ochre mixed with salt water), muffle their heads with a red, or yellow, *malo,* and then squeak and talk in an attenuated, falsetto tone of voice. By making this kind of a display of themselves and by fixing themselves up to resemble a shark, they caused great terror, and people were afraid lest they be devoured by them. Some people were completely gulled by these artifices.

8. The *kahus* of the *Pele* deities also were in the habit of dressing their hair in such a way as to make it stand out at great length, then, having inflamed and reddened their eyes, they went about begging for any articles they took a fancy to, making the threat, "If you don't grant this request Pele will devour you." Many people were imposed upon in this manner, fearing that Pele might actually consume them.

9. From the fact that people had with their own eyes seen persons bitten by sharks, solid rocks, houses and human beings melted and consumed in the fires of Pele, the terror inspired by this class of deities was much greater than that caused by the other deities.

10. The majority of people were terrified when such deities as *Pua*[3] and *Kapo*[4] took possession of them as their *kahu*, for the reason that, on account of such obsession, a person would be afflicted with a swelling of the abdomen (*opu-ohao*) which was a fatal disease. Many deaths also were caused by obstruction of the bowels (*pani*), the result of their work. It was firmly believed that such deaths were caused by this class of deities.

11. *Hiiaka*[5] caused hemorrhage from the head of the *kahu* of whom she took possession. Sometimes these deities played strange tricks when they took up their residence in any one; they would, for instance, utter a call so that the voice seemed to come from the roof of the house.

12. The offices of the *akua noho* were quite numerous. Some of them were known to have uttered predictions that proved true, so that confidence was inspired in them; others were mere liars, being termed *poo-huna-i-ke-aouli,* which merely meant tricksters (heads in the clouds).

13. Faith in the *akua noho* was not very general; there were many who took no stock in them at all. Sometimes those who were skeptical asked puzzling questions (*hoohuahua lau*) of the *akua noho,* at the same time making insulting gestures (*hoopuukahua*)—such as protruding the thumb between the fore and middle finger, or swelling out the cheek with the tongue—doing this under the cover of their tapa robe; and if the *akua noho,* i.e., the *kahuna,* perceived their insolence they argued that he was a god of power (*mana*); but if he failed to detect them they ridiculed him.

14. Others who were skeptical would wrap up some article closely in tapa and then ask the *akua noho* "what is this that is wrapped up in this bundle?" If the *akua noho* failed to guess correctly the skeptic had the laugh on the *akua noho.*

15. There was a large number, perhaps a majority of the people, who believed that these *akua noho* were utter frauds, while those who had faith in them were a minority.[6]

16. The consequence was that some of those who practiced the art of obsession, or *hoonohonoho akua,* were sometimes stoned to death, cruelly persecuted and compelled to flee away.

17 It is said that some practiced this art of *hoonohonoho akua* in order to gain the affections of some man or woman.

18. The practice of *hoonohonoho akua* was of hoary antiquity and a means of obtaining enormous influence in *Hawaii nei*.

19. Some of these miserable practices of the ancient Hawaiians were no doubt due to their devotion to worthless things (idols?)

Notes on Chapter XXXII

1. It would be an equally correct expression in Hawaiian, and would at the same time better convey to the foreign mind the idea intended, to say *hoonohonoho akua* instead of *akua noho*. Because according to the theory of obsession held by the Hawaiians themselves the role of the *akua* was ofttimes an entirely passive one, the *kahuna*, or sorcerer being the active agent; it was he who put the spirit or akua into the human body or bundle of bones by means of his incantations and *hoomanamana*, afterwards feeding him with offerings and with flattery, until he had grown powerful.

2. Sect. 2. *Unihipili, Aumakua*—While it will not do to hold too rigidly to lines of definition in dealing with such matters as *unihipili* and *aumakua*, yet it is evident that Mr. Malo does not give a clear idea as to the differences between the *unihipili* and the *aumakua*. In general an *aumakua* was an ancestral deity, whose worship and mutual service was handed down from father to son. It was, as a rule, an *akua* without an image. Ku, Kane, Kanaloa and Lono were *aumakuas* as were a host of lesser gods. A man might have several *aumakuas*. This was a useful and necessary precaution, that a man might not be left in the lurch at a critical time because the *aumakua* to whom he appealed for help might be giving ear to the prayer of some one else. The gods of Hawaii did not seem to have been able to be and do in two places at the same time.

As a safeguard against the possibility that his *aumakua*, the one on whom the *kahuna* depended to bless the herbs and simples which he gathered for use in his medical practice, might fail him the *kahuna* was wont to keep on hand a supply of these needed things on which the blessing of the *aumakua* had already been secured. Thus the *kahuna* was not left in the lurch at a critical juncture wise man!

To speak now of the *unihipili*, that was purely an artificial deity or devil rather—the work of the *kahuna* or worshipper, created by *hoomanamana*, the miraculous effect of his prayers and sacrifices.

The same person might consistently have two, or more, *unihipilis* at the same time. If one oracle was dumb he might be able to get voice from another.

The *Unihi-pili* then was a deity that was supposed to have been induced by incantation to take up its residence in an image, a dead body, or bundle of bones, and that was endowed with malignant power, *mana*, as a result of the *hoo-mana-mana*, prayers and sacrifices, that were offered to it. When the worship and offerings ceased its power and subserviency to its *kahu,* care-taker and author, came to an end. But such neglect on the part of the *kahu* was likely to result in his death from the vengeance of the offended *Unihi-pili.*

3. Sect. 10. *Pua* was a female deity, principally observed on Molokai.

4. Sect. 10. *Kapo* was also a female deity largely worshipped on Maui.

5. Sects. 8, 9, 10, 11. All of the *akua noho* mentioned by name are of the female sex.

6. Sect. 15. There were probably very few Hawaiians in ancient times who did not look with awe upon the manifestations of the *akua noho,* whatever may have been their misgivings as to the genuineness of all their pretensions.

XXXIII

THE HOUSE—ITS FURNITURE AND ITS CONSECRATION

1. The house was a most important means of securing the wellbeing of husband, wife and children, as well as of their friends and guests.

2. It was useful as a shelter from rain and cold, from sun and scorching heat. Shiftless people ofttimes lived in unsuitable houses, claiming that they answered well enough.

3. Caves, holes in the ground and overhanging cliffs were also used as dwelling places by some folks, or the hollow of a tree, or a booth. Some people again sponged on those who had houses. Such were called *o-kea-pili-mai*,[1] or *unu-pehi-iole*.[2] These were names of reproach. But that was not the way in which people of respectability lived. They put up houses of their own.

4. Their way was to journey into the mountains, and having selected the straightest trees, they felled them with an axe and brought them down as house-timber. The shorter trees were used as posts, the longer ones as rafters. The two end posts, called *pou-hana*,[3] were the tallest, their length being the same as the height of the house.

5. The posts standing alongside of the *pouhana*, called *kukuna*, rays, were not so high as the *hana*.[4] The *kaupaku*, ridge-pole, was a rafter that ran the whole length of the house. On top of the ridge-pole was lashed a pole that was called the *kua-iole*. The upright posts within the house were called *halakea*. The small sticks to which the thatch was lashed were called *a'ho*. This completes the account of the timbers and sticks of the house.

6. The house-posts, or *pou*, and the roof-beams, or *o'a*, were jointed to fit each other in the following manner. At the upper end and at the back of each post was fashioned a tenon (*wahi oioi*), and just below it and also on the back of the post, was cut a neck, leaving a chin-like projection above, called an *auwae* (chin). Corresponding to this at the lower end of each rafter, or roof-beam (*o'a*), was fashioned a mortise in the shape of a prong to receive the tenon of the post; likewise at the same end, and at the back of the rafter, was cut another chin-like projection, or *auwae*. (Fig. 2.)

The corner posts having been first planted firmly in the ground, a line was stretched from one post to another at top and bottom to bring the posts in line with each other.

The corner posts having been first planted firmly in the ground, a line was stretched from one post to another at top and bottom to bring the posts in line with each other.

8. Then the spaces between one post and another were measured and made equal, and all the posts on one side were firmly planted; then those on the other side; after which the plate, or *lohelau*, of the frame was laid on top of the posts from one corner post to another.

9. The posts were then lashed to the plates, *lohelau*, after which the tall posts at each end of the house, *pouhana*, were set up. This done, the *kau-paku*, ridge-pole, was laid in its place and lashed firmly with cord, and then the posts called *halakea*, uprights that supported the ridge-pole, were set in place. After this the rafters, or *o'a*, were laid in position and measured to see at what length they must be cut off.

10. The rafters were then taken down and cut to the proper length. A neck having been worked at the upper end of each rafter, they were lashed firmly in position, after which the *kua-iole*, a sort of supplementary ridge-pole, was fastened above the real ridge-pole.

11. The different parts of the frame were now bound together with cord, and the small poles, called *aho*,[5] on which to bind the thatch, were lashed in place. This done, the work of putting on the thatching was begun. The thatch was sometimes of *pili* grass, sometimes sugar-cane leaves, and sometimes the leaves of the *ti* plant, according to circumstances.[6]

12. The next thing was to thatch and bonnet the ridge-pole, after which the opening for a doorway was made, and the door itself was constructed. In making a door the top and bottom pieces were rabbetted along the edge, and then the ends of the boards were set into the grooves.

13. Holes were drilled through the end along the groove with a drill of human bone, into which holes wooden pegs were then driven. The middle part was sewed together with cord. The door-frame was then constructed, having a grooved piece above and below in which the door was to slide. After this a fence, or *pa*, was put up to surround the house and its grounds.

14. On the completion of this part of the work, the *kahuna pule*, or priest was sent for to offer the prayer at the ceremony of trimming the thatch over the door. This prayer was called the *pule kuwa*,[7] and

when it had been recited the man entered into his house and occupied it without further ado (*me ka oluolu*).

15. It was the custom among all respectable people, the chiefs, the wealthy, those in good standing (*koikoi*) and in comfortable circumstances to have their houses consecrated with some religious ceremony before living in them.

16. People who were of no account (*lapuwale*) did not follow this practice. They went in and occupied their houses without any such ceremony. Such folks only cared for a little shanty, anyway; the fire-place was close to their head, and the *poi*-dish conveniently at hand; and so, with but one house, they made shift to get along.

17. People who were well off, however, those of respectability, of character, persons of wealth or who belonged to the *alii* class, sought to do everything decorously and in good style; they had separate[8] houses for themselves and for their wives.

18. There was a special house for the man to sleep in with his wife and children (*hale noa*), also a number of houses specially devoted to different kinds of work, including one for the wife to do her work in (*hale kua*). There was the *halau*, or canoe-house, the *aleo*[9] a kind of garret or upper story, in which to stow things, also the *amana*, consisting of three houses built about a court.

19. This way of living corresponded with what the Hawaiians regarded as decent and respectable.

20. The bowls and dishes, *ipu*, used by the ancient Hawaiians in house-keeping were either of wood or of gourd (*pohue*).

21. Those who were skilled in the art carved bowls and dishes out of different woods; but the *kou* was the wood generally used for this purpose. After the log had been fashioned on the outside it was either deeply hollowed out as a calabash, or *umcke*, or as a shallow dish or platter, an *ipukai*, to hold fish—or meat. A cover also was hollowed out to put over the *ipukai* and the work was done.

22. The dish was then rubbed smooth within and without with a piece of coral, or with rough lava (*oahi*), then with pumice, or a stone called *oio*. After this charcoal was used, then bamboo-leaf, and lastly it was polished with bread-fruit leaf and *tapa*—the same was done to the cover, and there was your dish. Sometimes a *koko* or net, was added as a convenient means of holding and carrying, and the work was then complete. The *umeke* was used for holding *poi* and vegetable food (*ai*), the *ipukai* to hold meats and fish (*ia*).

23. The calabash, or *pohue,* was the fruit of a vine that was specially cultivated. Some were of a shape suited to be *umeke,* or *poi* containers, others *ipukai,* and others still to be used as *huewai* or water-containers. The pulp on the inside of the gourd was bitter; but there was a kind that was free from bitterness. The soft pulp within was first scraped out; later, when the gourd had been dried, the inside was rubbed and smoothed with a piece of coral or pumice, and thus the calabash was completed. A cover was added and a net sometimes put about it.

24. In preparing a water-gourd, or *hue-wai,* the pulp was first rotted, then small stones were shaken about in it, after which it was allowed to stand with water in it till it had become sweet.

25. Salt was one of the necessaries and was a condiment used with fish and meat, also as a relish with fresh food. Salt was manufactured only in certain places. The women brought sea-water in calabashes or conducted it in ditches to natural holes, hollows, and shallow ponds (*kaheka*) on the sea-coast, where it soon became strong brine from evaporation. Thence it was transferred to another hollow, or shallow vat, where crystallization into salt was completed.

26. The *papalaau* was a board on which to pound *poi.*

27. Water, which was one of the essentials of a meal, to keep one from choking or being burned with hot food, was generally obtained from streams (and springs), and sometimes by digging wells.

28. Vegetables (*ai*), animal food (*i'a*), salt and water—these are the essentials for the support of man's system.

29. Sharks' teeth were the means employed in Hawaii nei for cutting the hair. The instrument was called *niho-ako-lauoho.* The shark's tooth was firmly bound to a stick, then the hair was bent over the tooth and cut through with a sawing motion. If this method caused too much pain another resource was to use fire.

30. For mirrors the ancient Hawaiians used a flat piece of wood highly polished, then darkened with a vegetable stain and some earthy pigment. After that, on being thrust into the water, a dim reflection was seen by looking into it. Another mirror was made of stone. It was ground smooth and used after immersion in water.

31. The cocoanut leaf was the fan of the ancient Hawaiians, being braided flat. An excellent fan was made from the *loulu*-palm leaf. The handle was braided into a figured pattern. Such were the comforts of the people of Hawaii nei. How pitiable!

32. There are a great many improvements now-a-days. The new thing in houses is to build them of stone laid in mortar—mortar is made of lime mixed with sand. In some houses the stones are laid simply in mud.

33. There are wooden houses covered with boards, and held together with iron nails; there are also adobe houses (*lepo i omoo-mo ia*); and houses made of cloth. Such are the new styles of houses introduced by the foreigners (*haole*).

34. For new dishes and containers, *ipu,* we have those made of iron, *ipuhao,* and of earthenware or china, *ipu keokeo.* But some of the new kinds of ware are not suited to fill the place of the *umeke* or calabash.

35. The new instrument for hair-cutting which the *haole* has introduced is of iron; it is called an *upa,* scissors or shears (literally to snap, to open, or to shut); a superior instrument this. There are also new devices in fans that will open and shut; they are very good.

36. The newly imported articles are certainly superior to those of ancient times.

Notes on Chapter XXXIII

1. Sect. 3. *O-kea-pili-mai,* sand that collects about a thing.

2. Sect. 3. *Unu-pehi-iole,* a stone or shard to throw at a rat, a thing of no consequence.

3. Sect. 4. *Pou-hana,* the name applied to the two upright posts situated one at each gable of the house, which supported the ends of the ridgepole. *Pou-hana* was used almost as a title of distinction in ancient *meles* and *pules,* indicating that it was regarded with almost superstitious reverence, probably at one time being looked upon as a *kupua,* or deity. Like the other posts of the Hawaiian house, they were firmly planted in the ground; they also inclined slightly inward.

The *pou-hana* stood detached from the other sticks in the frame of the house, save that it was lashed at its top to the *kaupaku* and *kua-iole.*

4. Sect. 5. When the two *hana* posts had been set in the ground, one at each end of the house, the next thing was to lash the ridge-pole, or *kaupaku,* from the head of one *hana* to the other. To facilitate this lashing, a neck was cut at the top of each *hana* as well as the *kaupaku.*

5. Sect. 11. *Aho,* small sticks, saplings, which were bound across horizontally on the outside of the posts and rafters of the house, and to which the thatching was lashed.

6. Sect. 11. The best thatch used by the Hawaiians was *pili* grass; next came the leaf of the pandanus, *lau-hala;* then the leaf of the sugar-cane, and lastly the *ti* leaf, and a number of inferior grasses.

7. Sect. 14. Of the prayer called *kuwa* there were undoubtedly different forms used on the different islands and by the different priests. This remark is true not merely of this service but of nearly every service and prayer that can be mentiioned.

The *kahuna* stood on the outside of the house, ax in hand, and holding a block under the thatch to obtain a solid object on which his blow should fall, he timed the strokes of his ax to the cadence of the prayer. Having inquired of the house-owner if everything was ready, and if it was his wish to proceed with the ceremony, and having received an affirmative answer, the kahuna began the utterance of his prayer, and at the same time let his ax fall on the thatch, suiting the time of his blow to the cadence of his utterance.

> *Ku lalani ka pule a Kcoloalu i ke akua,*
> *O Kuwa wahi'a i ke piko o ka hale o Mea.*
> *A ku! A wa! A moku ka piko,**
> *A moku, a moku iho la!*

Orderly and harmonious is the prayer of the multitude to God.
Kuwa cuts now the *piko* of the house of Mea.
He stands! He cuts! The thatch is cut!
It is cut! Lo it is cut!

* This beautiful ceremony, as indicated in the prayer itself, was generally known as *ka oki ana o ka piko o ka hale,* the cutting of the navel string of the house. It is more easy to imagine than to describe the analogy between the cutting of a child's umbilical cord and the trimming of the thatch over the doorway of a new house. The completion of this symbolical ceremony was the signal for feasting by the whole company.

8. Sect. 17. Every self-respecting Hawaiian who desired to live up to the system of *tabu* was obliged to build for himself and family a number of houses, the chief motive being to separate the sexes entirely from each other while eating, as well as to provide suitable places for carrying on the various occupations incident to a self-sustaining savage life. First may be mentioned the *mua*, which was the men's eating house and was *tabu* to females; second the *hale noa*, which was the one place where the family mingled on familiar terms during the day and where they slept at night; third, the *hale ai'na*, the women's eating house, which was *tabu* to the men. If the woman of the house was given to that sort of thing, she must have. 4th, a *hale kua*, which was the place in which she would beat out tapa, braid mats, and carry on a variety of domestic arts. 5th, the *hale pea*, a place where the women isolated themselves during their monthly periods of impurity. To these might be added. 6th, a family chapel, or *heiau*, the place of which was in most cases probably filled by the *mua*. The family *heiau* seems in some cases to have been a simple enclosure, unroofed, open to the elements. The practice in this regard evidently differed in different

places. No fixed and fast rules can be laid down. If the man of the house were a fisherman, he would naturally have a *halau*, a long house or shed in which to house his canoe and fishing tackle.

9. Sect. 18. *Alco*: Hawaiian houses were built with but one story, but a sort of garret was sometimes made by flooring a certain space with some sort of lattice-work (*hulili ia*) in the upper part of the house. This was called an *aleo* and here it was that a man might keep his treasures, spears, weapons and family heir-looms.

The ceremony of *oki ana ka piko o ka hale* was performed only after the house was completely furnished and ready for habitation. On the Island of Molokai the following prayer was used on such an occasion, being repeated while the priest was cutting the long thatch that overhung the doorway, and which was called the piko or umbiblical cord:

> *A moku ka piko i ele-ua, i ele-ao,*
> *I ka wai i Haakula-manu la.*
> *E moku!*
> *A moku ka piko o kou hale la,*
> *E Mauli-ola!*
> *I ola i ka noho-hale,*
> *I ola i ke kanaka kipa mai,*
> *I ola i ka haku-aina,*
> *I ola i na 'lii,*
> *Oia ke ola o kau hale, e Mauli-ola;*
> *Ola a kolo-pupu, a haumaka-iole,*
> *A pala-lau-hala, a ka i koko.*
> > *Amama, ua noa.*

Severed is the *piko* of the house, the thatch that sheds the rain, that wards
  off the evil influences of the heavens,
The water-spout of Haakula-manu, oh!
Cut now!
Cut the *piko* of your house, *o Mauli-ola!*
That the house-dweller may prosper,
That the guest who enters it may have health,
That the lord of the land may have health,
That the chiefs may have long life.
Grant these blessings to your house, *o Mauli-ola.*
To live till one crawls hunched up, till one becomes blear-eyed,
Till one lies on the mat, till one has to be carried about in a net.
> Amen. It is free.

(a) Line 1—*Ele-ua*: The root-word *ele* means to protect; hence to shed *ua*, rain. The outside, protecting leaf that covered the *pai-ai*, bundle of hard *poi*, was called *la-ele* (*la* is a contraction from *lau*, leaf).

(b) Line 1—*Ele-ao*: Warding off the (evil) influences of the clouds, *ao*.

(c) Line 2—*Haakula-manu,* a water spout, a cloud-burst, a destructive fall of rain, idealized into a demi-god, a *kupua*.

(d) Line 10—*Mauli-ola,* a *kupua,* i.e., a superhuman power, a personification of health, something like Hygeia.

Fig. 1.
Interior View of Gable of Hawaiian House.

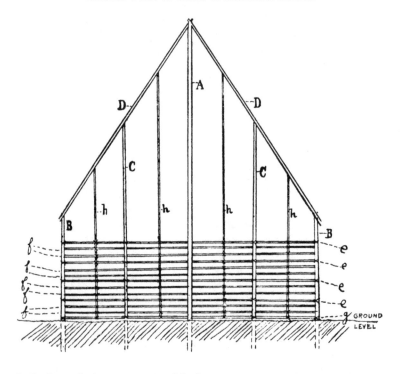

A, *Pouhana,* the important post of the house.

B, *Pou-kihi,* corner post.

C, *Kukuna,* or *Pou-kukuna.*   (*kukuna* : :ray).

D, *O'a,* rafter.

e, *Aho-pueo,* the *aho* were small sticks to which the thatch was lashed. At short intervals an *aho* of a somewhat larger size than the average was introduced. This was called an *aho-pueo* (pueo : :owl).

f, *Aho-kele, an aho* of the average size, generally spoken of as an *aho*.

h, *Aho-hu'i, an aho* lashed on outside and vertically, to hold the *ahos* fast.

Fig. 2.

Showing Tenon and Mortise joining Rafters, *oa*, of Roof to the Uprights, *Pou*, of the side of the house, also Ridge-pole, etc., in section.

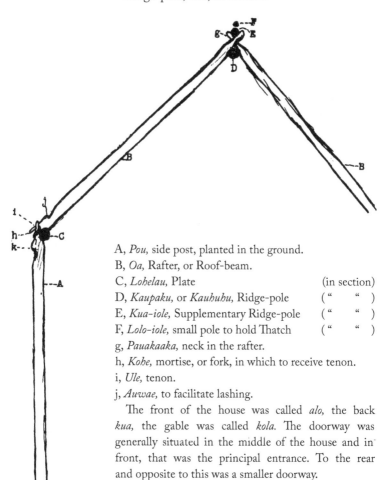

A, *Pou*, side post, planted in the ground.

B, *Oa*, Rafter, or Roof-beam.

C, *Lohelau*, Plate (in section)

D, *Kaupaku*, or *Kauhuhu*, Ridge-pole ("   ")

E, *Kua-iole*, Supplementary Ridge-pole ("   ")

F, *Lolo-iole*, small pole to hold Thatch ("   ")

g, *Pauakaaka*, neck in the rafter.

h, *Kohe*, mortise, or fork, in which to receive tenon.

i, *Ule*, tenon.

j, *Auwae*, to facilitate lashing.

The front of the house was called *alo*, the back *kua*, the gable was called *kola*. The doorway was generally situated in the middle of the house and in front, that was the principal entrance. To the rear and opposite to this was a smaller doorway.

XXXIV

The Hawaiian Canoe

1. The Hawaiian *wa'a*, or canoe, was made of the wood of the *koa* tree. From the earliest times the wood of the bread-fruit, *kukui, ohia-ha*, and *wiliwili* was used in canoe-making, but the extent to which these woods were used for this purpose was very limited. The principal wood used in canoe-making was always the *koa*. (*Acacia heterophylla*.)

2. The building of a canoe was an affair of religion. When a man found a fine *koa* tree he went to the *kahuna kalai wa'a* and said, "I have found a *koa* tree, a fine large tree." On receiving this information the *kahuna* went at night to the *mua*,[1] to sleep before his shrine, in order to obtain a revelation from his deity in a dream as to whether the tree was sound or rotten.

3. And if in his sleep that night he had a vision of some one standing naked before him, a man without a *malo*, or a woman without a *pau*, and covering their shame with the hand, on awakening the *kahuna* knew that the *koa* in question was rotten (*pupa*), and he would not go up into the woods to cut that tree.

4. He sought another tree, and having found one, he slept again in the *mua* before the altar, and if this time he saw a handsome, well dressed man or woman, standing before him, when he awoke he felt sure that the tree would make a good canoe.

5. Preparations were made accordingly to go into the mountains and hew the *koa* into a canoe. They took with them, as offerings, a pig, cocoanuts, red fish (*kumu*), and *awa*.

Having come to the place they camped down for the night, sacrificing these things to the gods with incantations (*hoomana*) and prayers, and there they slept.

6. In the morning they baked the hog in an oven made close to the root of the *koa*, and after eating the same they examined the tree. One of the party climbed up into the tree to measure the part suitable for the hollow of the canoe, where should be the bottom, what the total length of the craft.

7. Then the *kahuna* took the ax of stone and called upon the gods:

"*O Ku-pulupulu*,[2] *Ku-ala-na-wao*,[3] *Ku-moku-halii*,[4] *Ku-ka-ieie*,[5] *Ku-palalake*,[6] *Ku-ka-ohia-laka*."[7]—These were the male deties. Then he called upon the female deities:

"O Lea[8] and Ka-pua-o-alaka'i,[9] listen now to the ax. This is the ax that is to fell the tree for the canoe." . . .

8. The *koa* tree was then cut down, and they set about it in the following manner: Two scarfs were made about three feet apart, one above and one below, and when they had been deepened, the chips were split off in a direction lengthwise of the tree.

9. Cutting in this way, if there was but one *kahuna*, it would take many days to fell the tree; but if there were many *kahunas*, they might fell it the same day. When the tree began to crack to its fall, they lowered their voices and allowed no one to make a disturbance.

10. When the tree had fallen, the head *kahuna* mounted upon the trunk, ax in hand, facing the stump, his back being turned toward the top of the tree.

11. Then in a loud tone he called out, "Smite with the ax and hollow the canoe! Give me the *malo!*"[10] Thereupon the *kahuna's* wife handed him his ceremonial *malo,* which was white; and, having girded himself, he turned about and faced the head of the tree.

12. Then having walked a few steps on the trunk of the tree, he stood and called out in a loud voice, "Strike with the ax and hollow it! Grant us a canoe!"[11] Then he struck a blow with the ax on the tree, and repeated the same words again; and so he kept on doing until he had reached the point where the head of the tree was to be cut off.

13. At the place where the head of the tree was to be severed from the trunk he wreathed the tree with *ie-ie.* Then having ered from the trunk he wreathed the tree with *ie-ie,* (*Freycinetia Scandens*). Then having repeated a prayer appropriate to cutting off the top of the tree, and having again commanded silence and secured it, he proceeded to cut off the top of the tree. This done, the *kahuna* declared the ceremony performed, the tabu removed; thereupon the people raised a shout at the successful performance of the ceremony, and the removal of all tabu and restraint in view of its completion.

14. Now began the work of hewing out the canoe, the first thing being to taper the tree at each end, that the canoe might be sharp at stem and stern. Then the sides and bottom (*kua-moo*) were hewn down and the top was flattened (*hola*). The inner parts of the canoe were then planned and located by measurement.

15. The *kahuna* alone planned out and made the measurements for the inner parts of the canoe. But when this work was accomplished the

restrictions were removed and all the craftsmen took hold of the work (*noa ka oihana o ka waa*).

16. Then the inside of the canoe was outlined and the *pepeiao,* brackets, on which to rest the seats, were blocked out, and the craft was still further hewn into shape. A *maku'u,*[12] or neck, was wrought at the stern of the canoe, to which the lines for hauling the canoe were to be attached.

17. When the time had come for hauling the canoe down to the ocean again came the *kahuna* to perform the ceremony called *pu i ka wa'a,* which consisted in attaching the hauling lines to the canoe-log. They were fastened to the *maku'u.* Before doing this the *kahuna* invoked the gods in the following prayer:

"*O Ku-pulupulu, Ku-ala-na-wao,* and *Ku-moku-halii!* look you after this canoe. Guard it from stem to stern until it is placed in the *halau.*" After this manner did they pray.

18. The people now put themselves in position to haul the canoe. The only person who went to the rear of the canoe was the *kahuna,* his station being about ten fathoms behind it. The whole multitude of the people went ahead, behind the *kahuna* no one was permitted to go; that place was tabu, strictly reserved for the god of the *kahuna kalai wa'a.*

Great care had to be taken in hauling the canoe. Where the country was precipitous and the canoe would tend to rush down violently, some of the men must hold it back lest it be broken; and when it got lodged some of them must clear it. This care had to be kept up until the canoe had reached the *halau,* or canoehouse.

21. In the *halau* the fashioning of the canoe was resumed. First the upper part was shaped and the gunwales were shaved down; then the sides of the canoe from the gunwales down were put into shape. After this the mouth (*waha*) of the canoe was turned downwards and the *iwi kaele,* or bottom, being exposed, was hewn into shape. This done, the canoe was again placed mouth up and was hollowed out still further (*kupele maloko*). The outside was then finished and rubbed smooth (*anai ia*). The outside of the canoe was next painted black (*paele ia*).[13] Then the inside of the canoe was finished off by means of the *koi-owili,* or reversible adze (commonly known as the *kupa-ai ke'e*).

22. After that were fitted on the carved pieces (*na laau*) made of *ahakea* or some other wood. The rails, which were fitted on to the gunwales and which were called *mo'o* (lizards) were the first to be fitted and sewed fast with sinnet or *aha.*

The carved pieces, called *manu*, at bow and stern, were the next to be fitted and sewed on, and this work completed the putting together of the body of the canoe (*ke kapili ana o ka waa*). It was for the owner to say whether he would have a single or double canoe.

23. If it was a single canoe or *kaukahi*, (cross-pieces), or *iako* and a float, called *ama*, were made and attached to the canoe to form the outrigger.

The ceremony of *lolo-waa*, consecrating the canoe, was the next thing to be performed in which the deity was again approached with prayer. This was done after the canoe had returned from an excursion out to sea.

24. The canoe was then carried into the *halau*, where were lying the pig, the red fish, and the cocoanuts that constituted the offering spread out before the *kahuna*. The *kahuna kalai-waa* then faced towards the bows of the canoe, where stood its owner, and said, "Attend now to the consecration of the canoe (*lolo ana o ka waa*), and observe whether it be well or ill done." Then he prayed:

25.   *O Ku-wa*[14] *o ka lani, o Ku-wa o ka honua,*
        O Ku-wa o ka mauna, o Ku-wa o ka moana,
        O Ku-wa o ka po, o Ku-wa o ke ao,
        O Malualani ke Ku-wa, o Malua-hopu ke Ku-wa,
        Aia no ia ko'i la ke Ku-wa.
        Ka wa'a nei o ka luahine makua.
        Ka luahine! Owai?
        O ka luahine o Papa, wahine a Wakea.
        Nana i kuwa,[15] *nana i hainu,*
        Nana i hele, nana i a'e,
        Nana i hoonoanoa.
        Noa ke kuwa[16] *o ka wa'a o Wakea.*

26.   *O ka wa'a nei o ka luahine makua.*
        Ka luahine! Owai?
        Ka luahine o Lea, wahine a Moku-halii.
        Nana i kuwa, nana i hainu,
        Nana i hele, nana i a'e,
        Nana i hoonoanoa.
        Noa ke kuwa o ka wa'a o Mokuhalii.
        Hinu helelei aku,
        Hinu helelei mai.
        He miki oe Kane,

He miki oe Kanaloa.
O Kanaloa hea oe?
O Kanaloa inu awa.
Mai Kahiki ka awa,
Mai Upolu ka awa,
Mai Wawau ka awa.
E hano awa hua,
E hano awa pauaka.
Halapa i ke akua i laau wai la.
Amama, ua noa.
Lele wale aku la.

25.   Uplifter of the heavens, uplifter of the earth,
Uplifter of the mountains, uplifter of the ocean,
Who hast appointed the night, appointed the day,
Malualani is the Kuwa and Maluahopu,
That ax also is a kuwa.
This is the ax of our venerable ancestral dame.
Venerable dame! What dame?
Dame Papa, the wife of Wakea.
She set apart and consecrated, she turned the tree about,
She impelled it, she guided it,
She lifted the tabu from it.
Gone is the tabu from the canoe of Wakea.
The canoe this of our ancestral dame.
Ancestral dame! What dame?
Dame Lea, wife of Moku-halii;
She initiated, she pointed the canoe;
She started it, she guided it;
She lifted the tabu from it,
Lifted was the tabu from the canoe of Wakea.
Fat dripping here;
Fat dripping there.
Active art thou Kane;
Active art thou Kanaloa.
What Kanaloa art thou?
Kanaloa the awa-drinker.
Awa from Tahiti,
Awa from Upolu,
Awa from Wawau.

Bottle up the frothy awa,
Bottle up the well strained awa.
Praise be to the God in the highest heaven (laau)!
The tabu is lifted, removed.
It flies away.

28. When the kahuna had finished his prayer he asked of the owner of the canoe, "How is this service, this service of ours?" Because if any one had made a disturbance or noise, or intruded upon the place, the ceremony had been marred and the owner of the canoe accordingly would then have to report the ceremony to be imperfect. And the priest would then warn the owner of the canoe, saying, "Don't you go in this canoe lest you meet with a fatal accident."

29. If, however, no one had made a disturbance or intruded himself while they had been performing the *lolo*[17] ceremony, the owner of the canoe would report "our spell is good" and the kahuna would then say, "You will go in this canoe with safety, because the spell is good" (*maikai ka lolo ana*).

30. If the canoe was to be rigged as part of a double canoe the ceremony and incantations to be performed by the kahuna were different. In the double canoe the *iakos* used in ancient times were straight sticks. This continued to be the case until the time of *Keawe*[18], when one Kanuha invented the curved *iako* and erected the upright posts of the the *pola*.

31. When it came to making the lashings for the outrigger of the canoe, this was a function of the utmost solemnity. If the lashing was of the sort called *kumu-hele*, or *kumu-pou* it was even then tabu; but if it was of the kind called *kaholo*, or *Luukia* (full name *pa-u o Luukia*), these kinds, being reserved for the canoes of royalty, were regarded as being in the highest degree sacred, and to climb upon the canoe, or to intrude at the time when one of these lashings was being done, was to bring down on one the punishment of death.

32. When the lashings of the canoe were completed a covering of mat was made for the canoe (for the purpose of keeping out the water) which mat was called a *pa-u*[24].

The mast (*pou* or *kia*) was set up in the starboard canoe, designated as *ekea*, the other one being called *ama*. The mast was stayed with lines attached to its top. The sail of the canoe, which was called *la*, was made from the leaves of the pandanus, which were plaited together, as in mat-making.

33. The canoe was furnished with paddles, seats, and a bailer. There were many varieties of the *waa*. There was a small canoe called *kioloa*.[19]

A canoe of a size to carry but one person was called a *koo-kahi,* if to carry two a *koo-lua,* if three a *koo-kolu,* and so on to the the *koo-walu* for eight.

34. The single canoe was termed a *kau-kahi,* the double canoe a *kau-lua.* In the time of Kamehameha I a triple canoe named *Kaena-kane,* was constructed, such a craft being termed a *pu-kolu.* If one of the canoes in a double canoe happened to be longer than its fellow, the composite craft was called a *ku-e-e.*

35. In case the carved bow-piece, *manu-ihu,* was made very broad the canoe was called a *lele-iwi.*[20] (See fig. 2.) A canoe that was short and wide was called a *pou.* Canoes were designated and classified after some peculiarity. If the bow was very large the canoe would be termed *ihu-nui;*[22] one kind was called *kupeulu.*

36. In the reign of Kamehameha I were constructed the canoes called *peleleu.*[23] They were excellent craft and carried a great deal of freight. The after part of these crafts were similar in construction to an ordinary vessel (i.e. was decked over). It was principally by means of such craft as these that Kamehameha succeeded in transporting his forces to Oahu when he went to take possession of that part of his dominion when he was making his conquests.

37. In these modern times new kinds of sea-going craft have multiplied, large, fine vessels they are, which we call *moku* (an island, a piece cut off).

38. A ship was like a section of the earth quietly moving through the water. On account of their great size, when the first ships arrived here, people flocked from remote districts to view them. Great were the benefits derived from these novel craft, the like of which had never been seen before.

39. Some of these vessels, or *moku,* were three-masted, some two-masted, some schooner-rigged, and some had but one mast.

40. The row boat, or *waa-pa* (*waa-pa'a*), is one of this new kind of craft. But even some of these new vessels, including row-boats, sometimes perish at sea.

41. It is not, however, so common an occurrence for this to happen to them as it used to be for canoes to founder in every part of this ocean.

42. Many blessings have come to this race through these new sea-going craft. It was by them the word of God was conveyed to these shores, which is a blessing greater than any sought for by the ancients.

43. What a pity that the ancients did not know of this new blessing, of the word of God and the great salvation through Jesus the blessed Redeemer.

Notes on Chapter XXXIV

1. Sect. 2. *Hele oia i mua ma ka po e hoomoe ma kona heiau.* This passage confirms the statement made in the notes to Chap. XXXIII, p. 123, that the family *heiau,* or shrine, was probably in some part of the *mua.* The references made by Mr. Malo in this book to the *mua* as a place to which the *kahuna,* or any one desiring to consult his *aumakua,* or to receive warning or council from heaven in a dream, would go to spend the night, these references, I say, are so numerous that there seems to be no doubt that the *mua* and the *heiau* were integrally one. At the same time I am assured that the family *heiau* was ofen an open-air, unroofed enclosure. No doubt the practice in this matter was as various as in some others, in regard to which uniformity has been claimed. It must not be forgotten that two swallows do not make a summer.

2. Sect. 7. *Ku-pulupulu,* Ku, the rough one or the chip-maker, one of the gods of the waa.

3. Sect. 7. *Ku-ala-na-wao,* Ku-ae-la-na-wao, there stand the forests, a woodland deity, one of the gods of the waa.

4. Sect. 7. *Ku-moku-hali'i,* Ku that bedecks the island.

5. Sect. 7. *Ku-ka-ieie,—Ieie* was a parasitic evergreen much used in decorating.

6. Sect. 7. *Ku-palala-ke,* or *Kupa-ai-kee,* the reversible ax, used by the Hawaiians in hollowing the canoe.

7. Sect. 7. *Ku-ka-ohia-laka,—*The *ohia* tree was used in making idols. **Laka* was the mythical hero who made the famous canoe in which he went in search of his father's bones. He was one of the gods of the *wa'a.*

* This derivation is incorrect. Sec note 5, Chapter XXIII. *Laka* = the Tahitan name for the *lehua* tree.

8. Sect. 7. *Lea,* wife of (*Ku*) *Moku-halii,* was a patroness of the canoe. She was supposed to appear in the form of the wood-pecker, *elepaio,* whose movements when she walked upon the newly felled tree were attentively observed, and were ominous of good, or ill, luck. *Lea* seems to have been the same as Laia.

9. Sect. 7. *Ka-pua-o-alakai:* The more correct orthography is probably *Ka-pu-o-alakai,* the knot of guidance, i.e., the knot by which the hauling line was attached to the *maku'u,* q. v. sect. 16.

10. Sect. 11. *"E ku a ca! Homai he malo!"* A Molokai authority informs me that on that island the variant to this prayer was:

E ku a ea! Eia ka waa, he iho-ole pau-lua.
E ala, e ku, e hume i kou malo!

Stand up in your strength! Here is the canoe, a solid log without pith. Arise, stand up, gird on your malo!

His wife then gave him his sacerdotal *malo,* with the words:

> *Eia kou malo la, he malo keokeo.*
> Here is your *malo,* your white *malo.*

11. Sect. 12. According to the same Molokai practice the words uttered by the *kahuna* when he struck up the tree were:

> *Homai he wa'a, e ku a i'a!*
> *He wa e ulu.**
> *Ulu i ka aoao a nui.*

> Grant a canoe that shall be swift as a fish!
> To sail in stormy seas,
> When the storm tosses on all sides!

* *Ulu:* literally to grow, derivatively to kick up a storm.

12. Sect. 16. *Maku'u:* This was also called the *moamoa,* or *mo-moa,* and on the island of Molokai it was called *pau-akaaka.* The *momoa* was at the stern of the canoe. In every genuine Hawaiian canoe of the old fashion the *maku'u* is still clearly visible.

13. Sect. 21. This Hawaiian paint had almost the quality of a lacquer. Its ingredients were the juice of a certain euphorbia, the juice of the inner bark of the root of the *kukui* tree, the juice of the bud of the banana tree, together with charcoal made from the leaf of the pandanus. A dressing of oil from the nut of the *kukui* was finally added to give a finish. I can vouch for it as an excellent covering for wood.

14. Sect. 25. The meaning of the word *kuwa,* or *ku-wa,* here translated by uplifter, is involved in some doubt and obscurity. In opposition to the orthography of Mr. Malo, which, as often remarked, is anything but orthodox, and cannot be depended upon, I have ventured to unite the two parts and make of them one word.

In chapter XXXIII, section 14, the prayer uttered by the *kahuna* at the finishing and consecration of the house, symbolized by the trimming of the thatch over the doorway, was called *pule kuwa.* (See note to Chap. XXXIII.) As explained, the term *kuwa* is applied to that prayer because while performing the act and reciting the prayer the *kahuna* stood—*ku*—in the space—*wa*—of the doorway.

The opening words of the prayer, according to David Malo, are,

> *O ku wa o ka lani, o ku wa o ka honua.*

After diligent study and inquiry I am convinced that the correct orthography is *kuwa* or perhaps *ku-wa,* if one pleases, and that its meaning has reference to the lifting up of the heavens, the putting of a space between the heavens and the earth. This is a matter that is very prominent in the mythology of southern Polynesia.

NOTE.—The word *wa* in many of its uses is evidently intended to express the idea of interval, and *ku-wa* probably means in some instances to set in order, to place at orderly intervals. Another meaning is an echo. A derivative, secondary meaning is to set apart, consecrate.—N. B. E.

15. Sect. 25. *Nana i kuwa. . . kuwa* is here used as a verb. Among the various hypotheses that have been considered in the attempt to define the meaning of this multi-meaning word was that of hollowing out the canoe, thus putting a *wa* between one side and another of the canoe (*wa'a*). It seems, however, as if the most reasonable and obvious meaning—when once it is pointed out—is that of consecraating and setting apart the *wa'a*, making it ready for its use.

16. Sect. 25. *Noa ke kuwa o ka wa'a a Wakea.* The meaning of the word *kuwa* in this connection is slightly different in this passage from the one previously assigned to it. Here it evidently refers to the function of consecration now being performed by the priest. I have endeavored to express that meaning in my translation.

17. Sect. 29. *Lolo* ceremony: The expression in the text is *maikai ka lolo ana.* When a priest, or canoe-maker, or *hula*-dancer, or practitioner of any profession or art has acquired the greatest preliminary skill, before beginning the practice of his new art, or profession, he is by means of certain incantations and peculiar rites put to a test, and if he comes out successfully it is said *ua ai lolo,* that is, he has eaten brains, acquired great skill. The *lolo* ceremony is not merely a bestowing of good luck on the craft, it is rather an inquiry of heaven as to the fate or luck in store for the canoe.

18. Sect. 30. Keawe II, whose son Kanuha built the hale o Keawe, was of the last quarter of the 17th century. (See "Brief History of the Hawaiian People" by W. D. Alexander, p. 46).

19. Sect. 33. The *kio-loa* was a long, narrow canoe, principally used for racing.

20. Sect. 35. The classic model of the *manu,* the carved piece which adorned the bow and the stern of every worthy Hawaiian *waa,* a form which has been handed down to modern times, was as shown in Fig. 1; the model of the *lele-iwi* is as shown in Fig. 2. The *lele-iwi* canoe was principally for display, *hanonano.*

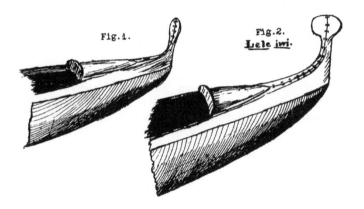

Fig. 1.

Fig. 2.
Lele iwi.

21. Sect. 31. *Pa-u o Luukia:* This was a highly decorative lashing by which the *iako* was bound to the canoe. *Luukia* was a famous beauty, who, though wife to another man, so fascinated *Moikeha,* a king of Hawaii, that he sailed with her to Tahiti. One of her would-be lovers, hoping to win her favor by alienating her against Moikeha, cunningly slandered that prince to Luukia. He so far succeeded that he aroused in her an aversion to the young man. As a consequence she sought to defend herself against the further approaches of her royal lover by wearing about her loins some sort of woven corset or *pa-u.* Hence the term *pa-u o Luukia,* corset or skirt of Luukia, applied by the old salts, canoe-men, of the sixteenth century to the most aesthetic and decorative style of canoe-lashing employed.

22. Sect. 35. In this kind of a canoe the bow, contrary to usual practice, was made at the butt end of the log. It was usually put at the small end.

23. Sect. 36. The *peleleu* were a fleet of very large war-canoes which Kamehameha I had made from koa trees felled in the forests back of Hilo, Hawaii. Their construction was begun about the year 1796. In spite of the fact that the Hawaiian historian, Malo, speaks of the *peleleu* with a certain pride and enthusiasm, they are to be regarded rather as monstrosities, not belonging fully to the Hawaiiian on whose soil they were made, nor to the white men who, no doubt, lent a hand and had a voice in their making and planning.

24. Sect. 32. *Pa-u:* Some times the *pa-u* covered the opening of the canoe from stem to stern, each paddle-man putting his head and body through a hole in the same. This would be in stormy weather. In ordinary times only the waist of the craft, where the baggage and freight were stowed, was covered in this way. The following was the manner of fastening the mat: A number of holes, called *holo,* were made in the upper edge of the canoe. By means of small cords passed through these holes a line, called *alihi pa-u,* was lashed in place. Through the loops of this *alihi* was run a line that criss-crossed from one side to the other and held the *pa-u* or mat in place. This last line was called a *haunu.*

XXXV

Religious Ceremonies Performed by the Aliis to Secure Off-Spring

1. The efforts of the kings to secure offspring were associated with the worship of the gods; but these religious performances related only to the first born,[1] because such held the highest rank as chiefs.

2. In the case of high chiefs the affair was conducted as follows; a high chief of the opposite sex was sought out and, after betrothal, the two young people were at first placed (*hoo-noho*)[2] under keepers in separate establishments, preparatory to pairing for offspring, the purpose being to make the offspring of the highest possible rank. Worship was paid to the gods, because it was firmly believed that the genius, power and inspiration (*mana*) of a king was like that of a god.

3. When the princess had recovered from her infirmity and had purified herself in the bath, she was escorted to the tent made of tapa, which had been set up in an open place in the sight of all the people.

4. To her now came the prince, bringing with him his *akua kaai*.[3] This *akua kaai* was set up outside of the tent, where were keeping watch the multitude of the people, and the assembled priests were uttering incantations and praying to the gods that the union of the two chiefs might prove fruitful.

5. When the princess has returned from her bath, the prince goes in unto her and remains in her company perhaps until evening, by which time the ceremony called *hoomau keiki* is completed. Then the prince takes his leave, the princess returns home, the people disperse, the kahunas depart, the chiefs retire and the tent is taken down. This ceremony is enacted only in the case of the very highest chiefs, never those of inferior rank.

6. If after this it is found that the princess is with child, there is great rejoicing among all the people that a chief of rank has been begotten. If the two parents are of the same family, the offspring will be of the highest possible rank.[4]

7. Then those who composed *meles* (*haku mele*[5]) were sent for to compose a *mele inoa* that should eulogise and blazon the ancestry of the new chief to-be, in order to add distinction to him when he should be born.

8. And when the bards had composed their *meles* satisfactorily (*a holo*[6] *na mele*), they were imparted to the hula dancers to be committed to memory. It was also their business to decide upon the attitudes and gestures, and to teach the *inoa* to the men and women of the hula (i.e. the chorus).

9. After that the men and women of the hula company danced and recited the *mele inoa* of the unborn chief with great rejoicing, keeping it up until such time as the prince was born; then the hula-performances ceased.

10. When the time for the confinement of the princess drew near the royal midwives (themselves chiefesses) were sent for to take charge of the accouchement and to look after the mother. As soon as labor-pains set in an offering was set before the idol (the *akua kaai* named *Hulu*), because it was believed to be the function of that deity to help women in labor.

11. When the expulsory pains became very frequent,[7] the delivery was soon accomplished; and when the child was born, the father's *akua kaai* was brought in attended by his priest. If the child was a girl, its navel-string was cut in the house; but if a boy, it was carried to the *heiau*, there to have the navel-string cut in a ceremonious fashion.

12. When the cord had first been tied with *olona*, the kahuna, having taken the bamboo (knife), offered prayer, supplicating the gods of heaven and earth and the king's *kaai* gods, whose images were standing there. The articles constituting the offering, or *mohai*, were lying before the king, a pig, cocoanuts, and a robe of tapa. The king listened attentively to the prayer of the kahuna, and at the right moment, as the kahuna was about to sever the cord, he took the offerings in his hands and lifted them up.

13. Thereupon the kahuna prayed as follows:

O ka ohe keia o ka piko o ka aiwaiwa lani.

This is the bamboo for the navel-string of the heaven-born chief.

The kahuna then took the bamboo between his teeth and split it in two (to get a sharp cutting edge), saying,

*O ka uhae keia o ka ohe o ka piko o ka aiwaiwa lani. * * * O ka moku keia o ka piko o ka aiwaiwa lani.*

This is the spliting of the bamboo for the navel-string of the heaven-born chief. * * * This is the cutting of the navel-string of the heaven-born one.

14. Thereupon he applies the bamboo-edge and severs the cord; and, having sponged the wound to remove the blood (*kupenu*), with a pledget of soft olona fibre, *oloa,* the kahuna prays:

> *Kupenu ula,*
> *Kupenu lei,*
> *Kumu lei,*
> *Aka halapa i ke akua i laau wai la.*

> Cleanse the red blood from the stump;
> Cleanse it from the cord;
> Bind up the cord;
> It is for God to safeguard this child,
> To make him flourish like a well-watered plant.

15. When the prayer of the kahuna was ended, the royal father of the child himself offered prayer to the gods:

O Ku, Lono, Kane and Kanaloa, here is the pig, the cocoanuts, the malo. Deal kindly with this new chief; give him long life; protect him until the last sleep of unconsciousness. Long may he reign and his kingdom extend from the rising to the setting of the sun.

Amen; it is free: the tabu is lifted.

The king then dashed the pig against the ground and killed it as an offering to the gods, and the ceremonies were ended.

16. The child was then taken back to the house and was provided with a wet nurse who became its *kahu.* Great care was taken in feeding the child, and the *kahus* were diligent in looking after the property collected for its support. The child was subject to its *kahus* until it was grown up. The young prince was not allowed to eat pork until he had been initiated into the templeservice, after which that privilege was granted him. This was a fixed rule with princes.

17. When the child had increased in size and it came time for him to undergo the rite of circumcision, religious ceremonies were again performed. The manner of performing circumcision itself was the same as in the case of a child of the common people, but the religious ceremonies were more complicated.

18. When the boy had grown to be of good size a priest was appointed to be his tutor, to see to his education and to instruct him in matters religious; and when he began to show signs of incipient

manhood, the ceremony of purification (*huikala*) was performed, a *heiau* was built for him, and he became a temple-worshipper (*mea haipule*) on his own account. He was then permitted to eat of pork that had been baked in an oven outside of the *heiau,* but not of that which had been put to death by strangulation, in the manner ordinarily practiced, and then baked in an oven outside of the *heiau* without religious rites. His initiation into the eating of pork was with prayer.

19. Such was the education and bringing up of a king's son. The ceremonies attendant on the education and bringing up of the daughters were not the same as those above described;—(At this point there is an ambiguity in the language of the manuscript, and it is not clear whether it is of the daughters alone or of the younger sons also that he speaks, when he says)—*E hana ia no nae ke oki piko ana, a me kekahi mau mea e ae, aole no e like me ko ka mua hana ana*—but the ceremony of cutting the navel-string, as well as some other ceremonies, was performed on them. The ceremonies, however, were not of the same grade as in the case of the first born, because it was esteemed as a matter of great importance by kings, as well as by persons of a religious turn of mind, that the first born should be devoted to the service of the gods.

20. The birth of a first child was a matter of such great account that after such birth chiefish mothers and women of distinction, whether about court or living in the back districts, underwent a process of purification (*hooma'ema'e*) in the following manner.

21. After the birth of the child the mother kept herself separate from her husband and lived apart from him for seven days; and when her discharge was staunched she returned to her husband's house.

22. During this period she did not consort with her husband, nor with any other man; but there was bound about her abdomen a number of medicinal herbs, which were held in place by her malo. This manner of purification for women after childbirth was termed *hoopapa.*

23. While undergoing the process of purification the woman did not take ordinary food, but was supported on a broth made from the flesh of a dog. On the eighth day she returned to her husband, the discharge (*walewale*) having by that time ceased to flow.

24. The woman, however, continued her purification until the expiration of an *anahulu,* ten days, by which time this method of treatment, called *hoopapa,* was completed. After that, in commemoration of the accomplishment of her tabu, the woman's hair was cut for the first time.[8]

25. Thus it will appear that from the inception of her pregnancy she had been living in a state of tabu, or religious seclusion, abstaining from all kinds of food that were forbidden by her own or her husband's gods. It was after this prescribed manner that royal mothers, and women of rank, conducted themselves during the period of their first pregnancy. Poor folks did not follow this regime.

26. The women of the poor and humble classes gave birth to their children without paying scrupulous attention to matters of ceremony and etiquette (*me ka maewaewa ole*).

Notes on Chapter XXXV

1. Sect. 1. This *hoomau* ceremony, as stated, was generally performed only apropos of the first child, but there were exceptions to this rule.

2. Sect. 2. *Hoonoho ia*, put in an establishment, placed under the care of a guardian or of a duenna. Such an establishment was surrounded by an enclosure, *pa*, made of the sacred *lama*, a tree whose wood in color and fineness of grain resembles boxwood. Hence this special care or guardianship was called *palama*. It is said that an establishment of this kind was anciently placed at that suburb of Honolulu which for that cause to this day bears the name of *Ka-pa-lama*. The word *pulama*, to care for, to guard, to foster, to cherish, is akin to *palama* in meaning, but it is generally used in a physical sense and applied to inanimate objects. A child would be *palama'd*, the care bestowed on one's spears, weapons, ornaments, etc., would be expressed by the word *pulama*.

3. Sect. 4. The *akua kaai* was represented by a short staff, on top of which was carved a figure representing the deity. The lower end was sharp to facilitate its being driven into the ground. *Hulu* was the name of one of the *kaai* gods whose special function it was to assist at childbirth.

4. Sect. 6. It is said that when the union was fruitful, neither party was allowed to have further sexual intercourse until the birth of the child and the purification of the mother had been accomplished.

5. Sect. 7. *Haku mele*, literally to weave a song. A *mele* for the glorification of a king, born or still unborn, was called a *mele inoa*. This was a eulogy or panegyric of the ancestral and personal virtues, real or fictitious, of a king or princeling, whether full fledged or still in his mother's womb. *Ko-i-honua* was not, as mistakenly supposed, a particular kind of *mele*. If related to the tone or manner of utterance of the *mele inoa;* it meant that the *inoa* was to be recited in an ordinary conversational tone, and not after the manner called *oli,* that is applied to a singing tone. The *ko-i-honua* manner of reciting a *mele inoa* made it more intelligible and therefore more acceptable to the king who might be an old man and hard of hearing, whether it was uttered in praise of himself or of some child or grand-child. The conversational tone, at any rate, made the

words and meaning more intelligible. In making out the origin of the phrase *ko–i–honua*, the *ko* seems to be the causative, as in such words as *ko–ala*, *ko–pi*, *ko–kua; i*, to utter, as in the sentence *I mai ke alii; honua*, the earth, earthly, as distinguished from an inflated, or stilted, manner of speech used in the singing tone of the *oli*. Following is an example of a

MELE INOA

> *O ke kulei*[a] *ula ce;*
> *O ke ahua lana moku,*
> *Ka ohe lana*[b] *a ke Kanaloa,*
> *Ke Kanaloa a Kane,*[c]
> *O Kane Ulu–hai–malama,*[d]
> *Malama ia o Kaelo.*[e]

> A garland strung of red flowers thou,
> The bank on which rests the island,
> The bamboo buoys of the Kanaloa,
> The Kanaloa of Kane,
> Kane of the fruitful growing month,
> Month that of Kaelo.

a. *ku–lei:* The full form of this word would be *kui–lei; kui*, a needle or sharp stick, used in stringing flowers for a *lei*, garland.

b. *ohe lana:* Bamboo joints were used as floats or buoys. As to the floats of Kanaloa, I cannot learn what they were.

c. *Kanaloa a Kane:* Kanaloa was the son of Kane, or according to some, his younger brother.

d. *Ulu–hai–malama*, said to be the *kahu*, or keeper, of the image of the god Kane, the man himself being oftenest spoken of as *Ulu*. The whole phrase seems to have the meaning given in the translation.

e. *Kaelo* was the month corresponding to October or November, the beginning of the rainy season, when vegetation began to freshen.

The *mele inoa* of which this is a fragment, was, I am told, an heirloom composed in honor of Liloa, handed down by him to Umi, and passed on to *Kalani–nui–a–mamao.*

6. Sect. 8. When the bards, *poe haku mele*, had composed their *meles*, they met at the *ni–o*, a house where were assembled also the critics, *poe loi*, the wise men, literati and philosophers, *kaka–olelo*, who were themselves poets; and the compositions were then recited in the hearing of this learned assembly, criticized, corrected and amended, and the authoritative form settled.

Ni–o (pronounced *nee-o*). and *lo–i* (pronounced (*low-ee*) are nearly synonymous, meaning to criticize. *Nema* or *nema-nema* is to be particular or finicky in criticism.

7. Sect. 11. *Kua-koko* literally bloody back.

8. Sect. 24. I am informed that virgins and young women before marriage wore the hair at full length on the head; but that all respectable women, who regarded the conventions of good society, and especially women about court, after marriage and the birth of their first born, had the hair trimmed short over the back-head, while over the forehead it was allowed to grow long enough to be gathered into a tuft, in which shape it was retained by a dressing of the mucilaginous juice of the *ti* root mixed with *ku-kui* gum. It was also the fashion to bleach and change the color of the hair by the application of lime mixed with the same *ti* juice. (Such is my information; but in rgeard to the prevalence of such a fashion I am very skeptical. There is surely no sign of it at the present day among the Hawaiians. It may have been local; I do not believe it was general.)

(It is fully described by M. Choris, artist of Kotzebue's first voyage in 1816, and shown in some of his portraits of Hawaiian women. The fashion still prevails in Samoa and other southern groups.—W. D. A.)

XXXVI

CONCERNING THE MAKAHIKI

1. The *makahiki*[1] was a time when men, women and chiefs rested and abstained from all work, either on the farm or elsewhere. It is was a time of entire freedom from labor.

2. The people did not engage in the usual religious observances during this time, nor did the chiefs; their worship consisted in making offerings of food. The king himself abstained from work on the *makahiki* days.

There were four days, during which every man, having provided himself with the means of support during his idleness, reposed himself at his own house.

3. After these four days of rest were over, every man went to his farm, or to his fishing, but nowhere else, (not to mere pleasure-seeking), because the *makahiki* tabu was not yet ended, but merely relaxed for those four days. It will be many days before the *makahiki* will be *noa*, there being four moons in that festival, one moon in *Kau*, and three moons in *Hooilo*.

4. The *makahiki* period began in *Ikuwa*, the last month of the period called *Kau*, and the month corresponding to October, and continued through the first three months of the period *Hooilo*, to-wit: *Welehu, Makalii* and *Kaelo*, which corresponded with November, December and January.

During these four months, then, the peopel observed *makahiki,* refraining from work and the ordinary religious observances.

5. There were eight months of the year in which both chiefs and commoners were wont to observe the ordinary religious ceremonies, three of them being the *Hooilo* months of *Kaulua, Nana,* and *Welo,* corresponding to February, March and April; and five, the *Kau* months of *Ikiiki Kaaona, Hinaiaeleele, Hilinaehu,* and *Hilinama,* which corresponded to May, June, July, August and September.

6. During these eight months of every year, then, the whole people worshipped, but rested during the four Makahiki months. In this way was the Makahiki observed every year from the earliest times.

7. Many and diverse were the religious services which the *aliis* and the commoners offered to their gods. Great also was the earnestness and sincerity (*hoomaopopo maoli ana*) with which these ancients conducted their worship of false gods.

8. Land was the main thing which the kings and chiefs sought to gain by their prayers and worship (*hoomana*), also that that they might enjoy good health, that their rule might be established forever, and that they might have long life. They prayed also to their gods for the death of their enemies.

9. The common people, on the other hand, prayed that the lands of their *aliis* might be increased, that, their own physical health might be good, as well as the health of their chiefs. They prayed also that they might prosper in their different enterprises. Such was the burden of their prayers year after year.

10. During the tabu-days of *Ku* (the 3rd, 4th, and 5th of each month), in the month of *Ikuwa* (corresponding to October) flags were displayed from the *heiaus* (temples), to announce the coming of the makahiki festival; the services at the royal *heiaus* were suspended, and the chiefs and people who were wont to attend the worship, betook themselves to sports, games and the pursuit of pleasure. But the priests, the *kahus* (keepers) of images and the ruler at the head of the government pursued another course.

11. There were twelve months, consisting of nine times forty days, in a year; and four tabu-periods, or *pules*, in each month. Two nights and a day would be tabu, and at the end of the second night the tabu would be off.

12. During the tabu of *Hua*, (the 13th, and 14th days), in the month *Ikuwa*, was performed the ceremony of breaking the coconut² of the king.

This was part of the observance of Makahiki and was to propitiate the deity. When this had been done he went to his pleasures.

13. When the *Ku*-tabu of the month of *Welehu* had come it went by without religious service; but on the *Hua*-tabu of that month the commoners, and the chiefs of lower ranks performed the ceremony of breaking the cocoanut-dish. The temples were then shut up and no religious services were held.

14. In the succeeding days the Makahiki-taxes were gotten ready against the coming of the tax-collectors for the districts known as *okanas, pokos, kalanas,* previously described, into which an island was divided.

15. It was the duty of the *konohikis* to collect in the first place all the property which was levied from the *loa* for the king; each konohiki also brought tribute for his own landlord, which was called *waiwai maloko.*

16. On *Laaukukahi* (18th day), the districts were levied on for the tax for the king, *tapas, pa-us, malos,* and a great variety of other things.

Contributions of swine were not made, but dogs were contributed until the pens were full of them. The *aliis* did not eat fresh pork during these months, there being no temple service. They did, however, eat such pork as had previously been dressed and cured while services were being held in the temples.

17. On *Laaupau*, (20th day), the levying of taxes was completed, and the property that had been collected was displayed before the gods (*hoomoe ia*): and on the followng day (*Oleku-kahi*), the king distributed it among the chiefs and the companies of soldiery throughout the land.

18. The distribution was as follows: first the portion for the king's gods was assigned, that the *kahus* of the gods might have means of support; then the portion of the king's *kahunas;* then that for the queen and the king's favorites, and all the *aialo* who ate at his table. After this portions were assigned to the remaining chiefs and to the different military companies.

19. To the more important chiefs who had many followers was given a large portion; to the lesser chiefs, with fewer followers, a smaller portion. This was the general principle on which the division of all this property was made among the chiefs, soldiery (*puali*) and the *aialo.*

20. No share of this property, however, was given to the people. During these days food was being provided against the coming of the Makahiki, preparations of cocoanut mixed with taro or breadfruit, called *kulolo,* sweet breadfruit-pudding, called *pepeiee,* also poi, bananas, fish, awa, and many other varieties of food in great abundance.

21. On the evening of the same day, *Olekukahi,* the feather gods were carried in procession, and the following evening, *Olekulua,* the wooden gods were in turn carried in procession. Early the following morning, on the day called *Olepau,* (23rd), they went at the making of the image of the *Makahiki* god, *Lonomakua* (See sec. 25). This work was called *ku-i-ke-pa-a.*

22. This Makahiki-idol was a stick of wood having a circumference of about ten inches and a length of about two fathoms. In form it was straight and staff-like, with joints carved at intervals resembling a horse's leg; and it had a figure carved at its upper end.

23. A cross-piece was tied to the neck of this figure, and to this cross-piece, *kea,* were bound pieces of the edible *pala*[3] fern. From each end of this cross-piece were hung feather *leis* that fluttered about, also feather imitations of the *kaupu*[5] bird, from which all the flesh and solid parts had been removed.

24. The image was also decorated with a white *tapa*[4] cloth made from wauke *kakahi,* such as was grown at *Kuloli.* One end of this tapa was basted to the cross-piece, from which it hung down in one piece to a length greater than that of the pole. The width of this tapa was the same as the length of the cross-piece, about sixteen feet.

25. The work of fabricating this image, I say, was called *kuikepaa.*[6] The following night the chiefs and people bore the image in grand procession, and anointed it with cocoanut oil. Such was the making of the Makahiki god. It was called *Lono-makua* (father Lono), also the *akua loa.* This name was given it because it made the circuit of the island.

Captain Cook was named Lono after this god, because of the resemblance the sails of his ship bore to the tapa of the god.

26. There was also an *akua poko* (short god); so called because it was carried only as far as the boundary of the district and then taken back; also an *akua paani*[7] (god of sports), which accompanied the *akua loa* in its tour of the island and was set up to preside at the assemblies for boxing, wrestling, and other games.

By evening of that same day (Olepau), the making of the *akua loa* was completed. (See sect. 21.)

27. On the morning following the night of Olepau, fires were lighted along the coast all round the island, and everybody, people and chiefs, went to bathe and swim in the ocean, or in fresh water; after which they came to bask and warm themselves about the fires, for the weather was chilly. The bathing was continued until daylight. This practice was called *hiuwai.*[8]

28. The Makahiki tabu began on sunrise of that same day, *Kaloa-kukahi* (the 24th). Every body rested from work, scrupulously abstaining even from bathing in the ocean or in a fresh water stream. One was not permitted to go inland to work on his farm, nor to put to sea, for the purpose of fishing in the ocean. They did no work whatever during those days. Their sole occupation was to eat and amuse themselves. This they continued to do for four days.

29. That same day (*Kaloa-kukahi*) the Makahiki god came into the district—it had to be carried by men, however. The same day also the high priest at *Kaiu* (said to be a place in Waimea, where was a famous shrine) began the observance of a tabu which was to continue for five days. His eyes were blindfolded with tapa during that whole time, and only at its expiration were they unbound to allow him to look upon the people.

30. By the time the Makahiki god had arrived, the *konohikis* set over the different districts and divisions of the land, known as *kalanas, okanas, pokos,* and *ahu-puaas,* had collected the taxes for the Makahiki, and had presented them as offerings to the god; and so it was done all round the island.

31. This tax to the Makahiki god consisted of such things as feathers of the *oo, mamo,* and *i'iwi,* swine, tapas and bundles of pounded taro, *paiai,* to serve as food for those who carried the idol. On the large districts a heavy tax was imposed, and on the smaller ones a lighter tax. If the tax of any district was not ready in time, the konohiki was put off his land by the tax-collector. The konohiki was expected to have all the taxes of the district collected beforehand and deposited at the border of the *ahu-pua'a,* where was built an altar.

32. In making its circuit of the island the *akua-loa* always moved in such a direction as to keep the interior of the island to its right; the *akua-poko* so as to keep it on the left; and when the latter had reached the border of the district it turned back. During the progress of the Makahiki god the country on its left, i.e., towards the ocean, was tabu; and if any one trespassed on it he was condemned to pay a fine, a pig of a fathom long; his life was spared.

33. As the idol approached the altar that marked the boundary of the *ahu-puaa* a man went ahead bearing two poles, or guidons, called *alia.*

34. The man planted the *alia,* and the idol took its station behind them. The space between the *alia* was tabu, and here the konohikis piled their *hookupu,* or offerings, and the tax-collectors, who accompanied the *akua-makahiki,* made their complaints regarding deliquent tax-payers. All outside of the *alia* was common ground (*noa*).

35. When enough property had been collected from the land to satisfy the demands of the tax-collector, the kahuna who accompanied the idol came forward and uttered a prayer to set the land free. This prayer was called *Hainaki* and ran as follows:

36.   Your bodies, O Lono, are in the heavens,
       A long cloud, a short cloud,
       A watchful cloud,
       An overlooking cloud—in the heavens;
       From Uliuli, from Melemele,
       From Polapola, from Ha'eha'e,
       From Omao-ku-ulu-lu,

From the land that gave birth to Lono.
Behold Lono places the stars
That sail through the heavens.
High resplendent is the great image of Lono;
The stem of Lono links our dynasties with Kahiki,
Has lifted them up,
Purified them in the ether of Lono.
Stand up! gird yourselves for play.

The people then responded:

Gird yourselves!

The kahuna says:

Lono—

The people respond:

The image of Lono!

The Kahuna says:

Hail!

The people respond:

Hail to Lono!

And thus ended the service.

Pule Hainaki

36. The kahuna said:

Ou kinoi Lono i ka lani,
He ao loa, he ao poko,
He ao kiei, he ao halo,

He ao hoo-pua i ka lani;
Mai Uliuli, mai Melemele,
Mai Polapola, mai Ha' ha'e,
Mai Omao-ku-ulu-lu,
Mai ka aina o Lono i hanau mai ai.
Oi hookui aku o Lono ka hoku e miha'i ka lani,
Amoamo ke akua laau nui o Lono.
Kuikui papa ka lua mai Kahiki,
Ha paina, kukaa i ka hau miki no Lono!
E ku i ka malo a hi'u!

People respond:

Hiu!

Kahuna says:

O Lono—

People respond:

Ke akua laau

Kahuna says:

Aulu!

People respond:

Aulu, e Lono!

37. By this ceremony the land under consideration was sealed as free. The idol was then turned face downwards and moved on to signify that no one would be troubled, even though he ventured on the left hand side of the road, because the whole district had been declared free from tabu, *noa*. But when the idol came to the border of the next *ahu-puaa* the tabu of the god was resumed, and any person who then went on the left hand-side of it subjected himself to the penalties of the law. Only when the guardians of the idols declared the land free did it become free.

38. This was the way they continued to do all round the island; and when the image was being carried forward its face looked back, not to the front.

39. When the Makahiki god of the *aliis* came to where the chiefs were living they made ready to feed it. It was not, however, the god that ate the food, but the man that carried the image. This feeding was called *hanai-pu* and was done in the following manner.

40. The food, consisting of *kulolo, hau,* preparations of arrowroot, bananas, cocoanuts and awa, (for such were the articles of food prepared for the Makahiki god), was made ready beforehand, and when the god arrived at the door of the *alii's* house, the kahunas from within the house, having welcomed the god with an *aloha,* uttered the following invocation:

41. Welcome now to you, O Lono! (*E weli ia oe Lono, ea!*) Then the kahuna and the people following the idol called out, *Nauane, nauane,* moving on, moving on. Again the kahunas from within the house called out, Welcome to you, O Lono! and the people with the idol answered, moving on, moving on (*Nauane, nauane*). Thereupon the kahunas from within the house called out, This way, come in! (*Hele mai a komo, hele mai a komo*).

42. Then the carrier of the idol entered the house with the image, and after a prayer by the kahuna, the *alii* fed the carrier of the image with his own hands, putting the food into the man's mouth, not so much as suffering him to handle it, or to help himself in the least. When the repast was over the idol was taken outside.

43. Then the female chiefs brought a malo, and after a prayer by the kahuna, they proceeded to gird it about the god. This office was performed only by the female chiefs and was called *Kai-olo-a*.

44. By this time the god had reached the house of the king, the means for feeding the god were in readiness, and the king himself was sitting in the mystic rite of Lono (*e noho ana ke alii nui i ka Iui o Lono*); and when the feeding ceremony of *hanaipu* had been performed the king hung about the neck of the idol a *niho-palaoa*. This was a ceremony which the king performed every year. After that the idol continued on its tour about the island.

45. That evening the people of the villages and from the country far and near assembled in great numbers to engage in boxing matches, and in other games as well, which were conducted in the following manner.

46. The whole multitude stood in a circle, leaving an open space in the centre for the boxers, while chiefs and people looked on.

47. As soon as the tumult had been quieted and order established in the assembly, a number of people on one side stood forth and began a reviling recitative: "Oh you sick one, you'd better lie abed in the time of *Makalii* (the cold season). You'll be worsted and thrown by the veriest novice in wrestling, and be seized *per lapides*,[17] you bag of guts you."

48. Then the people of the other side came forward and, standing in the midst of the assmebly, reviled the first party. Thereupon the two champions proceeded to batter each other; and whenever either one was knocked down by the other, the whole multitude set up a great shout.

49. This performance was a senseless sport, resulting in wounds and flowing of blood. Some struggled and fought, and some were killed.

50. The next day, *Koloa-kulua* (25th), was devoted to boxing, *holua* sledding, rolling the *maika* stone, running races (*kukini*), sliding javelins (*pahee*),[18] the *noa*[18]—or *puhenehene*—and many other games, including *hula* dancing.

51. These sports were continued the next day, which was *Kaloa-pau*, and on the morning of the following day, *Kane*, the *akua-poko*, reached the border of the district, traveling to the left, and turning back, arrived home that evening. The *akua-loa* kept on his way about the island with the god of sport (*akua-paani*).

52. The return of the *akua-poko*[19] was through the bush and wild lands above the travelled road, and they reacehd the temple sometime that evening. Along its route the people came trooping after the idol, gathering *pala* fern and making back-loads of it. It is said that on the night of Kane the people gathered this fern from the woods as a sign that the tabu was taken from the cultivated fields.

53. The keepers of the god Kane, whether commoners or chiefs, made bundles of *luau* that same night, and having roasted them on embers, stuck them up on the sides of their houses, after which their farms were relieved from tabu, and they got food from them.

54. The kahus of Lono also did the same thing on the night Lono (28th), after which their farms also were freed from tabu and they might take food from them. Likewise the kahus of the god *Kanaloa* did the same thing on the night of *Mauli* (29th). This ceremony was called *o-luau*, and after its performance the tabu was removed from the cultivated fields, so that the people might farm them. But this release from tabu applied only to the common people; the king and chiefs practiced a different ceremony.

55. With the *aliis* the practice was as follows: On the return of the *akua-poko*, which was on the day Kane (27th), *pala* fern was gathered; and that night the bonfire of *Puea*[20] was lighted—Puea was the name of an idol deity—and if the weather was fair and it did not rain that night, the night of Puea, it was an omen of prosperity to the land. In that case, on the following morning on the day Lono (28th), a canoe was sent out on a fishing excursion; and on its return, all the male chiefs and the men ate of the fresh fish that had been caught; but not the women. On that day also the bandages, which had covered the eyes of the high-priest were removed.

56. On the morning of Mauli (29th) the people again went after pala-fern, and at night the fire of Puea was again lighted. On the morning of the next day, Muku, the last of the month, the fishing canoe again put to sea. The same thing was repeated on the following day, Hilo, which was the first of the month, the new month Makalii, and that night the fires of Puea were again lighted, and the following morning the fishing-canoe again put to sea.

57. The same programme was followed the next day, and the next, and the day following that, until the four *Ku* (3rd, 4th, 5th and 6th), as well as the four days of the *Ole*-tabu, (7th, 8th, 9th, and 10th) were accomplished. On each of these days a fresh supply of pala-fern was gathered; each night the signal fires of Puea burned, and on each following morning the fishing canoe put forth to get a fresh supply of fish. This was also done on *Huna* (11th); and that day the queen and all the women ate of the fresh fish from the ocean. This observance was termed *Kala-hua*.[21]

58. On the morning of *Mohalu* (12th), the tabu set in again and continued through the days *Hua, Akua*, and *Hoku*, during which period no canoe was allowed to go afishing. On the following day, *Mahealani*, the Makahiki god returned from making the circuit of the island.

59. On that day the king for the first time again bathed in the ocean. It was on the same evening that the Makahiki god was brought back to the *luakini*.[22]

60. That same evening the king sailed forth in a canoe accompanied by his retinue and his soldiery, to meet the Makahiki god on his return from his tour, a ceremony which was called *ka-lii*.[23]

61. When the king came to where the Makahiki god was, behold there was a large body of men, with spears in their hands, drawn up at the landing as if to oppose him.

62. The king was accompanied on this expedition by one of his own men who was an expert in warding off spears. This man went forward

in advance of the king. And as the king jumped ashore, one of the men forming the company about the Makahiki god came on the run to meet him, holding in his hands two spears bound at their points with white cloth called *oloa*.

63. One of these he hurled at the king and it was warded off by the one who went in advance. The second spear was not thrown, the man merely touched the king with it.

64. That same afternoon they had a sham-fight with spears, which was termed a *Kane-kupua*. After that the king went into the temple of *Waiea*[24] to pay his respects to the Makahiki god *Lono-makua*, as well as to the *akua-poko*.

65. When the king came into the presence of these gods he offered a pig as a sacrifice. It was put upon the *lele* before the idols, and then the king went home for the night.

The next day was *kulu* (17th), and that evening a temporary booth, called a *hale kamala*, of *lama* wood, was put up for *Kahoalii*,[25] directly in front of the temple, Waiea, and in it Kahoalii spent the night. This hut was called the net-house, of Kahoalii (*ka hale koko o Kahoalii*).

66. That same night a very fat pig, called a *puaa hea*, was put into the oven along with preparations of cocoanut, called *kulolo*, and at daybreak, when the process of cooking was complete, all the people feasted on it; and if any portion was left over, it was carefully disposed of. This was on the morning of Laau-kukahi, and that same day the following work was done:

67. Namely, the entire dismantling of the Makahiki idols, leaving nothing but the bare images; after which they and all their appurtenances were bundled up and deposited in the luakini. The men who carried the idols were then fed, and the kahunas closed the services of the day with prayer.

68. A net with large meshes was then made, which, being lifted by four men supporting it at the four corners, was filled with all kinds of food, such as taro, potatoes, bread-fruit, bananas, cocoanuts, and pork, after which the priests stood forth to pray.

69. When the kahuna in his prayer uttered the word *hapai*, (lift) the men lifted the net and shook it back and forth, to make the food drop through the meshes, such being the purpose of the ceremony. This was called the net of *Maoloha*.[26] If the food did not drop from the net, the kahuna declared there would be a famine in the land; but if it all fell out he predicted that the season would be fruitful.

70. A structure of basket-work, called the *waa-auhau*,[27] was then made, which was said to represent the canoe in which Lono returned to Tahiti.

The same day also a canoe of unpainted wood, called a *waa kea*, was put to sea and coursed back and forth. After that the restrictions of the Makahiki were entirely removed and every one engaged in fishing, farming, or any other work.

71. On that same day orders were given that the timber for a new heiau, called a *kukoae*,[28] should be collected with all haste.

The next day was Laau-kulua, and on the evening of the following day, Laau-pau, the 20th, the king announced the tabu of *Kalo-ka-maka-maka*, which was the name of the prayer or service. This pule, or service, continued until Kaloa-kulua, the 25th, when it came to an end, was *noa*.

72. On the morning of Kaloa-pau, 26th, the king performed the ceremony of purification. He had built for himself a little booth, called a *hale-puu-puu-one*,[29] performing its ceremony of consecration and ending it that day; then another small house, or booth, called *oeoe*;[30] then a booth covered with pohue vine; then one called *palima*;[31] and last of all a heiau called *kukoa'e-ahuwai*.[32] Each of these was consecrated with prayer and declared *noa* on that same day by the king, in order to purify himself from the pleasures, in which he had indulged, before he resumed his religious observances.

73. On the morning of the next day, which was Kane (27th), the king declared the tabu of the heiau he had built, which was of the kind called *kukoa'e*, because it was the place in which he was to cleanse himself from all impurities, *haumia*, and in which he was to eat pork. This heiau was accordingly called a *kukoa'e* in which to eat pork, because in it the king resumed the use of that meat.

74. During the tabu period of Ku, in the month of Kaelo, people went their own ways and did as they pleased; prayers were not offered. During the tabu period of Hua in Kaelo the people again had to make a *hookupu* for the king. It was but a small levy, however, and was called the heap of Kuapola. (*Ka pu'u o Kuapola.*)

75. It was in this same tabu-period that *Kahoalii*[33] plucked out and ate an eye from the fish *aku*,[34] together with an eye from the body of the man who had been sacrificed. After this the tabu was removed from the aku and it might be eaten; then the opelu in turn became tabu, and could be eaten only on pain of death.

76. During this same tabu or *pule* the king and the high priest slept in their own houses. (They had been sleeping in the *heiau*.) On the last

day of the tabu-period the king and kahuna-nui, accompanied by the man who beat the drum, went and regaled themselves on pork. The service at this time was performed by a distinct set of priests. When these services were over the period of Makahiki and its observances were ended, this being its fourth month. Now began the new year.[35]

77. In the tabu-period of Ku of the month Kaulua, the king, chiefs, and all the people took up again their ordinary religious observances, because religion, i.e. *haipule*,[36] has from the very beginning of Hawaiian history been a matter of the greatest concern.

78. In the tabu-period Ku, of the month Kaulua, or it might be of the month Nana, the king would make a *heiau* of the kind called a *heiau-loulu*, or it might be, he would put up one of the kind called a *ma'o*. He might prefer an ordinary *luakini;* or, he might see fit to order the building of a temple to propitiate the gods for abundant harvets, that would be a *luakini houululu ai;* or he might order the building of a war-temple, a *luakini kaua*.[37] It was a matter which lay with the king.

Notes to Chapter XXXVI

1. The word *Makahiki* means a year of twelve months. In addition to this it was used to designate the festival-period which it is the purpose of this chapter to describe.

In order to understand the matters treated of in this chapter it is necessary to consider the calendar and the divisions of the year in use among the Hawaiians.

The Hawaiian year had in it three hundred and sixty days, and was divided into twelve months, or moons, *mahina*, of nominally thirty days each. The *mahina* was supposed to begin on the first appearance of the new moon in the west, which day, or night rather, was named *Hilo*, a filament or twist.

It should be noted that apparently in order to piece out the twenty-nine and a half days of the lunar month into the thirty days of the Hawaiian calendar month, either the first day *Hilo*, or the thirtieth, *Muku*, must, as it would seem, have been counted in alternate months.

In each month there were four *tabu*-periods, called *kapus*, also called *pules* (by David Malo), which were named the 1st *Ku*, 2nd *Hua*, 3rd *Kanaloa* or *Kaloa*, and the 4th *Kane*. The first three of these came at intervals of ten days; that of *Ku* on the 3rd, 4th and 5th; that of *Hua* on the 13th and 14th; that of *Kanaloa* on the 24th and 25th. The *kapu-Kane* was appointed irregularly on the 27th and 28th. The general disposition and arrangement as to time of these sacred periods points to and argues strongly in favor of a decimal scale and a division of time into periods of ten days, *anahulus*, three of which constituted a *mahina*. The word *anahulu* (ten days) is of frequent occurrence in the old *meles*, *pules* and *kaaos*. See Chap. XII.

The names of the days in the month differed somewhat on the different islands. The following table is based on the authority of W. D. Alexander, who differs slightly from David Malo, as will be seen in the fable:

Kapu-Ku
1. Hilo.
2. Hoaka. ⎫ Kapu Ku,
3. Ku-kahi. ⎭ D. Malo.
4. Ku-lua.
5. Ku-kolu.
6. Ku-pau.
7. Ole-ku-kahi.
8. Ole-ku-lua.
9. Ole-ku-kolu.
10. Ole-ku-pau, (or Ole-pau. D. M.)
11. Huna.

Kapu Hua
12. Mohalu. ⎫ Kapu Hua
13. Hua. ⎭ in D. Malo
14. Akua.
15. Hoku. (Hokupalemo, or Hoku-ill.)

16. Mahealani.
17. Kulu, or Kulua, in D. Malo.
18. Laau-ku-kahi.
19. Laau-ku-lua.
20. Laau-pau.
21. Ole-ku-kahi.
22. Ole-ku-lua.
23. Ole-pau ⎫ Kapu Kaloa.
Kapu-Kaloa or Kanaloa ⎰ 24. Kaloa-ku-kahi ⎭ in D. Malo,
25 Kaloa-ku-lua.
26. Koloa-pau.
Kapu Kane ⎰ 27. Kane.
28. Lono.
29. Mauli.
30. Muku.

2. Ka niu a ke'lii nui. I am informed that this was a carved cocoanut dish of rare workmanship, highly polished, which contained a number of choice things.

3. Sect. 23. *Pala* fern, (*Marattia alata*). This was obtained from the butt-end of the leaf-stalk, at its attachment to the stem. It was much eaten in times of famine. The extent to which the Maoris of New Zealand depended upon the fern as a means of sustenance suggests the question whether there is not a reminiscence of that fact in the mystical and religious use to which the fern is evidently put in this ceremony, as well as in other ceremonies to be described later.

4. Sect. 24. The *Makahiki* idol. The accompanying sketch is a representation of the *Akua loa, Akua makahiki,* or *Lono makua,* as the Makahiki god was called. The figure follows the descriptions given by experts in Hawaiian antiquities and tallies with that given by David Malo.

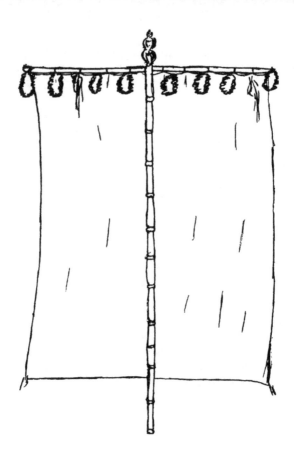

The resemblance of the *tapa*-banner to the sail of a ship, remarked by Malo in Sect. 25, is evident.

5. Sect. 23. The *kaupu* was a sea-bird. It was spoken of as *kaupu auhai ale*. It was the gannet or solan goose.

6. Sect. 21 and 25. *Ku-i-ke-paa*: to halt, to stand still. The application of the word to this use is due to the fact that in going after the tree from which to make the *akua loa,* when the procession, at the head of which was the high priest, bearing a feather-idol, came to where the tree was growing, the priest halted, and, planting the staff that bore the idol in the ground, gave the order *Ku i ke paa,* and the whole company came to a standstill. During the felling of the tree and the carving of it to make the idol, the feather-god was always present, the staff that supported it being planted in the ground.

7. Sect. 26. *Akua paani*: there are said to have been two of these, consisting of spears, the heads' of which were surrounded with a sort of basket-work intertwined and decorated with *leis* and streamers of white and yellow *tapa*. It

DAVID MALO

is said that the games of the festival were directed by gestures made with these poles.

8. Sect. 27. The Hawaiians of the present day have a sport which both sexes engage in while bathing together in the water. It is called *hiuwai*, and consists of dashing water at and splashing each other.

8½. Sect. 28. According to Kamakau of Kaawaloa, during these four days all things were *kapu* to *Lono-nui-akea*, land and sea and sky.—W. D. A.

9. Sect. 33. *Alia*, meaning to wait, hold on.

10. Sect. 36. *Ou kino*—In archaic Hawaiian the form of the singular number is often used in place of the plural, as in the present instance. David Malo himself shows a fondness for the use of the singular form of nouns when the plural evidently is meant.

Mr. S. Percy Smith informs me that *ou kino,* which in Maori would be *ou tino,* is a plural form, *ou* being the plural form of the second personal adjective. Thus in Maori *tou whare* is thy house, *ou whare* is your houses. This argues in favor of the view that the form *ou* in the passage is a survival from the old Maori.

11. Lines 5, 6 and 7.—*Uliuli, Melemele and Omaokuululu* are said to be the names of places in Puna, Hawaii; but as used here they stand for mystical places in the far off *Kukulu o Kahiki*.

Mele-mele: Of these names *Mere-mere* is known to Maoris and is connected with very ancient myths, located, say, in Malaysia, or India.

The above I have from S. Percy Smith of New Plymouth, N. Z.

12. Line 13.—*E ku i ka malo a hiu.* These words are addressed to the people. The religious services of the Hawaiians were to a large extent responsive, being heartily entered into by the people, as instanced in the service here described.

There are difficulties in the translation of this line. A *malo* bifurcated at its end was called, it is said, *he malo a hiu;* such a *malo* belonged to a *kahuna*.

13. Sect. 41. *Weli,* or *welina,* as more often found in modern Hawaiian, is a form of greeting of earlier usage than the present *aloha*.

14. The invitation to enter and have food is eminently Hawaiian. In a *mele o Hiiaka* occur the following verses:

> *E kipa maloko e hanai ai,*
> *A hewa ae ka waha.*
> *A eia ka uku, ka leo.*

> Come in and have food,
> And loosen the tongue.
> And the pay,—your voice.

15. Sect. 43. *Kaioloa,* said to be a choice kind of *malo* made from *wauke.*

16. Sect. 47. The epithets which the champions and their partisans hurl at each other. I venture to give, as a sample of heathen billingsgate, in spite of their

coarseness. *E mai nui, moe wale i ka wa o ka Makalii! Moe ae oe ia ka ai kauai, huki'a ka pauaka ko meamea, e he mai nui e!*

17. Sect. 47. *Per lapides:* This was a favorite hold with the contestants in the savage game of *lua*, one by means of which they sought to take the life out of a man and make him cry "mercy." The Hawaiians as a rule had no sense of fairness. No blow was foul, no advantage unfair in their eyes.

18. Sect. 50. This is but an imperfect list of the games played. *Pahe'e* was played with short, blunt darts of wood, or even with sugarcane tops, which were darted along the ground.

Noa was the name given the pebble with which the celebrated game of *puhenehene* was played. It was held in the hand of the player who in the view of the other side and of the spectators that were assembled passed his hand successively under the different bundles of tapa, five in number, that were ranged in front of him, hiding it under one of them. It was for the other side to guess correctly the bundle under which the *noa* was hidden, failing to do which, they must pay the forfeit. It was of course a betting game, like all Hawaiian sports. The forfeits of *puhenehene* were often of an immoral nature. (For further account of the games see Chap. XLI. pp. 220–240).

19. Sect. 52. *Akua poko.* Among the unnamed idols I have met with is one which I believe to be the *akua poko.* This is a staff of *kauila,* having a small figure in the form of a man arrayed with the *mahi-ole,* feather helmet. The lower end of the staff is sharpened, as if for thrusting into the ground. About midway of the staff is an opening with a head in relief adorning each aspect of the fenestra. The length of the staff is about three feet four inches.

20. Sect. 55. *Puea.* These bonfires of Puea were lighted on an eminence, so as to be visible to all the fishermen far and near along the coast. They were beacons, and guided their actions. If the night was rainy, it was accepted as an inauspicious omen, and the fires were alllowed to go out as a signal that no fishing canoe was to be put to sea; but if the weather was fair, the fires were kept burning brightly, and at day-break the canoes were to be seen at their fishing grounds.

21. Sect. 57. *Kala-hua,* the removal of tabu from the fruits—of the sea apparently, as well as of the land.

22. Sect. 59. *Lua-kini*—A *heiau* of the highest class, a war-temple, in which human sacrifices were offered; named from a pit, *lua,* and *kini,* many; into which the mouldering remains were finally cast.

23. Sect. 60. *Ka-'lii.*—This might be interpreted, doing the king-act, or acting the king. It is said that Kamehameha I, disdaining the assistance of another, as he jumped ashore caught the first spear in his hands, and with it warded off the others that were hurled at him in quick succession.

24. Sect. 64. The *luakini* of *Waiea* was unique. It was, I am informed, the abode of the *akua Makahiki, Lono-makua,* the *akua poko,* the *akua paani,* and of no other gods. On Hawaii this temple was located in Puna, on Maui at Kipahulu, on Molokai at Kaunakakai, on Kauai at Maka-weli.

25. Sect. 65. *Kahoalii* was a mythical hero who, according to one tradition, occupied the subterranean regions through which the sun travelled at night during its passage from West to East. (See the story of Maui.) He is represented as having a very dark complexion, and stripes or patches of white skin, perhaps painted, on the inside of his thighs. He was personated by a man entirely naked. "Nudity is the sacred garb of deity." (Lady Beaulieu.)

26. Sect. 69. *Koko a Maoloha*, the net of Maoloha. The expression is used *Ke koko a Maoloha i ka lani*. Tradition says that the first appearance of the koko of Maoloha was in a time of famine, when Waia was king on Hawaii. In view of the famine that distressed the land, Waia, who was a *kupua*, possessed of superhuman powers, let down from heaven a net whose four corners pointed to the North, South, East and West, and which was filled with all sorts of food, animal and vegetable. This done he shook the net and the food was scattered over the land for the benefit of the starving people.

27. Sect. 70. *Waa auhau*. This was a wicker-work crate, or basket, made out of peeled *wauke* sticks, which having been filled with all kinds of food, was lashed between the two *iakos*, or cross-beams that belong to the out-rigger of a canoe, and being taken out to sea, was cast off and allowed to drift away. It was also called *ka waa o Lono*, Lono's canoe.

Waa' Auhau, or *Waa o Lono.*

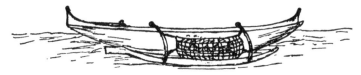

Apropos of the net of *Maoloha* (Sect. 69) at the time the net filled with food was lifted and shaken, the following responsive service, called *ka Pule koko,* the prayer of the net, was celebrated.

The net is lifted and the kahuna opens the service saying—

> *E uliuli kai, e Uli ke akua e!*
> *E uli kai hakoko!*
> *Koko lani e Uli!*
> *Uli lau ka ai a ke akua.*
> *Piha lani koko; e lu—!*

Then the people respond—

> *E lu ka ai a ke akua!*
> *E lu ka lani!*
> *He kau ai keia.*

E lu ka honua!
He kau ai keia.
Ola ka aina!
Ola ia Kane,
Kane ke akua ola.
Ola ia Kanaloa!
Ke akua kupueu.
Ola na kanaka!
Kane i ka wai ola, e ola!
Ola ke alii Makahiki!
Amama, ua noa.

Kahuna—*Noa ia wai?*
People—*Noa ia Kane.*

Oh deep-blue sea, Oh god Uli!
Oh blue of the wild, tossing sea!
Net of heaven, oh Uli.
Green are the leaves of God's harvest fields.
The net fills the heavens—Shake it!

Then the people respond—

Shake down the god's food!
Scatter it oh heaven!
A season of plenty this.
Earth yield thy plenty!
This is a season of food.
Life to the land!
Life from Kane,
Kane the god of life.
Life from Kanaloa!
The wonder-working god.
Life to the people!
Hail Kane of the water of life! Hail!
Life to the king of the Makahiki!
Amama. It is free.

Kahuna—Free through whom?
People—Free through Kane.

Then the kahunas stand up holding their hands aloft, and the people exclaim: "Ua noa. Ua noa. Ua noa." At the same time holding up the left hand, and at the utterance of each sentence, striking with the right hand under the left arm-pit.

When the kahuna utters the words *"E lu"*—in the 5th line—those who are lifting the net shake it and make its contents fall to the ground.

28. Sect. 71. The *Ku-koa'e* was a temple for purification. The meaning of the word seems to have reference to a standing apart, by itself. For an *anahulu*, ten days, the king must not enter into any other heiau.

29. Sect. 72. The *hale puu-puu-one* was a round thatched hut' of such a shape as a pile of sand would naturally assume when heaped up into a mound. Hence its name. It was for the use of the kahuna only. No one might partake of food, or allow himself to sleep while in the place. The entrance of a woman would have been an unspeakable defilement, punishable with death. One of the ceremonies performed in this sort of a heiau was the purification of the king or a chief, in case he had perhaps been defiled by the touch of a corpse, or other impurity.

33. Sect. 75. *Ka-hoa-lii*—literally the peer of the king; personated, before stated, by a man entirely naked. This man was for the time a god in the eyes of the people and therefore of course peer of the king.

34. Sect. 75. The *aku* and the *opelu* are said to have come with Paao from Samoa centuries before the white man came, and from that time to have been regarded with superstitious favor.

35. Sect. 76. *Ka makahiki hou.* I believe the meaning of this statement to be that the Hawaiian new year began with the month *Ka-ulua,* pretty nearly corresponding with our February, and not with *Makalii.*

35½. Sect. 77. Kamakau of Kaawaloa makes the following statement: "These are the names of the five war months, viz: Kaelo, Kaulua, Nana, Welo and Ikiiki," i.e., approximately from the first of January to the end of May.

Again he says: "These are the names of the months in which there could be no war, seven in number viz: Kaaona, Hinaiaeleele, Hilinaehu, Hilinama, Ikuwa, Welehu and Makalii, filling out the remainder of the year.

W. D. A.

36. Sect. 77. *Hai-pule.* The repeating of prayers. The same word continues to be in use today to mean religious devotion, prayer, and the external rites of religion, even the thing itself.

37. Sect. 78. This was the beginning of the year, the time also when men went to war, if so disposed. The complexion of the king's purpose and plan for the year on which he had entered, was to be seen in the manner of *heiau* he ordered built; whether a war-temple, whose reeking sacrifices were as significant as the open gates of the Roman Janus, or one of the peaceful sort, of which several are mentioned.

The *heiau loulu* was a temporary structure like a *lanai* thatched with leaves of the loulu palm. It was mostly open at the sides, but a part of the space, that at the top and bottom of the sides, was filled in with the same material, the broad leaves of the loulu. The roof was flat and was intended only to shelter from the rays of the sun. It could not shed the rain. The object of this sort of *heiau* was to propitiate the god or gods who presided over fishing that the people might have plenty of food. There was of course great need of this when for four months the productive industries of the land had been dried up, or diverted from useful channels, and the accumulated bounty of field and ocean had been lavished in religious offerings and feasting. The following prayer is one that was used at such times.

> *E Kane i ke au hulihia,*
> *Hulihia i ke ale ula.*
> *I ke ale lani,*
> *I ke pu-ko'a,*
> *I ka a'aka,*
> *I ke ahua o Lonomuku.*
> *Moku ka pawa o ka po e Kane.*
> *Eia ka alana la, e Kane,*
> *He puaa, he moa uakea.*
> *E ku ka i'a mai Ka-hiki mai,*
> *He opelu, ka i'a hele pu me ka la,*
> *He aku koko ia,*
> *He uwiuwi, he i'a lana kai,*
> *He aweoweo ku i ke kaheka.*
> *E Kane, e ku ka i'a,*
> *E ai ka maka-pehu.*
> *E ola ka aina.*
> *Amama. Ua noa.*

> O Kane of the time of overturning,
> Overturn the bright sea-waves.
> The high-arching sea-waves,
> The coral reefs,
> The bare reefs,
> The cave-floors of Lono-muku.
> Severed is the milky way of the night, Oh Kane!
> Here is an offering, Oh Kane,
> A pig, a white fowl.
> Drive hither the fish from Tahiti,
> The opelu, fish that travels with the sun,
> The aku pulled in by the line,
> The uwiuwi that swims near the surface,
> The aweoweo that haunts the pools;
> On Kane send us fish,
> That the swollen-eyed may eat it.
> Life to the land.
> Amen. It is free.

It was a kahuna *houluulu i'a* who performed this service, the prayer would not be known to an ordinary kahuna. The feast was then partaken of. "Let us eat this feast," said the priest, "and the bones and remnants we will bury in the ground." If any one, man, woman, or child, came near and looked in upon the scene of the feasting he must come in and partake with them of the feast. It would be an ill omen to allow him to turn away empty. A dog, however, was driven away; but it was a good omen to have the domestic animals frisking about and uttering their cries within hearing. If rain fell at the time of the feast, it was a good omen. When all were seated and ready to eat, the kahuna prayed as follows:

E Kane i ka wai ola,
E ola ia makou kau mau pulapula.
Eia ka mohai, he puaa,
He moa uakea, he niu,
He uala, he kalo mana.
E mana ia oe Kane,
E houlu i ka i'a,
I ola ka maka-pehu o ka aina.
E komo, e ai,
Eia ka ihu o ka puaa,
Ka huelo o ka puaa,
Ke ake niau o ka puaa,
Ka puu o ka moa,
Ka wai o ka niu,
Ka limu koko,
Ke kalo mana uakea.
Amama. Ua noa.

Oh Kane of the water of life!
Preserve us, thy offspring.
Here is an offering, a hog,
A white fowl, cocoanuts.
Potatoes, a *mana* taro,
The power is thine, Oh Kane!
To collect for us the fish,
And relieve the gauntness of the land.
Come in and eat of the feast.
Here is the snout of the pig;
The tail of the pig,
The spleen of the pig,
The neck of the fowl,
The juice of the cocoanut.
The red sea-moss,
The white-leafed mana taro,
Amen. It is free.

The articles composing this *alana*, or offering, were done up into five parcels and distributed about the posts that stood at the four corners and in the centre of the *heiau*. If in the next *anahulu*, ten days, an abundant haul of fish was not taken, there was something wrong with the service and it must be repeated.

Heiau ma'o. This sort of *heiau* was a temporary structure of small size for the use of the *aliis* only, any when its purpose was over, it was taken down. It was a slight structure covered with tapa cloth stained with *ma'o*, of a reddish color.

The *heiau mao* might also be used to perform the *ho-uluulu-ai* service, in which prayer to propitiate the gods of heaven and induce them to send abundant harvests of food. The following prayer is one that was used on such occasions:

> *E Kane auloli ka honua!*
> *Honu ne'e pu ka aina.*
> *Ulu nakaka, kawahawaha ka honua,*
> *Ulu ka ai hapu'u, e Lono,*
> *Ohi maloo, kupukupu,*
> *Ohi aa na uala o na pali,*
> *Pali-ku kawahawaha ka ua,*
> *Ka ua haule lani,*
> *He haule lani ka uala.*
> *He aweu ke kalo,*
> *He lauloa pili kanawao.*
> *O wao akua ka ai, e Kane!*
> *E Kane! e Lono! na akua mahiai,*
> *Hoola i ka aina!*
> *A poho ka ai,*
> *A ulu kupukupu,*
> *A ulu lau poo-ole;*
> *A o ka nui ia o ka ai*
> *Au, e Kane a me Lono.*
> *Amama. Ua noa.*

> O Kane, transform the earth,
> Let the earth move as one piece,
> The land is cracked and fissured.
> The edible fern yet grows, oh Lono,
> Let kupukupu cover the dry land,
> Gather potatoes as stones on the side-hills
> The rain comes like the side of a pali,
> The rain falling from heaven.
> The potato also falls from heaven.
> The wild taro is the only taro now,
> The taro of the mountain patches.
> The only food is that of the wilds, oh Kane!

Oh, Kane and Lono! Gods of the husbandmen,
Give life to the land!
Until the food goes to waste.
Until it sprouts in the ground;
Until the leaves cover the land;
And such be the plenty
Of you, O Kane and Lono.
The burden is lifted. We are free.

This service was performed in the open air; it was for the public weal. (Communicated by Polikapa of Auwai-o-limu, Honolulu, who obtained it from Rev. Kapohaku of Kula, Maui, who was a missionary to Nuuhiwa).

XXXVII

CONCERNING THE LUAKINI

1. It was a great undertaking for a king to build a *heiau* of the sort called a *luakini*, to be accomplished only with fatigue and redness of the eyes from long and wearisome prayers and ceremonies on his part.

2. There were two rituals which the king in his eminent station used in the worship of the gods; one was the ritual of Ku, the other that of Lono. The Ku-ritual was very strict (*oolea*), the service most arduous (*ikaika*). The priests of this rite were distinct from others and outranked them. They were called priests of the order of Ku, because Ku was the highest god whom the king worshipped in following their ritual. They were also called priests of the order of *Kanalu*, because that was the name of their first priestly ancestor. These two names were their titles of highest distinction.

3. The Lono-ritual was milder, the service more comfortable. Its priests were, however, of a separate order and of an inferior grade. They were said to be of the order of Lono (*moo-Lono*), because Lono was the chief object of the king's worship when he followed the ritual. The priests of this ritual were also said to be of the order of *Paliku.*

4. If the king was minded to worship after the rite of Ku, the *heiau* he would build would be a *luakini*. The timbers of the house would be of *ohia*, the thatch of *loulu*-palm or of *uki* grass. The fence about the place would be of ohia with the bark peeled off.

The *lananu'u-mamao*[1] had to be made of *ohia* timber so heavy that it must be hauled down from the mountains. The same heavy ohia timber was used in the making of the idols for the heiau.

5. The tabu of the place continued for ten days and then was *noa;* but it might be prolonged to such an extent as to require a resting spell, *hoomahanahana;*[2] and it might be fourteen days before it came to an end. It all depended on whether the *aha*[3] was obtained. If the *aha* was not found the heiau would not soon be declared *noa*. In case the men took a resting spell, a dispensation was granted and a service of prayer was offered to relax the tabu, after which the heiau stood open.

6. The body of priests engaged in the work stripped down the leaves from a banana-stalk—as a sign that the tabu was relaxed:—and when

DAVID MALO

the Ku-tabu of the next month came round, the tabu of the heiau was again imposed. Thus it was then that if the *aha* was procured the services of prayer came to an end; otherwise people and chiefs continued indefinitely under tabu, and were not allowed to come to their women-folk.

7. The tabu might thus continue in force many months, possibly for years, if the *aha* were not found. It is said that Umi was at work ten years on his heiau before the aha was found, and only then did they again embrace their wives. This was the manner of building a *heiau-luakini* from the very earliest times; it was *noa* only when the *aha* had been found.

It was indeed an arduous task to make a *luakini;* a human sacrifice was necessary, and it must be an adult, a law-breaker (*lawe-hala*).

8. If the king worshipped after the rite of Lono the heiau erected would be a *mapele*; or another kind was the *unu o Lono* The timber, in this case, used in the construction of the house, the fence about the grounds, and that used in constructing the *lananuu-mamao* was *lama,* and it was thatched with the leaves of the *ti* plant. (*Cordyline terminalis.*) There were also idols. The tabu lasted for three days, after which the place would be *noa,* provided, however, that the *aha* was found. If the *aha* were not found the same course was taken as in the case of the *luakini.*

9. The *mapele* was a thatched heiau in which to ask the god's blessing on the crops.[4] Human sacrifices were not made at this heiau; pigs only were used as offerings. Any chief in rank below the king was at liberty to construct a *mapele heiau,* an *unu o Lono,* a *kukoae,* or an *aka,* but not a *luakini.* The right to build a *luakini* belonged to the king alone. The *mapele,* however, was the kind of heiau in which the chiefs and the king himself prayed most frequently.

10. The *luakini* was a war temple, *heiau-wai-kaua,* which the king, in his capacity as ruler over all, built when he was about to make war upon another independent monarch, or when he heard that some other king was about to make war against him; also when he wished to make the crops flourish he might build a *luakini.*

11. It was the special temple in which the king prayed to his gods to look with favor upon him, and in the services of that heiau he obtained assurances of victory over his enemies, or received warnings of defeat at their hands.

12. If all the *ahas* of his luakini were obtained, then the king felt assured that he would have victory and rout his enemies, and he went

into battle with good courage. But if the *ahas* were not found, it meant his defeat, and he would not go out to attack the other king.

The building of a luakini for the king to worship in was conducted in the following manner.

13. The king in the first place inquired of his high priest in regard to building a luakini, whether he thought the old luakini would answer, provided the house and the fence were renewed; whether the old stone-wall should be allowed to remain, and whether the old idols should still continue to be used.

If the king's proposition was agreed to, the first thing was to perform the ceremony of purification—*huikala*—on the heiau, and make it *moa*, i e., free, to enable the workmen to enter it that they might put a new fence about it, and newly thatch the house with loulu-palm, or with uki.

14. If the king, the priests and others agreed that it was best to build an entirely new luakini, the *kahuna kuhi-kuhi-puu-one*[5] was sent for. It was his function to exhibit a plan of the heiau to the king; because this class of persons were thoroughly educated in what concerned a heiau. They were acquainted with the heiaus which had been built from the most ancient times, from Hawaii to Kauai; some of which had gone into ruins. These *kuhi-kuhi-puu-ones* knew all about these old temples because they had studied them on the ground, had seen their sites and knew the plans of them all.

15. They knew the heiau which a certain ancient king had built, as a result of which he gained a victory over another king. That was the heiau, the plan of which the *kuhi-kuhi-puu-one* explained to the king; and if the king was pleased, he first made a sort of plan of the heiau on the ground and exhibited it to the king with an explanation of all its parts, so that he could see where the fence was to run, where the houses were to stand, and where was the place for the *lana-nuu-mamao* with the idols.

16. Then a levy was made of people who should build the heiau from among those who ate at the king's table—the *aialo*—and the chiefs; and the work of hauling the ohia timber for the *lana-nuu-mamao*, and for making the idols themselves, was begun.

The work of carving the certain images was assigned to special chiefs. A stone wall was then put up which was to surround all the houses.

17. The plan of the luakini was such that if its front faced West or East the *Lana-nuu-mamao* would be located at the northern end. If

DAVID MALO

the heiau faced North or South, the *lana-nuu-mamao* would be located at the eastern end; thus putting the audience either in the southern or western part of the luakini.

18. Within this *lana-nuu-mamao* was a pit called a *lua-kini,*[6] or *lua-pa'u.* In front of the *lana-nuu* stood the idols, and in their front a pavement, *kipapa,* and the *lele* on which the offerings were laid.

19. In front of the *lele* was a pavement of pebbles, or framework, on which the offerings were deposited until they were offered up (*hai*), when they were laid upon the *lele.* In front of the lele was a house called *hale-pahu* with its door facing the *lele,* in which the drum was beaten. At the back of the *hale-pahu* stood a larger and longer house called *mana,* its door also opening towards the *lele.* To the rear again of the *hale-pahu* was another house which stood at the entrance of the heiau. In the narrow passage back of the drum-house, *hale pahu,* and at the end (*kala*) of the house called *mana* was a small house called *Waiea,* where the *aha*-cord was stretched.

20. At the other end (*kala*) of Mana was a house called *hale-umu,* in which the fires for the heiau were made. The space within the *pa,* or enclosure, was the court, or *kahua* of the heiau. Outside of the *pa,* to the North, was a level pavement, or *papahola,* and to the South, and outside of the *pa,* stood the house of *Papa.*[8] At the outer borders of the *papahola* crosses were set in the ground to mark the limits of the heiau.

21. After the stone-wall of the heiau was completed they proceeded to build the *lananuu;*[7] first setting up the frame and then binding on the small poles, or *aho;* after which they set up the idols of which there was a good number. Some of them were *makaiwa,*[9] images of great height. In the midst of these images was left a vacant space, in which to set up the new idol that was to be made, called the *Moi.*[10]

22. After all these things were done—the erection of the houses being deferred until a tabu was imposed—the *kahunas, aliis,* and certain other religious persons made preparations to purify themselves, which they did in the following manner.

23. During the days when the waning moon was late in rising over the island, that is during the nights of *Laaukukahi,* etc., they made for themselves temporary booths called *hale-puu-one,*[11] next booths covered with *pohue* vine, then an *oe-oe* booth, then a *palima,* then a *hawai.*[12] Each one of these was consecrated and made tabu, its ceremonies performed, and the place declared *noa* on the self-same day. After doing this the

purification of the priests, chiefs and others was completed and they were fit to enter the heiau.

24. The next thing was to purify the whole island. On the day *Kaloa-ku-kahi* the *mauka* road that extended round the island was cleared of weeds from one end to the other, each man who had land (abutting?) doing his share and all making a day of it about the whole island. They set up an altar of stone at the boundary of every *ahu-puaa*.

25. Then they carved a log of kukui wood in imitation of a swine's head. This image, called *puaa-kukui*, was placed on the altar, together with some *pai-ai*, i e., hard poi.

26. This done, every man went his way home and the road was left vacant. Then came the priest, smeared with red clay, *alaea*, mixed with water, accompanied by a man, who personated the deity and whose hair was done up after the fashion of *Niheu*.[13]

27. On coming to the altar on which was lying the pig's head carved in kukui, the priest having uttered a prayer[14] and having bedaubed the carving with *alaea*, they ate the *pai-ai* and the priest then declared the land purified, the tabu removed.

28. Then they left this land and went on to another, bedaubing with *alaea* the carved pigs' heads as they passed from one land to another, all that day—and the next day (Kane), and the next (Lono), and still another day, Mauli;—until the whole island was purified, and this ceremony relating to the luakini was performed. The ceremonies that remain were for other priests to perform.

29. On the evening of the next day, Muku, all those who were to attend the heiau, king, chiefs and commoners, came together in one place for purification, and when they had all assembled, a special priest, whose function it was to perform purification, came with a dish of water and a bunch of *pala* fern in his hands and conducted the following service:

30. The priest said,

A

Lele Uli e! lele wai e!
He Uli, he Uli, he wai, he wai!
A lele au i ke au, e Kane-mehane o Nehe-lani.
Nehe ia pika'na ka lani.
A lama, he mu oia.

The people responded,

> *He mu oia.*

The priest said,

> *He mu ka ai-ku.*
> *He mu ka aia.*
> *He mu ka ah'ula.*
> *He mu ka paani.*
> *He mu koko lana.*
> *I koko puaa,*
> *I koko ilio,*
> *I koko kanaka make.*
> *He mu oia.*

People— *He mu!*

C

Kahuna—*Elieli!*
People— *Kapu!*
Kahuna—*Elieli!*
People— *Noa!*
Kahuna—*Ia e!*
People— *Noa honua!*

30. The priest said:

> Fly, O Uli! fly, o water!
> Here is Uli, Uli! here is water! water!
> I fly to the realm of Kane, the benevolent, noiseless
> in the heavens.
> Heaven is appeased by the sprinkling.
> Light comes, he is gracious.

People respond:

> He is gracious.

Priest: Awed into silence are the unceremonious ones,
Awed into silence are the atheists,

Awed into silence are they who gather at the hula,
Awed into silence are those who sport,
Awed into silence are the hot-blooded ones.
Give the blood of swine!
Give the blood of dogs!
Give the blood of a human sacrifice!
These are of godlike power.

People: Of godlike power.
Priest: Finished—
People: The tabu.
Priest: Finished—
People: It is free.
Priest: O (god) Ia!
People: Freedom complete and instant!

The priest then sprinkled the water upon all the people, and the ceremony of purification was accomplished; after which every man went to his own house.

31. On the evening of the next day, Hilo, the first of the month—possibly on *Welo*—a tabu was laid on the luakini, and the king, chiefs, and all the people entered into the temple and were ordered to sit down by ranks and to make no noise.

32. Then another priest came forward to preside at the service, holding in his hand a branch of *ieie;* and standing in the midst of the people he offered a prayer called *Lupa-lupa.* When the priest uttered the words, *E ku kaikai na hikia* Stand up and hold aloft the spears, all the people responded, Hail! Then the priest said *Ia!* and the people responded, Hail, Hail, o Ku! (*Ola! ola, o Ku*). When this service was over all the people slept that night in the *heiau* under the restrictions of tabu. Not one, not even an *alii*, was allowed to go out secretly to sleep with his wife. If any one were detected in such conduct, he would be put to death.

33. On the morrow, which was Hoaka, the people were again seated in rows, as in the service led by the kahuna on the previous evening, and now another Kahuna stood forth to conduct the service. He repeated a *pule* called *Kau-ila Huluhulu* (rough *kauila* stick).

34. That night, Hoaka, still another kahuna conducted the service which was called *Malu-koi,* in which they consecrated the axes that were to be used in hewing the timber for the new idols, and laid them

DAVID MALO

over night (in the little house *Mana*). A fowl was baked for the use of the kahuna, another for the king, and a third for the deity; and then they slept for the night.

35. The next morning, *Ku-kahi*, the king, chiefs, people and the priests, including that priest who conducted the service of *Malu-koi*, started to go up into the mountains. The priest who performed the *Malu-koi* service with the ax was called *kahuna haku ohia*, because *Haku ohia* was a name applied to the idol which they were about to carve. Another name for the idol was *Mo-i*. That day the *kahuna haku ohia* began a fast which was to continue for six days.

36. In going up they took with them pigs, bananas, cocoanuts, a red fish—the *kumu*—and a man who was a criminal, as offerings to the deity.

37. A suitable ohia tree had previously been selected, one that had no decay about it, because a perfect tree was required for the making of the *haku-ohia* idol; and when they had reached the woods, before they felled the tree, the *kahuna haku-ohia* approached the tree by one route, and the man who was to cut the tree by another; and thus they stood on opposite sides of the tree.

38. The *kahuna* having the axe, and the king the pig—the people remained at a respectful distance, having been commanded to preserve strict silence. The *kahuna* now stood forth and offered the *aha*[18] prayer called *Mau haalelea*.[19]

39. On the completion of the prayer the king uttered the word *amana*, (equivalent to amen), and then killed the pig by dashing it against the ground; after which he offered the pig as a sacrifice. This done, the *kahuna* inquired of the king, "How was this *aha* of ours?" If no noise or voice, no disturbance made by the people had been heard, the king answered, "The *aha* is good." Then the *kahuna* declared: "Tomorrow your adversary will die. The incantation—*aha*—we have just performed for your god was a success. On the death of your adversary, you will possess his lands, provided this business is carried through."

40. The *kahuna*, having first cut a chip out of the tree, the criminal was led forth, and the priest, having taken his life by beheading, offered his body as a sacrifice. The tree was then felled; the pig put into the oven, and the work of carving the idol was taken up and carried to a finish by the image-carver. The pig when cooked was eaten by the king and people; and what remained, after they had satisfied their hunger, was buried, together with the body of the man, at the root of the tree from

which the image had been made. The man used as a sacrifice was called a man from *mau-Haalelea*. Thus ended this ceremony.

41. The people then went for *pala*-fern, making back-loads of it, and they gathered the fruit and flowers of the mountain-apple, the ohia, until the hands of every one were filled with the bouquets. Then, some of them bearing the idol, they started on their way down to the ocean with tumultuous noise and shouting.

42. Calling out as they went, "Oh Kuamu.[20] Oh Kuamumu. Oh Kuawa. Oh Kuawa-wa. I go on to victory, *u-o*." Thus they went on their wild rout, shouting as they went;—and if any one met them on their way, it was death to him—they took his life. On arriving at the *heiau* they put the image on the level pavement of the temple-court, and, having covered it with *ieie*-leaves, left it.

43. That evening they measured off the foundation of the house, *mana*, and determined where it should stand, where should be its rear, its front, and its gables. A post was then planted at the back of *mana*, directly opposite its door of entrance. This upright was termed a *Nanahua* post, and it marked the place where the image of Luamu was to be set. A post was also planted between the *Makaiwa*—images of Lono—at the spot where the image called Moi was to be set up. This post was called the pillar of Manu—*ka pou o Manu*.

44. The ensuing night stakes were driven to mark the four corner posts of *Mana*, after which the king and priest went to carry the measuring line (*e kai i ka aha helehonua*). The priest stood at the corner post of *Mana* while he repeated the prayer, and by him stood the king holding the sacrificial pig. When the prayer was over the *kahuna* stooped down and took the end of the line in his hands. . .

45. Then he ran from that stake to the next, gave the line a turn about the stake, then to the next and did the same thing there, thence he returned and rejoined the king at the spot where the prayer had been made. Then, having said *Amana*, the king despatched the pig by beating him against the ground.

46. This done, the priest inquires of the king, "how is our incantation—our *aha?*" and if no voice, no noise had been heard, the king answered, "the ceremony—the *aha*—was good." Thereupon the *kahuna* assured the king that his government was firmly established, "because," said he, "the land-grabbing ceremony (*aha hele honua*) has just been successfully performed." It was a special priest who officiated at this ceremony.

DAVID MALO

47. On the next day, *Kulu,* the people came in multitudes, bringing timber, cord, leaves of the *loulu*-palm, and *uki*-grass, with which to build and thatch the different houses, the drumhouse, the *waiea,* the *mana,* and the oven-house. When the frames of the houses had been set up, the thatching was left to be done after the *kauila* ceremony had been performed.

48. On the day *Kulua,* the *Kauila nui* celebration took place. It was conducted in this manner: The king and a company of men were stationed a short distance away at a place called *Kalewa,* the *kahuna* and the bulk of the people being by themselves and not far away.

49. This was on the level ground—*papahola*—outside of the *heiau,* the whole multitude of people being seated on the ground in rows.

50. Then the keepers of the *kaai*-gods came, each one bearing the *kaai*-god of his chief—the *kaai*-god of the king also was there. The number of these idols was very great. The god *Ka-hoa-lii* also was personated by a man in a state of nudity.

51. At this juncture, the *kaai*-gods being held aloft, each on his spear decorated with a banner, the *kahu* of each sat in front of the god of his charge, waiting for the signal to run in a circle about all the *kaai*-gods. If any *kahu,* however, made a mistake in this circuit-running he was put to death, and the duty of the running then devolved upon the *alii* to whom belonged the idol.

52. When all the people were ready, the high priest of the temple came forward, arrayed in a large, white *malo* and carrying in his hand a bunch of *pala*-fern. He was accompanied by a man carrying a human skull containing sea-water (*kai*). *Kai-a-po-kea* also was the name applied to the prayer which the *kahuna* now repeated—a very long prayer it was.

52. Silence was ordered and the high priest stood forth to conduct the service; and when he uttered the words, *"a hopu! a hopu!"* all the *kuhus* of the idols stood up and taking hold of their idols, held them to their front, standing the while in a well dressed line.

54. At the same time Kahoalii, the man-god, stood forth in front of the *kaai*-gods, his nakedness visible to the whole multitude, and the moment the priest uttered the following words of invocation:

55.   *Mau hoe e, ihe a Luakapu!*
        E Lukaluka e, he mau hoe e!
        Ihe a Luakapu, e Lukaluka, e Luka!
        O hookama ko haalauele, e Luka!

Strange paddles, spear of Luakapu!
Robed one, curious are your paddles!
Spear of Luakapu, oh Lukaluka,
Adoption will be to you a house, O Luka!

56. Kahoalii then started on the run in all his nakedness, and all the *kaai*-gods followed after in regular order. They took a circular course, all the time paying close attention to the prayer of the *kahuna;* and when he came to the words, *A mio i ka lani omamalu,*[24]

57. Kahoalii turned to the left, and all the *kaai*-gods following turned also and came back. On their return they came to where was standing a man with a staff in his hand, who joined their company, and they all came back together.

58. When the priest in his prayer uttered the words of invocation:

> *Kuku'i Kahiko i ka lani,*
> *A uwa i ka make o Manalu.*

> Kahiko assails heaven with petitions,
> An uproar at the death of Manalu,

all the *kaai-gods* with their *kahus* halted and stood in well dressed ranks facing the *kahuna* in profound silence, and the *kahuna* and all the assembly stood facing them.

59. The man whom they had met then took his station in the space between the people and the *kaai*-gods, still holding his staff in hand.

60. Then the high priest asked him in the words of the prayer, "To whom belongs the earth? To whom belongs the earth? (*Nowai honua? Nowai honua?*)

61. "The earth belongs to Ku," answered the priest; "a priest has ratified the transaction." (*Hana mai a mana ke kahuna.*) Then the *kahuna* again asked the question of this man, who was himself a *kahuna*, and he answered, "To Ku belong the small pieces of land." (*No Ku ka ha'i makaokao.*)

62. The *kahuna* then went through with a long service of the *Pule kai,* the full name of which was *Kai-o-po-kea;* but on account of its wearisome length it was nicknamed *Unuhi kai o po-kea;* and when their prayer was completed they sat down.

63. After that a priest of the order of Lono stood forth; he was called a *kahuna kuhi-alaea*—the kahuna bedaubed with clay. He held

in his hand a staff bound with a white cloth called *olo-a,* and recited a service of prayer.

64. This was also a tediously long service, and was called *Kai o Kauakahi,* salt water of *Kaua-kahi.* Toward the close of this prayer the *kahuna* uttered the words, Oh Ku! remove our perplexities!—*E Ku ka'ika'i na hihia!*

65. At this the whole assembly exclaimed, Hail! The priest then said, *Ia.* Thereupon the people responded, Hail, hail, Ku! (*Ola! ola! o Ku!*) With these words came to an end the part taken by this priest, also that portion of the service denominated *kauila* (*kauila ana*).

66. After this all the chiefs and the people returned to their own houses to refresh themselves with food. The material was now made ready for thatching the houses in the *luakini,* and when the arrangements were all completed, certain men climbed upon the houses, taking with them thatch-poles (*aho*), of a special kind called *auau.*

67 While this was going on the priest stood and recited a service for these *aho,* in which he used the expression, *kau na auau,*[29]—put the thatch-poles in place. When all these thatchsticks were lashed on, the priest concluded his service.

68. The houses were then thatched, the drum-house, the oven house, *waiea,* and *mana,* after which the people brought presents of pigs, cocoanuts, bananas, red fish, also *oloa* to serve as *malos* for the idols, braided sugar-cane for the thatch of the *anu'u-mamao* (same as the *lana-nuu-mamao*) as well as for the *mana.* This accomplished, all the people returned to their houses.

69. That same evening, *Kulua,* the *haku-ohia* idol, was brought in from the paved terrace, *papahola,*—(See sect. 42)—and set in the place which had been specially reserved for it, that being the spot where the pillar of Manu had been planted. (See sect. 43.)

70. The post-hole in which this idol (Haku-ohia) was set was situated between the *Makaiwa*[30] images, directly in front of the *lana-nuu-mamao,* and close to the *lele,* on which the offerings were laid. There it stood with no malo upon it.

71. At this time none of the idols had malos girded upon them; not until the evening, when this image, the Haku-ohia idol, had been arrayed in a malo, would the rest of them be so covered. While in this unclothed state, the expression used of them was, the wood stands with its nakedness pendent—*ua ku lewalewa ka laau.*

72. Then a priest stood forth and conducted a service for the setting in its place of this idol, which service was styled *ka Poupouana.* A man who

was a criminal[31] was first killed, and his body thrust into the hole where the idol was to stand. The man was sacrificed in order to propitiate the deity; and when the service was done the chiefs and the priests returned to their houses, keeping in mind the work to be done that night.

73. That evening all the people, commoners and chiefs, made themselves ready to pray to their own special gods for the success of the service, the *aha*, which was to be solemnized that night, being continued until morning.

74. The special burden of their prayers was that it might not rain that night, that there might be no wind, or thunder, or lightning, that there might be no heavy surf, that no fire should burn, that there should be no sound or outcry from voice of man or beast, that whole night until day; for thus would the conduct of the service be perfect. This was the character of the luakini-service from ancient times down.

75. That night some of the people left their houses and lay in the open air, for the purpose of observing the heavens; and if a cloud appeared in the sky they prayed that everything that could mar the ceremony of the night might be averted.

76. When the milky-way was visible and the sky became clear overhead, if it had perhaps been overcast, and all sounds were hushed, . . .

77. Then the king and the high priest went into the house, Waiea, and were there together by themselves to conduct the service—the *aha*. The multitude of the people remained at a distance in front of Mana, listening, lest any noise should be heard to make the ceremony nugatory (*o lilo ke kai aha ana*).

78. The king stood and held the pig and the priest stood and recited the service, which was called *hulahula*.[32] Until the close of the service, the king hearkened if every noise was quiet, and then he perceived that the *aha* was perfect.

79. The king then dashed the pig against the ground until it was dead and offered it to the gods, saying, "Oh Ku! Oh Kane! and Kanaloa! here is a pig. Keep and preserve me and safeguard the government. Amen. It is free. The tabu flies away."

80. Then the kahuna asked the king, "How is the *aha* you and I have performed?" He repeated the question, "How is the *aha* you and I have performed?" Then the king answered, "The *aha* is perfect."

81. The king and priest then went out to the people waiting outside, and the king put the question to them, "How is our *aha*?"

82. Thereupon they answered, "The *aha* is perfect; we have not heard the smallest sound (kini)." Then the whole assembly broke out into a loud shout, *"Lele wale ka aha e! Lele wale ka aha e!"* with frequent reiteration. "The *aha* is completely successful." (Literally—the *aha* flies away.)

83. Then the news was carried to the people outside of the temple, and everybody rejoiced that the king had obtained his *aha,* and all believed that the government would enjoy great peace and prosperity during the coming years.

84. The next morning, Kukolu, the high priest who had conducted the ceremony of *hulahula,* and who was the head-priest of the luakini, took it upon himself to join the priest of the *haku-ohia*-idol in a fast—that priest was already doing a fast in honor of the god. So they fasted together during those days.

85. During the days of fasting they sustained themselves on the honey of banana-flowers. The high priest was fasting in preparation for the ceremonies still remaining, the *haku-ohia*-priest in order to make the idol into a real god (*akua maoli*).[33]

86. On that same day—Kukolu—(*hai ka haina*)[39]—the people were called together and a feast declared. (This reading is somewhat conjectural.) Four pigs were baked. One pig was laid upon the *lele* as a sacrifice, one was devoted to the use of the kahuna, one for the use of the *kahu-akua,* and one for the king and his men. The one for the king was said to be the pig for the *iliili,* i.e., for the pavement of pebbles.

87. On that day also a few men climbed up on the roof of the house, Mana, taking with them bundles, *makuu,* of white tapa, four in number perhaps, which they fastened to the ridgepole, while all the priests, gathered beneath them, were reciting prayers. These two men were at the same time gesturing in pantomime as if performing a hula-dance. This ceremony was termed *Hoopii na aha limalima.*[34]

88. Then came the kahuna who was to trim the thatch over the door of Mana. The name of the service which he recited was *Kuwa.* After that an idol, named *Kahuanu'u-noho-n'io-n'io-i- ka pou-kua,* was set up in the back part of the house, just opposite the door, at the spot where the post called *Nanahua* had been planted, and thus ended this ceremony.

89. That night all the priests assembled at this place to perform a service of prayer, in which they were to continue until morning. This service was of a uniform character throughout. It had been committed to memory, so that, like a *mele,* the prayers and responses were all recited in unison. It was called *Kuili.*[35]

90. That night a large number of hogs, as many as eight hundred—*elua lau*—were baked; and—the priests being separated into two divisions, one on this side and one on that side of Mana—each division took part in the service alternately.

91. The pork also was divided into two portions, four hundred of the hogs being assigned to the priests seated at one end of the building and four hundred for the priests seated at the other end (*kala*). The priests and their men ate the flesh of the swine and continued their prayers without sleep until morning.

92. The next morning which was Kupau, the *Kuili* service was kept up and continued without intermission all day. That day four hundred pigs were served out to the worshippers, two hundred (*elima kanaha*) to those at one end of the temple and two hundred to those at the other end.

93. The service was still kept up during the ensuing night, two hundred and forty pigs being baked and served out—one hundred and twenty to the priests of this end of the temple and one hundred and twenty to those of the other end of the temple. The service continued all night.

94. During the next day, Olekukahi, the Kuili-service still went on, and four hundred pigs were baked and divided out equally between the priests at the two ends of the temple. Only the priests ate of this pork, not the chiefs; and that evening the Kuili-service of the kahunas came to a conclusion.

95. In the evening the king and high priest went, as they had done before, to hold a service (*aha*), called *Hoowilimoo.*[36] If this *aha* was successful it was a most fortunate omen for the luakini. The kahuna, having first besought the king for a piece of land for himself, then addressed the king in a hopeful and confident strain, saying:

96. "Your heavenly majesty, (*E ko lani,*) you have just asked the deity for a blessing on the government, on yourself and on the people; and, as we see, the god has granted the petition; the *aha* is perfect. After this if you go to war with any one you will defeat him, because your relations to the deity are perfect." (*Ua maikai ko ke akua aoao.*)

97. That same night a priest conducted a ceremony called *Ka-papa-ulua.*[36½] It was in this way: the priest, accompanied by a number of others, went out to sea, to fish for *ulua* with hook and line, using squid for bait.

98. If they were unsuccessful and got no *ulua,* they returned to land and went from one house to another, shouting out to the people within and telling them some lie or other and asking them to come outside.

If any one did come out, him they killed, and thrusting a hook in his mouth, carried him to the heiau. If there were many people in the house, they resisted and thus escaped.

99. The next morning they put a long girdle of braided coconut leaves about the belly of the *haku-ohia*-idol, calling it the navel-cord from its mother.

100. Then the king and the priest came to perform the ceremony of cutting the navel-string of the idol; and the priest recited the following prayer:

101. *O ka ohe keia o ka piko o ke Aiwaiwalani.*
O ka uhae keia o ka ohe o ka piko o ke Aiwaiwalani.
O ke oki keia o ka piko o ke Aiwaiwalani.
O ka moku keia o ka piko o ke Aiwaiwalani.

This is the bamboo for the navel-string of the wonderful idol.
This is the splitting of the bamboo for the navel-string of the wonderful idol.
This is the cutting of the navel-string of the wonderful idol.
This is the severing of the navel-string of the wonderful idol.

The priest then cut the cord, and having wiped it with a cloth, made the following prayer:

Kupenu ula, kupenu lei,
Aka halapa i ke akua i laau waila.

Sop the red blood, wear it as a wreath,
To the grace and strength of the deity.

Compare Chap. XXXV, Sect. 14.

The king then uttered the *amama* and the service was ended.

102. The next day, Ouekulua, took place the great feast. The chiefs contributed of their pigs, as also did the people. The contributions were arranged on the following scale. The high chiefs, who had many people under them, gave ten pigs apiece; the lesser chiefs, with a smaller number of followers, provided fewer.

103. In the same way, the people gave according to their ability. When all the pigs had been contributed and oven-baked the king and all the priests assembled for the ceremony of girding the malo upon the haku-ohia-idol (*e hoohume i ka malo o ke kii haku ohia*).

104. The whole body of priests recited in unison the *pule malo*, a prayer relating to the malo of the deity:

> *Hume, hume na malo e Lono!*
> *Hai ke kaua, hailea, hailono e.*

> Gird on, gird on the malo oh Lono!
> Declare war, declare it definitely, proclaim it by
>   messengers!

At the conclusion of the prayer they arrayed the idol in a malo, and a new name was given to it, *Moi*, lord of all the idols. After that all the idols were clothed with malos, and each one was given a name according to the place in which he stood.

105. When the pigs were baked, a fore-quarters of each pig was set apart for the kahunas, which piece was termed *hainaki*. Bundles of *pai-ai* were also set apart for the kahunas, that having been the custom from the most ancient times.

106. When the chiefs and the people had finished feasting on the pork, the king made an offering to his gods of four hundred pigs, four hundred bushels of bananas, four hundred cocoanuts, four hundred red fish, and four hundred pieces of oloa cloth; he also offered a sacrifice of human bodies on the *lele*.

107. Before doing this, however, the hair and bristles of the pigs were gathered up and burned, and the offal removed; then all the offerings were collected in that part of the court about the *lele* which was laid with pebbles, after which the offerings were piled upon the *lele*.

108. Then the *Ka-papa-ulua* priest (Sect. 97) entered the *lana-nuu-mamao* with the ulua—(This might be the fish, *ulua*, or it might be the man whom the priest had killed in its stead, as previously stated) and recited an *aha* which was of a different rite but belonged to his special service. When he had concluded his service he put to the king the question, how was our *aha?* The king answered, "It was excellent." "Most excellent indeed," said the priest to the king; the hook did not

break; your government is confirmed." Then the ulua was laid as an offering upon the *lele,* and the kahuna went his way.

109. After that the *lana-nuu-mamao* was dressed with white oloa. That day was called the day of great decoration (*la kopili nui*), because of this decoration of the *lana-nuu-mamao.*

110. Towards evening that same day the priests and the people, together with Kahoalii and the idols, made an excursion up into the mountains, to procure branches of the koa tree, In reality the koa-branches had been brought to a place not far away. When they had gotten the branches of the koa-tree they returned with great noise and uproar,[37] just as when they brought down the haku-ohia-idol.

111. On their return from the expedition, that same evening they made the koa branches into a booth and at the same time the *papa-ka-hui* was let down. That night they sacrificed the *puaa hea* for the consecration of the booth of koa branches (*hale lala koa*).

112. In the morning all the people assembled to eat of the *hea* pig. The fragments that were left over when they had finished their eating had to be carefully disposed of. It was not allowable to save them for eating at another time. On this occasion Kahoalii ate an eye plucked from the man whose body had been laid as an offering on the lele, together with the eyes of the pig (*puaa hea*).

113. By the following morning, Olekukolu, these solemn services were concluded, whereupon all the people, priests, chiefs, and commoners went to bathe in the ocean. They took with them the *kaai*-gods, which they planted in the beach. When they had finished their bathing they carried with them pieces of coral, which they piled up outside of the heiau.

114. On arriving at the luakini a number of pigs were baked, and all, chiefs, priests and people, being seated on the ground in an orderly manner, in front of the drum-house, they performed the service called *Hono.*

115. When everybody was in place the priest who was to conduct the ritual came forward and stood up to recite the service called *Hono;* and when he solemnly uttered the words, *O ka hoaka o ka lima aia iluna,* the palms of the hands are turned upwards, priests, chiefs and people, all, obedient to the command, held up their hands and remained motionless, sitting perfectly still. If any one stirred, he was put to death. The service was tediously long, and by the time it was over the pigs were baked; the people accordingly ate of them and then went home to their beds.

116. On the morning of the morrow, which was Olepau, all the female chiefs, relations of the king, came to the temple bringing a malo of great length as their present to the idol. All the people assembled at the house of *Papa,* to receive the women of the court. One end of the malo was borne into the heiau, (being held by the priests), while the women-chiefs kept hold of the other end; the priest meantime reciting the service of the malo, which is termed *Kaioloa.*[38]

117. All the people being seated in rows, the kahuna who was to conduct the service—(*nana e papa ka pule*)—stood forth; and when he uttered the solemn word, *Elieli,*—completed,—the people responded, *Noa.* The kahuna said, *Ia e!* Oh Ia! and the people responded, *Noa honua,* Freedom to the ground! The consecration of the temple was now accomplished, and the tabu was removed from it, it was *noa loa.*

With such rites and ceremonies as these was a *luakini* built and dedicated. The ceremonies and service of the luakini were very rigorous and strict. There was a proverb which said the work of the luakini is like hauling ohia timber, of all labor the most arduous.

118. The tabu of a luakini lasted for ten days, being lifted on Huna, nth, and on the evening of the following day, Mohalu, began another service of a milder cult—a *hoomahana-hana* service. This continued for three days; and with it terminated the special services of the king.

119. When the people and the priests saw that the services of the luakini were well conducted, then they began to have confidence in the stability of the government, and they put up other places of worship, such as the *Mapele,* the *Kukoea,* the *Hale-o-Lono.* These heiaus were of the kind known as *hoouluulu* (hoouluulu ai = to make food grow), and were to bring rain from heaven and make the crops abundant, bringing wealth to the people, blessing to the government, prosperity to the land.

120. After this the king must needs make a circuit of the island, building heiaus and dedicating them with religious services; traveling first with the island on his right hand (*ma ka akau o ka mokupuni e hele mua ai*). This progress was called *ulu akau,* growth to the right. When this circuit was accomplished another one was made, going in the opposite direction, to the left. This was termed *ho'i hema,* return on the left. It was likewise conducted with prayers to the gods.

121. All the *aliis* below the king worshipped regularly each month and from year to year in their heiaus.

122. If an *alii ai moku,* the king of an island, was killed in battle, his body was taken to the luakini and offered up to the gods by the other king (*hai ia*).

123. In such ways as these did the kings and chiefs worship the gods in the ancient tmes until the time of Liholiho, when idol worship came to an end.

Notes to Chapter XXXVII

1. Sect. 4. *Lana-nuu-mamao,* a tower-like frame, made of strong timbers, covered with *aho,* i.e. poles, but not thatched. It had three floors, or *kahuas,* of which the lowest was named *lana,* the next *nu'u,* and the highest *mamao.* The lowest, the *lana,* was used for the bestowal of offerings. The second, *nu'u,* was more sacred; the high priest and his attendant's sometimes stood there while conducting religious services. The third, the *mamao,* was the most sacred place of all. Only the high priest and king were allowed to come to this platform. When worship was being conducted at the *lana-nu'u-mamao* all the people prostrated themselves. It seems probable that the *lana-nu'u-mamao* was used as a sort of oracle.

2. Sect. 5. *Hoo-mahana-hana,* a relaxation of the rigor of *tabu,* a resting spell in which the priests and workmen took it easy and indulged in some informalities. It was analogous to Refreshment-Sunday in Lent. The following form of prayer is communicated to me as one that was used in entreating the gods to grant the dispensation for a period of *hoomahanahana.*

Pule Hoomahanahana

E Ku i ka lana mai nuu,
E Ku i ka ohia lele,
E Ku i ka ohia-lehua,
E Ku i ka ohia-ha uli,
E Ku i ka ohia moewai,
E Ku mai ka lani,
Ku i ke ao,
E Ku i ka honua,
E ka ohia ihi,
E Ku i ka lani-ka-ohia, ka haku-ohia,
A ku, a lele, ua noa.
A noa ia Ku.
Ua uhi kapa mahana,
Hoomahanahana heiau.
E noa, e noa.
Amama wale. Ua noa.

O god Ku, of the sacred altar!
O Ku of the scaffolding of *ohia*-timber!
O Ku carved of the *ohia-lehua!*
O Ku of the flourishing *ohia-ha!*
O Ku of the water-seasoned *ohia timber!*
O Ku, come down from heaven!
O Ku, god of light!
O Ku, ruler of the world!
O magnificent *ohia*-tree!
O Ku of the *ohia*-tree carved by a king, lord of *ohia*-gods!
It lifts, it flies, it is gone,
The *tabu* is removed by Ku.
Robed are we in warm *tapas,*
A warmth that relaxes the rigors of the *heiau.*
Freedom! freedom!
The load is lifted! there is freedom!

3. Sect. 5. *Aha,* often used to mean a prayer, an incantation, a service, or the successful performance of a service,—the slabness and goodness of it, in the present instance means a cord, or mat, braided out of a sea-tangle, which was found in the deep ocean far out to sea. Cocoanut fibre was combined with the sea-weed in braiding this *aha.* The sea-weed was perhaps more generally called *ahaaha.* This *aha* was used in the decoration of the shrine of Ku. The finding of the sea-tangle, with which to make the *aha,* was, of course, more or less a matter of good luck. Hence the uncertainty as to the length of the *kapu.*

4. Sect. 9. *Hoouluulu ai,* to bless the crops. Here is a sample of a prayer used on such an occasion.

Pule Hoouluulu ai, or Pule Hoomau

E Lono, alana mai Kahiki,
He pule ku keia ia oe e Lono.
E Lono lau ai nui.
E ua mai ka lani pili,
Ka ua houlu ai,
Ka ua houlu kapa,
Popo kapa wai lehua
A Lono i ka lani.
E Lono e! kuu'a mai koko ai, koko ua.
Ulua mai,
Houlu ia mai ka ai e Lono!
Houlu ia mai ka ia.
Ka moomoo, kiheaheapalaa e Lono!
Amama. Ua noa.

Oh Lono, gift from Tahiti,
A prayer direct to you oh Lono.
Oh Lono of the broad leaf,
Let the low-hanging cloud pour out its rain,
To make the crops flourish,
Rain to make the tapa-plant flourish,
Wring out the dark rain-clouds
Of Lono in the heavens.
Oh Lono shake out a net-full of food, a net-full of rain.
Gather them together for us.
Accumulate food oh Lono!
Collect fish oh Lono!
Wauke shoots and the coloring matters for tapa.
    Amen. It is free.

5. Sect. 14. *Kahuna kuhi-kuhi-pu'u-one,* literally the *kahuna* who pointed out the piles of sand. Sand was the material used in making a model, or plan of a *heiau.*

6. Sect. 18. *Lua-kini, Lua,* a pit, and *kini* 400,000. It was this undoubtedly which gave the name to this kind of a *heiau.* Into this pit it is said, that the decayed bodies of the offerings were finally thrown. It is a singular thing that the name *luakini* should often he used to mean a Christian church, or temple, whereas the word *heiau* is never, to my knowledge, so applied. It seems to prove, however, that the *luakini* was the highest grade of *heiau.*

7. Sect. 21. *Lana-nuu,* the same as *lana-nuu-mamao.*

8. Sect. 20. The house of *Papa.—Papa* was a mythical character, wife of Wakea.—See Chap. XLV. The *Hale o Papa* was the place where the women-chiefs had their services.

9. Sect. 21. *Makaiwa:* Images with eyes of pearl.

10. Sect. 21. *Mo-i,* sovereign, a word used in the days of the monarchy to designate the king or queen.

11. Sect. 23. *Halc-puu-one:* so called because it was of the same shape that sand would take if piled evenly in one spot. *i.e.,* of a conical shape, like the old-fashioned Sibley tent, used in the army of the Potomac in the early years of the great Civil War.

12. Sect. 23. *Hawai:* a long gabled house in which the women priests of the order of Papa, assembled with the king and priests to perform a service of purification,—*Pule huikala,*—after which they separated, to remain strictly apart until the *luakini* was *noa.* The prayer used on such an occasion was probably of the *Moo-Lono,* rite of Lono, as follows:

> *E Lono i ka oualii,*
> *E Lono uli moe,*
> *E Lono uli lani,*

E Lono ka lana mai nuu,
E Lono i ka makaiwa,
E Lono i ke one lau ea,
E huli e Lono,
E kala e Lono,
Kala ia na hala o ke alii kane.
E kala i ka hala o ke alii wahine.
E kala i ka hala o na kahuna.
E kala i ka hala o ka hu, ka makaainana,
He pule kala keia ia oe Lono.
Kuu'a mai ka ua pono,
Ka wai ola,
Ka alana pono.
Pono i kukini ia Lono,
Lono-a, ke akua mana.
      Amana.   Ua noa.

Response—   *Ua noa ke kino.*
Kapu ia kou heiau, e ke akua.
Hu a noa.
Noa, noa, ua lele,
A lele ia Lono, ke akua mana.
      Amana.

Oh Lono, tender offshoot of deity,
Oh Lono, consort of Uli,
Oh Lono-Uli, the heavenly pair,
Oh Lono, comforter of this fleshy temple,
Oh Lono, the discerning one,
Oh Lono, who abides with one to the last sand,
Turn to us, o Lono.
Forgive, oh Lono,
Pardon the sins of the men chiefs,
Pardon the sins of the women-chiefs,
Pardon the sins of the kahunas,
Pardon the sins of the boor, the plebeian, (*hu*).
This is a petition to you for pardon, oh Lono.
Send gracious showers of rain, oh Lono.
Life-giving rain, a grateful gift,
Symbols of Lono's blessing,
Lono-a, the mighty god.
Amen. It is noa.

Response—   The bodies are purified,
Your temple is tabu, oh God.

Purification for the multitude.
Purification, purification.
Salvation by Lono, the mighty god. Amen.

13. Sect. 26. *Niheu:* The hair was mixed with red clay—*alaea*—and skewered on top of the head. The hair of another person, it is said, was sometimes added to the natural hair.

14. Sect. 27. *Pule huikala no ka aina.* A prayer to purify the land.

> *E Lono ma ka uli lani,*
> *Eia ka ai, eia ka ia,*
> *He alana, he mohai,*
> *He nuhanuha, he alana ia oe e Lono.*
> *Houlu ia ka ai i keia ahupua'a,*
> *E ulu a maka-ole ke kalo,*
> *E ulu a muaiwa ka uala.*
> *A eia ka puaa,*
> *He puaa kukui nau e Lono.*
> *E kui a ko ahu puaa,*
> *A palahu ka ai i waena,*
> *A o kau ola ia e ke akua.*
> *E Lono, nana i kou pulapula.*
> > *Amana. Ua noa.*

O Lono of the blue firmament!
Here are vegetables, here is meat,
An offering of prayer, a sacrifice,
An offering of fat things to you, o Lono!
Let the crops flourish in this *ahu-puaa!*
The taro stay in the ground till its top dies down,
The potato lie in its hill till it cracks.
And here is the pig,
A pig carved in *kukui* wood for you, o Lono,
Let it remain on your district-altar
Until the vegetables rot in the fields.
Such is thy blessing, o God.
O Lono, look upon your offspring!
The burden is lifted! Freedom!

(A) Sect. 30. *Uli,* an *au-makua,* the chief agent of the *kahuna anaana,* a goddess, often addressed as *"Uli nana pono. Uli nana hewa."* She was also employed to do other criminal work. In the expression *Lele Uli!* That goddess is appealed to to speed on her errand.

(B) Sect. 30. The word *Mu* here refers, it would seem, to Kane previously mentioned. The meaning is not very clear, but after sifting the various conjectures that have been offered, I think the most plausible is that it adheres to the generic meaning of *mu*, as I take it to be, i.e. silent, and by silence giving consent. In the following verse, *He mu ka ai-ku*, and in those following to the 11th verse inclusive the word *mu* is used in a somewhat different sense. I take it, viz., that the *ai-ku*, those who eat standing, act unceremoniously; the *ai-a*, infidels, sinners; and all the other bad ones are now quiet, awed into silence. In consulting Hawaiian scholars as to the meaning of this word I have found that they either had no opinion about it or that no two of them agreed. I have also found that the same person held a different opinion at different times. It should be added that *mu* also means a gentle murmur, like the buzzing of insects, as in the following extract from *Ka mele o ka Nalu mai Kahiki mai*, which is said to be an old mele revamped by an old bard named Manu who lived in the time of Kalakaua:

> *Mu olelo ke kai o Kuhia;*
> *Ke wa mai la la i ka laa-laau,*
> *A lohe ka huakai hele o Puuloa.*

> Faint murmurs the ocean at Kuhia,
> Spraying upon the shrubs,
> Heard by the travellers to Puuloa.

(C) Sect. 30. *Elieli: Eli* is to dig. The following instance of its use in a counting out rhyme sometimes used by children is quoted to me:

> *Eli-eli, ku-pala-la!*
> *Nowai? nowai*
> *Ka lima i hawa-hawa?*
> *No kahupoka.*

The above is repeated in connection with a play, or trick more properly that is played on some novice. A number of piles of sand are heaped up, in one of which is hidden something foul or disagreeable. To each of the players is assigned a heap of sand, the one containing the filth being given to the green-horn or simple one, and at the word each one sets to dig, while one repeats the ditty. When the unfortunate one soils his hands, his name is at once called in the final line.

15. Sect. 32. Lupalupa, full of leaves, shaggy, flourishing; having reference also to the branch in the hand of the priest.

16. Sect. 32. *Ia*: Hawaiian authorities are able to throw no light, and conjecture but little light on the true meaning of this word. It is evidently the name, or appellation, or stands to represent some deity. The only name of a deity corresponding in form to this is the Hebrew JAH. Ps. 68:4.

17. Sect. 34. *Malu koi:* After a prayer the axes were laid within the lintels of the door of Mana and a sacrifice was offered of three fowls.

The following is a *Pule malu koi:*

> *E Kane uakea*
> *Eia ka alana,*
> *He moa ualehu,*
> *He moa uakea,*
> *He moa ulahiwa,*
> *He alana keia ia oe Kane,*
> *No ke koi kalai,*
> *Koi kua,*
> *Koi kikoni,*
> *Koi lou,*
> *He koi e kai e kalai ai ke kii,*
> *He koi ou e Kane, ke akua ola,*
> *Ke akua mana,*
> *Ke akua noho i ka iuiu,*
> *Ke akua i ke ao polohiwa,*
> *E ike i au ia. . .*
> *Ke kahuna kalai kii,*
> *A ku ke kii o Lanaikawai,*
> *O ka wai ola loa a Kane.*
> *E Kane eia kou hale la, o Mauliola,*
> *E ola ia. . . , ke alii heiau,*
> *E ola i a'u ia. . . , ke kahuna,*
> *E ola i na kahuna kapu heiau a pau,*
> *He ai kapu ka moa o ke alii.*
> *E ai noa ka moa o ke akua me ke kahuna.*
> *A lele, ua noa.*
> *A noa i ke akua.*
> *Amama.*

> Oh Kane the blond one,
> Here is an offering of prayer to you,
> A snuff-colored fowl for you,
> A fowl of a light-yellow color,
> A fowl of a red color.
> These are offerings for you oh Kane,
> For the benefit of the carpenter's adze,
> The woodman's adze,
> The little adze,
> The reversible adze,
> An adze to finish off the image,

The image of you, oh Kane, the god of life.
The God of power,
The God who dwells in the unapproachable heavens,
The god surrounded with clouds and darkness.
Look upon me, the kahuna Kalai-kii,
Until the image of Lanaikawai is set up,
Water of eternal life of Kane,
Oh Kane, here is your house, Mauliola.
Etc., etc.

18. Sect. 38. *Pule aha:* This was one of that class of prayers, for the ceremonial perfection of which absolute silence and freedom from disturbance was essential. The worshippers and the spectators, or listeners, whether within the same enclosure or outside of it, must preserve the most profound silence and attention. The charm of the service would be broken by the crowing of a cock, the barking of a dog, the squeaking of a rat, or the hooting of an owl. The intrusion of a woman was strictly forbidden and was punishable with death. An *aha*-prayer was a direct appeal to heaven to indicate by certain signs and phenomena the answer to the petition. Rain, thunder and lightning were generally regarded as unfavorable omens.

19. Sect. 38. *Mau-haa-lelea:* An entire turning away, repentance.

20. Sect. 42. *Kua-mu, Kua-wa* and *Kua-wao* were gods of the woodlands. It was *Kua-mu* who felled a tree in silence. *Kua-wa* did it with noise and shouting. *Kua-wao,* not mentioned in this prayer, felled a tree anywhere and everywhere and as he pleased. This tumultuous and joyous rout down the mountain was a farewell to these woodland deities.

21. Sect. 52. The following is a prayer such as is called

Pule O Kai-A-Pokea

E Kane, e Lono i ke kai uli,
Ke kai kea, ke kai haloiloi,
Ke kai nalu-poi,
Ke kai, e Ku, e lana i Kahiki.
E Ku i ke kai i Kahiki!
He kai kapu,
He kai a Po-kea.
E apo i ka hua.
Oia ke kai e lolo ai,
Ka ohia, ohia Kua-mu, Kua-wao, Kua-wa, Kua-lana,
E kaa ai ke akua kaei
O ke kahua aha-ula kuhonua,
O ka ohia haku-ohia,
Ke kii e lele ai a pau ka aina,

Nana e kulai ka hoa paio.
E Kane, eia kou kai ola,
Ai ia, inu ia, penu ia.
E ola i ke alii, e ola i na kahuna,
E ola i na mea a pau i moe-kapu i ka heiau!
A lele! A noa!
A mama! Ua noa!
Noa ia Kane, ke akua ola!

Oh Kane, oh Lono of the blue sea,
The white sea, the rough sea,
The sea with swamping breakers,
The sea, oh Ku, that reaches to Tahiti,
Oh Ku of the ocean at Tahiti,
The sacred ocean,
Sea of the bleached skull.
Take of the sea-foam
That is the brine wherewithal to consecrate,
Consecrate the ohia, ohia of Kuamu,
Of the woodland deities, Kua-wao Kua-wa, and Kua-lana,
That the kaei god may make his circuit
About the pavement guarded by the *aha ula* obedient
    only to royalty.
The ohia, god-image of ohia,
God-image that shall fly to the conquest of the whole land.
That shall overthrow all enemies.
Oh Kane, here is your life-giving brine,
To be mixed with food to be drunk, to be sopped up.
Long life to the king! Long life to the kahunas.
Long life to all true worshippers in the temple!
It is lifted, there is freedom!
The load is removed! Freedom!
Freedom through Kane, the life-giving one!

a. *Pokca:* probably from *poo kea,* white head, i.e., a bleached skull. The dish that held the brine was a skull.

b. *Aha ula:* the kind of aha here meant is the cord braided with much art, of many colored strands—one of them red, *ula*—which was stretched as a mystic protection about the residence of an alii with a kapu. It was claimed that if a tabu chief came to it, the aha would of itself fall to the ground, out of respect due to the tabu of the chief; but the strength of the chief's tabu must be such as to warrant it. Of course it would be death to any one who laid unconsecrated hands upon it.

c. *Haku-ohia:* this was a name applied to the idol called Moi, spoken of in section 21, which was carved from ohia wood. *Haku* means lord or head.

N. B. It will be perceived that I have divided line 10 into two. The exigencies of translation made this necessary.

22. Sect. 53. *Hopu*, seize, a word of command uttered by the officiating priest, the meaning being, *take, gods*, as in a military command, such for instance, as *carry arms*.

23. Sect. 55. *Mau hoe e, ihe a Luakapu*, etc. Needless to say, the difficulties of this passage are doubled by the inaccuracy of the etymology and absurdities of punctuation. The language is highly figurative, the key to its meaning being found in the veiled allusions to the nakedness of the man-god, *Kahoalii. Ihe, a* euphuism for *membrum virile* of Kahoalii. *Luakapu*, synonym of *Kahoalii. Lukaluka*, a fold of tapa cloth, worn by priests and others about the loins in a manner similar to the *pau* worn by the women. *Hookama* is to adopt as a son. *Haalauele* means a house, an archaic word.

24. Sect. 56. *A mio i ka lani omamalu (ia Kahiko).* The words in parenthesis are not quoted by Malo, though they belong to the verse, as I am informed.

25. Sect. 58. *Kuku,i Kahiko i ka lani*, &c. The text is in the literal form quite meaningless. It is as follows: *"Kukui, kahiko, i ke lani au, wai la make o manalu."* Kahiko was a king of Hawaii in ancient times. Tradition says of him that he was at first a good king. A head showed itself in the heavens and a voice was heard from it asking the question, "What man is there on earth who is just and upright in his life?"—(*Owai ke kanaka olalo i pono ka noho ana?*) The people answered *"Kahiko."* Later in his reign, when he had taken to evil ways, the same head appeared and asked the question, "What man is there on earth who leads a bad life?" Again the people answered, "Kahiko." "What is his fault?" asked the voice. "He commits murder; he robs the people of their hair; his life is corrupt, and now he instructs the people to pray to him, that all power is his." Manalu is said to have been the high priest of Kahiko. He is described as a very selfish person, not contented to suffer another priest to conduct a service without his interference and impertinent disturbance, grimacing and making insulting gestures. His fellow priests finally raised heaven and earth and besought the king that he might be put to death.

Apropos of this the following *pule* has been communicated to me:

> *Make Kane ia hii,*
> *Hii luna i ka lani o Kane,*
> *Hii ka honua ia Kane,*
> *Hii ke ao opulepule,*
> *Pule ola i o Kane e.*
> *O Kane ke akua ola.*
> *Amama Kahiko ia Kane.*
> *E ola o Kane.*
> *Amama. Ua noa.*

Response (?).   *Noa o Kane, ke akua o ke kupulau,*
> *Io welo Kahiko o Kane,*

O Kane i o Manaele.
Maeleele ka lani,
Ka lani, ka honua, ua kapu no Kane.
Amama. Ua noa.

Kane wearies himself to death with care,
Care for the government of his own heavenly kingdom,
The earth is governed by Kane,
Kane cares for the mottled scirrus clouds.
Pray to Kane for life.
Kane is the god of life.
Kahiko said *amama* to Kane
Hail Kane!
Amama. It is noa.

Response— The freedom of Kane, God of the shooting herb.
Through Kahiko, successor of Kane,
Darkened were the heavens.
Kane transmitted it to Manaele.
The heavens, the earth, are sacred to Kane.
Amama. It is noa.

26. Sect. 61. The phrase. *Hana, mai a mana ke kahuna,* which I have translated, a priest ratified it, is so ungrammatically put in the text that some ingenuity is necessary to make any sense at all of it. The writing of the words is in a different hand from the rest of the text. I am told that it was the custom, when land was made over to any one, for a priest to ratify the transaction by some appeal to heaven.

27. Sect. 61. The response made by the man puts one in mind of the passage, "The earth is the Lord's, and the fullness thereof."

28. Sect. 64. *Hihia* literally means entanglements. Perhaps in the present instance it might better be translated burdens. The word *ka'i,* or its reduplicated form *kaikai,* as here, literally means to bear, to carry.

29. Sect. 66. The expression, *"kau na auau,"* is said to be very old.
The following example of its archaic use is communicated to me:

Aulana auau ka aho!
Hoa kupukupu ka uki wailana!
Lanalana, hauhoa ka aha,
I ke kua o ke oa o ka hale o Lono!
E Lono, eia ko hale la, o Mauliola,
He hale ka-uki
E hoano, hoano e Kane!
Hoano i ko hale!
He luakini kapu,

He ana nau e Kane.
E ola! e ola! e ola Kane!
Hoano! Ua noa!

Above the level of the ground floats the thatch-pole,
Lash with a tight loop the uki leaf to this thatch-pole!
Bind and lash the cord firmly
To the back of the rafters of Lono's house!
Oh Lono, here is a house for you, the house Mauliola!
A house finished with uki leaf.
Consecrate! consecrate, oh Kane!
Consecrate this house!
A sacred temple,
A cave-temple for you, oh Kane!
Life! life! life through Kane!
Consecrated! The work is done!

30. Sect. 70. *Makaiwa,* pearl-eyed, a term descriptive of the images.

31. Sect. 72. That a criminal was chosen for this sacrifice is not to be credited. In order to fulfill this function worthily, the victim must be perfect and blameless. An infant, or an aged person, a female, or one in anywise deformed would not fill the bill.

32. Sect. 78. The following is communicated to me as as a

Pule Hulahula

Kai-ku ka lani, kakaa ka honua, alaneo ke kula.[a]
Ua moe ka ia, ua alaneo ka lani,
Hoomamalu ka lani Ia,
E Ku! e Kane! e Lono!
E Lono i ka po lailai,
Kuu'a mai ka alaneo!
Eia la he mohai,
He puaa no ka aha maka,[b]
He aha hula no ke alii,
No ka hale o ke akua.
Ea ka lani, ea ka honua,
Ea ia Kane ka waiola,
E ola i ke kini o ke akua!
Hoano! hoano! ua ola! ola!
Ola ke alii, ola na akua.
Eia ka mohai la, he puaa.
A make ka puaa, nau e ke akua.
A noa! Ua ola!

Resplendent the heavens, crystalline the earth, mirror-like
  earth's plane,
The milky way inclines to the West, refulgent are the heavens.
The heavens are guarded by the milky way.
Oh Ku! Oh Kane, Oh Lono!
Oh Lono of the clear night,
Keep the brightness of the heavens undimmed!
Here is an offering,
A swine sacrificed for this performance in public[b]
The celebration of a hula, a hula in honor of the king.
In honor of the house of the god.
The king comes forth, the people gather together,
Kane comes with the water of life,
Life through the multitude of the gods!
Sacred! sacred! Life! life!
Life through the king! life through the gods!
Behold the sacrifice, a pig!
Sacrificed is the pig, it is thine O God!
It is done! We are saved!

a. When the heavens were clear and free from clouds it was a good omen.

b. This performance was called *aha maka*, a performance for the eye, *maka*. All previous performances had been in secret and for rehearsal.

33. Sect. 85. *Akua maoli:* The carving of an idol did not produce a real god, *akua maoli*. To accomplish this sacrifice, worship, prayer, *hoo-mana*, were required. It was a work of time, patience, and faith.

34. Sect. 87. *Aha linalina*: said properly to be *aha limalima:* so called from the finger-like tassels or points which hung from it. It was a decorative, net-like arrangement of cords, fringed with tassels (*lima-lima*). This was hung over the ridge-pole. The prayer which was uttered was said to be as follows, and was called

PULE KUWA

E Ku i ka lani,
*Ke aha o makuu-halala.**
E Ku i kaupaku o Hanalei, makuu oloa,
E pu, e hikii, c paa ia oloa,
O oloa hulihia ka mana,
He mana puki no ka aha oloa,
E mana i ke akua.
E oki i ka piko o Mana.
Ua mana, mana ka aha linalina
I ka hale o ke akua o Kane.

Oki'a ka piko!
  A noa! ua noa!

O Ku in the heavens!
Behold the cord done into the all-including knot!
Oh Ku of the mystic, wonderful ridge-pole of Hanalei!
Bind, tie with the knotted oloa!
It is the oloa that shall overturn the power.
Power is wrapped up in the oloa cord.
Let power go forth to the god-image!
Cut now the navel-cord of the house Mana!
Virtue, virtue resides in the knotted oloa cord
That decorates the house of god Kane.
Cut now the navel-string!
  Done! It is done!

* *Ke aha o makuu halala.* Mr. S. Percy Smith finds in this a reference to the ancient Maori saying, *"Here ki te here o Matuku-tako-tako, te taca te wewete."* "Bind with the binding of Matuku-tako-tako, which cannot be undone." It is a long story.

35. Sect. 89. *Kuili:* this word means, I am told, that everyone talks, or prays at once. In this case the reference is to the fact, so said, that all utter their prayers at the same time. Whether this applies only to the priests, or also includes the people, I am not able to say

Pule Kuili

> *Kuili ka pule lani o Ku,*
> *E Kane, e Lono i ka ouli lani,*
> *Lani kuwa, e Kane,*
> *Kane ke akua mana,*
> *Mana e hehi ka aha hulahula.*
> *Kuili ia ka leo paa,*
> *Ka leo wi, ka leo ohe, ka leo ohia,*
> *Haku-ohia o uka e!*
> *Kuili ia i paa,*
> *E paa i ka lani,*
> *A mana i ka lani*
> *A ulu i ka lani,*
> *A lu i ka lani, lani ku.*
> *Oili ka pule.*
> *Kuili! kuhano!*
> *He lani pakaua kukahi.*
> *Ua noa!—E hui ka pule!*

Unite now in the prayers of the king to Ku!
Oh Kane, oh Lono of the portent-showing heavens,
Heavens that have been lifted up O Kane,
Kane the god of power,
Power to foot it in the assembly of the dancers.
Restrain now the voice and suppress it,
The voice of hunger, the sound of the bamboo, the sound of the
    ohia trees,
Ohia-god of the mountain forests.
Lift up your prayers that they may be approved!
Approved in the heavens!
Have power in the heavens!
Flourish in the heavens!
Scatter blessings from the heavens, the upper heavens!
The prayer unrolls itself.
The prayer is uttered; Kane reigns over all.
A heaven that is a walled stronghold.
The prayer is finished.—Let all pray!

36. Sect. 95. In this ceremony a long line of sinnet made of coconut fibre
was hung about the inside of the house *Mana*, from which were suspended a
number of strips of tapa of the sort called *mahuna*. The literal meaning of the
phrase *hoowili-moo* is to twist the serpent or lizard. But symbolical expressions
that have made departures as far from the original starting point as the serpent-
land of Asia is from serpent-free Hawaii, have as a rule precious little of the
original literalism left in their meaning. The following is communicated to me
as a

Pule Hoowilimoo

Hauli lani ka aha ka apipi o Kane,
O Kane ulu lani, hakoikoi ka lani,
Lani ku, ka alana o aha ula Hoowilimoo,
Moo lani, moo lani aukuku ka honua.
Ua wela ka hoku Kaelo ia Makalii,
Ka auhuhu paina,
O Hoowilimoo ka aha nani,
Nani Kukulu o Kahiki,
Ua nani ka aha,
Ua moe kaoo ka leo kanaka.
E kai ka aha no ke alii,
He aha noa, he aha lele,
He aha kapu, he aha ku,
Kulia ka aha no ke alii,

A make ka hoa paio.
Kulia ka aha, ola no ke alii.
A lu, a ola, ola ka aina
Ia oe Kane, ke akua ola.
E ola ia'u, ia (Mahoe) ke alii.
Ua noa! Ua ka'i ka aha!

From heaven fell the aha to the spot favored by Kane.

Kane who arched the heavens, mottled with clouds the whole heavens.

Gift of the sacred red aha of Hoowilimoo of the upper heavens.

Heavenly portent! heavenly portent! that fills the earth with blessings.

The star, Kaclo, blazes in the season of Makalii,

The bitter *auhuhu* scorched to brittleness,

Hoowilimoo is the beautiful service.

Beautiful is Tahiti,

Favorable are the omens for the service.

The voice of the multitude is at rest.

Now must we perform the service for the king

An acceptable service, one that reaches its end,

A sacred service that shall not fail.

The assembly stands before the king.

His enemies shall melt away before him.

Pour abundance! life! life to the land

Through you Kane, the god of life!

Life to me, to (Mahoe) the king!

It is accepted! The service is accomplished!

36½. Sect. 97. *Ka-papa-ulua*: This peculiar custom, seeming relic, surviving echo perhaps of old-time, South-sea cannibalism, was called by this name because in going out the rowers who occupied the forward part of the canoe were in the habit of striking (*ka*) vigorously against the side (*papa*) of the canoe, at the same time the one who held hook and line sat in the stern. The name *ka-papa-ulua* was also applied to the *kahuna* who hooked the human *ulua*. In going through the village the *kahuna* used the same means to wake up and bring out the human prey as he did in the ocean. He struck with his paddle on the door of the house at the same time calling out some blind phrase perhaps, as "*haha ulua, haha mano*," signifying a big catch of that kind of fish, on which the occupants of the house, would, if green, run out to see the sight, and thus give the murderous priest his opportunity. A dead man, not a woman, with a hook in his mouth answered very well as an *ulua*. In fact it was more desired by the priests, though it was euphemistically called by the same name.

37. Sect. 110. The occasion of bringing down the *koa* tree, like that of fetching the *haku-ohia*-idol from the mountains, was a scene of riot and tumultuous joy, like the procession of a Bacchic chorus, or shouting the harvest-home. The following is communicated to me as a sample of the wild song and chorus shouted by the multitude on such an occasion:

Mele Hookanikani-Pihe

	Stand up in couples!
One—*I ku mau mau!*	It moves, the god begins to run!
All—*I ku wa!*	Stand at intervals!
One—*I ku mau mau!*	Stand in couples
I ku huluhulu!	Haul with all your might!
I ka lanawao!	Under the mighty trees!
All—*I ku wa!*	Stand at intervals!
One—*I ku lanawao!*	Stand up among the tall forest trees!
All—*I ku wa!*	Stand at intervals!
I ku wa! huki!	Stand at intervals! and pull!
I ku wa! ko!	Stand at intervals! and haul!
I ku wa a mau!	Stand in place! and haul!
A mau ka eulu!	Haul branches and all!
E huki, e!	Haul now!
Kuli'a!	Stand up my hearties!
Umi'a ka hanu!	Hold your breath now!
A lana, ua holo ke akua!	It moves, the god begins to run!

38. Sect. 116. *Kai-oloa:* Any tapa that was bleached with seawater was called *kai-oloa.* The following is communicated to me as a

Pule Kaiolo'a

Malo lani kailolo'a,
Ka malo o ke akua, o Uli.
Uliuli kai, e Hina!
Hinaluuloa ka malo o Hina.
He ua lele ka malo o Ku,
Ku i ka lalani heiau.
Aulana ka malo o Lono!
Hume! hume ka malo o Lono-kaiolohia!
E lei ana ka malo o Lono-honua.
Honua-ku-kapu ka malo o Io-uli.
Ka malo puhano, kukapu, e Kane-auhaka,
Hume ia ko malo!
Eia la he malo kapu, he olo'a.

Oloa lani ke ola o na' lii wahine.
Hikii ia a paa i ka heiau,
Heiau ku, heiau lani,
No ke alii, no Umi a Liloa.
E ola ke alii!
E lanakila kee alii a make ka hoapaio!
E hume ke kii i ka malo!
Ua noa! a noa ka maka, maka aha o ke alii!

Malo of the king, bleached in the ocean,
Malo of god Uli!
Dark blue the sea, oh Hina!
Bright red the malo of Hina.
Lace-like as a mist-scud the malo of Ku,
Ku, the god of many temples.
Pass between the thighs the malo of Lono!
Gird! gird on the malo of Lono, the variegated!
They are bearing on their shoulders the malo of Lono-honua.
Decorated at its ends is the malo of the bird-god Io-uli,
Leaf embroidered the malo of long-limbed Kane,
Gird on your malo!
Lo here is a sacred malo, bleached by the ocean!
The sacred malo of the king is life to the women chiefs.
Bind it fast to the heiau!
An ordinary heiau, a royal heiau,
A heiau for the king, for Umi, son of Liloa.
Long live the king!
May he be victor, and put down all his enemies!
Array now the god-image in the malo!
It is accepted, the ceremony, the ceremony of the king is accepted.

39. Sect. 86. *Hai ka haina:* made a report to the king that everything, including the omens, was going on well, and was favorable.

XXXVIII

The Civil Polity

1. The word *kalaimoku* related to the civil polity, or government, of the land. The government was supposed to have one body (*kino*). As the body of a man is one, provided with a head, with hands, feet and numerous smaller members, so the government has many parts, but one organization.

2. The corporate body of the government was the whole nation, including the common people and chiefs under the king. This is seen to be the case from the fact that in a country where there are no people there is no government, as on Kaula and Niihoa.* The king was the real head of the government; the chiefs below the king the shoulders and chest. The priest of the king's idol was the right hand, the minister of interior (*kanaka kalaimoku*) the left hand of the government. This was the theory on which the ancients worked.

3. The soldiery were the right foot of the government, while the farmers and fishermen were the left foot. The people who performed the miscellaneous offices represented the fingers and toes. The unskilled and ignorant mass of people were sometimes termed *hu*, sometimes *makaainana*.

4. There were two strong forces, or parties, in the government; one the *kahunas*, who attended to the idol-worship, the other the *kalaimoku*, or king's chief councillor. These two were the ones who controlled the government, and led its head, the king, as they thought best. If the head of the government declined to follow their advice, the government went to another, on account of the fault of its head, that is the king. The high priest,—*kahuna o na kii*[1]—controlled the king in matters of religion—*haipule*—(He was keeper of the king's conscience). The *kalaimoku*, chief councillor or prime minister, guided him in regulating the affairs of administration, and in all that related to the common people.

5. In time of war the high priest—*kahuna kii*—was the first one to advise the king through his spiritual offices. The high priest would instruct the king that it was necessary to erect a heiau-luakini, in order

---

* Two rocky islets inhabited only by sea-birds.

that he might first learn by the services at the heiau whether it was advisable, or proper—*pono*—to go to war. If the priest perceived that it was not best to make war, he would tell the king "it is not best to go to war."

6. The high priest had many methods by which to obtain omens for the guidance of the king; there were also many priests under him, and each priest had a different function, the whole service, however, was under the direction of one priest.

7. Many were the duties entrusted to the priest under the king's government, the temple-service of the *luakini,* (a war temple) and that of the *kukoa'e,* (a temple to propitiate heaven for food), and the Makahiki celebration, also the distribution of the piles of goods from the taxes as well of the things given as sacrifices, the conduct of religious services and the uttering of suitable prayers—*kau mihau ana*[2]—in the day of battle; in fact everything that touched the worship of the gods.

8. It was the duty of the high priest to urge the king most strenuously to direct his thoughts to the gods, to worship them without swerving, to be always obedient to their commands with absolute sincerity and devotedness; not to be led astray by women; not to take up with women of low birth; but to serve only the gods.

9. One thing which the priest urged upon the king was to kill off the ungodly people, those who broke tabu and ate with the women, or who cohabited with a woman while she was confined to her infirmary, and the women who intruded themselves into the heiau.

10. Another thing he urged was that the woman who beat tapa on a tabu day, or who went canoeing on a tabu day should be put to death; also that the man who secretly left the service at the temple to go home and lie with his wife should be put to death; that the men and women who did these things, whether from the backwoods—*kuaaina*—or near the court should be put to death.

11. That any man, woman, or child, who should revile the high priest, or a keeper of the idols, calling him a filth-eater, or saying that he acted unseemly with women (*i ka ai mea kapu*), should be put to death, but he might ransom his life by a fine of a fathom-long pig.

12. Again, that if the king by mistake ate of food or meat that was ceremonially common or unclean—*noa*—the king should be forgiven, but the man whose food or meat it was should be put to death, if the king was made ill. In such a case a human sacrifice was offered to appease the deity, that the king might recover from his illness.

13. Again that certain kinds of fish should be declared tabu to the women as food, also pork, bananas and cocoanuts; that if any large fish—a whale—or a log strapped with iron, should be cast ashore, it was to be offered to the gods (i.e., it was to be given to the priests for the use of the king).

14. Again, in time of war the first man killed in battle, who was termed a *lehua,* and the second man killed, who was termed a *lua one,* were to be offered as sacrifices to the gods.

There were a great many ceremonies and services ordered by the kahuna, in order to establish the best relations with the gods, as the kahuna averred.

15. For six months of the year the *opelu* might be eaten and the *aku* was tabu, and was not to be eaten by chiefs or commoners. Then again, for other six months the *aku* might be eaten, and the *opelu* in turn was tabu. Thus it was every year.

16. Again during the observance of *Makahiki* the services at all the heiaus of the chiefs were omitted for two months and twenty-six days; after which all the chiefs returned and worshipped the idols.

17. After the *aliis* resumed their religious services the king must build a *luakini,* that is a large *heiau.* It was a common saying that this caused a famine[3] in the land, due to the fact that the inner bark of the *ohia* was red. For that reason the king after that built a *mapele,* it being believed that this sort of a *heiau* would bring prosperity to the land, because the bark of the *lama,* which was the wood used in building every *mapele heiau,* was black.

18. After these *heiaus* were built, the king went on a tour about the island, putting up heiaus as he went. This circuit was called a *palaloa.*[4] Next the king made an *unu o Lono,* and each of the chiefs erected an *eweai,* which was a *heiau* to bring rain.

19. At this time a light was kept burning all night in the house of the king while prayers[5] were constantly recited to the gods, beseeching that the misfortunes of the land might be relieved and averted, that it might be cleansed from pollution, its sins blotted out, the blight and mildew that affected it removed, that it might be protected from decay, destruction and barrenness. Then instead one might see the shooting forth of the buds, the weeding of the ground, the earth covered with the growing vines, the separation of the vines from different vines interlocking with each other as they grow together, the offering of the first fruits to God.

20. If all these matters relating to the worship of the gods were attended to, then the king was highly commended as a righteous king. And when the people perceived this, they devoted themselves with diligence to their farms and their fishing, while the women-folk industriously beat out and printed their tapas. Thus it was that the king worked away in the worship of the gods year after year.

21. It was on these lines that the high priest constantly used his authority and influence to guide the king; and when he saw that the king followed all his instructions, he took courage, and some day when they were conducting a service together successfully, he ventured to beg of the king a piece of land.

22. If the people saw that a king was religiously inclined (*haipule*), strict in his religious duties, that king attained great popularity. From the most ancient times religious kings have always been greatly esteemed.

23. From the earliest times down to the time of Kamehameha I., not one of the kings who has subjugated under his rule an entire island has been irreligious; every one of them has worshipped the gods with faith and sincerity.

24. If the services of religion under any king were conducted in a slack or slovenly manner, it would be the general opinion that that government would pass into the hands of a king under whom the services of religion would be strictly and correctly performed. It was firmly believed that a religious king was possessed of mighty power, because it was matter of observation, that kings who were attentive to their religious duties conducted all their affairs in a becoming manner, while irreligious kings neglected the affairs of their government.

25. There were many matters in regard to which the high priest used his office to lead the king in such ways as he thought right.

26. The high priest was a man whose father had also been a priest. While some of the priests were of priestly parentage, others were chosen to that office by the priest himself. The son of a priest was not allowed to be nourished with common food—the *kalaimoku* also was not allowed to be nourished with food that was common.

27. The principal duties of the *Kalaimoku's*[6] office were comprised under two heads; to look after the king's interests and to look after the people's interests. The one who filled the office of *kalaimoku* made it his first business to counsel the king in the regulation of these two departments.

28. The Kalaimoku's manner of procedure was as follows: He first made secret inquiries of the keepers of the genealogies—*poe kuauhau*—

and informed himself as to the pedigree of all the chiefs. Because the Kalaimoku believed that the king was to be compared to a house. A house indeed stands of itself, but its *pa,* or stockade, is its defence. So it was with the king; the chiefs below him and the common people throughout the whole country were his defence.

29. The office of an independent king (*Alii ai moku,* literally one who eats, or rules over, an island) was established on the following basis: He being the house, his younger brothers born of the same parents, and those who were called fathers or mothers (uncles and aunts) through relationship to his own father or mother, formed the stockade that stood as a defence about him.

30. Another wall of defence about the king, in addition to his brothers, were his own sisters, those of the same blood as himself. These were people of authority and held important offices in the king's government. One was his *kuhina nui,* or prime minister, others generals (*pu-kaua*), captains (*alihi-kaua*), marshals (*ilamuku*), the king's executive officers, to carry out his commands.

31. Again the king's uncles and aunts and the male and female cousins of his immediate line also formed part of this wall of defence.

32. Besides this the king's own brothers-in-law, the husbands of his sisters or of his cousins, also constituted a part of this defence about him.

33. The distant relatives of the king's parents and grandparents also were a protection and re-enforcement to his strength.

34. A *Hale Naua*[7] was then built for the king, and when this was accomplished an investigation was entered into at the house as to what persons were related to the king. The doings at the house were conducted in the following manner. When the king had entered the house and taken his seat, in the midst of a large assembly of people including many skilled genealogists, two guards were posted outside at the gate of the *pa.* (The guards were called *kaikuono.*)

35. When any one presented himself for admission to the Hale Naua, or king's house, the guards called out "here comes So-and-so about to enter." Thereupon the company within called out, "From whom are you descended, Mr. So-and-so Naua? Who was your father Naua? Who was your father Naua?" To this the man made answer, "I am descended from So-and-so; such and such a one is my father."

36. The question was then put to the man, "Who was your father's father, Naua?" and the man answered, "Such an one was my father's father, he was my grand-father." "Who was the father of your grand-father,

Naua?" and the man answered "Such an one was my grand father's father." Thus they continued to question him until they reached in their inquiry the man's tenth ancestor.

37. If the genealogists who were sitting with the king recognized a suitable relationship to exist between the ancestry of the candidate and that of the king he was approved of.

38. When another candidate arrived the outside guards again called out, "Here enters such an one." Thereupon those sitting with the king in a loud tone made their inquiries as to the ancestry on the mother's side. "Who was your mother? Naua?" And the man answered, "I am descended from such an one; So-and-so was my mother." Again the question was put to him, "Who was the mother of your mother? Naua?" Whereupon he answered, "Such a person was my grand-mother."

39. The questions were kept up in this manner until they had come to the tenth ancestor in their inquiry. When the genealogists had satisfied themselves as to the closeness of the man's pedigree to that of the king, special inquiries having been made as to his grand-father and grand-mother, the candidate was approved of.

40. On the satisfactory conclusion of this investigation the the commoner, or chief, was admitted as a member of the *Hale Naua,* another name for which was *Ualo malie.*[7]

41. In this way they learned who were closely related to the king, who also were in his direct line, as well as the relative rank of the *aliis* to each other and to the king.

42. A plan was then made as to what office the king should give to one and another chief or commoner who were related to him.

43. To the chiefs that were his near relations the king assigned districts; to others *kalanas, okanas, pokos, ahupuaas* and *ilis.*

44. To the commoners were given such small sections of land as the *ahupuaa,* or the *ili.*

45. The heavy work on the lands fell to the chiefs and their men, to the *makaainana.* The king did no work; his food was brought to him cooked. It was a rare thing for an *alii* to engage in agriculture.

46. One thing which the Kalaimoku impressed upon the king was to protect the property of the chiefs as well as that of the common people; not to rob them, not to appropriate wantonly the crops of the common people.

47. If the king made a tour about the island, when night fell, the proper thing for him to do was to camp down by the highway, and the

next morning to proceed on his journey. It was not right for him to enter the house of a commoner to pass the night; that was all wrong and was termed *alaiki*, the short way.

48. The wrong lay in the fact that when the king entered the house of a common man his men entered with him. They ate of the commoner's food, helped themselves to his goods, seduced or ravished the females, acted disgracefully, and raised the devil generally.

49. Their counsel to the king was that when, in travelling along the *alaloa*, he came to a branch-road, he was not to follow the branch, because that was a bad practice. The branch-road was called a *mooa*, or a *meheu*. (*Mooa*, a bending of the grass; *meheu*, a trail, a trace.)

50. The evil lay in the fact that when the king left the beaten way, the people followed along with him. The path led probably to a little farm—*mahina ai*—and as soon as the king's men saw it they pulled the crops, helping themselves to the sugar-cane, etc., and the blame for the outrage fell upon the king.

51. Another reason why the king should not turn aside to follow a by-path was because it might lead to a house where women were beating tapa—*hale kuku*—and if the king's men found her to be a handsome looking woman, they might ravish her, in which case the king would be blamed for the deed.

52. The proper course for the king was to camp at night by the highway. If the people put up a house for him, well and good. If not, let his own retinue set up for him a tent, and let him eat the food he brought with him. The king who would follow this plan would not have to issue any orders to the districts for food; he would be called a king of superior wisdom. (*Alii noeau loa*), a prudent king.

53. Again when the king went on a canoe-voyage around the island, he should not let his canoes tack back and forth, off and on, in towards the land and out to sea again, lest, by so doing, they should come across a fleet of fishing canoes, and the fishermen, being robbed of their fish, should lay the blame upon the king.

54. The right plan in sailing would be to keep the canoe on a straight course from the cape just passed to the one ahead, and when that was doubled to steer directly for the next cape, and so on until the destination was reached.

55. When the people bring presents of food to the king, the best course for him to pursue is to eat of the food then and there, so as to make it easy for the people. It were a wise thing for the king to invite

all of the people to partake of the food, that they might not go away fasting.

56. The king might well take as his own the *ahupuaas* on the borders of the districts, such an one, for instance, as *Kaulanamauna,* on the border of Kona, and *Manuka,* which lies on the border of Kau: (These were very rocky and rather sterile tracts of country,) and when the king had found a suitable man, let the king put the lands in his charge.

57. It would also be a wise thing for the king to keep as his own the *ahupuaas* or districts in which the *kauila,*[9½] or the *aala,* or the *auau*[9] is plentiful; together with any rocky and inhospitable tracts of land. He might entrust these lands into the hands of good men to farm them for him.

58. It is proper for the king to make frequent circuits of the island, that he may become well acquainted with the young people in the out-districts, that he may be able to choose from among them suitable ones to be taken into his train as intimates (*aikane*),[10] and to be brought up at court. Thus he will increase the number of his followers.

59. It is well for the king to gather many people about him. Both he and his queen should deal out food and meat, as well as *tapas* and *malos* with a liberal hand. Thus he will dispose the men to be as a shield to him in the day of battle.

The servants (*kanaka*)[11] of the king were known under the following designations: *malalaioa,*[11] *uh,*[11] *ehu,*[11] *kea,*[11] *lawa,*[11] kapii,[11] *kae,*[11] *kalol,*[11] *niho-mauole, puali, uha-kakau, hamohamo, haakualiki, olu-kelo-aho-o, kamoena, kuala-pehu, makai kauoe.*[11] Probably other names should be added.

60. The chiefs below the king also should gather men about them, the same as the king himself; and these men should be constantly practiced in the arts of war, with the short spear, *ihe,* the long spear, *pololu,* the club, *laau palau,* the *kuia,* in the use of the sling, *ka-ala,* in boxing and in the practice of temperance.[12]

61. If the Kalaimoku should see that the king's people were becoming stout, so as to be clumsy, he would urge the king to have the men run races, roll the *maika,* practice the game called *pahee,* drink awa, go to where food was scarce, in order to reduce their flesh.[13]

62. The largest districts were not generally assigned to the highest chiefs, lest they might thus be enabled to rebel against the government. Kamehameha I., however, entrusted the largest districts to his highest chiefs.

63. It was the practice for kings to build store-houses in which to collect food, fish, tapas, malos, pa-us, and all sorts of goods.

DAVID MALO

64. These store-houses were designed by the Kalaimoku as a means of keeping the people contented, so they would not desert the king. They were like the baskets that were used to entrap the *hinalea* fish. The *hinalea* thought there was something good within the basket, and he hung round the outside of it. In the same way the people thought there was food in the storehouses, and they kept their eyes on the king.

65. As the rat will not desert the pantry (*kumu-haka*)[14] where he thinks food is, so the people will not desert the king while they think there is food in his store-house.

66. The king had the right to select for himself fleet runners, men to paddle his canoes, canoe-makers, and spies to keep watch of the law-breakers and criminals in all parts of the land.

67. It is the king's duty to seek the welfare of the common people, because they constitute the body politic. Many kings have been put to death by the people because of their oppression of the *makaainana.*

68. The following kings lost their lives on account of their cruel exactions on the commoners: *Koihala*[15] was put to death in Kau, for which reason the district of Kau was called the weir (*Makaha*).

69. *Koha-i-ka-lani*[16] was an *alii* who was violently put to death in Kau. *Halaea* was a king who was killed in Kau. *Ehunui-kai-malino* was an *alii* who was secretly put out of the way by the fishermen in Keahuolu in Kona. *Kamaiole* was a king who was assassinated by Kalapana at Anaehoomalu in Kona.

70. King Hakau was put to death by the hand of Umi at Waipio valley in Hamakua, Hawaii. *Lono-i-ka-makahiki,* was a king who was banished by the people of Kona. *Umi-o-ka-lani* also was a king who was banished by the Konaites.

71. It was for this reason that some of the ancient kings had a wholesome fear of the people. But the commoners were sure to be defeated when the king had right on his side.

72. In every district, *okana,* and *poko,* certain pieces of land, called *koele,* were set apart for the king. The pigs in these lands had their ears mutilated in a certain fashion to designate them as belonging to the king.

73. It was to these lands that the king looked for his supply of pork and not to the common people. But some of the kings seized the pigs belonging to other people and appropriated them to their own uses.

74. In the same way the kings sometimes appropriated the fruits of the people's farms. The *makaainana* were not pleased with this sort of

conduct on the part of the king. They looked upon such work as acts of tyranny and abuse of authority.

75. The *kalaimoku* did not usually live with the king, but quite apart from him. If he wished to speak with the king he went to the king's *hale manawa*, whence he sent a message to the king by the king's *lomi-lomi*, requesting an interview. On the arrival of the king their interview was kept entirely private. This secret consultation was called *kuka malu*, and when it was over each one went his way.

76. If the lesser *aliis* desired to consult with the king on some important affair of government, it might be war, the king would send a message to the *kalaimoku* to come and hold a privy council with him; and, having given attention to what they had to say, the king dismissed them.

77. When the king met the whole body of his chiefs in conference it was his custom to give close attention to what each one had to say; and if he perceived that the counsel of any one of them agreed with that which his Kalaimokus had given him in secret, he openly expressed his approval of it.

78. If, however, the king saw that what the chiefs advised was in disagreement with the counsels of his Kalaimokus, given him in secret, he openly expressed his disapproval. This was the manner in which the assembly,—parliament of the chiefs[17] (*aha olelo o na' lii*) conducted their deliberations.

79. The *kalaimokus* were well versed in the principles of warfare. They knew how to set a battle in order, how to conduct it aright, how to adapt the order of battle to the ground.

80. If the battle-field was a plain, level and unbroken, (*malae-lae*) the order of battle suitable was that called *kahului*.[18] If it was a plain covered with scrub, the proper order of battle would be the *makawalu*.[19]

81. The Kalaimokus were also acquainted with the famous instances in which ambuscade (*poi-po*) had been used; what sort of a terrain was suited to the battle-order called *kukulu*,[20] to that called *kapae*,[21] and to that called *moemoe*.[22]

82. The kalaimokus were versed in all the manoeuvres of battle. They were called *kaakaua*,[23] defenders, also *lau-aua*,[24] strategists.

83. A small army or body of men should not be marshalled or brought into battle in the *makawalu*-order of battle, nor in the *kahului*.[25]

A small force which would not be able to stand before a force of larger size in a battle by day, might be able to make its escape if the battle were at night.

84. In making the dispositions for battle, the vanguard was composed of a small body of men and was called *huna-lewa*.[26] A larger body was placed to their rear, which was called *huna-pa'a*.

85. To the rear of them were stationed the *waakaua*,[27] the *pu-ulu-kaua*,[28] the *papa-kaua*,[29] and the *poe kaua*.[30] The king took his station in the midst of the *poe kaua*. Immediately in front of the body of soldiery that surrounded the king were stationed several ranks of men, armed with a long spear called a *pololu*. Now the *pololu* was called a powerful weapon of defense, a *kuau paa*.

86. The king stood in the midst of the *poe kaua*, with his wife, his *kaai*-gods, and his dearest friends. But if the order of battle was the *makawalu* the king would be stationed in the midst of the *huna-pa'a*.

87. When the forces were in position the *kilo-lani*, or astrologer, was sent for, and on his arrival the king asked him what he thought about the battle. Thereupon the astrologer made a study of the heavens to see whether the indications were favorable for the battle.

88. If he found the appearances favorable, he said to the king, "This is a day of clear vision (*he au keia no ka la*), a day in which your enemy will be delivered into your hands for defeat; because," said he, "this day is *apuni*, a day inauspicious to your foes." He thereupon urged the king strenuously to give battle.

89. But if the *kilo* saw that the day was unpropitious, he warned the king not make the battle against the other king.

90. When the armies drew near to each other, the priests were sent for to offer sacrifices to the king's gods, for the king himself could not offer sacrifice at such a time.

The ceremony was done in this manner: Two fires were built, one for each army, in the space between the two armies. The pig, having been killed by strangling, was offered to the idoldeities by the priest, the king uttering the *amama*. The pig was called an *umihau* pig.

91. When this ceremony was over the battle was begun. The kalaimokus were the principal advisers of the king in the conduct of a battle.

92. These kalaimokus were a class of people who did not care much for luxury and display, nor for distinction, wealth, or land.

93. They had no desire for great emoluments from the king. They were only intent on serving the king by their secret councils.

94. If the kalaimokus saw that the king had too many people about him they led him into the wilderness where food was scarce, that the

king might be the only one supplied with food, and all the people then would set their hearts upon the king.

95. If the kalaimokus saw that the king was eating too much soft poi they advised against it, because hard[31] poi is better and taro best of all to make one fleet of foot if defeated.

96. All the chiefs in the government were trained in military exercises until they had attained greater skill than was possessed by any of the common people.

97. There were two great reasons why a kalaimoku had superior ability as a councillor to others. In the first place, they were instructed in the traditional wisdom of former kalaimokus, and in the second place their whole lives were spent with kings. When one king died, they lived with his successor until his death, and so on. Thus they became well acquainted with the methods adopted by different kings, also with those used by the kings of ancient times.

98. Some of those who were skilled in the art of government were people from the back country. For while living in the outer districts they had been close students of the ways of some of the kings and had become thoroughly acquainted with them. The people of the country districts were really shrewd critics of the faults as well as the virtues of the kings.

99. If the common people after observing a king, disapproved of him, it was because he was really bad; but if, after studying him, they believed in him, it proved him to be a good man.

100. Great fault was found with a king who was a sluggard, or a pleasure-seeker, or who was contentious, used reviling language, was greedy, oppressive, or stingy.

101. The king who was gentle and quiet in manner, condescending and gracious, was the king who was greatly desired and beloved by the people.

102. Kings who were unjust in their government were not beloved by any of their subjects; but the king who ruled honestly was ever regarded with affection.

103. The *alii* who lived an honest life had great authority merely because he was right. The *alii* who slandered another *alii* was convicted of wrong out of his own mouth.

104. If one king speaks evil of another king without cause, he committs a wrong.

105. The king who lives righteously will be blameless. So it has been from the most ancient times.

Notes on Chapter XXXVIII

1. Sect. 7. *Kau mihau ana.* I am informed that when an army went forth to battle a priest went on ahead bearing a branch of the *hau* tree. This was set upright in the ground by the priest and guarded in that position by him as a favorable omen or sign for his side. Each side religiously respected the emblem of the enemy, and did not interfere with their *mihau.* So long as the branch was kept erect it meant victory to its side. If the battle finally went against them the hau was allowed to fall. There was a proverbial expression *"Ua puali ka hau nui i ka hau iki."* The great *hau* is broken by the small *hau,* meaning the large force is defeated by the small. The kahuna who performed this *mihau* service was in reality the chaplain of the army. While he was doing this service on the field of battle, the great body of the priests were in the heiau beseeching the gods by prayers and sacrifices for victory on their side.

1. Sect. 4. *Kahuna o na kii:* This is not a legitimate expression. The high priest is undoubtedly meant by the writer. There is, however, no warrant in Hawaiian usage for the employment of such an expression to designate that functionary.

3. Sect. 17. There might well be a famine in the land after such a prolonged interruption of all fruitful industries and so great a misuse of all its resources. (See sections 90–94, Chap. XXXVII.)

4. Sect. 18. *Palaloa,* the same in meaning as *palala,* to give gifts to the king. These gifts were not a regular tax. But they were none the less a burden, though supposed to be entirely voluntary offerings.

6. Sect. 27. In spite of the somewhat ambiguous language used by the author, a king had but one kalaimoku at a time.

7. Sect. 34. *Hale Naua:* There has been much discussion over the meaning of this word *naua.* It may throw some light on the subject to state that "Naua?" was the word of challenge which was addressed to every one who presented himself for admission to this society, the meaning of which it being a question, was, whence are you? what is your ancestry? To this the answer might be. *"Auwae pili,"* meaning a relative; or it might be, *"Auwahi la,"* meaning that the relationship was more distant; or, if the relationship of the candidate to the king was close and undisputed, as in case he were the king's brother, or other near relative, he would answer, *"Pilipili ula,"* referring to the red *ula* that was common to the veins of each. Answer having been made, as above indicated, the candidate was admitted, and was then put through an examination as to his ancestry; the first question asked him being, *"Owai kou papa?"* what is your line of ancestry? The candidate thereupon recited his ancestral claims in the form of a *mele inoa.* This *mele inoa* was not a thing to be hawked about at every festival, nor to be recited in public when the notion seized one to make a display of his claims. On the contrary, it was a sacred legacy from one's ancestors, to be recited only in the audience of one's peers. It is, therefore to be distinguished from that other *mele inoa,* which might be given forth in public. The whole matter

has been cheapened and made ridiculous in modern times. The following has been communicated to me as a fragment from a true *mele inoa* belonging to Kakuhihewa, an ancient king of Oahu, or rather to one of his descendants.

> *Aohe au e loaa i ka ui mai,*
> *He ipu aholehole,*
> *Na Kuhihewa, ka moi o Oahu nei,*
> *A Meehanau,*
> *Mai lalo mai a luna nei,*
> *Moe ia Kanui-a-panee,*
> *Puka o Ka-ua-kahi-a-ka-ola,*
> *He akua-olelo,*
> *A loaa ka I,*
> *A Kukaniloko...*

I am not one to give my name to every challenger,
A calabash of aholehole fish, (for the king)
Descended from Kahuhihewa, king of this island of Oahu,
And from Meehanau,
He was the first king of his line
Paired with Ke-a-nui-a-panee.
The issue Ka-ua-kahi-a-ka-ola,
A god eloquent in speech.
To him was born the I,
At Kukaniloko...

The Hale Naua is represented to have been a non-partisan, peaceful, organization. Its purpose was to prevent bloodshed by uniting the chiefs under the bonds of kinship, friendship, and rank. It was strictly an aristocratic society. The assertion made by Malo, in section 40, that a candidate might be a commoner as well as a chief, is in my opinion, and in it I am supported by intelligent Hawaiian critics, entirely erroneous. The doings of the so-called Hale Naua, instituted in the reign of King Kalakaua, are not to be regarded as an argument to be considered in the question. The Hale Naua did not sit as a court to discipline or expel its members. Once a member, always a member, was the rule. The most perfect and decorum must be observed at all the meetings. This canon of politeness was expressed in the phrase given in Sect. 40, as another name for the Naua Society. *"Ualo malie,"* the meaning of which is the gentle entreaty. Before leaving this matter, it should be remarked that membership in the Hale Naua was by no means confined to the relatives of the reigning family, as is implied by the statements of David Malo. It was open to every high-rank chief of whatever line.

5. Sect. 19. The text in the Hawaiian is as follows: "A ma ia mau po hoa mau ia ke kukui o ko ke alii nui hale, me ka pule mau i ke akua kii; he pule ia o holoi ana i ka poino o ka aina, ame ka pale ae i pau ko ka aina haumia; he

pule ia e hoopau ana i na hewa o ka aina a pau; i pau ke ae[a], me ke kawau[b]; i pau ke kulopia[c], a me ka peluluka[d]; i pau ka hulialana[e]; alaila nihopeku[f], hoemu[g], huikala[h], malapakai[i], kamauli hou i ke akua."[j] There is much difficulty in making out the meaning of this passage. By some it is regarded as having a figurative meaning, to be taken in a spiritual sense. I prefer to take it literally as referring to the crops. (a) Looked at it in this light, *ae* means blight: *kawau* means mildew, mould: (c) *kulopia* means decay, a condition worse than the one before mentioned: (d) *peluluka* a still worse condition, destruction of the entire crop by decay: (e) *hulialana* represents the resulting barrenness of the fields. Now comes the contrasting description of a luxuriant harvest, (f) *nihopeku*, the bud shooting from the soil like a tooth from the gum: (g) *hoemu*, the weeding of the tender plants: (h) *huikala*, the ground is covered with the herbage, leaves and vines: (i) *malapakai*, the interlacing vines have to be separated and turned back to their own hills, so rank is the growth: (j) *kamauli hou i ke akua*, the prayer being answered, and an abundant crop secured, the first fruits of the land are offered as a thank-offering to God.

8. Sect. 34. I am informed that the two outer guards were called *kaikuone*. The head of the *hale naua*, the king, was styled *Ikulani*. I am also informed (by J. K. K.) that there were four officers called *ulualono*, who acted as *kuauhau*, or keepers of the chronologies. They were also called the *kakaolelo*. The same one also says that when a candidate was introduced an officer called an *uluamahi* threw at him an *ipuaho*, which was nothing more or less than an ornamental ball of twine If this struck the candidate squarely, it was a sign that he was worthy. It is clear that the ideas of J. K. K. are too much influenced by the *hale naua* which Kalakaua founded.

9. Sect. 57. *Auau*, the straight light poles of the hau. These were very useful in training men in the spear practice. The head of the spear was blunted and wrapped with tapa to make its impact harmless. The young soldiers began practice with these. When they had acquired skill and proficiency with these harmless weapons, they were allowed to try their hand at the heavy, sharp-pointed, kauila spears, which were those used in battle.

9½. Sect. 57. *Kauila.* The *Kauila* was a famous wood for spears; its color like that of mahogany. Aala is said to be fragrant. Perhaps the Ala-a is the tree in question. Auau was a tree specially useful for the *ahos* or small poles that it furnished.

10. Sect. 58. The *aikane* meant primarily a male intimate of the most disreputable sort, but it came to mean also a male friend in a respectable sense. I take it that the word is used in the latter sense in the present instance.

11. Sect. 59. The following list of servants and people or attendants about the king's court has the double disadvantage, first, of being incomplete, confessedly so; second, of attaching itself to no principle of classification, besides which it is merely a list of names without significance or explanation. The following translation or explanation is given as the best I can do towards elucidating the subject.

Malalaioa, people who had acquired skill in any trade or occupation. It probably did not include soldiers, though it is claimed by some that it did.

Uli, people with straight black hair. Black was the acceptable color for hair.

Ehu. Persons with reddish or blond hair were not considered so comely as the former and were not retained about court. Though they might be employed about the menial offices, such as making ovens and cooking food.

Kea, a class of persons with unusually light skins. They were favorites, much desired at court.

Lawa, a name applied to a class of men of great strength. It was said that there was but a slight interval between their ribs and their hips.

Kapii. Persons with curly hair. These were regarded as strong bodied and were greatly desired in this regard.

Kae. This was a term applied to the old and worn-out.

Kalole. Persons who were stupid and inefficient. They could not get married because they could not support a wife.

Niho mauole, persons of either sex who had outlived their usefulness. So named from the loss of most of their teeth.

Puali. This applied to soldiers. They were tightly belted with the malo which they wore rather higher than was the custom among the common people. Hence the name *puali,* cut in two, from the smallness of the waist. It was regarded as a sign of readiness for any enterprise to have the malo tightly girded about one. The expression was *"ku ka puali o mea,"* such an one has his loins girded, he's ready for the fight.

Uha-kakau This is probably a wrong orthography, and should be *uhaheke.* The meaning is with thighs bent, consequently on the alert. They are contrasted with those who squat down on the ground. They generally carried some weapon concealed about them.

Hamohamo, I am told (by Kapule) that in Muolea, in the district of Hana, grew a poisonous moss in a certain pool or pond close to the ocean. It was used to smear on the spear-points to make them fatal. These men were the ones who did the job, hence they were called *hamohamo,* the smearers. This moss is said to be of a reddish color and is still to be found. It grows nowhere else than at that one spot. Kapule thinks it was about the year 1857 that he was in Hana and saw this moss. It was shown him by an old man named Peelua, the father-in-law of S. M. Kamakau. This is a revelation and a great surprise to me. I never heard of such a thing before. Manu covered it with stones.

Haa-kua-liki. The meaning is probably the same as the word *haa-kua-lii,* which is a later form. This class of people were dwarfish in figure, but of great strength and approved valor.

Olukeloa-hoo-kaa-moena. These were those who were highly skilled in the art of *lua* and *haihai,* in which wrestling, bone-breaking and dislocating joints were combined in one art. They were a very important part of the army.

Kuala-pehu. These were men who were very powerful with the fist. They fought with the naked fist. Extravagant statements are, of course, made of their prowess.

Maka-i. Persons who were skilled detectives, who were quick to interpret detective signs. They were valuable as spies.

Ka'u-o. Probably the same as *ka'u-koe,* persons who went as spies into the enemies' country. They carried no weapons with them. *Ka'u* meant fearful, unwilling; *koe* meant requested, bidden; persons therefore who went reluctantly, and only because they were commanded.

12. Sect. 60. The *ihe* was a spear to be thrown from the hand. According to my present informant, who is a very intelligent man from Molokai, the *ihe* was a long spear. A spear in my collection, which measures about 12½ feet is, he says, an *ihe* to be thrown.

The *pololu* was a spear of less length than the *ihe* and was not to leave the hand. It was generally wielded with both hands. It was generally a little longer than the man.

The *laau palau* was a club of various length, a yard or a fathom. It of course was intended to remain in the hand.

The *kuia* was a short sharp pointed stick, a dagger. It might be carried thrust into the girdle.

Ka ala meant to sling. It was a very important weapon in warfare.

(The Molokai man was certainly mistaken. The long spear was the *pololu,* the short spear or javelin was the *ihe.* See Sect. 60 and Sect. 85, above. W. D. A.)

13. Sect. 61. Awa drinking is not known to be an efficient means of reducing the flesh. No wise stateman, *kalai-moku,* even in ancient times would be likely to give such a foolish piece of advice as this.

14. Sect. 65. The *kumuhaka* was a shelf on which to keep provisions. It was either suspended by cords, or supported on legs.

15. Sect. 68. *Koihala.* I have two different statements in regard to this king. Which of them, or whether either, is correct. I know not. One of them is that Koihala was the successor to Keoua in Kau, who was the opponent of Kamehameha I., and was murdered at Kawaihae with the conqueror's connivance. According to that account the works with which he made the people of Kau to sweat and groan were the building of the heavy stone-walls about several fish ponds, of which are mentioned those at the coast of Hilea, at Honuapo, and Ninole. He also robbed the fishermen of their fish. The story is that he compelled his canoemen to paddle him about here and there where the fleets of fishing canoes were. The wind was bleak and his men suffered from the wet and cold, he being snugly housed in the *pola.* One day he had his men take his canoe out towards the South cape where was a fleet of fishing canoes. His own canoe, being filled with the spoils of his robbery, began to sink, and he called out for help. The fishermen declined all assistance; his own men left him and swam to the canoes of the fishers leaving him entirely in the lurch. He was drowned.

The other account represents him as a king of the ancient times. Where lies the truth of history in regard to this man, I am at a loss to say.

16. Sect. 69. *Koha-i-ka-lani.* The account I have of this king is that he kept his people ground down by hard work. It is said that he would start his people

off on a long tramp into the mountains to cut ohia timber for images; and before the work was done he ordered them at the work of carving stone images in some other direction. But no sooner had they got settled to the new job than he sent them back to finish their uncompleted work in the mountains. Finally he set off on a tour with all his wives and retinue, and ordered the serfs, his common people, to meet him at a specified place with a supply of food. When the people came to the appointed place with their burdens of food the king and his party were not there; they had moved on and the king had left word directing the people to carry the food to a place many miles distant. On arriving at the place now indicated the people, who had been smarting under the affliction, found themselves again ordered to bear their heavy loads to a place many hours' journey distant. Their patience was now exhausted. They consumed the food, filled the bundles with stones and on arriving at length in the presence of the king, with feigned humility laid the bundles at the king's feet. But when the bundles were opened the man that was in them broke forth. The king and his court were killed and covered under the stones.

(Both of the above traditions are given by M. Jules Remy, in his "Recits d'un Vieux Sauvage." They are undoubtedly very ancient). W. D. A.

17. Sect. 78. *Aha olelo o na 'lii.* Very little is known about this *aha olelo o na 'lii* more than this statement. There is no doubt, however, but what the king did consult with his chiefs as to certain important matters of policy, perhaps as to the waging of war. But the latter was more likely decided by the King in consultation with his Kalaimoku.

18. Sect. 80. *Kahului.* The Kahului was a disposition or order of battle, in which the main body of the soldiers were drawn up in the form of a crescent, with the horns pointing forwards. This name was, undoubtedly derived from the place of the same name. The region of Kahului was flat and treeless.

19. Sect. 80. *Makawalu,* an order of battle in which the soldiers were irregularly grouped into bands or companies to suit the ground.

20. Sect. 81. The *Kukulu* was a battle in which the opposing forces were formally drawn up in line against each other. It is said that in such cases the opposing forces would consult each other's convenience as to the time for beginning the action; and it was even postponed to accomodate one or the other. This reminds of the days of chivalry when men fought for *"Honour,"* when the captain of one side would step to the front, and, adressing the other side, say "Are you ready, gentlemen?" and, being answered in the affirmative, turning to his own men, said "Prepare to Fire." "Fire!"

21. Sect. 81. *Kapae* was not an order of battle, but a truce, or cessation of hostilities. It might be found out, for instance, there being no urgent reason for battle, that the two forces were led perhaps by men who were near relatives, or who had been at one time great friends; or, after a prolonged and bloody contest, in which the two forces were proven to be so nearly equal in strength and valor that neither party could hope for victory, prudence and a more reasonable view of things suggested the desirability of bringing the trial of strength and

endurance to a close. In such a case there would be a general shaking of hands—the right hand, as with us, or both hands, might be used, if there was strong emotion, sometimes embracing and touching noses, though that was not the general custom.

(The custom of shaking hands was first introduced here by white men, in modern times). W. D. A.

22. Sect. 81. *Moemoe*, a night attack. The Hawaiians were not given to placing sentinels and keeping watch at night in their military campaigns in ancient times. Possibly Kamehameha followed a stricter rule in this regard, for which reason a night attack must have proved very successful when it was tried.

23. Sect. 82. *Kaakaua* is said also to mean one who stimulated the men to brave deeds and enthusiasm by gesticulations and shouts, especially perhaps by brandishing or twirling a spear in the front of battle. Such actions were as legitimate as one of Napoleon's war proclamations.

24. Sect. 82. *Lau-aua* also means one who concealed his strength or skill until the time of battle. Is not that strategy? To hide one's power from one's enemies, even if one's friends are kept in the dark at the same time, what is that but strategy?

25. Sect. 83. A sound observation. Naturally it would not do to divide a small force, as would be done in *makawalu*, nor to draw up such a force in the form of a crescent, as in *kahului.*

26. Sect. 84. The *huna-lewa* were what might be called the skirmishers, those furthest in the advance and who were in very open order.

27. Sect. 85. *Waa-kaua*. In this an army was formed into bodies of men numbering perhaps 1000 each.

28. Sect. 85. *Puulu-kaua*, a close body, a phalanx.

29. Sect. 85. *Papa-kaua*, probably a body of picked men. chiefs and men of rank, who were armed with the *pololu*. which was probably the best offensive as well as defensive weapon employed by the Hawaiians. It seems probable to me that these were the men who surrounded the king, and I am informed that such was the case.

30. Sect. 85. *Poe kaua*, said to be the half-trained, light-armed soldiers.

31. Sect. 95. In order to make sense out of what would otherwise be an evidently foolish passage. I have found it necessary to substitute soft for hard, and hard for soft, poi, in this passage.

XXXIX

Agriculture

1. Agriculture was a matter of great importance in Hawaii, because by it a man obtained the means of supporting himself and his wife, his children, friends and domestic animals. It was associated, however, with the worship of idols.

2. In the Hawaiian Islands agriculture was conducted differently on lands where there were streams of water and on dry lands. On lands supplied with running water agriculture was easy and could be carried on at all times, and the only reason for a scarcity of food among the people on such lands was idleness. Sometimes, however, the water-supply failed; but the drought did not last long.

3. On the *kula*[1] lands farming was a laborious occupation and called for great patience, being attended with many drawbacks. On some of these were grubs, or caterpillars, or blight, *hauoki,* (frost), or *kahe,* (freshets), or the sun was too scorching; besides which there were many other hindrances.

4. On the irrigated lands wet patches were planted with *kalo* (taro, the *Arum esculentum,* or *Colocasia antiquorum* of the botanists). Banks of earth were first raised about the patch and beaten hard, after which water was let in, and when this had become nearly dry, the four banks were re-enforced with stones, coconut leaves and sugar-cane tops, until they were water-tight. Then the soil in the patch was broken up, water let in again, and the earth was well mixed and trampled with the feet.[2]

5. A line was then stretched to mark the rows, after which the *huli,* or taro-tops, were planted in the rows. Sometimes the planting was done without the rows being lined in. Water was then constantly kept running into the patch. The first two leaves appear called *laupai;* the taro attains full size, but it is not until twelve months are past that the tubers are ripe and ready to be made into food.

6. If potatoes were to be planted, the field was furrowed and water let in, after which the potato-stalks were set out, or, it might be, bananas, yams, or some other things.

7. When the land has become dry after the first watering, water is turned on again.[3] The plants are kept weeded out and hilled, and

water is turned on from time to time for six months, by which time the potatoes are ripe and fit for food. Such is the cultivation of all irrigable lands.

8. The cultivation of *kula* lands is quite different from that of irrigable lands. The farmer merely cleared of weeds as much land as he thought would suffice. If he was to plant taro (upland taro), he dug holes and enriched them with a mulch of ku-kui leaves, ashes or dirt, after which he planted the taro. In some places they simply planted without mulch or fertilizer.

9. Taro was constantly weeded until it had grown to be of good size, when it was fit to be made into poi or used as food in some other way. It was twelve months before it was mature and ready for pulling to be made into food.

10. If a field of potatoes[4] was desired, the soil was raised into hills, in which the stems were planted; or the stems might merely be thrust into the ground any how, and the hilling done after the plants were grown; the vines were also thrown back upon the hill. In six months the potatoes were ripe. Such was the cultivation of *kula* land.

11. On the *kula* lands the farms of the *aliis* were called *koele, hokuone,* or *kuakua,* those of the people, *mahina-ai.*

12. The island of Niihau was mostly *kula* and the principal crops were accordingly sweet potatoes, yams, and sugar-cane. There were, however, some taro patches at Waiu, on the windward side, but their extent was small. The people of that island were energetic farmers. They would clear the land and mulch it for many months, until the ground was thickly covered and the mulch had rotted, after which they planted such crops as sweet potatoes, yams, or sugar-cane.

13. There is *kula* land on parts of Kauai, Oahu, Molokai, and Lanai, just as on Niihau. The chief crops of these lands are sweet potatoes. There is wet taro-land, however, at Maunalei—on Lanai—and an abundance of taro. Kahoolawe is made up of *kula* land, and the principal vegetable is the potato, besides which yams and sugar-cane are produced, but no taro.

14. There is *kula*-land on parts of Maui and Hawaii. Kona is the part of Hawaii most exposed to the sun. Because of the prolonged dryness of the weather they frequently suffer from famine in that district. In time of famine the people of Kona performed religious ceremonies with great diligence, and carefully reckoned the months in which to plant.

15. There were different kinds of farmers. Those who really made a business of it and worked until sunset were called *ili-pilo.* Those who

kept at it for only a short time and did not do much at it were called *ili-helo* (dry skin).

16. Some husbandmen were provident of the food which they raised, while others wasted it. Those who raised an abundance of food, but used it improvidently, soon came to want because of their wastefulness.

17. The farmer who raised but little, but was economical in the use of his food did not soon come to want. Those who were economical in the use of their food were nicknamed *hoopi*—stingy; they did not often come to want.

18. One reason why people soon ran out of food was because they planted it all at once, so that when it ripened it ripened all at one time. While they were eating of one part another part also was ripe, so they invited their neighbors to help themselves to the food. This was one of the causes why some speedily came to want.

19. Some farmers did not plant a great deal at a time. They would plant a little now, and, after waiting a few months, they planted more land. So they continued to plant a little at a time during the months suitable for planting. The food did not all ripen at once, and by this plan the supply was kept up for a long time, and they had no lack of food. The necessity of furnishing food to the landlord was a reason for not taxing the land, and it was a means of averting famine from the farmers. Food was a child to be cared for, and it required great care.

20. Farmers were well acquainted with the seasons, the dry and the rainy season, the months suitable for planting potatoes, and those suitable for planting taro.

21. It was the custom with all farmers, when a crop of food has ripened, to peform a religious service to the gods. Those who worshipped Ku built their fire during the tabu period of Ku; those who worshipped Kane, built the fire during the tabu of Kane. If Lono was the god they worshipped, they built the fire on his day, and if Kanaloa was their God they built the fire in Kaloa.

22. While they were rubbing for fire and kindling it, no noise or disturbance must be made, but this tabu was removed so soon as fire was obtained. The contents of the oven were made up of vegetables and some sort of meat or fish as well.

23. When the food was cooked, the whole company were seated in a circle, the food was divided out and each man's portion was placed before him. Then the idol was brought forth and set in the midst of them all, and about its neck was hung the *ipu o Lono*. (See Chap XXIV, Sec. 5.)

24. Then the *kahuna* took of the food and offered it to heaven (*lani*), not to the idol; because it was believed that the deity was in the heavens, and that the carved image standing before them all was only a remembrancer.

25. When the priest had offered the food all the people ate until they were satisfied, after which what was left was returned to the owner of it. Such was the practice among those who were religiously inclined; but those who were without a god just ate their food without lighting the sacrificial fire and without performing any service of worship to the gods.

26. After this ceremony of fire-lighting the man's farm was *noa*, and he might help himself to the food at any time without again kindling a fire. But every time the farmer cooked an oven of food, before eating of it, he offered to the deity a potato or a taro, laying it on the altar, or putting it on a tree.

27. Every farmer with a god worshipped him at all times, but the farmers who had no gods did not worship.

Notes on Chapter XXXIX

1. Sect. 3. *Kula* was the name applied to such lands as were dry and inaccessible to water except from irrigation. The greater part of every one of the Hawaiian Islands is made up of what is called kula land. The word kula has been adopted by the English-speaking people of the Hawaiian Islands.

Kula, N. Z., *tura,* means bald. A long story is told of a man named *Tura,* who was said to have been the first bald-headed man.

2. Sect. 4. The trampling was to make the ground water-proof, i.e. so that the water would not soak entirely away.

3. Sect. 7. It seems unaccountable that Malo should give no description of, nor make direct allusion to, the method of irrigation by ditches with the Hawaiians used with great success, and in which they displayed not a little engineering skill. The course of old, historic irrigation canals can still be pointed out across lands that are dry at the present day, and that for generations have not received a supply of water from any such source.

4. Sect. 10. The Hawaiians were not acquainted with the so-called Irish potato, which is in reality an American potato, until its introduction by the white man. Their potato was the sweet potato, the *kumara* of Maori-land, the *uala* of Hawaii.

(N. B.) Lono was the god whose benignity chiefly commended him to the confidence of the farmer. The great god Ku, whose name and character suggest a resemblance to Zeus, was also a frequent object of worship by the same class. There were also many other gods worshipped by farmers.

XL

CONCERNING FISHING

1. Fishermen, or those skilled in the art of catching fish, were called *poe lawaia*. Fishing was associated with religious ceremonies, or idolatrous worship. The heiaus or altars, at which fishermen performed their religious ceremonies, were of a class different from all others.

2. There were many different methods of fishing: with nets; with hook and line; with the *pa*, or troll-hook; with the *leho*, or cowry; with the *hina'i*, or basket; the method called *ko'i;*[1] and with the hand thrust into holes in the rocks.

3. The heiau at which fishermen worshipped their patron deity for good luck was of the kind called *Kuula;*[2] but as to the gods worshipped by fishermen, they were various and numerous—each one worshipping the god of his choice. The articles also that were tabued by one god were different from those tabued by another god.

4. The god of one fisherman tabued everything that was black, and that fisherman accordingly would not allow anything colored black to appear in what he wore; his wife would not put on a *tapa* or a *pa-u* that had black in it, nor have anything black about her house. A line would be stretched about the house to prevent anyone who was robed, or *maloed* or *pa-ued*, in black, from entering the enclosure about their establishment. Nor would he allow any black to appear upon his fishing tackle.

5. Turmeric was an article that was tabued by some fishing gods, a red earth called *alaea* by others. Accordingly fishermen who looked to these gods as their patrons would not suffer the prohibited articles to appear in the apparel of man or woman in their family, and they stretched a line about their establishments to keep from entering therein anyone who had these things about them; nor would they suffer these things to be about their tackle.

6. The gods of this craft then were of many kinds and their tabus various; but they were all alike in the fact that they always worshipped before going forth to fish, and in a manner appropriate to the kind of fish.

7. The religious ceremonies centered specially about the *opelu* and *aku*, and were repeated at every fishing season. There were religious rites relating to other fishes also, but they were not so strict and rigorous as

those that related to the opelu and the aku, and this will appear from the fact that their rite formed part of the observances of the Makahiki. (See Chap. XXXVI.) The fish eaten during the summer months of *Kau* were different as to kind from those eaten during the winter, *Hooilo*. During Kau the opelu was taken and used for food, during Hooilo the aku—bonito or albicore.

8. In the month of Hina'iaeleele (corresponding to July) they took the opelu by means of the *kaili*[3] net and used it for food. The aku was then made tabu, and no man, be he commoner or alii, might eat of the aku; and if any chief or commoner was detected in so doing he was put to death. The opelu was free and might be used as food until the month of Kaelo or January.

9. Kaelo was the month in which was performed the ceremony of plucking out and eating the eye of the aku. (Chap. XXXVI: 75.) After that was done the aku might be eaten and the opelu in its turn became tabu and might not be eaten, save under pain of death.

10. Before starting out to fish for the opelu the fishermen would assemble at the *kuula heiau* in the evening, bringing with them their nets, of the sort called *aei,* pigs, bananas, coconuts, poi, and their sleeping apparel, that they might spend the night and worship the god of fishing.

11. While engaged in this ceremony all the people sat in a circle, and the kahuna, bringing a dish of water that had in it a coarse sea-moss, *limu kala,* and turmeric, stood in their midst and uttered a prayer for purification (*pule huikala*). At the close of the service the kahuna called out,

> *Hemu*[7] *oia.*
> Defend us from them.

The people responded:

> *Hemu.*
> Defend us.

The priest said:

> *Hemu na moe inoino, na moemoea,*
> *na punohunohu,*[4] *na haumia.*
> *Hemu oia.*

> Save us from night-mare, from bad-luck-dreams,
>   from omens of ill.
> From such deliver us.

The people responded:

> *Hemu!*
> Defend us!

The priest said:

> *Elieli!*
> Speedily and entirely!

The people responded:

> *Noa!*
> It is free!

The priest said:

> *Ia e!*
> Oh, Ia!

The people responded:

> *Noa honua.*
> Freedom complete, absolute.

With this the ceremony of purification was ended.

12. All the people slept that night about the sanctuary (*imua*). It was strictly forbidden for any one to sneak away secretly to his own house to lie with his wife. They had to spend that night at the sanctuary in the observance of tabu.

13. When this service was performed the canoes could put to sea, and the pigs were then laid into the ovens for baking. On the return of the men with their fish, the kahunas having offered prayer, the pork, bananas, coconuts and vegetables were laid upon the *lele,* and the function of the kahuna was ended.

14. After that the people feasted themselves on the food and religious services were discontinued by express command (*papa*), because the prayers had been repeated and the whole business was *noa*, fishing was now free to all.

15. Thus it was that fishermen, whether those who took the aku with the troll-hook, the *pa*, or those who used nets, performed their ceremonies of worship. But the godless, i.e., the irreligious or skeptical ones went to their fishing without any religious ceremony whatever.

16. There was a great variety of implements, apparatus and methods employed by fishermen; large nets and small nets, large baskets and small baskets; some used nets and some used hooks. Those who used nets sometimes dived under water with them while fishing, but those who used hooks did not dive, unless to clear the hook when it had caught in the reef, and then only if the water was shallow.

17. The following kinds of fish-nets were used: the *papa-hului*, to surround a school of fish, in conjunction with a net called *au-mai-ewa*,[8] the *aulau*, the *pakuikui*, the *papa-olewalewa*, the *laau melomelo* and possibly the *kahekahe*.

18. Of nets there was also the *kupo*,[9] the *ka-waa*, the *kuu*, the *aei*, the *pouono*, the *akiikii*, the *lu'elu'e*, the *kaihi*, the *hano-malolo*, the *hano-iao*, the *kaeeohua*, the *kaeepaoo*, the *kaili*, the *pahu*, and the *haoa-puhi*. Then there was *lawaia upalupalu* (or ordinary angling), and the *upena uluulu*.

19. Of arrangements of fish-hooks, there was the *kaka*,[19] used in taking the *ahi*, the *kahala*, the method called *kukaula*, the *luhe'e*, the *hi-aku*, the *ka-mokoi*, the *ku-mano*, *lawaia-palu*, the *haoa-puhi*, and *lawaia-upapalu*.

20. Of methods of basket fishing there were the *kala* basket, the eel basket, the *hinai-houluulu*,[11] the basket for taking *hinalea*, the *kawa'a* basket, the *pa'iohua* basket, and the *pa'i-o'opu*. Probably some of the baskets have failed of mention.

21. Some fish were taken by diving for them. Of such were the turtle, the lobster, the *manini*, the *kala*, and others for which the fishermen dived when they saw them entering holes in the rocks.

22. There were some who engaged in fishing on a large scale, and were called *Lawaia nui*, while those who worked on a small scale were called *lawaia liilii*.

23. The professional fisherman, who worked on a large scale and was in comfortable circumstances, carried such tackle as hooks, lines, etc., in a calabash or *ipu*, (the full name of which is *ipu-holoholona*), while the

petty fisherman who worked on a small scale, carried his tucked away in the bight or knot (*hipu'u*) of his malo, and such fishermen were called *lawaia-pola-malo*.

24. The name *ko'a* or *ko'a-lawaia* was applied to certain places in the deep sea where fish haunted. Thus the place where the *ahi* were wont to be found was called a *ko'a-ahi*, and that where the *aku* or the *kahala* or *opelu* were to be found, was called a *ko'a-aku* or a *ko'a-kahala* or a *ko'a-opelu*, and so on.

25. These *ko'a-lawaia* were so deep under water that the eye failed to perceive them, nor could the fish be seen when swimming over them, nor when they seized the hook. In order to find them it was necessary to take one's bearings from the land. Two bearings were required, and where these were found to intersect, there was the *ko'a*, and there the fisherman let down his hook or his net.

26. When the fish took the hook, a quiver ran along the line and was communicated to the hand of the fisherman, whereupon he at once pulled in the line. Such was deep sea fishing.

27. When the fish were in shoal water their presence could be detected, if it were a sandy bottom. Among the fishes that haunted waters with a sandy bottom were the *weke, oio, welea, akule,* and many other kinds of fish.

28. If it was on a bank that the fish were seen, then they were probably of the kind known as *ma'oma'o* or *palapala*.

29. Some fish played about on the surface of the water, as did the flying fish, *malolo,* the *puhikii, ua'u, iheihe, keke'e, aha,* and many others.

30. Some kinds of fish haunted caverns and holes, as did the shark, eel, lobster, squid and many others. There were fishermen who took every kind of fish except the whale; that was not taken by Hawaiian fishermen.

Notes to Chapter XL

1. Sect. 2. *Koi'*: This was a method of fishing in which a long, stiff pole was usel, with a strong line and hook attached. The hook was baited by preference with a tough fish such as the *paoo*. The baited hook was then drawn back and forth over the surface of the water to attract the prey. From this word comes no doubt the familiar word *mokoi'*, to angle with pole, hook and line.

2. Sect. 3. *Kuula:* this was generally a mere rude pile of stones, often placed on a promontory or elevation overlooking the sea. Coral or some sort of limestone was preferred to any other variety of stone. The altar itself was commonly called a *ko'a,* Kuula being the name of the chief patron deity of

fishermen. The number of gods and godlings worshipped by fishermen is too numerous for mention.

Remark. Altars of stone were erected and visible until a recent date at Maliko, Honuaula, Oloalu. and Kaupo on Maui; on the island of Kahoolawe; at Kaena and Kaohai on Lanai; at Waimea, Ka-lae-o-ka-oio, Kua-loa and Waimanalo on Oahu; at Hanalei, Mana, and Moloaa on Kauai; and at very many other places. A notable place was at the promontory south-east of Waimea, Oahu.

3. Sect. 8. *Kaili:* a name applied to the fine-mouthed net used for taking the *opelu.* It was also called *aei.* The mouth of the net was kept open by means of two sticks of the elastic *ulei* wood. After the net had been let down under water, it's mouth was made round by means of two lines that were attached to the ends of the sticks. On pulling these lines the sticks were bent, and the mouth of the net was drawn into a circular form.

4. Sect. 5. *Alaea;* the Hawaiian word shows the loss of consonants. The Tahitian word is *araca,* the Maori, *Karamea.*

5. Sect. 11. *Punohunohu:* clouds, especially the bright piled up clouds seen in early morning, which were looked upon as ominous of something.

6. Sect. 11. This prayer is very similar to that given in Chapter XXVII, Sect. 13, and it seems to me that *"He mu"* should be written here as two separate words, as it is in that passage. Its meaning is discussed in the note (No. 5) following that chapter. See also Chapter XXXVII, Sect. 30, note B. W. D. A.

7. Sect. 20. *Oopu*—the New Zealand Maori *Kokopu.*

8. Section 17. *Au-mai-ewa.* This net had a large mouth, and was placed at the wings of the *papa-hului* to receive the fish that were gathered by the former. The *aulau* consisted of leaves thickly strung to a long line, used to pen up the fish and drive them to the net.

Pakuikui: in this a net is laid in a hollow or ravine in the coral through which the fish must pass in their retreat sea-ward, the water being at the same time beaten to drive them towards the net.

Papa-olewalewa; a net used in much the same way as the *pa-kuikui,* but in deep water and in conjunction with the *laau melo-melo.*

Laau melo-melo; a clublike stick, which after being charred, was anointed with oils whose odor was attractive to the fish, and then thrust into the water to draw the fish by its fragrance.

Kahekahe; a method in which a large net was placed in deep water, in a place where the current or some opportunity for feeding caused the fish to assemble.

Another method called by this same name, was that in which the fish were attracted to the net by bait artfully strewn in the water.

9. Sect. 18. *Kupo;* a long net stretched across the track of fish, one end being anchored in deep, the other in shoal water.

Ka-wa'a; a set used in the deep sea, the fish being driven in by thrashing the water or pelting it with stones.

Kuu; a generic name for almost' any kind of net that was let down into the water. The *aei,* said to be the same as the *kaili* described in Note (3).

The mouth was held open by long sticks of *ulei,* the fish being attracted with bait. *Pouono;* a long net that' was stretched across an ocean ravine or gully, while men beat the water with sticks.

Akiikii; a net of moderate size used in ambuscading fish. The rocks in front of the net were upturned to give the fish a new feeding ground. After waiting awhile, the water was beaten to drive the fish towards the net.

Lu'elu'e; a net of moderate size, in which bait having been placed, it was let down into deep water, out of sight of the fisherman. At the point of juncture of the two lines which cross the mouth of the net, where is attached the line that leads to the fisherman's hand, is also attached a short line with bait at its free end. When the fisherman feels the line quiver from the entrance of the fish or from its pulling at the bait, he hauls up the net.

Kaihi; said to be a fine meshed net that takes all kinds of fish, similar to the *kaili.*

Hano-malolo; a long net held by two canoes, while two others drove the fish into its open mouth.

Hano–iao; a fine meshed net for taking small fish, to be used as bait.

Kaee-ohua; a small net that was held open by means of two sticks held in the hands of the fisherman. It was used in shoal water.

Kaee-paoo; the same as the *kae -ohua,* only that it had but one stick for a handle. The *kaili,* already mentioned and the same as the *aei.* By some it is said to be a net with fine meshes, used only in shoal water and over a sandy bottom, and to take all kinds of fish, a grab-all.

Pahu; a net two or three fathoms long, used by two men in shoal water, who at the same time thrashed with long sticks at the wings of the net to drive in the fish. *Haoa-puhi;* a short piece of hard wood tapering to a sharp point at each end, with a line attached to its middle; it was baited and lashed to the end of a stick that served as a handle, by means of which it was thrust into the hiding places of the eel. On being swallowed by the fish, the line was drawn taut, and the *haoa* was turned crosswise in the gullet of the fish. *Upalupalu,* ordinary angling. When the baited hook was thrown as in fly fishing, to a particular spot on the surface of the water, it was called *pa aeo.* The *uluulu* is described as a small net having two sticks to open its mouth, one of which was held in each hand. With this the fisherman dived deep down under water.

10. Sect. 19. *Kaka,* in which a number of hooks are attached to a single line, much used in a deep-sea fishing.

Kahala, in which a net made of very strong cord is used to take the shark, called also the *hihi-mano.*

Kukaula. In this method the canoe was anchored in water said not to exceed ten fathoms in depth, that being about' the length of line at which the pull of a fish taking the hook could be detected at once by the hand of the fisherman. They did, however, fish at greater depths than this.

Luhe'e; a method of squidding in which a large cowry, coupled with a stone sinker, is attached to the hook, the color and lustre of the shell offering an irresistible fascination to the octopus. The instrument itself is called *leho-he'e*, the method *luhee*.

Hi aku; the use of the *pa* in trolling for the *aku*, (*pa hi aku*) being the full name for the instrument. It consists of a hook of human bone fixed to a plate of mother of pearl. Various modifications of this troll-hook are found in the different islands of the Pacific.

Ka-mokoi, ordinary fishing with hook, line and rod.

Ku-mano', taking the shark with bait and a noose.

Lawaia-palu, attracting fish by means of bait scattered on the water.

Lawaia-upapalu. In this as in fly fishing, the hook is thrown to a desired spot.

11. Sect. 20. *Hinai houluulu,* a basket with which a fisherman would dive down under water to take certain fish.

Hinalea, a small fish much esteemed for its flavor.

The *pai-o'opu* was a hat-shaped basket used to take the *oopu,* a sweet and delicate fish found in mountain streams and fresh water ponds.

12. Sect. 28. *Ma'oma'o* or *palapalai;* the fishes of this or allied species of fish were marked with stripes or patches of bright color, like ripe autumn leaves, one being the *lauhau.*

XLI

Sports and Games, Ume

1. From the most ancient times down to the reign of Liholiho, Kamehameha II, there was a great variety of games practiced by the people. In the month of *Ikuwa*,[1] October, the coming of the *Makahiki* season was indicated by the display of flags,[2] and the people left their *ordinary*[3] worship of idols, and joined with the chiefs in the practice of games and sports.

2. *Ume* was a pastime that was very popular with all the Hawaiians. It was an adulterous sport and was played in the following manner. A large enclosure,[4] or pa, was made in the midst of or close to the town.

3. This done, all the people took hold and helped to collect a large quantity of faggots; and when it came night a bonfire was started, which made it as light as day, and all the people gathered together.

4. When all were seated in a circle within the enclosure, a man stood forth as the president[5] of the assembly and called them to order. Another man also came forward and chaunted a gay and lascivious song, waving in his hand the while a long wand[6] which was trimmed at intervals with tufts of bird-feathers. He waved this to and fro as he moved about, repeating at the same time the words of his song.

5. As he made his circuit, passing in front of the people, he selected[7] the fine-looking women and the handsome men, and the man and woman whom he indicated by touching them with his wand went out and enjoyed themselves together.

6. A husband would not be jealous of or offended at his own wife, if she went out with another man, nor would a wife be angry with her own husband because he went out to enjoy another woman, because each of them would have done the same thing if they had been touched with the *ume-stick*.

7. During the nights while this game was being played the man consorted with the woman that pleased him, and the woman with the man that pleased her; and when daylight[8] came the husband returned to his own wife and the wife to her own husband.

8. Owing to these practices, the affections of the woman were often transferred to the man, her partner,[9] and the affections of the man to

the woman who was his partner; so that the man would not return to his former wife, nor the woman to her former husband. This was the way *ume* was played. Another name for this sport was *pili* = touched by the wand.

Notes to Chapter XLI

1. Sect. 1. *I-ku-wa,* the month corresponding to October or November, said to be so called from the thunder often heard at that time.

2. Sect. 1. This display of flags was a natural expression of joy and enthusiasm.

3. Sect. 1. The statement that the people at the time of Makahiki left their idol-worship and indulged in games, is misleading in more than one respect. 1st. The assumption that the worship of the Hawaiians was mere idol-worship is not for a moment to be credited; one has but to consider the prayers they offered to be convinced of the opposite. 2d. The same spirit of worship inspired the ceremonies of this Makahiki festival as pervaded the other tabu-periods of the year. N. B. E.

The Makahiki festival was sacred to Lono, and the worship of the other gods was suspended for the time. W. D. A.

See Chap. XXXVIII, Sect. 16.

3½. Sect. 1. *Ume* was a plebeian sport. No chief of high rank, or who greatly respected himself, would think of being present at the performance of this game. Not because of its immorality, not that, but because it was not a place where he would meet his peers. Chiefs of low rank went, because they were of low rank and did not greatly respect themselves. The sport of this nature at which the chief should attend was *kilu,* which will soon be described.

4. Sect. 2. It is an error to assert that *ume* was generally played in an open court or enclosure. It was in a house that it was chiefly played. In Honolulu—which by the way was in ancient times called *Kou*—the *hale ume* was situated where Bishop's Bank now stands.

5. Sect. 4. The president of the assembly was called the *ano-hale,* i.e., the one who kept the house quiet, orderly.

6. Sect. 4. The one who carried the wand was called the *mau*, and the wand itself was called the *maile*.

7. Sect. 5. The selection was not left to the uninfluenced judgment of the *mau*. The man indicated his choice to the *mau*, the wand-bearer, at the same time putting into his hands some thing of value as an inducement, to be given to the woman, perhaps to be passed on to her husband in return for his complaisance. Sometimes, when the pair got outside, the woman would refuse to have anything to do with the man, and they returned at once to the *hale ume.*

8. Sect. 7. The word *ho-ao,* which was the ancient word that meant the most legitimate form of marriage, was derived from this staying together until day-light, *ao.* For a man and woman to make a night of it together and to stay with

each other until *ao,* morning was equivalent to a declaration of marriage. This temporary union for a night was termed *omau,* in distinction from *hoao.*

Virgins and unmarried women did not as a rule attend at the *hale-ume. Ume,* as said before, was not a game for the *aliis,* but for the common people. The woman could of course do something in the way of management, but she could not actually refuse to go out with the man who had chosen her.

9. Sect. 8. If the man took his new wife to his home, it was for the new favorite to say whether the former woman might stay on the promises. The children belonged to the man.

The meaning of the word *u-me* is to draw, to attract. *"E ume mai ia'u; e hahai makou mamuli ou."* Draw me; we will run after thee. Song of Solomon, 4:1.

XLII

Sports and Games

Kilu

1. *Kilu* was a very favorite sport with the ancient Hawaiians. It was played in the same enclosure as *ume*. One night *ume* would be played, another night *kilu*. They were both licentious sports. The manner of playing *kilu* was as follows:

2. The company were seated in a circle within the enclosure. On one side were set a number of pobs, (broad-based, pointed cylinders), and opposite to them, on the other side, about ten fathoms away, an equal number of pobs.

3. The players sat immediately behind these pobs or posts, five or more on each side, together with the tally-keepers of the game. Then the one who acted as president of the game stood up and called aloud "Puheoheo"; and the whole assembly answered, "Puheoheo-heo."

4. Order was at once established; and if any one made a disturbance they set fire to his clothing. Silence having been secured, the *kilus*, with which the game was to be played, were placed in front of those who were to play the game.

5. The *kilu* was a gourd (or cocoanut shell) that had been cut obliquely from one end to the other. Before beginning the play, the tally-keeper, or *helu-ai*, holding a *kilu* in his hand, addressed the tally-keeper of the other side in a low tone of voice, and stated the name, or purpose of the *kilu*, saying, for instance, "this *kilu* is a love-token; it is a kissing *kilu* (*kilu honi*)."

6. The tally-keeper on the other side then replied in a low tone giving the name of some person on his side. (*O ka mea aloha kapa mai.*)

7. This done, the tally-keepers gave the *kilus* into the hands of the two players. Each of the players chanted an *oli* before he began to play. If the *kilu* thrown by one of the players hit the pob on the other side at which he aimed, his tally-keeper in a loud tone said,

> *A uweuwe ke ko'e a ke kae,*
> *Puehuehu ka la, komo inoino,*
> *Kakia, kahe ka ua ilalo.*

Now wriggles the worm to its goal,
What a towelling: a hasty entrance:
Pinned: down falls the rain.

8. The successful player then crossed over and claimed a kiss in payment for his success, because the forfeit of the *kilu* was to be kissing. They continued to play till one of them scored ten and that one was declared the winner. Sometimes one side would celebrate the victory by dancing. The play was kept up till morning and resumed the following night.

Notes to Chapter XLII

Notes. Kilu was a select and aristocratic game to which none but *aliis* were admitted. The king and queen were not above participating in the pleasures of this sport. Any chief of recognized rank in the *papa alii* was admitted. Once admitted to the hall in which the sport was indulged in. all were peers and stood on an equal footing as to the privileges and rules of the game. King nor queen could claim exemption from the rules of the game, nor deny to any one the full exercise of the privileges acquired under the rules.

There was a greater outward propriety and a certain show of regard for etiquette in the playing of *kilu*, which must have been wanting in *ume*, but the *motive* of the game was in each case the same.

The men sat grouped at one end of the hall, the women at the other. The players, five or more in number of each sex, sat facing each other in advance of the spectators, separated by an interval, which must have been less than the "ten fathoms" at which David Malo places it. The floor, at least that portion of it which lay between the players, was covered with matting. (In the game of *ume* it was strewn with rushes.) The players were probably selected by the president (Sect. 3), who was termed the *la-anoano*, i.e., quiet day. In front of each player was placed, what, for lack of a better name, I have termed a pob (following the terminology of the game of quoits), which was nothing more or less than a conical block of heavy wood broad at the base, to keep it upright. The *kilu*, with which the game was played, was a dish made by cutting in two an egg-shaped coconut shell obliquely from one side of the point to the eyes, thus making a somewhat one-sided dish. The object of the player was to cast his *kilu* so that it should travel with a sliding, and at the same time a rotary, motion, across the floor and hit the pob that stood in front of the woman of his choice. The woman also took her turn in playing after the man. A successful hit entitled a player to claim a kiss from his opponent, a toll which it was customary to demand the payment of at once. The successful making of ten points in the game entitled one to claim the same forfeit as in the game of *ume*. But such rights were often commuted for,—on grounds of wise policy, at the request of the victor,—by an equivalent of land or some other possession. Still no fault could be found if a player demanded the full payment of the forfeit. The two did not, however, retire for that purpose at the time—that would have been contrary to etiquette—but did so later in the night, after the company had separated.

A game of *kilu* was often gotten up by one *alii* as a compliment to distinguished visitors of rank. It was a supreme expression of hospitality, and was not an empty phrase, as when the Spanish don says to his guest "all that I have is yours." I have succeeded in obtaining the following specimen of an *oli* which is such as might have been recited by a contestant in *kilu* before playing (Sect. 7).

> *Ula Kala'e-loa* i ka lepo a ka makani,*
> *Hoonuanua na pua i Kalamaula,*
> *He hoa i ka La'i-a-ka-manu,†*
> *Manu ai ia i ka hoa laukona.‡*
> *I keke'e lauaua ia e ka moe*
> *E kuhi ana ia he kanaka e.*
> *Oau no keia mai luna a lalo.*
> *Huna ke aloha, pe'e maloko,*
> *Ike'a i ka uwe ana iho.*
> *Pela ka hoa kamalii,*
> *He uwe wale ke kamalii.*

Ruddy glows Kalae-loa* through the wind-blown dust.
Plump and lush are the flowers at Lamaula,
A partner in the songs of the birds,
A sea-bird that spoils the beauties, spite of the duenna,
His stinginess is that he is jealous of his protege's bed.
He was thinking me to be a stranger.
I am myself from crown to sole.
Hidden has been my love, pent up within,
Shown by my weeping over you.
That is the way with a child-friend.
A child weeps for a trifle.

N. B. In old times the site on which now stands Bishop's Bank was occupied by a house in which *kilu* and *ume* were wont to be played.

* *Kala'e-loa* was the full name of the place on Molokai ordinarily known as Kalae.

† *La'i-a-ka-manu* is the name of a land near Kala'e-loa. In the use of this word a double meaning is evidently intended, i.e., a reference both to the land so-called and to the song of the birds. Hawaiian poetry depended upon this trick to produce its chief effects.

‡ *Laukona,* applies to one who is jealous and watchful of one under his care.

REMARK. In justice to the ancient Hawaiians it should be stated that there existed a more respectable class among them, who disapproved of the debauchery of the *ume* and *kilu,* and endeavored to keep their children away from the places where those games were played.

W. D. A.

XLIII

Puhenehene, or Pa-Puhene

1. *Puhenehene* was a game that was played at night. The people were seated in two rows facing each other.

2. Then a long piece of tapa, made perhaps by stitching several pieces together, was stretched between one party and the other.

3. When the assembly had been brought to order the president whistled a call on the *puheoheo,* or called out "puheoheo," and all the company answered "puheoheo". This done a man stood forth and chanted a gay and pleasing song.

4. Then three men lifted up the long tapa, already described, and with it covered over and concealed from view one of the groups of players.

5. One of the men of the number who were concealed then hid the pebble which was called a *no'a.*[1] The tapa which curtained or covered them was then removed, and the men, one of whom had the *no'a,* then leaned forward and looked down.[2]

6. Then the other side made a guess where the *no'a* was. If the guess was correct it counted for them, if not for the other party. When either side scored ten it had the victory; somebody would then start up a hula-dance.

Notes to Chapter XLIII

1. Sect. 5. The *no'a* was a small pebble, and it was hidden on the person of one of the players.

2. Sect. 5. The purpose of leaning forward was to conceal the countenance as much as possible, because it was as much by the study of the countenance as in any other way that one was to judge which of the players had the *no'a* about him.

XLIV

Kukini—Running Foot-Races

1. Foot-racing, *kukini*, was a very popular amusement. It was associated with betting and was conducted in the following manner:

2. The *kukini*, or swift runners, were a class of men who were trained[1] with great severity and made to practice running very frequently, until they had attained great speed. When the people wished to indulge in betting a number of the fastest of this class were selected and two of this number were chosen to run a race.

3. Those who thought one man was the faster runner of the two bet their property on him, and those who thought the other was the faster, bet their property on him.

4. When people had made their bets, the experts came to judge by physical examination which of the two runners was likely to win, after which they made their bets. One man, after staking all his property, pledged his wife and his own body (*pili hihia*), another man bet property he had borrowed from another (*pili kaua*). When all the pledges had been deposited (*kieke*, literally bagged) the betting was at an end.

5. The runners (*kukini*) then took their station at the starting point and a pole with a flag was planted at the goal. The race might be over a long course or a short one; that was as the runners aggreed.

6. It was a rule of the game that if both runners reached the goal at the same instant, neither party won (*aole no eo*), it was a dead heat (*pai wale*). It was when one reached the goal ahead of the other that he was declared victor. In that case the winners made great exultation over their victory.

7. Sometimes a runner would sell out[2] the race to his opponent and let a third person stake his property on the other runner. This was the practice in *kukini*.

Notes to Chapter XLIV

1. Sect. 2. *Koi, ko'h-ee.* According to other authorities if should be *ka'i, ka'h-ee*, to practice, train, exercise. The runner was first exercised in walking on his toes, without touching the heel of the foot to the ground. Then he was set

to running, at first for a short distance and at a moderate pace. Finally he was made to run at full speed for great distances. While in training they were denied poi and all soggy, heavy food, but were fed on rare-done flesh of the fowl, and roasted vegetables, taro, sweet-potato, bread-fruit, etc.

Kaohele, son of Kumukoa, a king of Molokai who was cotemporary with Alapai-nui of Hawaii, was a celebrated *kukini.* It is related of him that he could run from Kaluaaha as far as to Halawa and return before a fish put on the fire at the time of his starting had time to be roasted. *"E kui ka mama' i loaa o Kaohele."* You must double (literally piece out) your speed to catch Kaohele.

Uluanui of Oahu, a rival and friend of Kaohele, was a celebrated foot-runner. It was said of him that he could carry a fish from the Kaelepulu pond in Kailua, round by way of Waialua and bring it in to Waikiki while it was still alive and wriggling.

Makoko was a celebrated runner of Kamehameha I on Hawaii. It was said of him that he could carry a fish from the pond at Waiakea, in Hilo, and reach Kailua before it was dead. The distance is a little over a hundred miles, making it, of course, an impossible story. But it would be unkind to take such statements with utter literalness.

2. Sect. 7. The Hawaiian text reads. *"O kekahi poe, nolunolu na hai ke eo, a na hai e lipi ka lakou waiwai, pela ka hana ana ma ke kukini."* Only by removing the comma after *poe* and rearranging the letters in the word *lipi,* which should evidently be *pili,* is it possible to make sense out of this passage. It is curious to note the same corrupt practice, of selling out a race, in ancient Hawaii, as prevails in the civilized world today.

XLV

The Game of Maika

1. Rolling the *maika stone* was a game on which much betting was done. The manner of conducting the game was as follows:

2. When people wanted the excitement of betting they hunted up the men who were powerful in rolling the *maika* stone, and every man made his bet on the one whom he thought to be the strongest player.

3. The experts also studied the physique of the players, as well as the signs and omens, after which the betting went to ruinous lengths.

Now the *maika* was a stone which was fashioned after the shape of a wheel, thick at the centre and narrow at the circumference—a biconvex disc. It was alsc called an *ulu,* this thing with which the game of *maika* was played.

4. The *ulu-maika* (by which name the stone disc, or the game itself was called) was made from many varieties of stone, and they were accordingly designed after the variety of stone from which they were made.

5. The game of *maika* was played on a road-way, or *kahua,* made specially for the purpose. When all had made their bets the *maika*-players came to the *maika*-course.

6. The *ulu* which the first man hurled was said to be his *kumu, mua,* i.e., his first basis or pledge; in the same way the *ulu* which the second player hurled, or bowled, was called his *kumu.*

7. If the second player outdid the first player's shot he scored. If they both went the same distance it was a dead heat.

8. But if the second player did not succeed in out-doing the first man's play the score was given to the first player.

Notes to Chapter XLV

The meaning of the language in sections 6, 7, and 8 is such that I can make no sense of it; and after diligent inquiry of those who are Hawaiian scholars and skillful in unraveling puzzles, I can find no one who can do anything with it. I give a literal copy of the original:

6. *O ke kanaka i pehi mua i kana ulu, oia kana kumu mua, o ke kana-naka i pehi hope mai, oia no hoi kana kumu.*

7. *O ke kanaka i pehi mua, pehi oia i ke kumu, a ka mea i pehi hope mai, ina pau iaia ke kumu a kela mea, helu oia, a pela nohoi kela mea, a i pa nohoi ka kekahi, ua pai maika.*

8. *Aka, i pau ole ke kumu a ke kahi, i kekahi, eo, kekahi i kekahi, pela ke ano o ka Maika.* Such is the Hawaiian as written by a Hawaiian.

The first thing in translating this is to utterly disregard the punctuation. That is entirely wrong and misleading.

The game of *maika* was a most worthy and noble sport. It is not an easy matter to obtain definite information as to some points in the game, whether sometimes the play was not to drive the *ulu* between two stakes set up at a distance, whether the *ulu-maika* of the first player was removed from the course as soon as it came to a standstill, by what means the point reached by the *ulu* was marked, if it was removed from the course in order to clear the track for the next player. These are some of the questions to which I have been able to obtain only partial and unsatisfactory answers. There was no doubt a great diversity of practice as to these points on the different islands, and even in the different parts of the same island.

The principal point to be made was, so far as I can learn, to send the *ulu* to as great a distance as possible. When an *ulu* had come to a standstill it was probably removed from the track and the place of its fall marked by a little flag, or stake, set in the ground opposite and outside of the track. According to some, however, the *ulu* was allowed to remain in the track as it fell, thus adding an obstacle to the success of the player who had the next throw. But this method is so clearly opposed to all fair play that I cannot believe it was the general practice.

The *ulu, maika,* or *ulu-maika* (for by all these names was the thing called) was of various sizes, being all the way from two and a quarter to six inches in diameter. The size most ordinarily used, if one may judge from specimens seen in museums and private collections, was perhaps from three to four inches. It was in some cases made one-sided to enable it to follow the bend of a curved track, one of which description I remember to have seen on the plains back of Kaunakakai, on Molokai. There is said to have been another of the same kind at Lanikaula, also on Molokai. There is said to be a *kahua-maika* at Ka-lua-ko'i, on the mountain of Maunaloa, at the western end of Molokai, which to this day remains in a fair state of preservation. There must also be many others scattered through the group.

N. B.—The half-grown bread-fruit, which is generally of a globular shape was much used in playing this game, and undoubtedly gave its name, *ulu,* both to the thing itself and to the sport. Spherical stones, evidently fashioned for use in this game, are object's occasionally met with. From the fact that the stone *ulu* is of spherical shape—in evident imitation of the fruit—as well as that all the specimens met with have been fashioned out of a coarse, vesicular stone that is incapable of smooth finish or polish, while the material from which the *maika* is made, has in the majority of cases been a close, fine-grained basalt, leads to the conclusion that the *ulu* was the early form, and the *maika* the product of later evolution.

Mr. S. Percy Smith suggests that the word *ulu* probably meant originally "round," "spherical," as in the word for "head."

XLVI

The Game of Pahee

1. The game of *pahee* was one which people played at odd times, whenever they were so inclined, and it was associated with betting.

2. A short javelin, made from the hard wood of the *ulei* or *kauila*, was the instrument used in playing pahee. It was made thick at the forward end, the head, and tapered off towards the tail-end. One man cast his javelin, and when it had come to a stand still, the other man cast, and whichever javelin went farther than the other, it counted for him who threw it.

3. After each one had made his bet the players went to the tail-end.

4. He who first scored ten won the game.

Note to Chapter XLVI

The *pahee* or javelin was cast on a roadway or piece of sward, in such a way as to slide or skip along, over the ground. It was a very interesting game. Betting was no doubt a very common fault of old Hawaiian life, but it is not exactly true that betting was an accompaniment to every game that was played in ancient Hawaii.

XLVII

Canoe-Racing

1. The ancient Hawaiians were very fond of betting on a canoe-race. When they wished to indulge this passion, people selected a strong crew of men to pull their racing canoes.

2. Each man then put up his bet on that crew which was in his opinion composed of the strongest canoe-paddlers, and, the betting being over, they started out for the race.

3. If the canoe was of the kind called the *kioloa* (a sharp and narrow canoe, made expressly for racing) there might be but one man to paddle it, but if it was a large canoe, there might be two, three, or a large number of paddlers, according to the size of the canoe.

4. The racing canoes paddled far out to sea—some, however, staid close in to the land (to act as judges, or merely perhaps as spectators), and then they pulled for the land, and if they touched the beach at the same time it was a dead heat; but if a canoe reached the shore first it was the victor, and great would be the exultation of the men who won, and the sorrow of those who lost their property.

XLVIII

He'e-nalu, Surf-Riding[5]

1. Surf-riding was a national sport of the Hawaiians, on which they were very fond of betting, each man staking his property on the one he thought to be the most skilful.

2. When the bets were all put up, the surf-riders, taking their boards with them, swam out through the surf, till they had reached the waters outside of the surf. These surf-boards were made broad and flat, generally hewn out of *koa;*[1] a narrower board, however, was made from the wood of the *wiliwili.*[2]

3. One board would be a fathom in length, another two fathoms, and another four fathoms, or even longer.[3]

4. The surf-riders, having reached the belt of water outside of the surf, the region where the rollers began to make head, awaited the incoming of a wave, in preparation for which they got their boards under way by paddling with their hands until such time as the swelling wave began to lift and urge them forward. Then they speeded for the shore until they came opposite to where was moored a buoy, which was called a *pua.*

5. If the combatants passed the line of this buoy together it was a dead heat; but if one went by it in advance of the other he was the victor.

6. *A i ka au hou ana, o ka mea i komo i ka pua hoomawaena mai oia, aole e hiki i ke kulana, o ka eo no ia nana; pela ka he'e nalu.*[4]

Notes to Chapter XLVIII

1. Sect. 2. *Koa,* the same wood as that of which the canoe was generally made.

2. Sect. 2. *Wili-wili,* a light, cork-like wood, used in making floats for the outriggers of canoes, for nets, and a variety of other similar purposes.

3. Sect. 3. The longest surf-board at the Bishop Museum is sixteen feet in length. It is difficult to see how one of greater length could be of any service, and even when of such dimensions it must have required great address to manage it. It was quite sufficient if the board was of the length of the one who used it. One is almost inclined to doubt the accuracy of David Malo's statement that it was sometimes four, or even more, fathoms in length. If any thinks it an easy matter to ride the surf on a board, a short trial will perhaps undeceive him.

4. Sect. 6. I am unable to give a satisfactory translation of this section.

It has been suggested to me that the meaning of Sect. 6 is that the victory was declared only after more than one heat, a rubber, if necessary. The Hawaiian text should be corrected as follows:

A i ka au hou ana i ka mea i komo i ka pu-a i ho-o mawaena mai oia aole e hiki i ke kulana o ka eo ia nana. Pela ka hee-nalu.

5. Surf-riding was one of the most exciting and noble sports known to the Hawaiians, practiced equally by king, chief and commoner. It is still to some extent engaged in, though not as formerly, when it was not uncommon for a whole community, including both sexes, and all ages, to sport and frolic in the ocean the livelong day. While the usual attitude was a reclining on the board face downwards, with one, or both arms folded and supporting the chest, such dexterity was attained by some that they could maintain their balance while sitting, or even while standing erect, as the board was borne along at the full speed of the inrolling breaker. Photographs can be given in proof of this statement.

XLIX

Holua-Sledding

1. Sliding down hill on the *holua*-sled was a sport greatly in vogue among chiefs and people, and one on the issue of which they were very fond of making bets, when the fit took them.

2. The *holua* was a long course laid out down the steep incline of a hill and extending onto the level plain.

3. Rocks were first laid down, then earth was put on and beaten hard, lastly the whole was layered with grass, and this was the track for the *holua-sled* to run on.

4. The runners of the holua-sled were made of *mamane*, or of *uhiuhi* wood, chamfered to a narrow edge below, with the forward end turned up, so as not to dig into the ground, and connected with each other by means of cross-pieces in a manner similar to the joining of a double-canoe.

5. On top of the cross-pieces boards were then laid, as in flooring the *pola* of a canoe. This done and the runners lubricated with oil of the kukui-nut, the sled was ready for use.

6. The bets having been arranged, the racers took their stations at the head of the track; the man who was ranged in front gave his sled a push to start it and mounted it, whereupon his competitor who was to his rear likewise started his sled and followed after. He who made the longest run was the victor. In case both contestants travelled the length of the course, it was a dead heat and did not decide who was victor.

7. The victory was declared for the player who made the best run.

Notes on Chapter XLIX

The course of an old-time *holua* slide is at the present writing clearly to be made out sloping down the foot-hills back of the Kamehameha School. The track is of such a width,—about 18 feet—as to preclude the possibility of two sleds travelling abreast. It is substantially paved with flat stones, which must have held their position for many generations. The earth that once covered them has been mostly washed away. The remains of an ancient *kahua holua* are also to be made out at Keauhou, or were a few years ago.

From the sample of the *holua* sled to be seen at the Bishop museum, it seems a wonder that any one was able to ride the sled down such a descent as either one of the two just mentioned, or to keep on the thing at all. The two runners are—in the specimen at the museum—twelve and a half feet long, are set about two and a half inches apart at the narrow, sliding edge, and about six inches apart on top, where the body of the man rests. A more difficult feat by far it must have been to ride on this tipsy affair at speed than to keep one's balance on the back of a horse, *a la* circus-rider; yet it is asserted that there were those who would ride down hill on the *holua*-sled at break-neck speed maintaining at the same time an erect position. It hardly seems credible. The swift rush of the toboggan is as nothing to this.

L

Noa

1. Noa was a sport that was extremely popular with people and chiefs. The number of those, including chiefs, who were beggared by this game was enormous.

2. The people are seated in two groups facing each other, and five bundles or tapa are placed (on a mat) between the two groups. These bundles are to hide the *noa* under, and beginning with the *Kihipuka*,[1] which completes the list.

4. Two well-skilled persons were chosen to hide the *noa*. This was a small piece of wood or of stone. Bets having been made, one side—by their player—hid their *noa* under one of the piles of tapa.

5. This done, the player sat still and shut his eyes.

6. The opposite side, who had attentively watched the man while he was hiding the *noa*, made a guess as to its position. If they guessed correctly, it counted for them. The other side then made their guess, and that side which first scored ten won the game.

7. Sometimes a man, when he lost his property and was reduced to poverty, took it so greatly to heart that he became bitter and desperate. He would then, perhaps, risk everything he had and become beggared, or actually go crazy through grief.

8. After losing everything else,[2] people would sometimes stake their wives, or children, speaking of the former as an old sow, and the latter as shoats. These were some of the results of *noa*.

Notes on Chapter L

1. Sect. 3. A Hawaiian who says he used to see the game of *noa* played in his boyhood on the island of Molokai, informs me that according to his recollection, the piles of tapa were named in this order: *Kihipuka, Pilimoe, Kau, Pilipuka, Kihimoe*. He gives me the following, which he heard recited by the man who was hiding the *noa*:

> *Aia la, aia la,*
> *I ke Kau, i ke Pili, i ka Moe,*
> *Ilaila e ku ai ka noa a kaua. E ku!*

> There it is, there it is,
> Under the *kau,* under the *pili,* under the *moe,*
> There is lodged our *noa.* It's lodged!

See also Andrews' Dictionary under the word *kau.*

2. Sect. 8. It was not an unknown thing for a man, having exhausted other resources, to stake his own body, *pili iwi* as it was called. If he lost he was at least the slave of the winner, who might put his body to what use he pleased. If put to death by his master he would be called a *moe-puu,* i.e., he joined the great heap, or majority of the dead, *"ka puu nui o ka make."* Death was the puu nui. There was evident allusion to the same thought in the expression *"moe puu,"* applied to the human sacrifices that were in ancient times made at the death of a king.

LI

Pukaula, Juggling

1. *Pukaula* or juggling was a great betting game. It was played by experts, through whose skill a great many people were taken in and victimized. An outsider stood no chance of winning from the slight-of-hand-performer, unless the juggler saw that the audience was too small, in which case he let some one win from him.

2. And after people began to think they had a show for winning they gathered in crowds about the jugglers and staked all their property, thinking they were sure to win. When the jugglers saw this and that the betting was heavy, they changed their tactics and managed it so that they themselves should win. In playing the game of *pukaula* an *olona* line several fathoms long was used (The author says a fathom long; but that is clearly impossible.) which is braided very closely and smoothly and was about the size of a watch-guard.

3. When the jugglers came on to the ground where they were to exhibit, they started in by repeating some sort of jingle (*kepakepa*[1]) which tickled the fancy of the people, and they accordingly crowded up and filled the place.

4. The performers very cunningly gave one end of the line into the hands of one man and the other end into the hands of another man to hold, and then did their tricks with the middle part of the line.[2]

5. The juggler artfully tied the middle part of the line up into a knot and then asked the people "what do you think about the knot?"

6. Being sure from their own observation that the knot was a tight one, they bet that it would hold. Then the juggler and the ones who made bets struck hands and pledged[3] themselves to stick to their bargain. The ends of the rope were then pulled, and according to whether the knot held or no, did the jugglers or the others win.

7. Men and women as well in large numbers were driven to desperation at their losses in this game. A woman would sometimes put her own body at stake and lose it to the juggler, in which case she became his property.

8. Men were affected with the same craze and likewise became the slaves of the jugglers. They were let off only when they paid a heavy ransom.

1. Sect. 3. *Kepakepa.* The meaning of this word is to amuse, amusement.

2. Sect. 4. The statement that the juggler allowed outsiders to hold the ends of the line is on the face of it absurd and improbable. So I am told by those who have seen something of the game.

3. Sect. 6. The pledge was, no doubt, in the form that was very commonly used in connection with solemn affirmations, *"Pau Pele, pau mano,"* as much as to say, Let me be destroyed by Pele, or by the shark, if I do not keep my oath.

My informant says the rope he once saw used in the play was three fathoms long.

4. Sect. 3. The following is communicated to me as a sample of a *Kepakepa,* recitative, it could hardly be called a jingle—such as was used by the pu-kaula or juggler in baiting and fascinating his audience. It is to all intents a prayer to Kana, the god of jugglery and of jugglers.

> *E Kana. E Kana.*
> *E mahulu-ku, e kii lalau,*
> *E kuhi a leo, e ka moe,*
> *Ka hanai a Uli.*
> *Kuu'a mai kou kapa kaula.*
> *Hoalu mai kou kapa kanaka,*
> *I ka pu a kaua, e Kana.*

> Oh Kana. Oh Kana.
> Rough line of hala-root, or bark of hau.
> Point and declare as to the sleeper,
> The foster child of Uli.
> Put on your rope-body,
> Lay off your human form
> In this trick of yours and mine, oh Kana,

Kana was a *kupua*—a word which has no exact equivalent in our language, though perhaps the word demi-god comes nearest to it: it was a being more than human or heroic and less than divine. His father was Hakalanileo, his mother Hina-ai-ka-malama. The scene of his nativity and chilhood was Hilo, on the island of Hawaii. His birth was remarkable. His little body at its first appearance seemed only a small piece of cord and was put one side as of no account. The goddess Uli, however, recognized the nature of the being and put him in a place of safety. The nutriment suitable for the sustenance and growth of a kupua are *hoomana,* i.e., adoration and worship, and *awa.* Through the care of Uli, his foster mother, the spiritual and physical necessities of Kana were well supplied and he grew apace. His growth was only in length, not in circumference. Under the stimulus of *hoomanamana* and *awa,* the growth of Kana was so great that after a time the house in which he had been placed grew too narrow for him and another one had to be built for his accommodation. To all appearance Kana was merely an enormous length of line; but he was a demi-god of tremendous power.

The following is a sample of the spiritual, or worshipful, incense, which was daily offered to him (without it any kupua must dwindle and fade into nothingness) and which was an *Inoa*, i.e., a name:

> *Ia moku kele-Kahiki i ke ao ua o Haka,*
> *O Hakalanileo hoowiliwili Hilo,*
> *Hookaka'a ka lani, kaka'a ka iloli,*
> *Wehiwehi ka opua, palamao*[a] *Kahiki,*
> *Wai-kahe ka mauna, kaikoo ka moana,*
> *I ka hanau ana o ka ui a Haka.*
> *Hanau ae o Kana he lino,*
> *He aho loa, he pauku kaula,*
> *He kaee koali, he awe pu-maia,*
> *He punawelewele.*
> *Hanai ia Uli a ka ihu pi,*
> *Ka ihu nana, ka mano hae,*
> *Ka ilio hae, keiki alala, keiki omino.*
> *Ku i koholua,*[b] *ku iki a Kana.*
> *Naue na koa,*[c] *ka elawa i kai,*
> *Ka pu-koa i kai, ka puoleolei,*
> *Ka nihi*[d] *moe lawa, ka auna*[e] *lele kai.*
> *Kou inoa e Kana.*

To the craft voyaging to Tahiti amid the rain-clouds of Kana,
King of Hilo, land of cloud-portents,
Portents in the heavens, commotions in the womb.
Open and clear are the heavenly signs, a mottling that reaches to Tahiti.
Freshets in the mountains, wild surf in the ocean
At the birth of the child of Haka.
Kana was born a four-stranded rope,
A long fish-line, a piece of cord,
A line of koali, a thread of banana fibre,
A spider's web,
Adopted by Uli, the cross one,
She of the up-tilted nose, a ravenous shark.
A barking dog, a puny wailing thing he,
To be lanced most delicately, this Kana.
The ocean-spearmen rally about him,
The ocean-reefs, the conchs of ocean,
The black shark, the sword-fish.
An ascription this to you, Oh Kana.

a. *Palamoa,* mottled, mackerel scales in the sky.

b. *Koholua,* a bone from near the tail of certain fishes, that was sharp and used as a lancet.

c. *Koa,* soldiers of the ocean, the hihimanu. A sharp bone near the tail.

d. *Nihi,* a contracted form of hiuhi, a monster shark.

e. *Auna,* sword-fish.

Kana had a younger brother named Niheu. When his mother was abducted by Kapepeekauila, a powerful *kupua* of Molokai, who had his seat in the inaccessible cliffs of that island, he concealed her at a place called Haupukele high up in the mountains. Hakalanileo mourned the loss of his wife so bitterly that Niheu made ready to start on an expedition for her rescue. Uli insisted that he must take his brother Kana with him. So they wrapped his body in a mat and put him in the canoe. On the voyage the sea-turtle did his best to overwhelm the canoe. Kana was the first one to call attention to the monster in the ocean that was threatening them, *"ka ea nui, kua–wakawaka."* Kana pierced the monster with his spear and he troubled them no more. Opposite the point of Halawa was a dangerous reef called Pu'upo'i. Warned in time by Kana Niheu turned the canoe aside and this danger was passed. Arrived at Pelekunu, the inaccessible heights of Haupu-kele-ka-pu'u towered above them. It was there Pepeekauila lived in security with his stolen bride. From this elevation he commanded a bird's-eye view of the party in the canoe, but to assure himself of their character and probable errand, he sent as messengers and spies the Ulili and Kolea birds to learn the truth. On their return they reported that it was not a war-canoe, there were no arms or warriors visible. The principal thing to be seen was a large roll of matting which occupied the waist of the canoe. The party on the hill were consequently off their guard.

At the request of Niheu Kana climbed the hill to bring away their mother. Hina-ai-ka-malama recognized her son and willingly went with him down to the canoe. Keoloewa, the king who had been keeping her as his wife or paramour, at first offered no objections to her departure; when, however, she had boarded the canoe, the sense of his loss came over him and he ordered the birds, Ulili and Kolea, to fly and fetch her back. When Kana saw that his mother was gone he took the form of a man, and standing with one foot in one canoe and the other foot in the other canoe, his tall form at first reached above the highest point of the mountain cliff, thus enabling him to seize the body of Hina-ai-ka-malama and restore her to the canoe. But in the effort he found that the hili kept growing in height and getting away from him. Keoloewa and his men hurled down great rocks upon those below. Kana's eyes were as big as the moon. As the hill grew in height Kana also stretched himself up, but the hill kept growing higher, and Kana wondered why. But feeling in the ocean at the roots of the mountain, he found that it was the turtle. *ka ea,* that was lifting it. Then he tore the *ea* in pieces and scattered them in the ocean, where they became sea-turtle of many species. From that moment the mountain ceased to grow in height. This ended the fight. Niheu and Kana sailed away in the canoe with their mother, who was thus restored to her husband, Haka-lani-leo.

LII

Pa-Pua, or Kea-Pua

1. Ke'a-pua was a pastime which was engaged in by great numbers of men, women and children when the Makahiki period came round, because that was the season when the sugar-cane put forth the flowers that were used in this game.

2. When the tassels were ripe the flower-stems were plucked and laid away to dry. The lower end of the stem was tightly bound with string, after which the point thus made was wetted in the mouth and then thrust into the dirt to become coated with clay.

3. Matches were then gotten up between different players, and bets were made in which the arrows themselevs might be the wagers, but it might be anything else.

4. A knoll of earth or sand was chosen from which to skate the arrows. One of them would project his arrow and then the other, and so they took turns.

5. The one who first scored ten points was the winner and took the bet.

Note to Chapter LII

A description is necessary to make this beautiful pastime intelligible. The arrow, made from the light and elegant stem of the sugar-cane flower was about two feet long. Posting himself so as to take advantage of a knoll or any slight eminence, the player, holding the arrow well towards its tail-end, ran forward a few steps in a stooping position, and as he reached the desired point, with a downward and forward swing of his arm, projected the arrow at such an angle that it just grazed the surface of the ground, from which it occasionally glanced with a graceful ricochet movement. It is a rare sight to see this game played nowadays, but twenty or thirty years ago, in the season of it it was all the rage from Hawaii to Niihau. It is a pity to see this elegant and invigorating pastime supplanted by less worthy sports.

The mythical hero Hiku, who, with his mother lived on the topmost parts of Hualalai, is said to have had the faculty of calling back to him the arrow he had sent to a distance. He uttered the call "pua-ne. Pua-ne." And the arrow immediately returned to his hand.

I am informed that the expression used to denote the pastime is *kca-pua, ka-pua,* or *pa-pua.*

LIII

Hoo-Haka-Moa, Cock-Fighting

1. Cock-fighting (*haka-moa*) was a very fashionable sport with the *aliis*, and was conducted in the following manner. A person who was a good judge of fowls would secure one which he thought to be a good fighter.

2. A roost was then made, on which to place the cock, and every night a small fire was started under him, to make him lively.[1]

3. Each game-keeper trained his fighting cock in the same manner, until they were paired for a fight.

4. The day having been set for the match, a multitude of people assembled to witness it, and to bet on the result. When the experts had studied the two cocks and had made up their minds which would fight to the death, they made their bets, betting all their own property, as well as all they could borrow.

5. When the betting was done, the president or *luna hoomalu*, of the assembly stood forth, and a rope was drawn around the cock-pit to keep the people out. Any one who trespassed within this line was put to death.

6. The cocks were then let loose and the multitude flocked about the cock-pit. If the cocks were equally matched it was a drawn battle (*pai wale*); but if one of them ran away from the other, that gave victory to the latter.

7. The winners always reviled those who lost with insulting and offensive language, saying "you'll have to eat chicken-dung after this," repeating it over and over.

Note to Chapter LIII

Note 1. Sect. 2. It was imagined that the motions made by the cock in thrusting his head to one side and the other, in his efforts to escape the heat and pungent smoke, were just the exercises needed to fit him for his duties as a fighter.

LIV

The Hula

1–2. The *hula* was a very popular amusement among the Hawaiian people. It was used as a means of conferring distinction upon the *aliis* and people of wealth. On the birth of an *alii* the the chiefs and people gave themselves up to the *hula*, and much property was lavished on *hula* dancers. The *hula* most frequently performed by the chiefs was the *kalaau* (in which one stick was struck against another).

3–4. The children of the wealthy were ardent devotees of the *hula*. Among the varieties of the *hula* were the *pa'i umauma*, (beating the chest), *hula pahu* (with a drum accompaniment), and the *hula pahu'a*, besides which there were also the *ala'a-papa*, the *pa'ipa'i*, the *pa-ipu*, the *ulili*, the *kolani*, and the *kielei*.

5. It was the custom of *hula* dancers to perform before the rich in order to obtain gifts from them.

Note to Chapter LIV

The *hula*, like all other savage, Polynesian institutions degenerated and went on the run to the bad the moment the white man appeared on the scene. The activity and heat of his passions started a fire that burnt up all the properties at once. The *hula* in the ancient times was no better, no worse than other of the Hawaiian, Polynesian institutions.

The modern *hula* is no more a fair and true representative of the savage Hawaiian, or Polynesian dance than the Parisian *cancan* is of a refined and civilized dance.

I regret that I cannot entirely concur with the view expressed above. I believe that the *hula* in Hawaii-nei. like the Areoi society in Tahiti, appealed largely to the baser instincts of the people, and had a debasing influence on them.

But I admit that there were different kinds of *hula* in ancient times, and that the worst form of it, (which had always been the most popular), is the one that has survived, and furthermore that foreign influence has helped to keep this relic of heathenism alive. W. D. A.

LV

Mokomoko or Boxing

1. During the Makahiki season, when the Makahiki god made his rounds, the people of different districts gathered at one place and held boxing matches.

2. The multitude being seated in a circle, the backers of one champion stood forth and vaunted the merits of their favorite, who thereupon came forward and made a display of himself, swaggering, boasting and doubling up his fists.

3. Then the other side followed suit, made their boasts, had their man stand forth and show himself; and when the champions came together they commenced to beat and pummel each other with their fists.

4. If one of the boxers knocked down his opponent a shout of exultation went up from those who championed him, and they grossly reviled the other side, telling him perhaps to "go and eat chicken-dung."

5. The one who fell was often badly maimed, having an arm broken, an eye put out, or teeth knocked out. Great misery was caused by these boxing matches.

Note to Chapter LV

The Hawaiians do not seem to have used the fore-arm, after the manner of modern practitioners of the "noble art." Each boxer sought to receive his opponent's blow with his own fist. This meeting of fist with fist was very likely the cause of the frequent broken arms.

LVI

Hakoko—Wrestling

1. *Hakoko* or wrestling was a very popular sport in ancient Hawaii. It was generally done in the midst of a large assembly of people, as the boxing game, *mokomoko,* was.

2. The multitude formed a circle, and the wrestlers took their stand in the centre, and then, having seized hold of each other, they struggled to trip each other with the use of their feet, striving with all their might to throw each other to the ground.

3. The one who was thrown was beaten. A man who was a strong and skillful wrestler was made much of. Wrestling was much practiced about court, very little in the country districts.

LVII

Sundry Minor Sports

1. In addition to the games mentioned, there were a great many little informal sports. One of these was *koi* (a child's game, played with a crooked stick, with which one dug into the earth or sand, at the same time repeating some word-jingle or other).

Panapana (a child's game played with a *niau,* the small midrif of the coconut leaf. This was bent into the form of a bow in the hand, and, being suddenly released, sprang away by its elasticity).

Honuhonu (a game in which one boy sat astride on the back of another boy who was down on all-fours).

Loulou. (Two persons would hook fingers together and then pull to see who would hold out the longest, without letting go or straightening out his finger).

Pahipahi (played by slapping hands together, as in the game "bean-porridge hot, bean-porridge cold," etc.).

Hookakaa (in which boys turned over and over or turned somersets on the grass or in the sand).

Lele-koali (swinging on a swing suspended by a single line, for which purpose the strong convolvulus vine, *koali,* was most often used. When permitted, youths of both sexes delighted to enjoy this sport together, the girl seated on the lap of the boy and facing him).

Lele-kawa (jumping off from a height into the deep water).

Kaupua (swimming or diving for a small, half-ripe gourd that would barely float in the water).

Pana-iole (shooting mice with bow and arrow. This was a sport much practiced by kings and chiefs. It was the only use which the Hawaiians made of the bow and arrow. A place somewhat like a cockpit was arranged in which to shoot the mice).

Kuialua. (This was an exhibition of *lua* for amusement. Lua was a murderous system of personal combat which combined tricks of wrestling with bone-breaking, the dislocation of limbs, and other thug-like methods that put it outside the pale of civilized warfare. It was used by robbers).

Notes to Chapter LVII

It seems remarkable that David Malo should make no mention of a large number of games that were of established vogue and popularity among the ancient Hawaiians. Such as—

Konane, a game played with black and white pebbles on a checkerboard laid out in squares at right angles to each other, the squares being represented by hollows for the pebbles to rest in. The game consists in moving one's pieces in such a way as to compel the opponent to take them. The number of squares on the *konane* board was not uniform. I have seen them with nine on a side, making eighty-one in all; I have also seen them with such a number that the board was longer in one direction than the other.

Hei, cat's cradle, is a game that deserves mention. There were many figures into which the string was worked. It was a game at which the genius of the Hawaiian was specially fitted to excel, for by nature he was a born rigger, skilled in manipulating and tying ropes and knots.

Kimo, jack-stones, a game at which the Hawaiian boy, and more especially the Hawaiian girl excelled.

This list might be greatly extended.

Hoolele-lupe, kite-flying, deserves special mention as a pastime that was dear to the Hawaiian heart, and the practice of which recurred with the regularity of the seasons.

LVIII

THE FLOOD

1. Long before the coming of the white people to Hawaii nei[1] the Hawaiians had heard about the deluge. The strange thing about it was that the Hawaiian kings did not know when this deluge (*kai-a-ka-hina-lii*), occurred, whether or not it was earlier than their arrival at the Hawaiian shores.

2. The story was as follows: There was a woman of the sea who lived in a land called *Lalohana,* which was far away in the ocean, for which reason she was called the woman of Lalohana.

3. There are two versions of this story given by the ancients. One tradition has it that the place where the woman lived was on a reef, named *Mauna,* situated in the ocean outside of Keauhou, in Kona, and that Lono was the name of the king who reigned over the land at that time. Other ancient authorities aver that this woman lived in the ocean outside of Waiakea, Hilo, and that Konikonia was the reigning king at the time. But this Lono and this Konikonia, where did they come from? Their names do not appear in the genealogies of the kings.

To take up the story of Konikonia, leaving that of Lono:

4. When Konikonia's fishermen on their excursions out to sea, let down their hooks to this fishing reef (*koa lawaia*[2]) on pulling up the lines their hooks were gone. They had not felt the tremor of the lines; the hooks had evidently been removed by this woman of the sea.

5. The fishermen returned and reported to Konikonia, saying, "The disappearance of our hooks was mysterious. The quiver of the line was not perceived; the hooks were cut away just as if there were a man down below on the reef." Now, there was at this time with Konikonia a man, named Kuula, the brother of Lalohana, who had come out of the ocean. But Konikonia was not aware that Kuula was from the ocean.

6. This Kuula explained to Konikonia and his fishermen that their hooks had been cut away by men, "Because," said he, "the place where you were fishing is a large town, in which men and women live under the ocean."

7–8. Then Konikonia asked Kuula, "Are you from that place?" "Yes, I come from there," said Kuula. "Have you a sister in the ocean?" said

Konikonia. "I have a sister," answered Kuula, "and she it was who cut away the hooks of your fishermen." "Go and ask your sister to be my wife," said Konikonia.

9. "She has a husband, a carved image, (*Kane kii*) named *Kiimaluahaku*,[3] and she loves him," replied Kuula. "Tell me of some way by which I can have that woman for myself," said Konikonia.

10, 11, 12, 13. "If you wish to get that woman for yourself, now, just carve a large image; smooth it off nicely and paint it of a dark color; let it have eyes of pearl; cover its head with hair and finally dress it in a malo. This done, lay this one image in the corner of the house with some tapas. Two other images must be placed at the door of the house, one on either side; two at the entrance of the *pa* (enclosure); other figures must be placed in line from the entrance of the *pa* down to the beach. This done, you must have trumpets blown on the canoes from the bay clear out to the fishing reef. Put an image in each boat in the line extending from the bay to the reef. Tie an image to a line and let it down into the water a fathom; then tie on another, and so on."

14. "Now this woman's husband, Kiimaluahaku, is absent just now at Kuku-lu-o-Kahiki[4] and it is likely that, when she sees the image coming down, she will think it is Kiimaluahaku, her husband, and she will accordingly go out to meet him, and thus she will come ashore here; for she is very fond of images."

15. Konikonia immediately set to work and made the images according to Kuula's directions, and when completed they were set up from the house to the reef, as directed.

16. All being ready, they sent down an image to the fishing reef, and when the woman saw it standing at the door of her house under the ocean, behold, said she to herself, it is my husband, Kiimaluakahaku.

17. Then she called out, "O Kii, O Kiikamaluakahaku, so you have been to Kukulu-o-Kahiki and returned, and here you are standing outside of our place. Come, come in to the house." But no; the image did not enter.

18. Then she approached the image to kiss it; and when she saw there was another image above it she left the first image and went up to kiss the second. So she went on, kissing one image after another, until she had risen from the bottom to the surface of the ocean, where the canoes were floating.

19–20. When the woman saw the images stationed in the line of canoes, she went along kissing one after the other until she came to the shore; and then she went on to kiss the images in succession that stood in line until she had reached the house. Then seeing the image that was lying in the corner of the house she went and lay down alongside of it.

21. The woman then fell into a deep sleep; and, the image having been taken away, Konikonia moved up close to her and lay by her side. When it came evening the woman awoke and seeing Konikonia lying at her side, they embraced each other. . .

22. Then the woman said to Konikonia, "I am hungry. Send a man to fetch my food. Let him go to my fishing reef and bring it. He must dive down and, having opened, he must enter the house that stands by itself, thence let him bring the coconut dish that he will find at one side of the house, but he must not open the dish." The man went and did as he was bidden.

23. On his return the woman opened the coconut dish—and instantly the food that was therein flew up into the heavens, and it was the moon of two days old. The crescent of the moon which shone clear and bright above, was *kena;* and that part that glimmered below was *ana.*[5] When the woman saw that her food was gone she was filled with regret.

24–25. On the fourth day of that same month the woman said to Konikonia, "I have been ashore here four days. My parents are now looking for me. They will search for me in the ocean, and, not finding me there, will proceed to hunt for me on the land." "Who are your parents?" asked Konikonia. "Kahina-lii is my father, and Hina-ka-alu-alu-moana is my mother," said she. "Will your parents come up here onto the land?" asked Konikonia.

26. "They will not come up in person," said she, "but this ocean that swims before us, that will come in search of me. This ocean will rise up and flood the whole land. In what place, pray, shall I be hidden, and you saved from this destructive deluge that is coming?"

27. "Is it the ocean itself that will seek you?" asked Konikonia. "It is my brothers, the *paoo* fish, that will come in search of me," said the woman, "but it is the ocean that will rise in order to lift them and enable them to advance and search for me." "Let us flee to the mountains," said Konikonia.

28. Then they fled to the mountains. "Let us take to the tallest trees," said the woman, whereupon they climbed the tallest trees and built houses in their tops.

29. After ten days had passed Ka-hina-lii sent the ocean, and it rose and overwhelmed the land from one end to the other.

30. The people fled to the mountains, and the ocean covered the mountains; they climbed the trees, and the waters rose and covered the trees and drowned them all.

31. The ocean kept on rising until it had reached the door of Konikonia's house, but Konikonia and his household were not drowned, because the waters then began to subside; and when the waters had retreated, Konikonia and his people returned to their land.

32. This is the story of the deluge which has been handed down by tradition from the ancients. Traditions are not as reliable as genealogies. Genealogies can be trusted to some extent. The ancients were misinformed. This we know because we have heard the story of Noah, and that does not tally with our tradition of the Kai-a-ka-hina-lii. For this reason this tradition of the Kai-a-ka-hina-lii can not be of Hawaiian origin. It was heard by the ancients and finally came to be accepted by them as belonging to Hawaii *nei*.

Notes to Chapter LVIII

1. Sect. 1. There is no doubt but that the Hawaiians, like all the other Polynesian tribes, had traditions regarding a flood. The conclusions properly to be deduced from this fact are well worthy of consideration; but not here and now.

2. Sect. 4. *Ko'a lawai'a; Ko'a,* was the same applied to any reef; a reef on which fish were taken was called a *ko'a lawai'a.* These *ko'a lawai'a* were generally quite a distance from land and were located by two cross ranges from points on land. Lawaia, from *lawe-ia,* i.e., to take fish. In the Maori this would be *toka-rawe-ika.* The change from *e* to *a* is, I think for euphony, a matter which very much concerned the Hawaiian ear; the Maori *r* has become *l* in Hawaiian; the *t* a *k;* and the *k* in the Maori form *toka* and *ika* has been dropped, gnawed away by the tooth of time.

3. Sect. 9. *Kii-ma-luahaku:* There is a god named *Ruahatu* mentioned in the Tahitian and Marquesan legends.

4. Sect. 14. *Kukulu o Kahiki*: In regard to this geographical expression, Mr. S. Percy Smith says *"Kukulu-o-Kahiki* is in my opinion the Fiji group. It would take too long to explain. In N. Z. we have *tuturu-o-Hiti,* (or *Whiti*) and *Te-mau-o-Hiti,* which mean the same, i.e., the original, permanent, true *Hiti."*

One cannot doubt the correctness of so eminent an authority in his exposition of the Maori view and meaning of the expression; but I canont escape the conviction that the phrase *kukulu-o-Kahiki,* like so many others which the Hawaiians brought with them from the South, imposing, however, their own linguistic modifications, came in time to have, as it evidently now has, a different meaning from that of its original use. I believe that it came to have a general reference to the region about Tahiti; even Tahiti came to be applied to almost any foreign land; but that was in comparatively late times, long after the period of communication, when it was not an uncommon thing for voyages to be made between Hawaii and the groups to the South. (See chapter V for what Mr. Malo has to say on this subject.) *Kukulu* meant an erection, applied therefore to a wall or vertical support, the pillars that supported the dome of heaven, according to the cosmogony of the ancient Hawaiians, as well as the Polynesians. Criticism of Hawaiian tradition must stand firmly on Hawaiian soil and take the Hawaiian point of view.

5. Sect. 23. *Kena,* means the satisfying of thirst, *ana* to drink sufficiently, to satiate, as with food. There is a myth—Hawaiian—of an old woman who, to get rid of her troubles, went up to the moon; but I do not see that this story has any reference to that, nor can I find any story that bears on this *kena* and *ana.*

LIX

Traditions Regarding the Ancient Kings

1. The histories of the ancient kings, from Ke-alii-wahi-lani[1] and his wife, La'ilai[2] down, from Kahiko[3] and his wife Kupu-lana-ka-hau[4] down, and from Wakea[5] and his wife Papa[6] down to the time of Liloa, are but scantily and imperfectly preserved. We have, however, it is true, a fragmentary, traditional knowledge of some kings. Of the kings from Liloa to Kamehameha I we have probably a fair historical knowledge.

2. *Genealogy of the Kings from Wakea to Liloa:*

1	Wakea,	26	Nanakaoko,
2	Haloa,	27	Nanakuae,
3	Waia,	28	Kapawa,
4	Hinanalo,	29	Heleipawa,
5	Nanakehili,	30	Aikanaka,
6	Wailoa,	31	Hema,
7	Kio,	32	Kahai,
8	Ole,	33	Wahieloa,
9	Pupue,	34	Laka,
10	Manaku,	35	Luanuu,
11	Lukahakoa,	36	Pohukaina;
12	Luanuu,	37	Hua,
13	Kahiko,	38	Pau,
14	Kii,	39	Huanuiikalailai,
15	Ulu,	40	Paumakua,
16	Nanaie,	41	Haho,
17	Nanailani,	42	Palena,
18	Waikulani,	43	Hanalaanui,
19	Kuheileimoana,	44	Lanakawai,
20	Konohiki,	45	Laau,
21	Wanena,	46	Pili,
22	Akalana,	47	Koa,
23	Maui,	48	Ole,
24	Nanamaoa,	49	Kukohou,
25	Nanakulei,	50	Kaniuhi,

51	Kanipahu,	56	Kohoukapu,
52	Kalapaua,	57	Kauhola,
53	Kahaimoelea,	58	Kiha,
54	Kalaunuiohua,	59	Liloa.
55	Kuaiwa,		

We have some traditional knowledge of these kings, but nothing very definite.

3. *WAKEA.* We have the following traditions regarding Wakea. He was the last child of Kahiko, the first born of Kahiko, and the elder brother of Wakea being Lihau-ula, to whom Kahiko bequeathed his land, leaving Wakea destitute.

4. After the death of *Kahiko, Lihau-ula*[7] made war against Wa-kea. The councillor of Lihau-ula had tried to dissuade him, saying, "Don't let us go to war with Wakea at this time. We shall be defeated by him, because this is a time of sun-light; the sun has melting power (*no ka mea he au keia no ka la, he la hee*).

5. Lihau-ula, however, considered that he had a large force of men, while Wakea had but a small force, his pride was up and he gave battle. In the engagement that followed Lihau-ula lost his life, killed by Wa-kea, the blond one, (*ka ehu*), and his kingdom went to Wa-kea.

6. After Wa-kea came to the government he had war with *Kane-ia-kumu-honua,*[8] in which Wa-kea was routed and obliged to swim out into the ocean with all his people.

7. Tradition gives two versions to the story of this war. According to one the battle took place in Hawaii; Wakea was defeated and Kane-ia-kumu-honua pursued him as far as Kaula, where Wakea and his followers took to the ocean (*au ma ka moana*).

8. Another ancient tradition has it that the battle was not fought in Hawaii, but in Kahiki-ku; and that Wakea, being routed, swam away in the ocean with all his people.

9. From swimming in the ocean Wakea and his followers were at length reduced to great straits, and he appealed to his priest (*kahuna-pule*), Komoawa, saying, "What shall we do today to save our lives?"

10, 11, 12. "Build a *heiau* to the deity," answered Komoawa. "There is no wood here with which to build a *heiau, noa a pig* with which to make a suitable offering to the god," answered Wakea. "There is wood and there is a pig," said Komoawa. "Lift up your right hand; hollow the palm of your hand into a cup, and then elevate the fingers." Wakea did so, and Komoawa said, "The house is built. Now pinch together the fingers of the left hand into a cone and put the finger-tips into the hollow of your right hand." When Wakea had done this, Komoawa declared, "The *heiau* is now completed; only the prayer is wanting."

13. "Gather all your people together," said Komoawa, and that was done, and the charm, or *aha*, of the ceremony was perfect.

14. Then Komoawa asked Wakea, "How was the *aha* of our ceremony?" "It was good," answered Wakea. "We are saved then," said Komoawa; "let us swim ashore."

15. Then Wakea and his people swam ashore with great shouting; and, on reaching the land, they renewed the battle with Kane-ia-kumu-honua, and utterly defeated him. In this way the government was permanently secured to Wakea.

There is a fanciful tradition that has come down from the ancients that some of those who went a swimming with Wakea are still swimming about, and that the name of one of them is Kamamoe.

16. There is a doubtful story about Wakea and Hoo-hoku-ka-lani.[9] A venerable tradition has it that Hoo-hoku-ka-lani was the daughter of Wakea and Papa, but that Wakea incestuously took her to wife.

17. Another tradition says that Hoo-hoku-ka-lani was the daughter of Komoawa, by his wife, Popo-kolo-nuha, and that Wakea was justified in consorting with Hoo-hoku-ka-lani, seeing she was of another family and not his own daughter.

18. It is asserted by tradition[10] of Wakea that he was the one who instituted the four seasons of prayer in each month, and that he also imposed the tabu on pork, coconuts, bananas and the red fish (*kumu*), besides declaring it tabu for men and women to eat together in the *mua*.

19. Because of Wakea's desire to commit adultery (incest) with his daughter, Hoo-kohu-ka-lani, he set apart certain nights as tabu, and during those nights he slept with Hoo-hoku-ka-lani. On Wakea's over-sleeping himself, his priest, seeing it was already daylight, called to Wakea with the following words of prayer to awake him:

20. *E ala-au aku, e ala-au mai,*
 E ala o Makia, o Makia a Hano,[11]
 A hano ke aka,[12] *o ke aka kuhea,*
 O ke aka kii i Hikina,
 Ku ka Hikina iluna ka lam
 Ka opua ulu nui, ka opua makolu, ua ka ua,
 Kahe kaa wai, mukeha,

Oili, olapa i ka lani poni,
Poni haa i ka mea.
Mo[13] *ka pawa, lele ka hoku,*
Haule ka lani,[14] *Moakaka i ke ao malamalama.*
Ala mai, ua ao e!

I call to you, answer me!
Awake Makia, Makia son of Hano!
Portentous is the shadow, the shadow of him who calls,
Shadow rising from the East,
Morning climbs the heavens.
The piled up clouds, the gloomy clouds, down pours the rain,
A rush of waters, a flood;
Lightning darts and flashes in the dark heavens;
Bound with a strong covenant to that one,
The curtains of night are lifted, the stars flee away,
The king's honor is dashed, all is visible in the light of day.
Awake! Lo the day is come!

21. Wakea did not awake, his sleep was profound. So the kahuna prayed more fervently, repeating the same prayer; but still Wakea did not awake.

22. When the sun had risen, Wakea arose and wrapped himself in his tapa to go to the *mua,* thinking that Papa would not see him. But Papa did see him, and, coming on the run, entered the *mua* to upbraid Wakea. Wakea then led her back to her own house, doing what he could to pacify her, and after that he divorced her.

(This poem has the ear-marks of great antiquity, to be seen both in its language and in the thought).

Notes to Chapter LIX

The subject matter of this chapter, in so far at least as it deals with Wakea and Papa, is almost wholly mythical. The names of the *dramatis personae* are, as I take it, figurative, such as are applicable to, or expressive of, the wonder-working convulsions, or the quieter, but equally mysterious, operations, of nature; as for instance:

1. Sect. 1. *Ke-alii-wahi-lani,* literally, the king who rends or breaks the heavens. The ancient Hawaiians conceived of the heavens, the visible sky, as a

solid dome. The exact meaning that lies back of this figurative expression, the *hyponoia*, as Max Muller would say, is open to different interpretations, and of course presents insuperable difficulties to any one who would try to define it; but it clearly refers to some heavenly phenomenon or phenomena. Diligent comparison with the myths of Southern Polynesia might help to clear up the intent of this expression. That *Wahi-lani* was, or came to be, regarded as a veritable personage is evident from the following ancient *mele:*

> *"O wahi-lani, o ke alii o Oahu,*
> *I holo aku i Kahiki,*
> *I na pae-moku o Moa-ulanui-akea,*
> *E keekeehi i ka houpu o Kane a me Kanaloa."*

> Wahi-lani, king of Oahu,
> Who sailed away to Tahiti.
> To the islands of Moa-ula-nui-akea,
> To trample the bosom[a] of Kane and Kanaloa.[b]

a. By the bosom of Kane and Kanaloa was probably meant the land and the sea; to trample them was therefore to travel by land and by sea.

b. Quoted to me as from a mele published in the '60's in *"Ka Hoku o ka Pakipika"*, a Hawaiian newspaper of Honolulu, edited by the late John M. Kapena, and issued under the management of Prince David, later King Kalakaua.

2. Sect. 1. *Lai-lai.* (1) physical, calm and peacefulness; (2) joy and light-heartedness.

3. Sect. 1. *Kahiko*, the ancient one. It is to be noted that in this account we find no mention of *Po*, Night, the original Darkness and Chaos that enveloped the world. *Ku, Kane, Kanaloa, Lono* and perhaps some of the other deities are said to be *no ka po mai*, to date back to the night, a time far antecedent to history and tradition.

4. Sect. 1. *Kupu-lana-ka-hau*, a phrase difficult of interpretation. To my mind it conveys the idea of fogs and floating mists, perhaps also of ice-masses. *Hau* at the present time means ice and snow. It is said to be a female element, receptive rather than active therefore. A Hawaiian of intelligence as well as of considerable critical faculty gives it as his opinion that in this word is typified the formation and development of land, though still in a wild and inhospitable condition, perhaps covered with ice and snow. He informs me that ice was formerly termed *wai-puolo-i-ka-lau-laau*, water-wrapped-up-in-leaves; the reason being that when ice or frozen snow was first met with the people who came across it in the mountains wrapped it up in leaves and, finding it reduced to water on reaching home, gave to it this name descriptive of their experience. *Ke-hau* is the name given to dew, it having absorbed the article *ke*. It is clear, it seems to me, that *kupu-lana-ka-hau* is expressive of some form of phenomenon due to water, either in the form of clouds or mists or frozen into ice and snow.

5. Sect. 1. *Wa-kea,* modern *awa-kea,* means noon, undoubtedly figurative of the sky, the light of day, the vivifying influence of the sun. In Sect. 5, Wakea is spoken of as the *ehu,* the blond, the bright, the shining one, an epithet that conveys the same idea as the Sanscrit deva. Wakea, it seems needless to remark, is represented to be the vivifying male element, which, as hinted at or plainly stated in the myths of Polynesia, was in the remote ages of *Po* torn from the close embrace of Papa, Earth, and placed in its present position.

6. Sect. 1. *Papa,* the female element, the generatrix, the plain or level of the Earth's surface, hence the Earth itself. Papa is the name applied to a stratum, a level formation, a table; it is a name frequently met with.

7. Sect. 4. *Lihau-ula:* The exact meaning of this word is not clear. It seems to refer to some effect of light shooting through the drifting clouds that remain undissipated. Wa-kea, the bright one, is still represented as being at war with the unsubdued elements of darkness and cold(?), which he finally overcomes, routing and driving out *Lihau-ula.* He thus gains possession of the kingdom of his father, Kahiko. His victory is ascribed to the fact that "it is a time of sunlight, the sun has power to melt"—*no ka mea he au keia no ka la, he la hee.*

8. Sect. 6. *Kane-ia-kumu-honua,* Kane the founder of the earth, or Kane at the foundations of the earth, sometimes spoken of as *Kane-lulu-honua,* Kane the shaker of the earth, the one who causes earth-quakes. Having gained the victory over darkness, clouds and cold, Wakea is for a time routed and put to flight by the deity that shakes the foundations of the earth, which may be naturally supposed to be a volcanic eruption, accompanied with earth-tremors and a darkening of the heavens, obscuring the light of the Sun on the land but leaving it bright at sea. It is well to remark that the religious services, incantations some would call them, which are performed to relieve the situation, are of the simplest form, suited to the occasion, a lifting of the hands, a prayer, a lesson to all formalists.

9. Sect. 16. *Hoo-hoku-ka-lani,* to bestud the heavens with stars, the starry sky, the stars of heaven, the offspring of Wakea and Papa, i.e., of Heaven and Earth. The action of the drama reaches its summit of interest in the passion of Wakea for his own daughter, *Hoo-hoku-ka-lani,* Star-of-heaven. It is to be noted as a proof of the simple faith with which David Malo accepts this tradition as based on a historic foundation of fact, that he actually seeks to extenuate Wakea's offense by ascribing the paternity of the maiden, Hoo-hoku-ka-lani, to the old priest, Komoawa. This story is evidently an after-thought, gotten up to save Wakea's reputation. To admit such evidence would be the spoiling of a fine solar myth (aside). The dalliance of the lovers is kept up to an unsafe time in the morning; daylight comes and they are still in each other's company—the stars of morning continue to shine after the sun is in the heavens. The priest comes with a friendly warning; Wakea sleeps on; Papa comes forth from her chamber and discovers the situation and the row is precipitated at once.

According to one version the divorce of Papa was accomplished by Wakea spitting in the face of the woman whom he turned away; according to another account it was Papa herself who did the spitting—who had more occasion?—and it almost seems as if something of the sort was indicated in the word *mukeha* in the 6th line. Having poured on Wakea the scorn and contempt which he deserved, Papa betook herself to the remote regions of *Kukulu-o-Kahiki,* while Wakea continued his intimacy with Hoo-hoku-ka-lani, by whom he had Molokai and Lanai as off-spring. Papa, according to the same version, had already given birth to Hawaii and Maui. But in the case of Papa blood proved thicker than water; she could not bear the thought of a fruitful rival taking her place in the affections of her husband, "her womb became jealous;" she returned to her husband: the result was the birth of Oahu, Kauai and Kauai's little neighbor, Niihau.

> *O Wakea noho ia Papa-hanau-moku,*
> *Hanau o Hawaii, he moku,*
> *Hanau o Maui, he moku*
> *Hoi hou o Wakea noho ia Hoo-hoku-ka-lani,*
> *Hanau o Molokai, he moku,*
> *Hanau o Lanai ka ula, he moku,*
> *Lili-opu-punalua o Papa ia Hoo-hoku-kalani,*
> *Hoi hou o Papa noho ia Wakea,*
> *Hanau o Oahu, he moku,*
> *Hanau o Kauai, he moku,*
> *Hanau o Niihau, he moku,*
> *He ula-a o Kahoolawe.*

> Wakea lived with Papa, begetter of islands,
> Begotten was Hawaii, an island,
> Begotten was Maui, an island,
> Wakea made a new departure and lived with Hoo-hoku-kalani,
> Begotten was Molokai, an island,
> Begotten was red Lanai, an island.
> The womb of Papa became jealous at its partnership with Hoo-hoku-ka-lani,
> Papa returned and lived with Wakea,
> Begotten was Oahu, an island,
> Begotten was Kauai, an island,
> Begotten was Niihau, an island,
> A red rock was Kahoolawe.

There are numerous variants to this story; one of them seeks to give a more human and historical turn to the narrative, and explains the opportunity by which Wakea gained access to his daughter's couch, or rather by which he smuggled her to his own cottage, by stating that, advised by his kahuna, he had imposed a *tabu* which separated him from his wife's bed at certain seasons of prayer in each month.

But the real significance of the narrative, as I understand it, lies not so much in the special human incidents which make up this sun-myth, as in the fact that there is a sun-myth at all, that the heavenly phenomena which daily and nightly unrolled themselves before these Polynesians, were at one time in the remote past translated by their poets and thinkers into terms of human passion. Granted the myth-making faculty at all—and most races seem to have possessed it at some time, the form the myth shall take and the human incidents with which it shall be clothed, will be determine by the habits and ruling propensities of the people themselves.

This solar myth from Polynesia reads as if it had been taken straight from Aryan head-quarters. Is this similarity to be explained, as in the case of the Hellenes, from their having rocked in the same race-cradle, aye sucked at the same paps, or, because they carried with them out into the Pacific the memory of those old myths that they learned from their masters, or from those who drove them forth from the plains of India? or, is it that being human, they had the same myth-making faculty that shows itself in the other races of the earth? The question whether the resemblance is the result of historical contact, or a coincidence of independent growth is a question beyond our power to answer. Whatever view one takes of it, there can be no doubt that the ancient Polynesians were the equals of the Aryans or the Hellenes in the art of projecting the lies, thefts and adulteries that embroidered their own lives into the courts of heaven.

10. Sect. 18. The assertion that the tabu-system originated in the concupiscence of Wakea is merely equivalent to saying that the origin of the system is not known.

11. Sect. 20. *Makia a Hano: Makia* is evidently a special name for Wakea, and *Hano,* a name belonging to some ancestor.

12. Sect. 20. *A hano ke aka:* There may perhaps be an intentional antithesis between *hano* and *kuhea. Hano* primarily means silent, while *kuhea,* a compound word from *ku,* to stand, and *hea,* to call, therefore to proclaim, to herald. Such antitheses are in fine accord with the genius of Hawaiian poetry.

13. Sect. 20. *Mo,* an elided form of *moku.*

14. Sect. 20. *Lani,* literally sky, a title frequently applied to a king or chief.

LX

Haloa, the Son of Wakea

1. We have a fragment of tradition regarding *Haloa*. The first born son of Wakea was of premature birth (*keiki alualu*) and was given the name of *Haloa-naka*. The little thing died, however, and its body was buried in the ground at one end of the house. After a while from the child's body shot up a taro plant, the leaf of which was named *lau-kapa-lili*, quivering leaf; but the stem wasgiven the name *Haloa*.

2. After that another child was born to them, whom they called *Haloa*, from the stalk of the taro. He is the progenitor of all the peoples of the earth.

LXI

Waia, the Son of Haloa

1. Tradition gives us some account of *Waia,* the son of Haloa.

2. According to the traditions handed down by the ancient Hawaiians, the government of Waia was extremely corrupt. He was so absorbed in the pursuit of pleasure that he disregarded the instructions of his father, to pray to the gods, to look well after the affairs of the kingdom, and to take good care of his people, so that the country might be prosperous.

3–4. It is said that during Waia's reign a portent was seen in the heavens, a head without a body, and a voice came from it, uttering the words, "What king on the earth below lives an honest life?" The answer returned was *"Kahiko."*[1] Then the voice came a second time from the head and asked the question, "What good has Kahiko done?"

5. Again came the answer from below, "Kahiko is well skilled in all the departments of the government; he is priest and diviner; he looks after the people in his government; Kahiko is patient and forbearing."

6. Thereupon the voice from the portent said, "Then it is Kahiko who is the righteous, the benevolent man."

7. Again the head asked, "What king on earth lives corruptly?" Then the people of the earth answered with a shout, "Waia[2] is the wicked king." "What sin has he committed?" asked the head.

8. "He utters no prayers, he employs no priests, he has no diviner, he knows not how to govern," said the people.

9. "Then he is the wicked king," said the head, and thereupon it withdrew into the heavens.

10. During Waia's reign Hawaii nei was visited by a pestilence. *ma'i ahulau,* which resulted in a great mortality among the people. Only twenty-six persons were left alive, and these were saved and cured by the use of two remedies, *pilikai* and *loloi.*

11. This pestilence was by the ancients called *Ikipuahola.*

12. Kama, the Hawaiian medicine-man (*kahuna-lapaau*), gave it as his opinion that the *ikipuahola* was of the same nature as the *oku'u,* the pestilence which appeared in 1804 in the reign of Kamehameha I.

13. Kama made this statement to his grandson Kuauau, and one year before the appearance of this pestilence Kama foretold its arrival. The circumstances were as follows:

14. Kamehameha was at Kawaihae making preparations for his *Peleleu* expedition to Oahu. At that time Kama was taken sick unto death when he made the following statement to Kuauau.

15. "I am about to die, but you will witness a great pestilence that is soon to make its appearance among us. You will doubtless be weary and worn out with your labors as a physician, because this is the same disease as that which raged in the time of Waia. Ikipuahola is the name of it. It is the same as that pestilence which slew all but twenty-six of the population of Hawaii."

16. "How do you know that this disease is the same as Ikipuahola?" asked Kuauau. To this Kama answered, "My instructor once told me that if a distemper associated with buboes[3] (*haha'i*), and a skin eruption (*meeau*), were to show itself, a short time thereafter this disease would make its appearance. So the ancients told him, and so my preceptor Kalua told me."

17. After that Kamehameha sailed for Oahu and the pestilence in truth made its appearance, raging from Hawaii to Kauai. A vast number of people died and the name *Oku'u* was applied to it.

18. After Waia's time another pestilence called *Hai-lepo* invaded the land and caused the death of a large number of the people. Only sixteen recovered, being saved by the use of a medicine which was composed of some kind of earth (*lepo*). The name of the king during whose reign this epidemic occurred has escaped me.

18. I have not heard the traditions of the kings that succeeded Waia, until we come to the time of Maui. The traditions that have come to me of Maui are false (*waha-hee*), lies, and I repeat no falsehoods.

20. The traditions of the kings that succeeded Maui, until we come to Kapawa, are not known. But tradition informs us with certainty of the place of birth and death of the kings from Kapawa to Paumakua.

Notes to Chapter LXI

1. *Kahiko*, the remote past. This answer smacks of the notion which locates the *golden age* in the remote past, a time when men were good and true and pure, a sentiment not confined to Hawaii.

2. *Wai-a'*: This word is now used in the sense of foul, polluted, Its use here is probably figurative.

3. Sect. 16. This symptom resembles the chief feature of bubonic plague.

LXII

Kapawa

1. Kapawa was a chief who was born at Kukaniloko,[1] district of Waialua, island of Oahu. He died at Lahaina, on Maui, and his bones were taken to Iao valley.

2. *Hele-i-pawa* was a chief who was born at Lelekea, Kaapahu, in Kipahulu on the island of Maui. He died at Poukela and his bones were deposited at Ahulili. (Fornander—The Polynesian Race, Vol. 2, p. 21,—regards Heleipawa as another name for Kapawa).

3. *Aikanaka* was a chief born at Holonokiu, Muolea, Hana, Maui. He died at Oneuli, Puuolai, Honuaula, and his bones were laid to rest at Iao. (According to the *Ulu* genealogy Aikanaka was the grand-son of Heleipawa.)

4. *Puna and Hema*[2] were chiefs who were born in *"Hawaii-kua-ula,"* at Kauiki, Maui. Hema died in Kahiki, i.e., foreign lands, and his bones were left at Ulupaupau.

5. *Kaha'i*[3] was a chief who was born at Kahalulukahi, Wailuku, Maui. He died at Kailikii in Kau; his bones were deposited in Iao.

6. *Wahieloa* was a king who was born at Wailau, in Kau, Hawaii; died at Koloa, in Punaluu, Kau; buried at Alae, in Kipahulu, Maui.

7. *Laka*[4] was a king who was born at Haili, Hawaii; died at Kualoa, Oahu; was buried at Iao.

8. *Lua-nuu* was a king who was born at Peekauai, in Waimea, on Kauai; he died at Honolulu, Oahu, and was buried in Nuuanu.

9. *Pohukaina,* a king, was born at Kahakahakea, in Kau, died at Waimea, Hawaii, and was buried at Mahiki.

10. *Hua* was a king, who was born at Kahona, Lahaina, Maui; died at Kehoni on the same island, and was buried at Iao.

11. *Pau,* the son of Hua, was a king who was born at a place in Kewalo on Oahu; died on Molokai and was buried at Iao.

12. *Hua (nui-i-ka-lailai),* the son of Pau, was a king who was born at Ohikilolo in Waianae, on Oahu. He died on Lanai and his bones were deposited at Iao.

13. *Paumakua*[6] was a king of Oahu who was born at Kua-aohe, on Oahu. He died on Oahu and his bones were laid to rest at Iao.

14. *Haho.*[7] Traditions regarding this king are scanty.

Of *Palena* tradition says that he had two sons, of whom the elder, called *Hana-laa-nui,* was in the line of the Hawaii kings, and the younger, *Hana-laa-iki,* was of the line of Maui kings.

15. *Puna-imua* was one of the ancestors of kings on Oahu and on Kauai, *Hema* of kings on Hawaii.

16. Of traditions regarding *Lanakawai, Laau, Pili, Koa, Ole, Kukohou, Kaniuhi,* I have heard none. Of Kani-pahu we have this:

17. *Kani-pahu* was from Hawaii, but, the kingdom being seized by Kamaiole, he left Hawaii and took refuge at Kalae on Molokai, where he lived incognito. He took to wife a woman of Kalae, and by his father-in-law was so frequently set to the work of carrying burdens—water and other things—that he contracted callosities on his shoulders.

18. Kani-pahu had two sons on Hawaii named *Kalapana* and *Kalahuimoku. Alaikauakoko* was the mother of Kalapana and *Hua-lani* the mother of *Kalahuimoku.*

19. Now these two boys had been brought up in retirement in the country, without the knowledge of Kamaiole, because if Kamaiole had known them to be the sons of king Kanipahu, he would have put them to death.

20. At that time Kamaiole reigned as king over Hawaii. It happened that while Kamaiole was making a tour of that island some of his boon companions abducted and seduced the good looking wives of certain country folk and took them for. themselves.

21. These people whose wives had been taken from them came before Kamaiole and appealed to him to have their women returned to them. But Kamaiole took the part of his own favorites and the women were not returned to their husbands.

22. Thereupon these men became greatly incensed against Kamaiole and they secretly consulted *Paao* that they might put Kamaiole to death. Paao's advice to them was, "Yes, he should be killed; but first secure another king."

23. Paao accordingly sent a messenger to Kanipahu, who was living at Kalae, on Molokai. On his arrival at Kalae the messenger went before Kanipahu, bearing in his hand a pig as a gift, and coming into his presence he said, "I have come to ask you to return and be the king of Hawaii. The people of Hawaii have rejected Kamaiole as unworthy."

24. Then Kanipahu considered the callous bunches on his neck (*kona hokua, ua leho*), and he was ashamed to return to Hawaii. His answer to the messenger was, "I will not return with you; but go to Waimanu; there you will find my peeping fledgeling (*ioio moa*) Kalapana. He will be a king for you. He is my own offspring, in the care of his mother Alaikauakoko, who lives at Waimanu. Make him your king."

Notes to Chapter LXII

1. Sect. 1. It was held to be a most distinguished honor to be born at Kukaniloko. Queens in expectation of motherhood were accustomed to go to Kukaniloko in advance that by undergoing the pains of labor in that place they might confer on their offspring this inestimable boon. Kapawa is mentioned in legends as *"Ke alii o Waialua,"* indicating that he may have passed his youth in that district. Tradition informs us that for some fault, whether of personal character or of government, we are not told, Kapawa was deposed from his government. A chief named Pili Kaaiea was prevailed upon by the king-maker Paao to come to Hawaii and assume kingly authority. Kapawa was undoubtedly a weak and degraded character. The fact that in spite of having been deposed from the throne he died at Lahaina, in peace so far as we know, and that his bones received the distinguished honor of sepulture in the royal burying place in Iao valley, argues that his unfitness for rule depended upon his own personal weakness and debasement rather than upon outbreaks of violence and cruelty. Kapawa was the last of his line, the Nana genealogy.

2. Sect. 4. It were a shame to allow this barren, truncated statement to pass current in its present form. It was the period of communication between Hawaii and the archipelagoes of the South Pacific. Great navigators, guided by the stars, steered their canoes and successfully voyaged from Hawaii to the lands, principally in the South, known to them as *Kukulu-o-Kahiki*.

Hawaii-kua-uli is a poetical expression meaning "verdure-clad-Hawaii." The following mele celebrates the deeds of Hema.

> *Holo Hema i Kahiki, ki'i i ke apo ula,*
> *Loa'a Hema, lilo i ka Aaia,*
> *Haule i Kahiki, i Kapakapakaua,*
> *Waiho ai i Ulu-pa'upa'u.*

Hema voyaged to Kahiki to fetch the red coronet,
Hema secured it, but he was caught by the Aaia,
He fell in Kahiki, in Kapakapakaua,
His body was deposited at Ulu-pa'upa'u.

The descendants of this old-time navigator Hema reigned over Hawaii and Maui, those of Puna over Oahu and Maui.

3. Sect. 5. *Kaha'i* also was a great navigator. If we can believe the legend he voyaged in search of his father, perhaps to avenge him. In Samoa, in the heroic period.

> *O ke anuenue ke ala o Kaha'i;*
> *Pii Kaha'i, koi Kaha'i,*
> *He Kaha'i i ke koi-ula a Kane;*
> *Hihia i na maka o Alihi.*
> *A'e Kaha'i i ke anaha,*
> *He anaha ke kanaka, ka waa;*
> *Iluna o Hana-ia-kamalama,*
> *O ke ala ia i imi ai i ka makua o Kaha'i.*
> *O hele a i ka moana wehiwehi,*
> *A haalulu i Hale-kumu-ka-lani,*
> *Ui mai kini o ke akua,*
> *Ninau o Kane, o Kanaloa,*
> *Heaha kau huaka'i nui*
> *E Kaha'i, i hiki mai ai?*
> *I imi mai au i ka Hema.*
> *Aia i Kahiki, aia i Ulupaupau,*
> *Aia i ka aaia, haha mau ia e Kane,*
> *Loaa aku i kukulu o Kahiki.*

The rainbow was the path of Kaha'i,
Kaha'i climbed, Kaha'i strove,
He was girded with the mystic enchantment of Kane,
He was fascinated by the eyes of Alihi.
Kaha'i mounted on the flashing rays of light,
Flashing on men and canoes.
Above was Hana-ia-kamalama
That was the road by which Kaha'i sought his father.
Pass over the dark-blue ocean,
And shake the foundation of heaven.
The multitude of the gods keep asking,
Kane and Kanaloa inquire,
What is your large travelling party seeking,
O Kaha'i, that you have come hither?
I come looking for Hema.
Over yonder in Kahiki, over yonder in Ulupa'upa'u,
Yonder by the Aaia constantly fondled by Kane,
I have travelled to the pillars of Tahiti.

4. Sect. 7. He is generally spoken of as "Laka, of Kipahulu, the son of Wahieloa." There is a very interesting legend about him relating to the building of a canoe, in which he sailed to discover the bones of his father.

5. Sect. 7. The names of Aikanaka, Puna, Hema, Kaha'i Wahieloa, Laka and Luanuu are celebrated in the New Zealand traditions. W. D. A.

6. Sect. 13. There was a Maui Paumakua, with whom Malo has evidently confounded this one of Oahu. They belonged to different lines. The deeds of the Oahu king seem to have been appropriated by the bards who in later times sang the praises of the Maui man. As claimed by Fornander—"The Polynesian Race," Vol. 2, pp. 24–27,—the Oahu Paumakua was a great traveller. His exploits are embellished by the bards in high flown language.

> O Paumakua, ka lani o Moenaimua,
> O ke alii nana i hele ke Kahiki,
> A Kahiki i ke kaiakea,
> O mimo, o momi, o ka mamio,
> O ka ia mailoko, o ka Auakahinu,
> O Auakamea ia lani.

Paumakua, the divinity of Moenaimua,
The king who voyaged to Tahiti,
Tahiti in the great ocean,
He the superb, the select, the magnificent.
The fish he brought away with him were Auakahinu
And Auakamea, the high born.

These captives (fish, *i-a*) whom Paumakua brought with him were said to have been white men and priests. They are described as *ka haole nui, maka alohilohi, ke a aholehole, maka aa, ka puaa keokeo nui, maka ulaula,* foreigners of large stature, fat cheeks, bright eyes, ruddy and stout. The introduction of circumcision is by some ascribed to Paumakua.

7. Sect. 14. He was the son of the Maui Paumakua, and is distinguished as the founder of the *Aha-Alii,* College or Assembly of Chiefs, admission to which was very strictly guarded, and was granted only to those who could prove their royal ancestry.

LXIII

Kalapana

1. We have the following scanty traditional information regarding Kalapana. The messengers above mentioned returned from their visit to Kanipahu; they reported to Paao, the commands of Kanipahu.

2. And when Paao had received the message he went in search of Kalapana. On his arrival at Waimanu valley, Paao inquired of Alaikauakoko, "Whereabouts in Waimanu lives the son of Kanipahu?"

3. Alaikauakoko, however, kept Kalapana in hiding, and would not reveal where he was, fearing that search was being made for him to kill him, and she replied to Paao, "Kanipahu has no son here." "He has a son," said Paao, "where is Alaikauakoko?" "I am Alaikauakoko," said the woman. Then Paao explained, "Kanipahu has advised me that his son, Kalapana, is here with you."

4. Thereupon Alaikauakoko yielded and presented Kalapana to Paao.

5. Then Paao took Kalapana away with him into Kohala, and there they lived secretly together, and they and the people sought for an opportunity to put Kamaiole to death.

6. By and by, when Kamaiole was about to voyage by canoe to Kona, they thought they saw their opportunity to kill him while he was boarding his canoe. The nature of this opportunity will be evident from the fact that it was a principle of royal etiquette in ancient times that the canoes bearing the royal party should tarry until the canoes of the people had started out to sea before the king's canoes left the beach.

7. So the people and Kalapana secretly waited the king's movements. Arriving at Anaehoomalu, in Kekaha, Kona, they spent the night, and at day-break the next day all the canoes started off, leaving those of Kamaiole behind.

8. Thereupon Kalapana and his people set upon Kamaiole and put him to death, and the government passed to Kalapana. Kalapana was nicknamed *kuu ioio moa*, after the expression used by his father, Kanipahu. No further tradition has been preserved in regard to Kamaiole (sic).

LXIV

Kalaunuiohua

1. It is said that in the reign of *Kalaunuiohua* there lived a prophetess, or *kaula,* of great power named Waahia.

2. Kalaunuiohua had frequently sought to put her to death, but without success. She had been thrown into the sea, beaten with rods, rolled down steep declivities, but still she survived, and the king's patience had become exhausted because she would not die.

3. Then this prophetess said to Kalaunuiohua, "Do you really wish me to die?" "Yes, that is my wish," said the king.

4. "I shall not die if you attempt to put me to death at any other place save one," said the woman. "If you are in earnest in your wish to kill me, thrust me into the *heiau* and burn me up with the temple, then I shall die," The heiau she meant was at *Keeku* in Kona.

5. "On the day you set fire to the heiau to destroy me you must stay quietly in the house from morning till night and by no means go out of doors. If the people make an outcry at some portent in the heavens you must not go out to look at it.

6. "Nor must you open the doors of the house in order to observe the heavenly phenomenon. If you do so you will die. You must wait patiently all day in the house, and only when night comes may you go out of doors. In this way will you and your kingdom be saved from destruction. But if you do not obey my injunctions, disaster will fall upon you and your kingdom.

7. "My god *Kane-ope-nui-o-alakai* will afflict you and your kingdom because of your disobedience to his wishes (*e like me ke akua*). He has granted your desire. I die by your hand." Thus ended her speech.

8. Then Kalaunuiohua had the woman burnt with fire, and the smoke of the burning heiau went up to heaven and took the shape of two gamecocks that fought together in the heavens.

9. When the people saw this portent they raised a great shout, and Kalaunuiohua asked, "What means this great uproar?" The answer was "It is a cloud in the heavens that resembles two cocks fighting." "I will look at it," said Kalaunuiohua.

10. "The prophetess strenuously commanded you not to look lest you die," said his men, and the king yielded. Then that appearance passed away and another portent made its appearance.

11. The same smoke-cloud assumed the shape of a pig which moved about from one place to another in the heavens. Again the people raised a great shout, and again Kalaunuiohua declared his wish to look; but his people entreated him not to look out until the thing had disappeared from the heavens.

12. After this the clouds took on a singular appearance, some were white, some glistening, some green, yellow, red, black, blue-black, black and glistening, and the sky sparkled and flashed with light. Again the people raised a shout and again Kalaunuiohua wished to look, but his men restrained him.

13. When it came evening and the sun was about to set two clouds resembling mud-hens flew down from the heavens, and, having alighted close to the end of Kalaunuiohua's house, stood and fought with each other, at the sight of which the people again raised a tremendous shout.

14. Kalaunuiohua had now become greatly excited and could no longer master his impatience. He reached out his hand to the side of the house and tearing away the thatch gazed upon the mud-hens (*alae*) of cloud.

15. Then the prophetess took spiritual possession of Kalaunuiohua's hand. The deity that inspired was *Kane-nui-akea*. Kalaunuiohua became very powerful, he had only to point with his hand and direct war against another country and that country would be at his mercy.

16. Kalaunuiohua pointed hither to Maui (*kuhi mai*[1]), and began to wage war against Kamaluohua, king of Maui, and he defeated him and added Maui to his possession.

17. Kamaluohua was not put to death, but appointed governor of Maui under Kalaunuiohua.

18. After that Kalaunuiohua pointed to Molokai; and he made war on *Kahakuohua*, and, having defeated him, he appointed Kahakuohua governor of Molokai under himself.

19. The hand of Kalaunuiohua next pointed at Oahu, and he made war on *Hua-i-pou-leilci* and overcame him, after which he made that king governor of Oahu.

20. His hand pointed next towards Kauai, and he waged war against that island, a war which was called *Ka-welewele-iwi*.

21. When Kalaunuiohua sailed on his campaign against Kauai to wage war upon Kukona, the king of that island, he was accompanied by Kamaluohua, Kahakuohua, and Huakapouleilei, (kings subject to him).

22. After the arrival of Kalaunuiohua at Kauai the deity (good luck) deserted that king's hand and took possession of Kauli'a, a man of Kauai. The hand of Kalaunuiohua lost the magic power it once had when it pointed.

23. In the battle with Kukona, king of Kauai, Kalaunuiohua was defeated, but his life and the lives of his allies, the *Huas*, were spared.

24. Kalaunuiohua and the other *Huas* lived peacefully on Kauai with Kukona and were treated by him with all kindness.

One time when Kukona was spending the day apart from his own people with these captive *Huas* about him, he was taken with a desire for sleep. He rolled himself in his blanket and lay down, but did not fall asleep,—he was setting a trap for them,—and was all the time alert and watching them from beneath his covering.

25. Kalaunuiohua and his fellow captives supposed that Kukona had really gone to sleep, and they began to grumble and find fault with Kukona and to plot against his life, at which they of Oahu, Molokai, and Hawaii nodded assent, agreeing that they should turn upon Kukona and put with to death.

26. But Kamaluohua, the king of Maui, said, "Let us do no hurt to Kukona, because he has been kind to us. Here we are in his hands, but he has not put us to death. Let us then treat him kindly."

27. Just then Kukona rose up and said to them, "What a fine dream I've just had while sleeping! I dreamed all of you were muttering and plotting my death, but that one pointing to Kamaluohua, defended me and preserved my life."

28. They all acknowledged the truth of his accusations. "Because, however, of Kamaluohua's kindness," continued Kukona, "and because of his determination that no evil should be done to me; because he appreciated that life and the enjoyment of peace were great blessings, I will not trouble you."

29. "Because Kamaluohua did right, I now declare all of you free to return to your homes with the honors of war (*me ka lanakila*), taking your own canoes with you. Do not think I shall oppress you in your own lands. Your lands shall be your own to live in as before."

30. So Ka-lau-nui-o-hua returned home to Hawaii, Huaipou-leilei to Oahu, Kahakuohua to Molokai, Kamaluohua to Maui; and they

lived peacefully in their own homes. This peace was called *ka la'i loa ia Kamaluohua,* the long peace of Kamaluohua.

31. Kamehameha I[2] had this affair of Kukona's in mind when he allowed Kaumualii to live at the time he met him in Honolulu, Oahu.

32. There is a lack of traditional knowledge of *Kuaiwa* and of *Kahoukapu;* but of Kau-hola-nui-mahu tradition gives us some information.

Notes to Chapter LXIV

1. Sect. 16. It may be inferred from the use of this word *mai* (hither) that David Malo himself lived on Maui at the time of writing this.

2. Sect. 31. This statement of David Malo is entirely contrary to the truth. Kamehameha basely plotted to take the life of Kaumualii by poisoning him while at a feast given in his honor when that noble king (Kaumualii) had come to Honolulu on an errand of peact. The life of Kaumualii was saved only by the interference of Isaac Davis, who warned the king of Kauai of his danger. For this act Isaac Davis was afterwards poisoned.

LXV

KAUHOLANUIMAHU

1. There was a king named Kahoukapu, whose wife being barren, they had no children.

2. But being very desirous of offspring, she went to consult with Paao, the priest, about it. "Here I am," said Paao. "What shall I do to beget a child?" asked La'akapu.

3. "You must go and fetch a fish as an offering to the deity for yourself," said Paao. Then she went away, and having obtained a fish, returned to Paao, saying, "Here is a fish for the deity." "What sort of a fish is it?" asked Paao.

4. "A *weke*," said La'akapu. "Throw it away," said Paao, "the deity will not eat such a kind of a fish as that. It is like a rat. It's full of bones; so is a rat. It has a beard; so has a rat. It is lean; so is a rat. Go and fetch another fish."

5. Laakapu then brought another fish to the priest. "What fish have you?" asked Paao. "It is a *moi*," answered she. "Throw it away," said he. "It is a rat, the rat *Makea*. It lives in sea foam (*hu'a-kai*); the rat makes his covert in the housethatch (*hua-hale);* the *moi* has whiskers; so has mister rat. Bring another fish."

6. Then Laakapu got another fish and brought it to Paao, who asked, "What fish have you?" "A squid." "Fling it away," said he; "it is the rat *Haunawelu.* He lives in holes under the ocean. Mr. Rat lives in holes in the rocks. Mr. Squid has arms (*awe);* Mr. Rat also has a tail. Fetch another fish."

7. La'akapu then brought a *ma'oma'o;* but Paao again declared it also was a rat. Laakapu, now discouraged and out of patience, said to Paao, "Tell me what sort of a fish you want." "A *pao'o;* that is no rat," said he.

8. Then Laa'kapu brought a *pao'o* to the priest, and in answer to his question as to what the fish was she answered, naming the fish, and then, obedient to his demand, gave it to him.

9. Then Paao offered the fish as a sacrifice to the idol diety with the prayer, "Grant a child unto La'akapu." And in due season La'akapu gave birth to a child. But it was of doubtful sex, and she named it *Kau-hola-nui-mahu.*[1]

10. On the death of Kahoukapu the kingdom passed into the hands of Kauholanuimahu. After reigning for a few years Kauholanuimahu sailed over to Maui and made his residence at *Honua-ula*. He it was that constructed that fish-pond at Keoneoio.

11. The wife of Kauholanuimahu remained on Hawaii and took to herself another husband; his kingdom also revolted from him but Kauholanuimahu returned to Hawaii and recovered it by war.

Note to Chapter XLV

1. *Mahu* means a hermaphrodite.

LXVI

Liloa

1. *Liloa,* the son of Kiha, had the reputation of being very religious, also of being well skilled in war. His reign was a long one. I have not gained much information about the affairs of his government.

2. Tradition reports the rumor that Liloa was addicted[1] to the practice of sodomy (*moe-ai-kane*); but it did not become generally known during his lifetime, because he did it secretly.

3. During Liloa's reign there was much speculation as to why he retained a certain man as a favorite. It was not apparent what that man did to recommend himself as a favorite (*puna-hele*) in the eyes of the king, and it caused great debate.

4. After the death of Liloa people put to this man the question, "Why were you such a great favorite with Liloa?" His answer was, *"He hana ma'i mai ia'u ma ku'u uha."*

5. When people heard this, they tried it themselves, and in this way the practice of sodomy became established and prevailed down to the time of Kamehameha I. Perhaps it is no longer practiced at the present time. As to that I can't say.

6. Liloa lived most of the time at Wai-pio,[2] and it was in that valley he died. When near to death Liloa directed that the government of Hawaii should go to Ha-kau.[3]

7. As for Umi, he was unprovided for by Liloa, though during the lifetime of the king he had been his great favorite.

8. The result was that Hakau acted very insultingly towards Umi, and constantly abused and found fault with him, until finally it came to war between them, and Hakau was killed by Umi.

Notes on Chapter XLVI

1. Sect. 2. The language is such as to make it appear that Liloa was the first Hawaiian inventor of this form of vice, and the one through whom it finally became popularized. As to its prevalence at the time when Mr. Malo wrote, it is safe to say that, like such a vegetable pest as the lantana, the introduction of a vice is more easy than its eradication, to forget is more difficult than to remember.

2. Sect. 6. Liloa is represented as an affable, pleasure-loving monarch, of easy manners, but a strict disciplinarian. He was much given to touring through the districts of his kingdom, by which means he acquainted himself with the needs of his people and was able to repress the arbitrary encroachments of the chiefs on the rights of the land-holders under their authority. In this way he gained popularity with the common people. The romantic incident relating to the parents and birth of Umi are related in the following chapter. In explanation of David Malo's statement that Liloa was counted a person of great piety, it may be remarked that in his reign the temple-service of the famous heiau of *Pa-ka'a-lana*, situated in the valley of Wai-pio, was maintained with great care and strictness. The sacred pavement,—of which Mr. Fornander speaks—and which perhaps formed a sort of roadway between the royal residence, called *Hau-no-ka-ma'a-hala*, and the heiau above mentioned, though built long anterior to Liloa's time, became so closely associated in mind with the glories of Liloa's reign, that it was thenceforward known as *ka Pae-pae-a-Liloa*. The celebrity of Waipio as a royal residence and the capital of the kingdom of Hawaii—the island—went into a decline at the death of Liloa; and the incoming of so narrow-minded and despicable a monarch as Hakau, was the finishing stroke to its primacy among the towns and places of the island-kingdom. There was peace on Hawaii during the long reign of Liloa.

3. Sect. 7. This statement conveys a wrong impression. It is true the territory of the kingdom was not divided, but provision was made for Umi—after a fashion—in that he was appointed the *kahu* of the idol, a fact which had an important influence over his life and fortunes. There is a certain similarity between the position occupied by Umi, after the death of Liloa, and that in which Kamehameha found himself after the death of Ka-lani-opu'u. Kamehameha, like Umi, was the *kahu* of the idol (*akua*)—probably in both cases the same, *Ku-kaili-moku*, Ku, the land-grabber; but Umi was left without resources with which to maintain his proper self-respect or to support the service of the idol, or divinity that was entrusted to his care. But in both instances genius, ability, was able to take care of itself.

LXVII

Umi

Umi was the son of Liloa, but not his first son. The name of his first son was Hakau, whom he begot by Pinea, the regular wife of Liloa. Hakau was considered a very high chief, because Pinea was of the same alii-rank as Liloa, owing to the fact that Liloa's mother, Waiolea, was the elder sister of Pinea.

2. Umi was the child of Liloa by a woman whom he seduced named *Akahi-a-kulcana*. She has often been spoken of as a person of no *alii* blood, but the fact was that she was of the same *alii* line as Liloa himself. They were both descendants of Kanipahu.

3. The genealogies of Akahi-a-kuleana and of Liloa from Kanipahu are as follows: Kanipahu first took to wife *Ala-i-kaua-koko*, as a result of which union was born Kalapana, the ancestor of Liloa. Afterwards Kanipahu took to wife Hualani, who gave birth to Ka-la-hu-moku, who was the ancestor of *Akahi-a-kuleana*.

4. Kalahumoku took to wife Laamea, and begot Ikialaamea.
Ikialaamea took to wife Kalama, and begot Kamanawa-a-akalamea.
Kamanawa-a-akalamea took to wife Kaiua, and begot Ua-kai-ua.
Ua-kai-ua took to wife Kua-i-makani, and begot Ka-nahae-kua-i-makani.
Ka-nahae-kua-i-makani took to wife Kapiko, and begot Kuleana-kapiko.

5. Kuleana-kapiko took to wife Keniani-a-hoolei, and begot Akahi-a-kuleana, who was wifed by Liloa, and gave birth to Umi.

6. Here is the genealogy from Kalapana:
Kalapana and Makeamalaehanae, begot Kahaimoeleaikai-kupou.
Kahaimoeleaikaikupou and Kapoakauluhailaa, begot Kalaunuiohua (k.).

Kalaunuiohua and Kaheka, begot Kuaiwa.

Kuaiwa and Kainuleilani, begot Kahoukapu.

Kahoukapu and Laakapu, begot Kauhola.

Kauhola took to wife Neulaokiha and Waiolea, and begot Liloa.

Liloa took to wife Akahiakuleana, and begot Umi.

7. The story of the birth of Umi is as follows: Liloa, the father of Umi, was at that time the king of all Hawaii and had fixed residence in the Waipio valley, Hamakua.

8. The incident happened while Liloa was making a journey through Hamakua toward the borders of Hilo to attend the consecration of the heiau of Manini. This heiau, which Liloa had been pushing forward to completion, was situated in the hamlet of Kohola-lele, Hamakua.

9. When the tabu had been removed he waited for a while, till the period of refreshment (*hoomahanahana*)[1] was over, and then moved on to the North of that place and staid at Kaawikiwiki, where he gratified his fondness for *pahee* and other games.

10. While staying at this place he went to bathe in a little stream that runs through Hoea, a land adjoining Kealakaha. It was there and then he came across Akahi-a-kuleana. She had come to the stream and was bathing after her period of impurity in preparation for the ceremony of purification, after which she would rejoin her husband, that being the custom among women at the time. Her servant was sitting on the bank of the stream guarding her *pa-u*.

11. When Liloa looked upon her and saw that she was a fine looking woman he conceived a passion for her, and, taking hold of her, he said, "lie with me." Recognizing that it was Liloa, the king, who asked her, she consented, and they lay together.

12. After the completion of the act, Liloa, perceiving that the woman was flowing, asked her if it was her time of impurity, to which she answered, "Yes, this is the continuation of it." "You will probably have a child then," said Liloa, and she answered that it was probable. Liloa then asked her whose she was and what was her name. "I am Akahi-a-kuleana," said she, "and Kuleanakapiko is the name of my father." "You are undoubtedly a relation of mine," said Liloa. "Quite likely," said she.

14. Then Liloa instructed her regarding the child, saying, "When our child is born, if it is a girl do you name it from your side of the family; but if it is a boy give to him the name Umi."

DAVID MALO

15. "By what token shall I be able to prove that the child is yours, the king's?"

16. Then Liloa gave into her hands his *malo*, his *niho-palaoa*, and his club (*laau palau*), saying, "These are the proofs of our child, and when he has grown up give these things to him."[2] To this arrangement Akahiakuleana gladly assented, and handed the things over to her maid, to be taken care of for the child.

17. Liloa then made for himself a substitute for a malo by knotting together some *ti*-leaves, with which he girded himself.

18. On returning to the house the people saw that he had a covering of ti-leaf, which was not his proper *malo* and they remarked to each other, "What a sight! Liloa is out of his head. That isn't his usual style; it's nothing but a ti-leaf makeshift for a *malo.*"

19. Liloa remained at this place until the period of refreshment (*hoomahana hana*) was over and then he went back to Waipio, his permanent residence.

20. A short time after this Akahi-a-kuleana found herself to be with child, the child Umi. Her husband, not knowing that Liloa was the true father of the child, supposed it to be his own,

21. When the boy was born his mother gave him the name Umi as she had been bidden to do by Liloa at the time of his conception.

22. And they fed and took care of the boy until he was grown of good size. The story is told that on one occasion, when his foster-father, the husband of Akahi-a-kuleana, returned to the house, after having been at work on his farm, and found that Umi had eaten up all the food that had been prepared, he gave the lad a beating.

23. Umi was regularly beaten this way every time it was found that he had consumed the last of the fish and poi, or any other kind of food. This was the way Umi's foster father treated him at all times, because he in good faith took the boy to be his own son.

But Umi and Akahi-a-kuleana were greatly disturbed at the treatment he received.

24. Then Umi privily asked his mother "Have I no other father but this one? Is he my only *makua?*"[3]

25. "You have a father at Waipio," answered his mother, "his name is Liloa." "Perhaps I had better go to him," said Umi. "Yes, I think you had better go," said his mother.

26. After that, on a certain occasion when Umi had consumed the food and his foster father (*makua kolea*)[4] had given him a drubbing,

Akahi-a-kuleana expostulated and said, "My husband, it is not your own son that you are all the time beating after this fashion."

27. Then her husband flamed into passion and sarcastically said, "Who, pray, is the father of this child of yours? is it King Liloa?" "Yes," said she, "Liloa is the father of my child."

28. "Where is the proof of the fact that this son to whom you, my wife, have given birth, belongs to Liloa?" demanded he.

29. Then Akahi-a-kuleana called to her maid-servant and ordered her to bring the things which Liloa had left for Umi.

30. "You see now," said she, "who is the real father of the boy," and the man was satisfied that he could not claim the paternity of the child.

31. Sometime after this explanation Akahi-a-kuleana carefully instructed Umi as to his going to Waipio to Liloa.

32. She girded him with Liloa's *malo,* hung about the boy's neck the *lei-palaoa,* and put into his hands the club, after which she carefully instructed Umi how he was to act.

33. "Go down into Waipio valley," said she, "and when you have reached the foot of the *pali* swim to the other side of the stream. You will see a house facing you; that is the residence of Liloa."

34. "Don't enter through the gate, but climb[5] over the fence; nor must you enter the house in the usual way, but through the king's private[5] door. If you see an old man, and some one waving a kahili over him, that is your father, Liloa; go up to him and sit down in his lap. When he asks who you are, tell him your name is Umi." Umi assented to all his mother's instructions.

35. Akahi-a-kuleana ordered her brother, Omao-kamau, to accompany Umi and to wait upon him. Omao-kamau readily agreed to this and followed him as a servant.

36. She also directed that Omao-kamau should take charge of the club which had been Liloa's, saying, "Keep this stick which was Liloa's."

37. When all the arrangements had been made, Umi and Omao-kamau started off on their journey by themselves.

38. On reaching Ke-aha-kea they came across a little boy named Pii-mai-waa, who asked them whither they were going. "To Waipio," they replied.

39. "I will adopt you as my boy, and you may ge along with us to Waipio," said Umi. "Agreed," said the lad, and they proceeded in company.

40. On reaching Waipio they descended into the valley by way of Koaekea, and coming to the foot of the *pali* they all swam across the Wailoa stream.

41. Gaining the other side they saw before them the residence of Liloa at a place called *Hau-no ka-ma'a a-hala,* with the entrance to the house facing them.

42. On nearing the house Umi said to the others, "You two tarry here and wait for me. I will go in to Liloa. If in my going to him I am killed, you must return by the way we came; but if I come back alive to you we shall all live." With these words Umi left them.

43. In his going Umi climbed over the fence that surrounded the residence of Liloa and entered the house by Liloa's private door, as his mother had bade him do when he left her.

44. When Liloa's officers (that stood guard about him) saw that the lad had forfeited his life (*laa*) because he had climbed over the fence, which was a sacred and tabu thing, they gave chase after him to kill him. Then Umi ran up to Liloa and made as if he would sit down in his lap; but Liloa spread his thighs apart so that Umi sat down upon the ground.

45. As he did so Liloa saw the *niho-palao* on Umi's neck, and his own *malo* about Umi's loins, and he asked, "What is your name? Are you Umi?" "Yes," answered he, "I am Umi, your son."

46. Then Liloa took Umi upon his lap and embraced and kissed him and inquired of him, "Where is Akahi-a-kuleana?"

47. "She it was," answered Umi, "who directed me to come to you." Then Liloa showed to the people the things of his which Umi had, saying, "This is my *malo* and my *palaoa*—but where is my club?" "It is outside, in the hands of my companion," answered the boy.

48. Then Liloa sent for Omaokamau and Pi'i-mai-wa'a.

49. And he said to all his people, "When we went to consecrate the *heiau* you called me a crazy one, because I wore a *malo* of *ti*-leaf."

50. "But here is that *malo* of mine, and that *niho-palaoa,* also that club. I left them for this one. He is my son, Umi."

51. Then all the people saw that Umi was the son of Liloa. The king then ordered to bring his idols that the ceremony of *oki-piko* might be performed on Umi, and it was done.

52. When Hakau, Liloa's first son, heard the sound of the drum, he asked what it meant, and the people answered, "It is the drum at the *oki-piko* of Liloa's new-found son, Umi."

53. On hearing that Liloa had a new son, Hakau was full of wrath, and he came to Liloa with the question, "Is this your son?" To this Liloa ayed assent and at the same time tried to placate Hakau, saying, "You will be king, and he will be your man. You will have authority over him." With words like these Liloa tried to soften Hakau's anger towards Umi. Hakau was outwardly appeased, but there was a hypocritical reservation within.

54. While Umi lived in the court of Liloa he gave the strictest obedience to his father's commands, and Liloa on his part took the greatest care of his son, Umi. This was noticed by Hakau.

55. And the very fact intensified the hatred of Hakau to Umi, so that he always treated him with rudeness, and thus it was so long as Liloa lived. Hakau's anger and constant hectoring of Umi continued through Liloa's life, and caused the king much pain and sadness.

56. When Liloa drew near to death he announced it as his will that Hakau should inherit all the land, but that the idols and the house of the gods should be given to Umi, to be under his care.

57. After the death of Liloa, Umi submitted dutifully himself to Hakau. Hakau, however, hated Umi cordially and treated him with great contempt and spitefulness (*hookae*).

58. Once when Umi rode upon Hakau's surf-board, Hakau said to him, "Don't you use my surf-board. Your mother was a common, plebeian woman of Hamakua. My board is tabu. I am an *alii*."

59. When Umi chanced on one occasion to put on a *malo* belonging to Hakau, Hakau insulted and upbraided him, saying, "Don't you wear my *malo*. I am an *alii*. Your mother was a low-class woman of Hamakua."

60. Thus it was that Hakau insulted and actually offered violence to Umi so that finally he made up his mind to leave the court of Hakau secretly, his two companions, Omaokamau, and Pi'imaiwa'a, who came with him from Hamakua, keeping him company in his flight.

61. The road they followed in their departure was the same as that they took in their coming.

62. After climbing Koae-kea and reaching Kukui-haele they found a boy named Koi, and Umi having adopted him as his own, son, he travelled along with them.

63. On reaching Kealakaha, which was Umi's birth-place, they did not put up with his mother. Their inclination was rather to wander still farther.

64. For that reason they travelled on in a northerly direction, and reaching the western bounds of Hilo, they entered a land called Wai-puna-lei.

65. It being now near the close of day they selected a place to camp down and spend the night; but at day-break they resumed their journey, for Umi had conceived the idea of living a vagabond life in some unknown and out-of-the-way place, because he was ashamed at having been so insulted by Hakau.

66. When it came bed-time the young women of the place saw that they were clean and wholesome-looking youths, and they chose them for husbands, and they spent the night with them (*a hoao ae lakou*).

67. There was a young woman to each of them, but Umi was such a handsome fellow that he had two.

68. While they stayed at this place they (the young men) agreed among themselves, after consulting together, that Umi's name should be kept secret; and on talking it over with each other again, they still further agreed that Umi should do no work. Umi accordingly performed no labor.

69. After they had been there awhile Pi'i-mai-wa'a. Koi and Omao-kamau went out to work in the farms of their fathers-in-law; but Umi did not go.[6]

70. When the young men came home at night from their farming, their fathers-in-law were delighted with their vigor as farmers.

71. But Umi's father-in-law was greatly disappointed that Umi did not work to help support his wife.

72. On one occasion they went down to the ocean at Lau-pa-hoe-hoe, and engaged in surf-bathing (*kaha-nalu*), in which Umi was of superior skill; and Umi raced with one Paiea.

73. And as they were coursing, Paiea rudely crowded over onto Umi, so that his board came violently in collision with Umi's shoulder and hurt him severely. This was the fault, on account of which Umi afterwards put Paiea to death, he having then succeeded to the government of the island.

74. When it came to the season for *aku*, Pi'i-mai-wa'a, Omaokamau and Koi went a-trolling for *aku* along with the men of the place.

75. Their fathers-in-law were delighted, when they got the fish, but the fathers-in-law of Umi were very much put out because he did not go for *aku* with the fishermen of the region.

76. Umi's fathers-in-law said to Umi's wives, "If this fat husband of yours were only a fisherman now, we would have some *aku* to eat, but as it is, you are wasting yourselves on this man."

77. On one occasion when the fishermen saw that Umi was a strong fellow they invited him to go *aku*-fishing with them, and he consented.

They did not know that he was an *alii*, though the disappearance of Umi had become notorious: nor did they know that his name was Umi.

78. While they were fishing, Umi noticed that when a fisherman took in a fish he passed it between his legs (*poho-lalo*) in putting it into the canoe, and when it came to the division of the fish, he would not use as food for himself such as had been treated in this way.[8]

79. But he exchanged the fish thus obtained for those of another fisherman, whose fish had been passed over the fisherman's shoulder, saying to him, "Give me your small fish, and take in exchange these large fish as yours;" to which the other readily agreed.

80. Umi would not eat of these fish, but took them as an offering to his god *Kaili*, which he kept in a secret place near the residence of *Ho-kuli.*

81. When Kalei-o-ku, the prophet, noticed that as often as Umi went a-fishing, which was very frequently, a rainbow[9] appeared over the patch of calm water in the ocean that surrounded him (malau), and he said to himself, "Perhaps this is Umi,"—for he had heard of Umi's disappearance.

82. Accordingly Kalei-o-ku came down to where Umi was living, bringing with him a pig, as an offering. And when he arrived at Umi's place of residence he found him living in a lordly fashion, and he said to himself, "This man is an *alii.*"

83. He immediately offered the pig, at the same time repeating this prayer, "Here is a pig, o God, a pig for the purpose of detecting an *alii.*" Then Kalei-o-ku released the pig, and it went and stood before[10] Umi; after which it came back to Kalei-o-ku.

84. Kalei-o-ku then put to him the question, "Are you Umi?" "I am he," said Umi. "Let us go then to my place," said Kaleioku, and Umi consented and went with him. Thereupon his fathers-in-law and all the people of the neighborhood said, "So then this man is an *alii,* and his name is Umi, the son of Liloa. He is that one of whom we heard some time ago that he was lost."

85. Then Umi and his wives, and Pi'i-mai-wa'a, Omao-ka-mau, and Koi, and their wives accompanied Ka-lei-o-ku to his residence.

The End

Notes to Chapter LXVII

1. Sect. 9. *Hoo-mahana-hana*, literally to warm, to cause to be warm. In this connection it probably refers to that relaxation from the rigors of temple-worship spoken of in connection with the *lua-kini*. See note 2, Sect. 5. Chap. XXXVII. It is probable that Liloa had been engaged in the pious work of consecrating some newly built temple.

2. Sect. 16. From the point of view of the time, the conduct of Liloa in this whole affair was not only non-reprehensible, but was at the same time marked with a fine sense of honor. The giving of the pledges into the hands of Akahi-a-kuleana, so far as they go, give color to this view.

3. Sect. 24. The term *makua* was applied to an uncle as well as to one's own father. It was a common thing for children to roam from one *makua* to another for the most trivial reasons. This was a vice, a weak point in the Polynesian social system.

4. Sect. 26. *Makua-kolea.* A very significant phrase, literally a plover-father. Apropos of the uncertainty of the parentage on the male side the Hawaiians have the saying, *"Maopopo, ka makuahine, maopopo ole ka makuakane,"* one can be sure of the mother, but not of the father.

5. Sect. 34. This daring act was intended as a rightful assertion of high *alii* rank. In Maori story, says S. Percy Smith, when a child goes to visit a heretofore unseen parent he does not enter by the main gateway, but over the fence of the pa.

6. Sect. 66, *A ho-ao ae lakou.* The study of the word *ho-ao* sheds a flood of light upon the manners and customs of the ancient Hawaiians. To remain with a woman until morning, broad daylight, was equivalent to declaring her one's wife. Apropos of this subject see note 7, Chap. XLI, on the game *ume.* In the Wakea sun-myth Wakea's relation to Hoohoku-ka-lani was regarded as one of marriage only when he had remained with her until day-light. (See Chap. XLIII, Notes.)

7. Sect. 69. "But Umi did not go." Polynesians were not behind some other races in that sort of devotion to aristocracy which thought it belittling to noble blood to soil the hands with labor. Umi did not, however, consistently live up to this notion. Kamehameha also broke away from this tradition, and set an example to husbandmen by farming it with his own hands.

8. Sect. 78. It was a race-trait of the Polynesians—and still is—to have unaccountable squeamish notions as to food, not merely superstitious ceremonialisms, but personal, finicky disgust's. In this case, however, it would seem as if it was something more than a personal whimsy, perhaps a delicate scruple as to the respect due his god, Kaili.

9. Sect. 81. The rain-bow was looked upon as one of the signs of royalty; so also was a thunder-storm, a heavy surf, or any unusual meteorological disturbance. In this attempt to weave into the story of Umi, a purely historical character, these omens and portents, we can, if I mistake not, detect a myth-making effort in its early stage. The attempt in this case is so well within the

historic period, so close to modern times, as to spoil the effect by raising the suspicion of self-consciousness.

10. Sect. 83. The pig had the reputation of being a capital detective of royalty. During the reign of Ka-la-kaua the "Board of Genealogy," of historic fame, employed the detective power of this animal to search out and reveal the hiding place, and establish the identity, of the long lost bones of the great Kamehameha. The effort was claimed to have been successful.

A Note About the Author

David Malo (1795–1853) was a Hawaiian scholar, educator, politician, and minister. Born in Keauhou, Malo was raised during the period of unification under Kamehameha I. As a young man, he served as oral historian and court genealogist of chief Kuakini and married A'alailoa, an older widow. In 1823, Malo became a student of Reverend William Richards on the island of Maui, learning to write in Hawaiian and English, as well as converting to Christianity. Following the deaths of his first and second wives, Malo married Lepeka, who took the name Rebecca and gave birth to a daughter, Emma, in 1846. In his official role, he composed laments—most notably, a grief chant on the death of Queen Ka'ahumanu—genealogies, and letters in the Hawaiian language. In addition, Malo worked to translate the Gospel of Matthew and formed the first Hawaiian Historical Society alongside Samuel Kamakau in 1841. That same year, he was elected to serve as a representative from Maui in the Legislature of the Hawaiian Kingdom.

A Note from the Publisher

Spanning many genres, from non-fiction essays to literature classics to children's books and lyric poetry, Mint Edition books showcase the master works of our time in a modern new package. The text is freshly typeset, is clean and easy to read, and features a new note about the author in each volume. Many books also include exclusive new introductory material. Every book boasts a striking new cover, which makes it as appropriate for collecting as it is for gift giving. Mint Edition books are only printed when a reader orders them, so natural resources are not wasted. We're proud that our books are never manufactured in excess and exist only in the exact quantity they need to be read and enjoyed.

Discover more of your favorite classics with Bookfinity™.

- Track your reading with custom book lists.
- Get great book recommendations for your personalized Reader Type.
- Add reviews for your favorite books.
- AND MUCH MORE!

Visit **bookfinity.com** and take the fun Reader Type quiz to get started.

Enjoy our classic and modern companion pairings!